Learning the vi and Vim Editors

Other resources from O'Reilly

Related titles   vi Editor Pocket Reference   The Productive Programmer
Unix in a Nutshell   Unix Power Tools
Classic Shell Scripting   Mac OS X for Unix Geeks

oreilly.com   *oreilly.com* is more than a complete catalog of O'Reilly books. You'll also find links to news, events, articles, weblogs, sample chapters, and code examples.

oreillynet.com is the essential portal for developers interested in open and emerging technologies, including new platforms, programming languages, and operating systems.

Conferences   O'Reilly Media brings diverse innovators together to nurture the ideas that spark revolutionary industries. We specialize in documenting the latest tools and systems, translating the innovator's knowledge into useful skills for those in the trenches. Visit *conferences.oreilly.com* for our upcoming events.

Safari Bookshelf (*safari.oreilly.com*) is the premier online reference library for programmers and IT professionals. Conduct searches across more than 1,000 books. Subscribers can zero in on answers to time-critical questions in a matter of seconds. Read the books on your Bookshelf from cover to cover or simply flip to the page you need. Try it today for free.

SEVENTH EDITION

Learning the vi and Vim Editors

Arnold Robbins, Elbert Hannah, and Linda Lamb

Beijing · Cambridge · Farnham · Köln · Sebastopol · Taipei · Tokyo

Learning the vi and Vim Editors, Seventh Edition
by Arnold Robbins, Elbert Hannah, and Linda Lamb

Copyright © 2008 Arnold Robbins, Elbert Hannah, and Linda Lamb. All rights reserved.
Printed in the United States of America.

Published by O'Reilly Media, Inc., 1005 Gravenstein Highway North, Sebastopol, CA 95472.

O'Reilly books may be purchased for educational, business, or sales promotional use. Online editions are also available for most titles (*http://safari.oreilly.com*). For more information, contact our corporate/institutional sales department: 800-998-9938 or *corporate@oreilly.com*.

Editor: Andy Oram	**Indexer:** Joe Wizda
Production Editor: Sarah Schneider	**Cover Designer:** Karen Montgomery
Copyeditor: Genevieve d'Entremont	**Interior Designer:** David Futato
Proofreader: Sarah Schneider	**Illustrator:** Robert Romano

Printing History:

July 2008:	Seventh Edition
November 1998:	Sixth Edition
October 1990:	Fifth Edition
June 1988:	Fourth Edition
August 1987:	Third Edition
April 1986:	Second Edition
February 1986:	First Edition

ISBN: 978-0-596-52983-3

[M]

1215018617

To my wife, Miriam, for your love, patience, and support.

—Arnold Robbins, Sixth and Seventh Editions

Table of Contents

Part I.   Basic and Advanced vi

Preface

Text editing is one of the most common tasks on any computer system, and vi is one of the most useful standard text editors on a system. With vi you can create new files or edit any existing text-only file.

vi, like many of the classic utilities developed during the early years of Unix, has a reputation for being hard to navigate. Bram Moolenaar's enhanced clone, Vim ("vi Improved"), has gone a long way toward removing reasons for such impressions. Vim includes countless conveniences, visual guides, and help screens. It has become probably the most popular version of vi, so this seventh edition of this book devotes seven new chapters to it in Part II, *Vim*. However, many other worthy clones of vi also exist; we cover three of them in Part III, *Other vi Clones*.

Scope of This Book

This book consists of 18 chapters and 4 appendixes, divided into 4 parts. Part I, *Basic and Advanced vi*, is designed to get you started using vi quickly, and to follow up with advanced skills that will let you use it effectively.

The first two chapters, Chapter 1, *The vi Text Editor*, and Chapter 2, *Simple Editing*, present some simple vi commands with which you can get started. You should practice these until they are second nature. You could stop reading at the end of Chapter 2, having learned some elementary editing tools.

But vi is meant to do a lot more than rudimentary word processing; the variety of commands and options enables you to shortcut a lot of editing drudgery. Chapter 3, *Moving Around in a Hurry*, and Chapter 4, *Beyond the Basics*, concentrate on easier ways to do tasks. During your first reading, you'll get at least an idea of what vi can do and what commands you might harness for your specific needs. Later, you can come back to these chapters for further study.

Chapter 5, *Introducing the ex Editor*, Chapter 6, *Global Replacement*, and Chapter 7, *Advanced Editing*, provide tools that help you shift more of the editing burden to the computer. They introduce you to the ex line editor underlying vi, and they show you how to issue ex commands from within vi.

Chapter 8, *Introduction to the vi Clones*, provides an introduction to the extensions available in the four **vi** clones covered in this book. It centralizes in one place the descriptions of multiwindow editing, GUI interfaces, extended regular expressions, facilities that make editing easier, and several other features, providing a roadmap to what follows in the rest of this book. It also provides a pointer to source code for the original **vi**, which can be compiled easily on modern Unix systems (including GNU/ Linux).

Part II, *Vim*, describes Vim, the most popular **vi** clone in the early part of the 21st century.

Chapter 9, *Vim (vi Improved): An Introduction*, provides a general introduction to Vim, including where to get binary versions for popular operating systems and some of the different ways to use Vim.

Chapter 10, *Major Vim Improvements over vi*, describes the major improvements in Vim over **vi**, such as built-in help, control over initialization, additional motion commands, and extended regular expressions.

Chapter 11, *Multiple Windows in Vim*, focuses on multiwindow editing, which is perhaps the most significant additional feature over standard **vi**. This chapter provides all the details on creating and using multiple windows.

Chapter 12, *Vim Scripts*, looks into the Vim command language, which lets you write scripts to customize and tailor Vim to suit your needs. Much of Vim's ease of use "out of the box" comes from the large number of scripts that other users have already written and contributed to the Vim distribution.

Chapter 13, *Graphical Vim (gvim)*, looks at Vim in modern GUI environments, such as those that are now standard on commercial Unix systems, GNU/Linux and other Unix work-alikes, and MS Windows.

Chapter 14, *Vim Enhancements for Programmers*, focuses on Vim's use as a programmer's editor, above and beyond its facilities for general text editing. Of particular value are the folding and outlining facilities, smart indenting, syntax highlighting, and edit-compile-debug cycle speedups.

Chapter 15, *Other Cool Stuff in Vim*, is a bit of a catch-all chapter, covering a number of interesting points that don't fit into the earlier chapters.

Part III, *Other vi Clones*, describes three other popular **vi** clones: **nvi**, **elvis**, and **vile**.

Chapter 16, *nvi: New vi*, Chapter 17, *Elvis*, and Chapter 18, *vile: vi Like Emacs*, cover the various **vi** clones—**nvi**, **elvis**, and **vile**—showing you how to use their extensions to **vi** and discussing the features that are specific to each one.

Part IV, *Appendixes*, provides useful reference material.

Appendix A, *The vi, ex, and Vim Editors*, lists all vi and ex commands, sorted by function. It also provides an alphabetical list of ex commands. Selected vi and ex commands from Vim are also included.

Appendix B, *Setting Options*, lists set command options for vi and for all four clones.

Appendix C, *Problem Checklists*, consolidates checklists found earlier in the book.

Appendix D, *vi and the Internet*, describes vi's place in the larger Unix and Internet culture.

How the Material Is Presented

Our philosophy is to give you a good overview of what we feel are vi survival materials for the new user. Learning a new editor, especially an editor with all the options of vi, can seem like an overwhelming task. We have made an effort to present basic concepts and commands in an easy-to-read and logical manner.

After providing the basics for vi, which are usable everywhere, we move on to cover Vim in depth. We then round out our coverage of the vi landscape by looking at nvi, elvis, and vile. The following sections describe the conventions used in this book.

Discussion of vi Commands

A picture of a keyboard button, like the one on the left, marks the main discussion of that particular keyboard command or of related commands. You will find a brief introduction to the main concept before it is broken down into task-oriented sections. We then present the appropriate command to use in each case, along with a description of the command and the proper syntax for using it.

Conventions

In syntax descriptions and examples, what you would actually type is shown in the Courier font, as are all command names. Filenames are also shown in Courier, as are program options. Variables (which you would not type literally, but would replace with an actual value when you type the command) are shown in *Courier italic*. Brackets indicate that a variable is optional. For example, in the syntax line:

    vi [*filename*]

filename would be replaced by an actual filename. The brackets indicate that the vi command can be invoked without specifying a filename at all. The brackets themselves are not typed.

Certain examples show the effect of commands typed at the Unix shell prompt. In such examples, what you actually type is shown in **Courier Bold**, to distinguish it from the system response. For example:

```
$ ls
ch01.xml ch02.xml ch03.xml ch04.xml
```

In code examples, *italic* indicates a comment that is not to be typed. Otherwise, *italic* introduces special terms and emphasizes anything that needs emphasis.

Following traditional Unix documentation convention, references of the form *printf*(3) refer to the online manual (accessed via the man command). This example refers to the entry for the `printf( )` function in section 3 of the manual (you would type man 3 printf on most systems to see it).

Keystrokes

Special keystrokes are shown in a box. For example:

```
iWith a  ESC
```

Throughout the book, you will also find columns of `vi` commands and their results:

Keystrokes	Results
ZZ	`"practice" [New file] 6 lines, 320 characters`
	Give the write and save command, ZZ. Your file is saved as a regular Unix file.

In the preceding example, the command ZZ is shown in the left column. In the window to the right is a line (or several lines) of the screen that show the result of the command. Cursor position is shown in reverse video. In this instance, since ZZ saves and writes the file, you see the status line shown when a file is written; the cursor position is not shown. Below the window is an explanation of the command and its result.

Sometimes `vi` commands are issued by pressing the CTRL key and another key simultaneously. In the text, this combination keystroke is usually written within a box (for example, CTRL-G). In code examples, it is written by preceding the name of the key with a caret (^). For example, ^G means to hold down CTRL while pressing the G key.

Problem Checklist

A problem checklist is included in those sections where you may run into some trouble. You can skim these checklists and go back to them when you actually encounter a problem. All of the problem checklists are also collected in Appendix C, for ease of reference.

What You Need to Know Before Starting

This book assumes you have already read *Learning the Unix Operating System* (O'Reilly), or some other introduction to Unix. You should already know how to:

- Log in and log out
- Enter Unix commands
- Change directories
- List files in a directory
- Create, copy, and remove files

Familiarity with **grep** (a global search program) and wildcard characters is also helpful.

Comments and Questions

Please address comments and questions concerning this book to the publisher:

> O'Reilly Media, Inc.
> 1005 Gravenstein Highway North
> Sebastopol, CA 95472
> 800-998-9938 (in the United States or Canada)
> 707-829-0515 (international or local)
> 707-829-0104 (fax)

To ask technical questions or comment on the book, send email to:

> *bookquestions@oreilly.com*

The web site for this book lists examples, errata, and plans for future editions. You can access this page at:

> *http://www.oreilly.com/catalog/9780596529833*

For more information about our books, conferences, software, resource centers, and the O'Reilly Network, see our web site:

> *http://www.oreilly.com*

Safari® Books Online

When you see a Safari® Books Online icon on the cover of your favorite technology book, that means the book is available online through the O'Reilly Network Safari Bookshelf.

Safari offers a solution that's better than e-books. It's a virtual library that lets you easily search thousands of top tech books, cut and paste code samples, download chapters, and find quick answers when you need the most accurate, current information. Try it for free at *http://safari.oreilly.com*.

About the Previous Editions

In the fifth edition of this book (then called *Learning the vi Editor*), the ex editor commands were first discussed more fully. In Chapters 5, 6, and 7, the complex features of ex and vi were clarified by adding more examples, in topics such as regular expression syntax, global replacement, .exrc files, word abbreviations, keyboard maps, and editing scripts. A few of the examples were drawn from articles in *Unix World* magazine. Walter Zintz wrote a two-part tutorial* on vi that taught us a few things we didn't know, and that also had a lot of clever examples illustrating features we did already cover in the book. Ray Swartz also had a helpful tip in one of his columns.† We are grateful for the ideas in these articles.

The sixth edition of *Learning the vi Editor* introduced coverage of four freely available "clones," or work-alike editors. Many of them have improvements over the original vi. One could thus say that there is a "family" of vi editors, and the book's goal was to teach you what you need to know to use them. That edition treated nvi, Vim, elvis, and vile equally.

The sixth edition also added the following features:

- Many minor corrections and additions were made to the basic text.
- For each chapter where appropriate, a command summary was added at the end.
- New chapters covered each vi clone, the features and/or extensions common to two or more of the clones, and multiwindow editing.
- The chapters for each vi clone described a bit of that program's history and goals, its unique features, and where to get it.
- A new appendix described vi's place in the larger Unix and Internet culture.

Preface to the Seventh Edition

This seventh edition of *Learning the vi and Vim Editors* retains all the good features of the sixth edition. Time has proven Vim to be the most popular vi clone, so this edition adds considerably expanded coverage of that editor (and gives it a place in the title). However, to be relevant for as many users as possible, we have retained and updated the material on nvi, elvis, and vile.

---

* "vi Tips for Power Users," *Unix World*, April 1990; and "Using vi to Automate Complex Edits," *Unix World*, May 1990. Both articles by Walter Zintz. (See Appendix D for the web location of these articles.)

† "Answers to Unix," *Unix World*, August 1990.

What's New

The following features are new for this edition:

- Once again, we have corrected errors in the basic text.
- Seven new chapters provide exhaustive coverage of Vim.
- The material on nvi, elvis, and vile has been brought up-to-date.
- The previous edition's two reference appendixes on ex and vi have been condensed into one and now contain selected additional material on Vim.
- The other appendixes have been updated as well.

Versions

The following programs were used for testing out various vi features:

- The Solaris version of vi for a "reference" version of Unix vi
- Version 1.79 of Keith Bostic's nvi
- Version 2.2 of Steve Kirkendall's elvis
- Version 7.1 of Bram Moolenaar's Vim
- Version 9.6 of vile, by Kevin Buettner, Tom Dickey, and Paul Fox

Acknowledgments from the Sixth Edition

First and foremost, thanks to my wife, Miriam, for taking care of the kids while I was working on this book, particularly during the "witching hours" right before meal times. I owe her large amounts of quiet time and ice cream.

Paul Manno, of the Georgia Tech College of Computing, provided invaluable help in pacifying my printing software. Len Muellner and Erik Ray of O'Reilly & Associates helped with the SGML software. Jerry Peek's vi macros for SGML were invaluable.

Although all of the programs were used during the preparation of the new and revised material, most of the editing was done with Vim versions 4.5 and 5.0 under GNU/Linux (Red Hat 4.2).

Thanks to Keith Bostic, Steve Kirkendall, Bram Moolenaar, Paul Fox, Tom Dickey, and Kevin Buettner, who reviewed the book. Steve Kirkendall, Bram Moolenaar, Paul Fox, Tom Dickey, and Kevin Buettner also provided important parts of Chapters 8 through 12. (These chapter numbers refer to the sixth edition.)

Without the electricity being generated by the power company, doing anything with a computer is impossible. But when the electricity is there, you don't stop to think about it. So too when writing a book—without an editor, nothing happens, but when the editor is there doing her job, it's easy to forget about her. Gigi Estabrook at O'Reilly is a true gem. It's been a pleasure working with her, and I appreciate everything she's done and continues to do for me.

Finally, many thanks to the production team at O'Reilly & Associates.

—Arnold Robbins
Ra'anana, ISRAEL
June 1998

Acknowledgments for the Seventh Edition

Once again, Arnold thanks his wife, Miriam, for her love and support. The size of his quiet time and ice cream debt continues to grow. In addition, thanks to J.D. "Illiad" Frazer for the great *User Friendly* cartoons.‡

Elbert would like to thank Anna, Cally, Bobby, and his parents for staying excited about his work through the tough times. Their enthusiasm was contagious and appreciated.

Thanks to Keith Bostic and Steve Kirkendall for providing input on revising their editors' chapters. Tom Dickey provided significant input for revising the chapter on vile and the table of set options in Appendix B. Bram Moolenaar (the author of Vim) reviewed the book this time around as well. Robert P.J. Day, Matt Frye, Judith Myerson, and Stephen Figgins provided important review comments throughout the text.

Arnold and Elbert would both like to thank Andy Oram and Isabel Kunkle for their work as editors, and all of the tools and production staff at O'Reilly Media.

—Arnold Robbins
Nof Ayalon, ISRAEL
2008

—Elbert Hannah
Kildeer, Illinois USA
2008

‡ See *http://www.userfriendly.org* if you've never heard of *User Friendly*.

Basic and Advanced vi

Part I is designed to get you started quickly with the **vi** editor and to provide the advanced skills that will let you use **vi** most effectively. These chapters cover the original, core **vi** and provide commands you can use on any version; later chapters cover popular clones. This part contains the following chapters:

- Chapter 1, *The vi Text Editor*
- Chapter 2, *Simple Editing*
- Chapter 3, *Moving Around in a Hurry*
- Chapter 4, *Beyond the Basics*
- Chapter 5, *Introducing the ex Editor*
- Chapter 6, *Global Replacement*
- Chapter 7, *Advanced Editing*
- Chapter 8, *Introduction to the vi Clones*

The vi Text Editor

Unix[*] has a number of editors that can process the contents of text files, whether those files contain data, source code, or sentences. There are line editors, such as ed and ex, which display a line of the file on the screen; and there are screen editors, such as vi and Emacs, which display a part of the file on your terminal screen. Text editors based on the X Window System are also commonly available and are becoming increasing popular. Both GNU Emacs and its derivative, XEmacs, provide multiple X windows; two interesting alternatives are the sam and Acme editors from Bell Labs. Vim also provides an X-based interface.

vi is the most useful standard text editor on your system. (vi is short for **vi**sual editor and is pronounced "vee-eye." This is illustrated graphically in Figure 1-1.) Unlike Emacs, it is available in nearly identical form on every modern Unix system, thus providing a kind of text-editing *lingua franca*.[†] The same might be said of ed and ex, but screen editors are generally much easier to use. (So much so, in fact, that line editors have generally fallen into disuse.) With a screen editor, you can scroll the page, move the cursor, delete lines, insert characters, and more, while seeing the results of your edits as you make them. Screen editors are very popular, since they allow you to make changes as you read through a file, like you would edit a printed copy, only faster.

To many beginners, vi looks unintuitive and cumbersome—instead of using special control keys for word processing functions and just letting you type normally, it uses all of the regular keyboard keys for issuing commands. When the keyboard keys are issuing commands, vi is said to be in *command mode*. You must be in a special *insert mode* before you can type actual text on the screen. In addition, there seem to be so many commands.

---

[*] These days, the term "Unix" includes both commercial systems derived from the original Unix code base, and Unix work-alikes whose source code is available. Solaris, AIX, and HP-UX are examples of the former, and GNU/Linux and the various BSD-derived systems are examples of the latter. Unless otherwise noted, everything in this book applies across the board to all those systems.

[†] GNU Emacs has become the universal version of Emacs. The only problem is that it doesn't come standard with most commercial Unix systems; you must retrieve and install it yourself.

Figure 1-1. Correct pronunciation of vi

Once you start learning, however, you realize that vi is well designed. You need only a few keystrokes to tell vi to do complex tasks. As you learn vi, you learn shortcuts that transfer more and more of the editing work to the computer—where it belongs.

vi (like any text editor) is not a "what you see is what you get" word processor. If you want to produce formatted documents, you must type in codes that are used by another formatting program to control the appearance of the printed copy. If you want to indent several paragraphs, for instance, you put a code where the indent begins and ends. Formatting codes allow you to experiment with or change the appearance of your printed files, and, in many ways, they give you much more control over the appearance of your documents than a word processor. Unix supports the troff formatting package.[‡] The TEX and LATEX formatters are popular, commonly available alternatives.[§]

(vi does support some simple formatting mechanisms. For example, you can tell it to automatically wrap when you come to the end of a line, or to automatically indent new lines. In addition, Vim version 7 provides automatic spellchecking.)

As with any skill, the more editing you do, the easier the basics become, and the more you can accomplish. Once you are used to all the powers you have while editing with vi, you may never want to return to any "simpler" editor.

What are the components of editing? First, you want to *insert* text (a forgotten word or a new or missing sentence), and you want to *delete* text (a stray character or an entire paragraph). You also need to *change* letters and words (to correct misspellings or to reflect a change of mind about a term). You might want to *move* text from one place

---

[‡] troff is for laser printers and typesetters. Its "twin brother" is nroff, for line printers and terminals. Both accept the same input language. Following common Unix convention, we refer to both with the name troff. Today, anyone using troff uses the GNU version, groff. See *http://www.gnu.org/software/groff/* for more information.

[§] See *http://www.ctan.org* and *http://www.latex-project.org* for information on TEX and LATEX, respectively.

to another part of your file. And, on occasion, you want to *copy* text to duplicate it in another part of your file.

Unlike many word processors, vi's command mode is the initial or "default" mode. Complex, interactive edits can be performed with only a few keystrokes. (And to insert raw text, you simply give any of the several "insert" commands and then type away.)

One or two characters are used for the basicIp commands. For example:

i

>   Insert

cw

>   Change word

Using letters as commands, you can edit a file with great speed. You don't have to memorize banks of function keys or stretch your fingers to reach awkward combinations of keys. You never have to remove your hands from the keyboard, or mess around with multiple levels of menus! Most of the commands can be remembered by the letters that perform them, and nearly all commands follow similar patterns and are related to each other.

In general, vi commands:

- Are case-sensitive (uppercase and lowercase keystrokes mean different things; I is different from i).
- Are not shown (or "echoed") on the screen when you type them.
- Do not require an ENTER after the command.

There is also a group of commands that echo on the bottom line of the screen. Bottom-line commands are preceded by different symbols. The slash (/) and the question mark (?) begin search commands, and are discussed in Chapter 3. A colon (:) begins all ex commands. ex commands are those used by the ex line editor. The ex editor is available to you when you use vi, because ex is the underlying editor and vi is really just its "visual" mode. ex commands and concepts are discussed fully in Chapter 5, but this chapter introduces you to the ex commands to quit a file without saving edits.

A Brief Historical Perspective

Before diving into all the ins and outs of vi, it will help you to understand vi's worldview of your environment. In particular, this will help you make sense of many of vi's otherwise more obscure error messages, and also appreciate how the vi clones have evolved beyond the original vi.

vi dates back to a time when computer users worked on terminals connected via serial lines to central mini-computers. Hundreds of different kinds of terminals existed and were in use worldwide. Each one did the same kind of actions (clear the screen, move the cursor, etc.), but the commands needed to make them do these actions were different. In addition, the Unix system let you choose the characters to use for back-space, generating an interrupt signal, and other commands useful on serial terminals, such as suspending and resuming output. These facilities were (and still are) managed with the stty command.

The original UCB version of vi abstracted out the terminal control information from the code (which was hard to change) into a text-file database of **term**inal **cap**abilities (which was easy to change), managed by the termcap library. In the early 1980s, System V introduced a binary **term**inal **info**rmation database and terminfo library. The two libraries were largely functionally equivalent. In order to tell vi which terminal you had, you had to set the TERM environment variable. This was typically done in a shell startup file, such as .profile or .login.

Today, everyone uses terminal emulators in a graphic environment (such as xterm). The system almost always takes care of setting TERM for you. (You can use vi from a PC non-GUI console too, of course. This is very useful when doing system recovery work in single-user mode. There aren't too many people left who would want to work this way on a regular basis, though.) For day-to-day use, it is likely that you will want to use a GUI version of vi, such as Vim or one of the other clones. On a Microsoft Windows or Mac OS X system, this will probably be the default. However, when you run vi (or some other screen editor of the same vintage) inside a terminal emulator, it still uses TERM and termcap or terminfo and pays attention to the stty settings. And using it inside a terminal emulator is just as easy a way to learn vi as any other.

Another important fact to understand about vi is that it was developed at a time when Unix systems were considerably less stable than they are today. The vi user of yesteryear had to be prepared for the system to crash at arbitrary times, and so vi included support for recovering files that were in the middle of being edited when the system crashed.‖ So, as you learn vi and see the descriptions of various problems that might occur, bear these historical developments in mind.

Opening and Closing Files

You can use vi to edit any text file. vi copies the file to be edited into a *buffer* (an area temporarily set aside in memory), displays the buffer (though you can see only one screenful at a time), and lets you add, delete, and change text. When you save your edits, vi copies the edited buffer back into a permanent file, replacing the old file of the same name. Remember that you are always working on a *copy* of your file in the buffer, and that your edits will not affect your original file until you save the buffer. Saving your edits is also called "writing the buffer," or more commonly, "writing your file."

‖ Thankfully, this kind of thing is much less common, although systems can still crash due to external circumstances, such as a power outage.

Opening a File

 vi is the Unix command that invokes the vi editor for an existing file or for a brand new file. The syntax for the vi command is:

```
$ vi [filename]
```

The brackets shown on the above command line indicate that the filename is optional. The brackets should not be typed. The $ is the Unix prompt. If the filename is omitted, vi will open an unnamed buffer. You can assign the name when you write the buffer into a file. For right now, though, let's stick to naming the file on the command line.

A filename must be unique inside its directory. A filename can include any 8-bit character except a slash (/), which is reserved as the separator between files and directories in a pathname, and ASCII NUL, the character with all zero bits. You can even include spaces in a filename by typing a backslash (\) before the space. In practice, though, filenames generally consist of any combination of uppercase and lowercase letters, numbers, and the characters dot (.) and underscore (_). Remember that Unix is case-sensitive: lowercase letters are distinct from uppercase letters. Also remember that you must press ENTER to tell Unix that you are finished issuing your command.

When you want to open a new file in a directory, give a new filename with the vi command. For example, if you want to open a new file called practice in the current directory, you would enter:

```
$ vi practice
```

Since this is a new file, the buffer is empty and the screen appears as follows:

```
~
~
~
"practice" [New file]
```

The tildes (~) down the lefthand column of the screen indicate that there is no text in the file, not even blank lines. The prompt line (also called the status line) at the bottom of the screen echoes the name and status of the file.

You can also edit any existing text file in a directory by specifying its filename. Suppose that there is a Unix file with the pathname /home/john/letter. If you are already in the /home/john directory, use the relative pathname. For example:

```
$ vi letter
```

brings a copy of the file letter to the screen.

If you are in another directory, give the full pathname to begin editing:

```
$ vi /home/john/letter
```

Problems Opening Files

- *When you invoke* vi, *the message* [open mode] *appears.*

  Your terminal type is probably incorrectly identified. Quit the editing session immediately by typing :q. Check the environment variable $TERM. It should be set to the name of your terminal. Or ask your system administrator to provide an adequate terminal type setting.

- *You see one of the following messages:*

  ```
  Visual needs addressable cursor or upline capability
  Bad termcap entry
  Termcap entry too long
  terminal:  Unknown terminal type
  Block device required
  Not a typewriter
  ```

  Your terminal type is either undefined, or there's probably something wrong with your terminfo or termcap entry. Enter :q to quit. Check your $TERM environment variable, or ask your system administrator to select a terminal type for your environment.

- *A* [new file] *message appears when you think a file already exists.*

  Check that you have used correct case in the filename (Unix filenames are case-sensitive). If you have, then you are probably in the wrong directory. Enter :q to quit. Then check to see that you are in the correct directory for that file (enter pwd at the Unix prompt). If you are in the right directory, check the list of files in the directory (with ls) to see whether the file exists under a slightly different name.

- *You invoke* vi, *but you get a colon prompt (indicating that you're in* ex *line-editing mode).*

  You probably typed an interrupt before vi could draw the screen. Enter vi by typing vi at the ex prompt (:).

- *One of the following messages appears:*

  ```
  [Read only]
  File is read only
  Permission denied
  ```

  "Read only" means that you can only look at the file; you cannot save any changes you make. You may have invoked vi in view mode (with view or vi -R), or you do not have write permission for the file. See the section "Problems Saving Files" on page 10.

- *One of the following messages appears:*

  ```
  Bad file number
  Block special file
  Character special file
  Directory
  Executable
  ```

```
Non-ascii file
file non-ASCII
```

The file you've called up to edit is not a regular text file. Type :q! to quit, then check the file you wish to edit, perhaps with the file command.

- *When you type* :q *because of one of the previously mentioned difficulties, this message appears:*

```
No write since last change (:quit! overrides).
```

You have modified the file without realizing it. Type :q! to leave vi. Your changes from this session will not be saved in the file.

Modus Operandi

As mentioned earlier, the concept of the current "mode" is fundamental to the way vi works. There are two modes, *command mode* and *insert mode*. You start out in command mode, where every keystroke represents a command. In insert mode, everything you type becomes text in your file.

Sometimes, you can accidentally enter insert mode, or conversely, leave insert mode accidentally. In either case, what you type will likely affect your files in ways you did not intend.

Press the ESC key to force vi to enter command mode. If you are already in command mode, vi will beep at you when you press the ESC key. (Command mode is thus sometimes referred to as "beep mode.")

Once you are safely in command mode, you can proceed to repair any accidental changes, and then continue editing your text.

Saving and Quitting a File

You can quit working on a file at any time, save your edits, and return to the Unix prompt. The vi command to quit and save edits is ZZ. Note that ZZ is capitalized.

Let's assume that you do create a file called **practice** to practice vi commands, and that you type in six lines of text. To save the file, first check that you are in command mode by pressing ESC, and then enter ZZ.

Keystrokes	Results
ZZ	`"practice" [New file] 6 lines, 320 characters`
	Give the write and save command, ZZ. Your file is saved as a regular Unix file.
ls	`ch01          ch02          practice`
	Listing the files in the directory shows the new file **practice** that you created.

You can also save your edits with ex commands. Type :w to save (write) your file but not quit vi; type :q to quit if you haven't made any edits; and type :wq to both save your edits and quit. (:wq is equivalent to ZZ.) We'll explain fully how to use ex commands in Chapter 5; for now, you should just memorize a few commands for writing and saving files.

Quitting Without Saving Edits

When you are first learning vi, especially if you are an intrepid experimenter, there are two other ex commands that are handy for getting out of any mess that you might create.

What if you want to wipe out all of the edits you have made in a session and then return to the original file? The command:

    :e! ENTER

returns you to the last saved version of the file, so you can start over.

Suppose, however, that you want to wipe out your edits and then just quit vi? The command:

    :q! ENTER

quits the file you're editing and returns you to the Unix prompt. With both of these commands, you lose all edits made in the buffer since the last time you saved the file. vi normally won't let you throw away your edits. The exclamation point added to the :e or :q command causes vi to override this prohibition, performing the operation even though the buffer has been modified.

Problems Saving Files

- *You try to write your file, but you get one of the following messages:*

      File exists
      File *file* exists - use w!
      [Existing file]
      File is read only

  Type :w! *file* to overwrite the existing file, or type :w *newfile* to save the edited version in a new file.

- *You want to write a file, but you don't have write permission for it. You get the message "Permission denied."*

  Use :w *newfile* to write out the buffer into a new file. If you have write permission for the directory, you can use mv to replace the original version with your copy of it. If you don't have write permission for the directory, type :w *pathname/file* to write out the buffer to a directory in which you do have write permission (such as your home directory, or /tmp).

- *You try to write your file, but you get a message telling you that the file system is full.*

  Type `:!rm junkfile` to delete a (large) unneeded file and free some space. (Starting an **ex** command with an exclamation point gives you access to Unix.)

  Or type `:!df` to see whether there's any space on another file system. If there is, choose a directory on that file system and write your file to it with `:w pathname`. (`df` is the Unix command to check a **d**isk's **f**ree space.)

- *The system puts you into open mode and tells you that the file system is full.*

  The disk with **vi**'s temporary files is filled up. Type `:!ls /tmp` to see whether there are any files you can remove to gain some disk space.[#] If there are, create a temporary Unix shell from which you can remove files or issue other Unix commands. You can create a shell by typing `:sh`; type CTRL-D or **exit** to terminate the shell and return to **vi**. (On modern Unix systems, when using a job-control shell, you can simply type CTRL-Z to suspend **vi** and return to the Unix prompt; type **fg** to return to **vi**.) Once you've freed up some space, write your file with `:w!`.

- *You try to write your file, but you get a message telling you that your disk quota has been reached.*

  Try to force the system to save your buffer with the **ex** command `:pre` (short for `:preserve`). If that doesn't work, look for some files to remove. Use `:sh` (or CTRL-Z if you are using a job-control system) to move out of **vi** and remove files. Use CTRL-D (or **fg**) to return to **vi** when you're done. Then write your file with `:w!`.

Exercises

The only way to learn **vi** is to practice. You now know enough to create a new file and to return to the Unix prompt. Create a file called **practice**, insert some text, and then save and quit the file.

Open a file called **practice** in the current directory:	`vi practice`
Insert text:	`i any text you like`
Return to command mode:	ESC
Quit **vi**, saving edits:	`ZZ`

[#] Your **vi** may keep its temporary files in `/usr/tmp`, `/var/tmp`, or your current directory; you may need to poke around a bit to figure out where exactly you've run out of room. Vim generally keeps its temporary file in the same directory as the file being edited.

## CHAPTER 2

Simple Editing

This chapter introduces you to editing with **vi**, and it is set up to be read as a tutorial. In it you will learn how to move the cursor and how to make some simple edits. If you've never worked with **vi**, you should read the entire chapter.

Later chapters will show you how to expand your skills to perform faster and more powerful edits. One of the biggest advantages for an adept user of **vi** is that there are so many options to choose from. (One of the biggest *disadvantages* for a newcomer to **vi** is that there are so many different editor commands.)

You can't learn **vi** by memorizing every single **vi** command. Start out by learning the basic commands introduced in this chapter. Note the patterns of use that the commands have in common.

As you learn **vi**, be on the lookout for more tasks that you can delegate to the editor, and then find the command that accomplishes it. In later chapters you will learn more advanced features of **vi**, but before you can handle the advanced, you must master the simple.

This chapter covers:

- Moving the cursor
- Adding and changing text
- Deleting, moving, and copying text
- More ways to enter insert mode

vi Commands

vi has two modes: command mode and insert mode. As soon as you enter a file, you are in command mode, and the editor is waiting for you to enter a command. Commands enable you to move anywhere in the file, to perform edits, or to enter insert mode to add new text. Commands can also be given to exit the file (saving or ignoring your edits) in order to return to the Unix prompt.

You can think of the different modes as representing two different keyboards. In insert mode, your keyboard functions like a typewriter. In command mode, each key has a new meaning or initiates some instruction.

There are several ways to tell vi that you want to begin insert mode. One of the most common is to press i. The i doesn't appear on the screen, but after you press it, whatever you type *will* appear on the screen and will be entered into the buffer. The cursor marks the current insertion point.* To tell vi that you want to stop inserting text, press ESC. Pressing ESC moves the cursor back one space (so that it is on the last character you typed) and returns vi to command mode.

For example, suppose you have opened a new file and want to insert the word "introduction." If you type the keystrokes iintroduction, what appears on the screen is:

    introduction

When you open a new file, vi starts in command mode and interprets the first keystroke (i) as the insert command. All keystrokes made after the insert command are considered text until you press ESC. If you need to correct a mistake while in insert mode, backspace and type over the error. Depending on the type of terminal you are using, backspacing may erase what you've previously typed or may just back up over it. In either case, whatever you back up over will be deleted. Note that you can't use the backspace key to back up beyond the point where you entered insert mode. (If you have disabled vi compatibility, Vim allows you to backspace beyond the point where you entered insert mode.)

vi has an option that lets you define a right margin and provides a carriage return automatically when you reach it. For right now, while you are inserting text, press ENTER to break the lines.

Sometimes you don't know whether you are in insert mode or command mode. Whenever vi does not respond as you expect, press ESC once or twice to check which mode you are in. When you hear the beep, you are in command mode.

Moving the Cursor

You may spend only a small amount of time in an editing session adding new text in insert mode; much of the time you will be making edits to existing text.

In command mode you can position the cursor anywhere in the file. Since you begin all basic edits (changing, deleting, and copying text) by placing the cursor at the text that you want to change, you want to be able to move the cursor to that place as quickly as possible.

---

* Some versions show that you're in input mode in the status line.

There are vi commands to move the cursor:

- Up, down, left, or right—one *character* at a time
- Forward or backward by blocks of *text* such as words, sentences, or paragraphs
- Forward or backward through a file, one *screen* at a time

In Figure 2-1, an underscore marks the present cursor position. Circles show movement of the cursor from its current position to the position that would result from various vi commands.

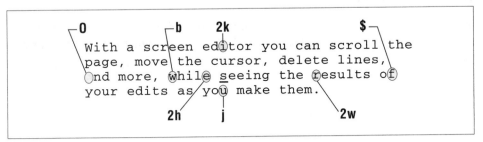

Figure 2-1. Sample movement commands

Single Movements

The keys h, j, k, and l, right under your fingertips, will move the cursor:

h

    Left, one space

j

    Down, one line

k

    Up, one line

l

    Right, one space

You can also use the cursor arrow keys (←, ↓, ↑, →), + and - to go up and down, or the ENTER and BACKSPACE keys, but they are out of the way. At first, it may seem awkward to use letter keys instead of arrows for cursor movement. After a short while, though, you'll find it is one of the things you'll like best about vi—you can move around without ever taking your fingers off the center of the keyboard.

Before you move the cursor, press ESC to make sure that you are in command mode. Use h, j, k, and l to move forward or backward in the file from the current cursor position. When you have gone as far as possible in one direction, you hear a beep and the cursor stops. For example, once you're at the beginning or end of a line, you cannot use h or l to wrap around to the previous or next line; you have to use j or k.[†] Similarly, you cannot move the cursor past a tilde (~) representing a line without text, nor can you move the cursor above the first line of text.

Numeric Arguments

You can precede movement commands with numbers. Figure 2-2 shows how the command 4l moves the cursor four spaces to the right, just as if you had typed l four times (llll).

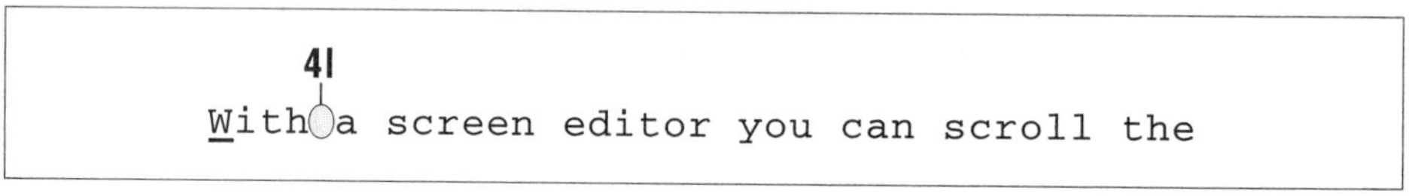

Figure 2-2. Multiplying commands by numbers

The ability to multiply commands gives you more options and power for each command you learn. Keep this in mind as you are introduced to additional commands.

Movement Within a Line

When you saved the file **practice**, **vi** displayed a message telling you how many lines are in that file. A *line* is not necessarily the same length as the visible line (often limited to 80 characters) that appears on the screen. A line is any text entered between newlines. (A *newline* character is inserted into the file when you press the ENTER key in insert mode.) If you type 200 characters before pressing ENTER, **vi** regards all 200 characters as a single line (even though those 200 characters visibly take up several lines on the screen).

As we mentioned in Chapter 1, **vi** has an option that allows you to set a distance from the right margin at which **vi** will automatically insert a newline character. This option is **wrapmargin** (its abbreviation is **wm**). You can set a **wrapmargin** at 10 characters:

```
:set wm=10
```

This command doesn't affect lines that you've already typed. We'll talk more about setting options in Chapter 7. (This one really couldn't wait!)

If you do not use **vi**'s automatic **wrapmargin** option, you should break lines with carriage returns to keep the lines of manageable length.

[†] Vim, with **nocompatible** set, allows you to "space past" the end of the line to the next one with l or the space bar.

0 Two useful commands that involve movement within a line are:

0 (digit zero)
> Move to beginning of line.

$
> Move to end of line.

In the following example, line numbers are displayed. (Line numbers can be displayed in vi by using the number option, which is enabled by typing :set nu in command mode. This operation is described in Chapter 7.)

```
 1  With a screen editor you can scroll the page,
 2  move the cursor, delete lines, insert characters,
    and more, while seeing the results of your edits
    as you make them.
 3  Screen editors are very popular.
```

$ The number of logical lines (3) does not correspond to the number of visible lines (5) that you see on the screen. If the cursor were positioned on the *d* in the word *delete*, and you entered $, the cursor would move to the period following the word *them*. If you entered 0, the cursor would move back to the letter *m* in the word *move*, at the beginning of line two.

Movement by Text Blocks

w You can also move the cursor by blocks of text: words, sentences, paragraphs, etc. The w command moves the cursor forward one word at a time, counting symbols and punctuation as equivalent to words. The following line shows cursor movement by w:

> Cursor, delete lines, insert characters,

You can also move by word, not counting symbols and punctuation, using the W command. (You can think of this as a "large" or "capital" Word.)

Cursor movement using W looks like this:

> Cursor, delete lines, insert characters,

To move backward by word, use the b command. Capital B allows you to move backward by word, not counting punctuation.

As mentioned previously, movement commands take numeric arguments; so, with either the w or b commands you can multiply the movement with numbers. 2w moves forward two words; 5B moves back five words, not counting punctuation.

To move to a specific line, you can use the G command. Plain G goes to the end of the file, 1G goes to the top of the file, and 42G goes to line 42. This is described in more detail later in the section "The G (Go To) Command" on page 43.

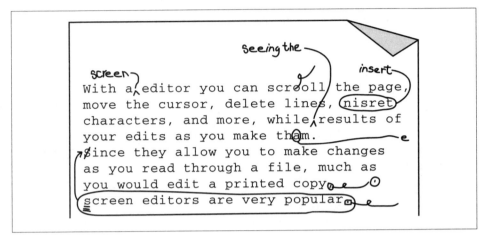

Figure 2-3. Proofreading edits

We'll discuss movement by sentences and by paragraphs in Chapter 3. For now, practice using the cursor movement commands that you know, combining them with numeric multipliers.

Simple Edits

When you enter text in your file, it is rarely perfect. You find typos or want to improve on a phrase; sometimes your program has a bug. Once you enter text, you have to be able to change it, delete it, move it, or copy it. Figure 2-3 shows the kinds of edits you might want to make to a file. The edits are indicated by proofreading marks.

In vi you can perform any of these edits with a few basic keystrokes: i for insert (which you've already seen); a for append; c for change; and d for delete. To move or copy text, you use pairs of commands. You move text with a d for "delete," then a p for "put"; you copy text with a y for "yank," then a p for "put." Each type of edit is described in this section. Figure 2-4 shows the vi commands you use to make the edits marked in Figure 2-3.

Inserting New Text

You have already seen the insert command used to enter text into a new file. You also use the insert command while editing existing text to add missing characters, words, and sentences. In the file **practice**, suppose you have the sentence:

```
you can scroll
the page, move the cursor, delete
lines, and insert characters.
```

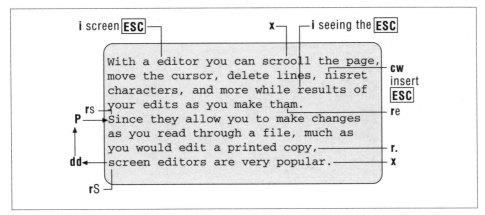

Figure 2-4. Edits with vi commands

with the cursor positioned as shown. To insert *With a screen editor* at the beginning of the sentence, enter the following:

Keystrokes	Results

2k	`You can scroll`
	`the page, move the cursor, delete`
	`lines, and insert characters.`
	Move the cursor up two lines with the k command, to the line where you want to make the insertion.

iWith a	`With a you can scroll`
	`the page, move the cursor, delete`
	`lines, and insert characters.`
	Press i to enter insert mode and begin inserting text.

screen editor
ESC
	`With a screen editor you can scroll`
	`the page, move the cursor, delete`
	`lines, and insert characters.`
	Finish inserting text, and press ESC to end the insert and return to command mode.

Appending Text

a You can append text at any place in your file with the append command, a. This works in almost the same way as i, except that text is inserted *after* the cursor rather than *before* the cursor. You may have noticed that when you press i to enter insert mode, the cursor doesn't move until after you enter some text. By contrast, when you press a to enter insert mode, the cursor moves one space to the right. When you enter text, it appears after the original cursor position.

Changing Text

c You can replace any text in your file with the change command, c. To tell c how much text to change, you combine c with a movement command. In this way, a movement command serves as a *text object* for the c command to affect. For example, c can be used to change text from the cursor:

cw
> To the end of a word

c2b
> Back two words

c$
> To the end of line

c0
> To the beginning of line

After issuing a change command, you can replace the identified text with any amount of new text, with no characters at all, with one word, or with hundreds of lines. c, like i and a, leaves you in insert mode until you press the [ESC] key.

When the change affects only the current line, vi marks the end of the text that will be changed with a $, so that you can see what part of the line is affected. (See the example for cw, next.)

Words

 To change a word, combine the c (change) command with w for word. You can replace a word (cw) with a longer or shorter word (or any amount of text). cw can be thought of as "delete the word marked and insert new text until [ESC] is pressed."

Suppose you have the following line in your file practice:

```
With an editor you can scroll the page,
```

and want to change *an* to *a screen*. You need to change only one word:

Keystrokes	Results
w	With a̲n editor you can scroll the page,
	Move with w to the place you want the edit to begin.
cw	With a̲$ editor you can scroll the page,
	Give the change word command. The end of the text to be changed will be marked with a $ (dollar sign).
a screen	With a scree̲n editor you can scroll the page,
	Type in the replacement text, and then press [ESC] to return to command mode.

cw also works on a portion of a word. For example, to change *spelling* to *spelled*, you can position the cursor on the *i*, type cw, then type *ed*, and finish with [ESC].

General Form of vi Commands

In the change commands we've mentioned up to this point, you may have noticed the following pattern:

>   (*command*)(*text object*)

command is the change command c, and *text object* is a movement command (you don't type the parentheses). But c is not the only command that requires a text object. The d command (delete) and the y command (yank) follow this pattern as well.

Remember also that movement commands take numeric arguments, so numbers can be added to the text objects of c, d, and y commands. For example, d2w and 2dw are commands to delete two words. With this in mind, you can see that most vi commands follow a general pattern:

>   (*command*)(*number*)(*text object*)

or the equivalent form:

>   (*number*)(*command*)(*text object*)

Here's how this works. *number* and *command* are optional. Without them, you simply have a movement command. If you add a *number*, you have a multiple movement. On the other hand, combine a *command* (c, d, or y) with a *text object* to get an editing command.

When you realize how many combinations are possible in this way, vi becomes a powerful editor indeed!

Lines

To replace the entire current line, use the special change command, cc. cc changes an entire line, replacing that line with any amount of text entered before pressing ESC. It doesn't matter where the cursor is located on the line; cc replaces the entire line of text.

A command like cw works differently from a command like cc. In using cw, the old text remains until you type over it, and any old text that is left over (up to the $) goes away when you press ESC. In using cc, though, the old text is wiped out first, leaving you a blank line on which to insert text.

The "type over" approach happens with any change command that affects less than a whole line, whereas the "blank line" approach happens with any change command that affects one or more lines.

C replaces characters from the current cursor position to the end of the line. It has the same effect as combining c with the special end-of-line indicator $ (c$).

The commands cc and C are really shortcuts for other commands, so they don't follow the general form of vi commands. You'll see other shortcuts when we discuss the delete and yank commands.

Characters

r One other replacement edit is given by the r command. r replaces a single character with another single character. You do *not* have to press ESC to return to command mode after making the edit. There is a misspelling in the line below:

```
▓ith a screen editor you can scroll the page,
```

Only one letter needs to be corrected. You don't want to use cw in this instance because you would have to retype the entire word. Use r to replace a single character at the cursor:

Keystrokes	Results
rW	`▓ith a screen editor you can scroll the page,`
	Give the replace command r, followed by the replacement character W.

Substituting text

s Suppose you want to change just a few characters, and not a whole word. The substitute command (s), by itself, replaces a single character. With a preceding count, you can replace that many characters. As with the change command (c), the last character of the text will be marked with a $ so that you can see how much text will be changed.

S The S command, as is usually the case with uppercase commands, lets you change whole lines. In contrast to the C command, which changes the rest of the line from the current cursor position, the S command deletes the entire line, no matter where the cursor is. vi puts you in insert mode at the beginning of the line. A preceding count replaces that many lines.

Both s and S put you in insert mode; when you are finished entering new text, press ESC.

R The R command, like its lowercase counterpart, replaces text. The difference is that R simply enters overstrike mode. The characters you type replace what's on the screen, character by character, until you type ESC. You can overstrike a maximum of only one line; as you type ENTER, vi will open a new line, effectively putting you into insert mode.

Changing Case

Changing the case of a letter is a special form of replacement. The tilde (~) command will change a lowercase letter to uppercase or an uppercase letter to lowercase. Position the cursor on the letter whose case you want to change, and type a ~. The case of the letter will change, and the cursor will move to the next character.

In older versions of **vi**, you cannot specify a numeric prefix or text object for the ~ to affect. Modern versions do allow a numeric prefix.

If you want to change the case of more than one line at a time, you must filter the text through a Unix command such as **tr**, as described in Chapter 7.

Deleting Text

You can also delete any text in your file with the delete command, **d**. Like the change command, the delete command requires a text object (the amount of text to be operated on). You can delete by word (**dw**), by line (**dd** and **D**), or by other movement commands that you will learn later.

With all deletions, you move to where you want the edit to take place, then give the delete command (**d**) and the text object, such as **w** for word.

Words

 Suppose you have the following text in the file:

```
Screen editors are are very popular,
since they allowed you to make
changes as you read through a file.
```

with the cursor positioned as shown. You want to delete one *are* in the first line:

Keystrokes	Results

2w	`Screen editors are are very popular,`
	`since they allowed you to make`
	`changes as you read through a file.`
	Move the cursor to where you want the edit to begin (*are*).

dw	`Screen editors are very popular,`
	`since they allowed you to make`
	`changes as you read through a file.`
	Give the delete word command (**dw**) to delete the word *are*.

dw deletes a word beginning where the cursor is positioned. Notice that the space following the word is deleted.

dw can also be used to delete a portion of a word. In this example:

```
since they allowed you to make
```

you want to delete the *ed* from the end of *allowed*.

Keystrokes	Results
dw	`since they allo you to make` Give the delete word command (dw) to delete the word, beginning with the position of the cursor.

dw always deletes the space before the next word on a line, but we don't want to do that in this example. To retain the space between words, use de, which deletes only to the end of a word. Typing dE deletes to the end of a word, including punctuation.

You can also delete backward (db) or to the end or beginning of a line (d$ or d0).

Lines

The dd command deletes the entire line that the cursor is on. dd will not delete part of a line. Like its complement, cc, dd is a special command. Using the same text as in the previous example, with the cursor positioned on the first line as shown here:

```
Screen editors are very popular,
since they allow you to make
changes as you read through a file.
```

you can delete the first two lines:

Keystrokes	Results
2dd	`changes as you read through a file.` Give the command to delete two lines (2dd). Note that even though the cursor was not positioned on the beginning of the line, the entire line is deleted.

The D command deletes from the cursor position to the end of the line. (D is a shortcut for d$.) For example, with the cursor positioned as shown:

```
Screen editors are very popular,
since they allow you to make
changes as you read through a file.
```

you can delete the portion of the line to the right of the cursor:

Keystrokes	Results
D	Screen editors are very popular, since they allow you to make changes█
	Give the command to delete the portion of the line to the right of the cursor (D).

Characters

x Often you want to delete only one or two characters. Just as r is a special change command to replace a single character, x is a special delete command to delete a single character. x deletes only the character the cursor is on. In the line here:

```
█You can move text by deleting text and then
```

you can delete the letter z by pressing x.[‡] A capital X deletes the character before the cursor. Prefix either of these commands with a number to delete that number of characters. For example, 5x will delete the five characters under and to the right of the cursor.

Problems with deletions

- *You've deleted the wrong text and you want to get it back.*

  There are several ways to recover deleted text. If you've just deleted something and you realize you want it back, simply type u to undo the last command (for example, a dd). This works only if you haven't given any further commands, since u undoes only the most recent command. Alternatively, a U will restore the line to its pristine state, the way it was before *any* changes were applied to it.

  You can still recover a recent deletion, however, by using the p command, since vi saves the last nine deletions in nine numbered deletion buffers. If you know, for example, that the third deletion back is the one you want to restore, type:

  ```
  "3p
  ```

  to "put" the contents of buffer number 3 on the line below the cursor.

  This works only for a deleted *line*. Words, or a portion of a line, are not saved in a buffer. If you want to restore a deleted word or line fragment, and u won't work, use the p command by itself. This restores whatever you've last deleted. The next few subsections will talk more about the commands u and p.

  Note that Vim supports "infinite" undo, which makes life much easier. See the section "Undoing Undos" on page 296 for more information.

[‡] The mnemonic for x is that it is supposedly like "x-ing out" mistakes with a typewriter. Of course, who uses a typewriter anymore?

Moving Text

In vi, you move text by deleting it and then placing that deleted text elsewhere in the file, like a "cut and paste." Each time you delete a text block, that deletion is temporarily saved in a special buffer. Move to another position in your file and use the put command (p) to place that text in the new position. You can move any block of text, although moving is more useful with lines than with words.

p The put command (p) puts the text that is in the buffer *after* the cursor position. The uppercase version of the command, P, puts the text *before* the cursor. If you delete one or more lines, p puts the deleted text on a new line(s) below the cursor. If you delete less than an entire line, p puts the deleted text into the current line, after the cursor.

Suppose in your file `practice` you have the text:

```
You can move text by deleting it and then,
like a "cut and paste,"
placing the deleted text elsewhere in the file.
each time you delete a text block.
```

and you want to move the second line, *like a "cut and paste,"* below the third line. Using delete, you can make this edit:

Keystrokes	Results
dd	```You can move text by deleting it and then,
placing the deleted text elsewhere in the file.
each time you delete a text block.```
	With the cursor on the second line, delete that line. The text is placed in a buffer (reserved memory).
p	```You can move text by deleting it and then,
placing that deleted text elsewhere in the file.
like a "cut and paste"
each time you delete a text block.```
	Give the put command, p, to restore the deleted line at the next line below the cursor. To finish reordering this sentence, you would also have to change the capitalization and punctuation (with r) to match the new structure.

 Once you delete text, you must restore it before the next change command or delete command. If you make another edit that affects the buffer, your deleted text will be lost. You can repeat the put over and over, so long as you don't make a new edit. In Chapter 4, you will learn how to save text you delete in a named buffer so that you can retrieve it later.

Transposing two letters

You can use xp (delete character and put after cursor) to transpose two letters. For example, in the word *mvoe*, the letters *vo* are transposed (reversed). To correct a transposition, place the cursor on *v* and press x, then p. By coincidence, the word *transpose* helps you remember the sequence xp; x stands for *trans*, and p stands for *pose*.

There is no command to transpose words. The section "More Examples of Mapping Keys" on page 107 discusses a short sequence of commands that transposes two words.

Copying Text

Often you can save editing time (and keystrokes) by copying a part of your file to use in other places. With the two commands y (for yank) and p (for put), you can copy any amount of text and put that copied text in another place in the file. A yank command copies the selected text into a special buffer, where it is held until another yank (or deletion) occurs. You can then place this copy elsewhere in the file with the put command.

As with change and delete, the yank command can be combined with any movement command (yw, y$, 4yy). Yank is most frequently used with a line (or more) of text, because to yank and put a word usually takes longer than simply to insert the word.

The shortcut yy operates on an entire line, just as dd and cc do. But the shortcut Y, for some reason, does not operate the way D and C do. Instead of yanking from the current position to the end of the line, Y yanks the whole line; that is, Y does the same thing as yy.

Suppose you have in your file **practice** the text:

```
With a screen editor you can
scroll the page.
move the cursor.
delete lines.
```

You want to make three complete sentences, beginning each with *With a screen editor you can*. Instead of moving through the file, making this edit over and over, you can use a yank and put to copy the text to be added.

Keystrokes	Results
yy	With a screen editor you can scroll the page. move the cursor. delete lines.
	Yank the line of text that you want to copy into the buffer. The cursor can be anywhere on the line you want to yank (or on the first line of a series of lines).
2j	With a screen editor you can scroll the page. move the cursor. delete lines.
	Move the cursor to where you want to put the yanked text.
P	With a screen editor you can scroll the page.

Keystrokes	Results

	`With a screen editor you can`
	`move the cursor.`
	`delete lines.`

	Put the yanked text above the cursor line with P.

jp	`With a screen editor you can`
	`scroll the page.`
	`With a screen editor you can`
	`move the cursor.`
	`With a screen editor you can`
	`delete lines.`

	Move the cursor down a line and put the yanked text below the cursor line with p.

Yanking uses the same buffer as deleting. Each new deletion or yank replaces the previous contents of the yank buffer. As we'll see in Chapter 4, up to nine previous yanks or deletions can be recalled with put commands. You can also yank or delete directly into up to 26 named buffers, which allows you to juggle multiple text blocks at once.

Repeating or Undoing Your Last Command

Each edit command that you give is stored in a temporary buffer until you give the next command. For example, if you insert *the* after a word in your file, the command used to insert the text, along with the text that you entered, is temporarily saved.

Repeat

Any time you make the same editing command over and over, you can save time by duplicating it with the repeat command, the period (.). Position the cursor where you want to repeat the editing command, and type a period.

Suppose you have the following lines in your file:

```
With a screen editor you can
scroll the page.
With a screen editor you can
move the cursor.
```

You can delete one line, and then, to delete another line, simply type a period.

Keystrokes	Results

dd	`With a screen editor you can`
	`scroll the page.`
	`move the cursor.`

	Delete a line with the command dd.
.	`With a screen editor you can` `scroll the page.`
	Repeat the deletion.

Older versions of vi have problems repeating commands. For example, such versions may have difficulty repeating a long insertion when wrapmargin is set. If you have such a version, this bug will probably bite you sooner or later. There's not a lot you can do about it after the fact, but it helps to be forewarned. (Modern versions do not seem to have this problem.) There are two ways you can guard against a potential problem when repeating long insertions. You can write your file (:w) before repeating the insertion (returning to this copy if the insertion doesn't work correctly). You can also turn off wrapmargin like this:

```
:set wm=0
```

In the later section "More Examples of Mapping Keys" on page 107, we'll show you an easy way to use the wrapmargin solution. In some versions of vi, the command CTRL-@ repeats the most recent insertion. CTRL-@ is typed in insert mode and returns you to command mode.

Undo

 As mentioned earlier, you can undo your last command if you make an error. Simply press u. The cursor need not be on the line where the original edit was made.

To continue the previous example, showing deletion of lines in the file **practice**:

Keystrokes	Results
u	With a screen editor you can scroll the page. Move the cursor.
	u undoes the last command and restores the deleted line.

U, the uppercase version of u, undoes all edits on a single line, *as long as the cursor remains on that line*. Once you move off a line, you can no longer use U.

Note that you can undo your last undo with u, toggling between two versions of text. u will also undo U, and U will undo any changes to a line, including those made with u.

> A tip: the fact that u can undo itself leads to a nifty way to get around in a file. If you ever want to get back to the site of your last edit, simply undo it. You will pop back to the appropriate line. When you undo the undo, you'll stay on that line.

Vim lets you use CTRL-R to "redo" an undone operation. Combined with infinite undo, you can move backward and forward through the history of changes to your file. See the section "Undoing Undos" on page 296 for more information.

More Ways to Insert Text

You have inserted text before the cursor with the sequence:

`itext to be inserted` `ESC`

You've also inserted text after the cursor with the **a** command. Here are some other insert commands for inserting text at different positions relative to the cursor:

A
> Append text to end of current line.

I
> Insert text at beginning of line.

o (lowercase letter "o")
> Open blank line below cursor for text.

O (uppercase letter "o")
> Open blank line above cursor for text.

s
> Delete character at cursor and substitute text.

S
> Delete line and substitute text.

R
> Overstrike existing characters with new characters.

All of these commands place you in insert mode. After inserting text, remember to press `ESC` to return to command mode.

A (append) and **I** (insert) save you from having to move your cursor to the end or beginning of the line before invoking insert mode. (The **A** command saves one keystroke over **$a**. Although one keystroke might not seem like much of a saving, the more adept —and impatient—an editor you become, the more keystrokes you will want to omit.)

o and **O** (open) save you from having to insert a carriage return. You can type these commands from anywhere within the line.

s and **S** (substitute) allow you to delete a character or a whole line and replace the deletion with any amount of new text. **s** is the equivalent of the two-stroke command **c** `SPACE`, and **S** is the same as **cc**. One of the best uses for **s** is to change one character to several characters.

R ("large" replace) is useful when you want to start changing text, but you don't know exactly how much. For example, instead of guessing whether to say **3cw** or **4cw**, just type **R** and then enter your replacement text.

Numeric Arguments for Insert Commands

Except for o and 0, the insert commands just listed (plus i and a) take numeric prefixes. With numeric prefixes, you might use the commands i, I, a, and A to insert a row of underlines or alternating characters. For example, typing 50i* ESC inserts 50 asterisks, and typing 25a*- ESC appends 50 characters (25 pairs of asterisk and hyphen). It's better to repeat only a small string of characters.§

With a numeric prefix, r replaces that number of characters with a repeated instance of a single character. For example, in C or C++ code, to change || to &&, you would place the cursor on the first pipe character and type 2r&.

You can use a numeric prefix with S to substitute several lines. It's quicker and more flexible, though, to use c with a movement command.

A good case for using the s command with a numeric prefix is when you want to change a few characters in the middle of a word. Typing r wouldn't be correct, and typing cw would change too much text. Using s with a numeric prefix is usually the same as typing R.

There are other combinations of commands that work naturally together. For example, ea is useful for appending new text to the end of a word. It helps to train yourself to recognize such useful combinations so that they become automatic.

Joining Two Lines with J

J Sometimes while editing a file you end up with a series of short lines that are difficult to scan. When you want to merge two lines into one, position the cursor anywhere on the first line, and press J to join the two lines.

Suppose your file **practice** reads:

```
With a
screen editor
you can
scroll the page, move the cursor
```

Keystrokes	Results
J	With a screen editor you can scroll the page, move the cursor J joins the line the cursor is on with the line below.
.	With a screen editor you can scroll the page, move the cursor Repeat the last command (J) with the . to join the next line with the current line.

§ Very old versions of vi have difficulty repeating the insertion of more than one line's worth of text.

Using a numeric argument with J joins that number of consecutive lines. In the example here, you could have joined three lines by using the command 3J.

Problem Checklist

- *When you type commands, text jumps around on the screen and nothing works the way it's supposed to.*

  Make sure you're not typing the J command when you mean j.

  You may have hit the CAPS LOCK key without noticing it. vi is case-sensitive; that is, uppercase commands (I, A, J, etc.) are different from lowercase commands (i, a, j), and if you hit this key, all your commands are interpreted not as lowercase but as uppercase commands. Press the CAPS LOCK key again to return to lowercase, press ESC to ensure that you are in command mode, and then type either U to restore the last line changed or u to undo the last command. You'll probably also have to do some additional editing to fully restore the garbled part of your file.

Review of Basic vi Commands

Table 2-1 presents a few of the commands you can perform by combining the commands c, d, and y with various text objects. The last two rows show additional commands for editing. Tables 2-2 and 2-3 list some other basic commands. Table 2-4 summarizes the rest of the commands described in this chapter.

Table 2-1. Edit commands

Text object	Change	Delete	Copy
One word	cw	dw	yw
Two words, not counting punctuation	2cW or c2W	2dW or d2W	2yW or y2W
Three words back	3cb or c3b	3db or d3b	3yb or y3b
One line	cc	dd	yy or Y
To end of line	c$ or C	d$ or D	y$
To beginning of line	c0	d0	y0
Single character	r	x or X	yl or yh
Five characters	5s	5x	5yl

Table 2-2. Movement

Movement	Commands
←, ↓, ↑, →	h, j, k, l
To first character of next line	+
To first character of previous line	-
To end of word	e or E
Forward by word	w or W

Movement	Commands
Backward by word	b or B
To end of line	$
To beginning of line	0

Table 2-3. Other operations

Operations	Commands
Place text from buffer	P or p
Start **vi**, open file if specified	vi *file*
Save edits, quit file	ZZ
No saving of edits, quit file	:q!

Table 2-4. Text creation and manipulation commands

Editing action	Command
Insert text at current position	i
Insert text at beginning of line	I
Append text at current position	a
Append text at beginning of line	A
Open new line below cursor for new text	o
Open new line above cursor for new text	O
Delete line and substitute text	S
Overstrike existing characters with new text	R
Join current and next line	J
Toggle case	~
Repeat last action	.
Undo last change	u
Restore line to original state	U

You can get by in **vi** using only the commands listed in these tables. However, in order to harness the real power of **vi** (and increase your own productivity), you will need more tools. The following chapters describe those tools.

## CHAPTER 3

Moving Around in a Hurry

You will not use **vi** just to create new files. You'll spend a lot of your time in **vi** editing existing files. You rarely want to simply open to the first line in the file and move through it line by line; you want to get to a specific place in a file and start working.

All edits start with you moving the cursor to where you want to begin the edit (or, with **ex** line editor commands, by identifying the line numbers to be edited). This chapter shows you how to think about movement in a variety of ways (by screens, by text, by patterns, or by line numbers). There are many ways to move in **vi**, since editing speed depends on getting to your destination with only a few keystrokes.

This chapter covers:

- Movement by screens
- Movement by text blocks
- Movement by searches for patterns
- Movement by line number

Movement by Screens

When you read a book, you think of "places" in the book in terms of pages: the page where you stopped reading or the page number in an index. You don't have this convenience when you're editing files. Some files take up only a few lines, and you can see the whole file at once. But many files have hundreds (or thousands!) of lines.

You can think of a file as text on a long roll of paper. The screen is a window of (usually) 24 lines of text on that long roll.

In insert mode, as you fill up the screen with text, you will end up typing on the bottom line of the screen. When you reach the end and press ENTER, the top line rolls out of sight, and a blank line appears on the bottom of the screen for new text. This is called *scrolling*.

In command mode, you can move through a file to see any text in it by scrolling the screen ahead or back. And, since cursor movements can be multiplied by numeric prefixes, you can move quickly to anywhere in your file.

Scrolling the Screen

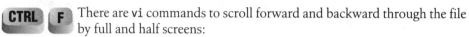 There are vi commands to scroll forward and backward through the file by full and half screens:

^F

Scroll forward one screen.

^B

Scroll backward one screen.

^D

Scroll forward half screen (down).

^U

Scroll backward half screen (up).

(In this list of commands, the ^ symbol represents the CTRL key. So ^F means to hold down the CTRL key and press the f key simultaneously.)

There are also commands to scroll the screen up one line (^E) and down one line (^Y). However, these two commands do not send the cursor to the beginning of the line. The cursor remains at the same point in the line as when the command was issued.

Repositioning the Screen with z

If you want to scroll the screen up or down, but you want the cursor to remain on the line where you left it, use the z command.

z ENTER

Move current line to top of screen and scroll.

z.

Move current line to center of screen and scroll.

z-

Move current line to bottom of screen and scroll.

With the z command, using a numeric prefix as a multiplier makes no sense. (After all, you would need to reposition the cursor to the top of the screen only once. Repeating the same z command wouldn't move anything.) Instead, z understands a numeric prefix as a line number that it will use in place of the current line. For example, z ENTER moves the current line to the top of the screen, but 200z ENTER moves line 200 to the top of the screen.

Redrawing the Screen

CTRL L Sometimes while you're editing, messages from your computer system will display on your screen. These messages don't become part of your editing buffer, but they do interfere with your work. When system messages appear on your screen, you need to redisplay, or redraw, the screen.

Whenever you scroll, you redraw part of (or all of) the screen, so you can always get rid of unwanted messages by scrolling them off the screen and then returning to your previous position. But you can also redraw the screen without scrolling, by typing CTRL-L.

Movement Within a Screen

H You can also keep your current screen, or view of the file, and move around within the screen using:

H
> Move to home—the top line on screen.

M
> Move to middle line on screen.

L
> Move to last line on screen.

*n*H
> Move to *n* lines below top line.

*n*L
> Move to *n* lines above last line.

H moves the cursor from anywhere on the screen to the first, or "home," line. M moves to the middle line, L to the last. To move to the line below the first line, use 2H.

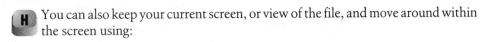

Keystrokes	Results
| L | ```
With a screen editor you can
scroll the page, move the cursor,
delete lines, insert characters, and more,
while seeing the results of your
edits as you make them.
Screen editors are very popular,
since they allow you to make changes
█s you read through a file.
``` |

Move to the last line of the screen with the L command.

| 2H | ```
With a screen editor you can
█croll the page, move the cursor,
delete lines, insert characters, and more,
while seeing the results of your
edits as you make them.
Screen editors are very popular,
since they allow you to make changes
as you read through a file.
``` |

Movement by Line

 Within the current screen there are also commands to move by line. You've already seen j and k. You can also use:

ENTER

Move to first character of next line.

+

Move to first character of next line.

-

Move to first character of previous line.

These three commands move down or up to the first *character* of the line, ignoring any spaces or tabs. j and k, by contrast, move the cursor down or up to the first position of a line, even if that position is blank (and assuming that the cursor started at the first position).

Movement on the current line

Don't forget that h and l move the cursor to the left and right, and that 0 (zero) and $ move the cursor to the beginning or end of the line. You can also use:

^

Move to first nonblank character of current line.

n|

Move to column *n* of current line.

As with the line movement commands shown earlier, ^ moves to the first *character* of the line, ignoring any spaces or tabs. 0, by contrast, moves to the first position of the line, even if that position is blank.

Movement by Text Blocks

 Another way that you can think of moving through a vi file is by text blocks— words, sentences, paragraphs, or sections.

You have already learned to move forward and backward by word (w, W, b or B). In addition, you can use these commands:

e

Move to end of word.

E

    Move to end of word (ignore punctuation).

(

    Move to beginning of current sentence.

)

    Move to beginning of next sentence.

{

    Move to beginning of current paragraph.

}

    Move to beginning of next paragraph.

[[

    Move to beginning of current section.

]]

    Move to beginning of next section.

To find the end of a sentence, vi looks for one of these punctuation marks: ?, ., or !. vi locates the end of a sentence when the punctuation is followed by at least two spaces or when it appears as the last nonblank character on a line. If you have left only a single space following a period, or if the sentence ends with a quotation mark, vi won't recognize the sentence.

A paragraph is defined as text up to the next blank line, or up to one of the default paragraph macros (.IP, .PP, .LP, or .QP) from the troff MS macro package. Similarly, a section is defined as text up to the next default section macro (.NH, .SH, .H 1, or .HU). The macros that are recognized as paragraph or section separators can be customized with the :set command, as described in Chapter 7.

Remember that you can combine numbers with movement. For example, 3) moves ahead three sentences. Also remember that you can edit using movement commands: d) deletes to the end of the current sentence, 2y} copies (yanks) two paragraphs ahead.

Movement by Searches

One of the most useful ways to move around quickly in a large file is by searching for text, or more properly, a *pattern* of characters. Sometimes a search can be performed to find a misspelled word or to find each occurrence of a variable in a program.

The search command is the special character / (slash). When you enter a slash, it appears on the bottom line of the screen; you then type in the *pattern* that you want to find: */pattern*.

A pattern can be a whole word or any other sequence of characters (called a "character string"). For example, if you search for the characters *red*, you will match *red* as a whole word, but you'll also match occurred. If you include a space before or after *pattern*, the spaces will be treated as part of the word. As with all bottom-line commands, press ENTER to finish. vi, like all other Unix editors, has a special pattern-matching language that allows you to look for variable text patterns: for example, any word beginning with a capital letter, or the word *The* at the beginning of a line.

We'll talk about this more powerful pattern-matching syntax in Chapter 6. For right now, think of a *pattern* simply as a word or phrase.

vi begins the search at the cursor and searches forward, wrapping around to the start of the file if necessary. The cursor will move to the first occurrence of the pattern. If there is no match, the message "Pattern not found" will be shown on the status line.[*]

Using the file practice, here's how to move the cursor by searches:

Keystrokes	Results
/edits	With a screen editor you can scroll the page, move the cursor, delete lines, insert characters, and more, while seeing the results of your █dits as you make them.
	Search for the pattern *edits*. Press ENTER to enter. The cursor moves directly to that pattern.
/scr	With a █creen editor you can scroll the page, move the cursor, delete lines, insert characters, and more, while seeing the results of your edits as you make them.
	Search for the pattern *scr*. Press ENTER to enter. Note that there is no space after *scr*.

The search wraps around to the front of the file. Note that you can give any combination of characters; a search does not have to be for a complete word.

To search backward, type a ? instead of a /:

> ?*pattern*

In both cases, the search wraps around to the beginning or end of the file, if necessary.

Repeating Searches

The last pattern that you searched for stays available throughout your editing session. After a search, instead of repeating your original keystrokes, you can use a command to search again for the last pattern:

n

> Repeat search in same direction.

---

[*] The exact message varies with different vi clones, but their meanings are the same. In general, we won't bother noting everywhere that the text of a message may be different; in all cases the information conveyed is the same.

N

> Repeat search in opposite direction.

/ ENTER

> Repeat search forward.

? ENTER

> Repeat search backward.

Since the last pattern stays available, you can search for a pattern, do some work, and then search again for the same pattern without retyping it by using n, N, /, or ?. The direction of your search (/ is forward, ? is backward) is displayed at the bottom left of the screen. (nvi does not show the direction for the n and N commands. Vim puts the search text into the command line too, and lets you scroll through a saved history of search commands, using the up and down arrow keys.)

To continue with the previous example, since the pattern *scr* is still available for search, you can do the following:

Keystrokes	Results
| n | ```
With a screen editor you can Scroll the
page, move the cursor, delete lines, insert
characters, and more, while seeing the
results of your edits as you make them.
``` |
| | Move to the next instance of the pattern *scr* (from *screen* to *scroll*) with the n (next) command. |
| ?you | ```
With a screen editor You can scroll the
page, move the cursor, delete lines, insert
characters, and more, while seeing the
results of your edits as you make them.
``` |
| | Search backward with ? from the cursor to the first occurrence of *you*. You need to press ENTER after typing the pattern. |
| N | ```
With a screen editor you can scroll the
page, move the cursor, delete lines, insert
characters, and more, while seeing the
results of Your edits as you make them.
``` |
| | Repeat the previous search for *you* but in the opposite direction (forward). |

Sometimes you want to find a word only if it is further ahead; you don't want the search to wrap around earlier in the file. vi has an option, **wrapscan**, that controls whether searches wrap. You can disable wrapping like this:

```
:set nowrapscan
```

When **nowrapscan** is set and a forward search fails, the status line displays the message:

```
Address search hit BOTTOM without matching pattern
```

When **nowrapscan** is set and a backward search fails, the message displays "TOP" instead of "BOTTOM."
```

Changing through searching

You can combine the / and ? search operators with the commands that change text, such as c and d. Continuing with the previous example:

Keystrokes	Results
d?move	With a screen editor you can scroll the page, ▊our edits as you make them.
	Delete from before the cursor up to and through the word *move*.

Note how the deletion occurs on a character basis, and whole lines are not deleted.

This section has given you only the barest introduction to searching for patterns. Chapter 6, will teach you more about pattern matching and its use in making global changes to a file.

Current Line Searches

[f] There are also miniature versions of the search commands that operate within the current line. The command f*x* moves the cursor to the next instance of the character *x* (where *x* stands for any character). The command t*x* moves the cursor to the character *before* the next instance of *x*. Semicolons can then be used repeatedly to "find" your way along.

The inline search commands are summarized here. None of these commands will move the cursor to the next line:

f*x*
> Find (move cursor to) next occurrence of *x* in the line, where *x* stands for any character.

F*x*
> Find (move cursor to) previous occurrence of *x* in the line.

t*x*
> Find (move cursor to) character *before* next occurrence of *x* in the line.

T*x*
> Find (move cursor to) character *after* previous occurrence of *x* in the line.

;
> Repeat previous find command in same direction.

,
> Repeat previous find command in opposite direction.

With any of these commands, a numeric prefix *n* locates the *n*th occurrence. Suppose you are editing in practice, on this line:

> ▊ith a screen editor you can scroll the

Keystrokes	Results
fo	`With a screen edit`o`r you can scroll the`
	Find the first occurrence of *o* in your current line with f.
;	`With a screen editor y`o`u can scroll the`
	Move to the next occurrence of *o* with the ; command (find next *o*).

dfx deletes up to and including the named character *x*. This command is useful in deleting or yanking partial lines. You might need to use dfx instead of dw if there are symbols or punctuation within the line that make counting words difficult. The t command works just like f, except that it positions the cursor before the character searched for. For example, the command ct. could be used to change text up to the end of a sentence, leaving the period.

Movement by Line Number

Lines in a file are numbered sequentially, and you can move through a file by specifying line numbers.

Line numbers are useful for identifying the beginning and end of large blocks of text you want to edit. Line numbers are also useful for programmers, since compiler error messages refer to line numbers. Finally, line numbers are used by ex commands, which you will learn in the next chapters.

If you are going to move by line numbers, you must have a way to identify them. Line numbers can be displayed on the screen using the :set nu option described in Chapter 7. In vi, you can also display the current line number on the bottom of the screen.

The command CTRL-G causes the following to be displayed at the bottom of your screen: the current line number, the total number of lines in the file, and what percentage of the total the present line number represents. For example, for the file practice, CTRL-G might display:

    "practice" line 3 of 6 --50%--

CTRL-G is useful either for displaying the line number to use in a command or for orienting yourself if you have been distracted from your editing session.

Depending upon the implementation of vi you're using, you may see additional information, such as what column the cursor is on, and an indication as to whether the file has been modified but not yet written out. The exact format of the message will vary as well.

The G (Go To) Command

 You can use line numbers to move the cursor through a file. The G (go to) command uses a line number as a numeric argument and moves directly to that line.

For instance, 44G moves the cursor to the beginning of line 44. G without a line number moves the cursor to the last line of the file.

Typing two backquotes (``) returns you to your original position (the position where you issued the last G command), unless you have done some edits in the meantime. If you have made an edit and then moved the cursor using some command other than G, `` will return the cursor to the site of your last edit. If you have issued a search command (/ or ?), `` will return the cursor to its position when you started the search. A pair of apostrophes ('') works much like two backquotes, except that it returns the cursor to the beginning of the line instead of the exact position on that line where your cursor had been.

The total number of lines shown with CTRL-G can be used to give yourself a rough idea of how many lines to move. If you are on line 10 of a 1,000-line file:

    "practice" line 10 of 1000 --1%--

and you know that you want to begin editing near the end of that file, you could give an approximation of your destination with 800G.

Movement by line number is a tool that can move you quickly from place to place through a large file.

Review of vi Motion Commands

Table 3-1 summarizes the commands covered in this chapter.

Table 3-1. Movement commands

Movement	Command
Scroll forward one screen	^F
Scroll backward one screen	^B
Scroll forward half screen	^D
Scroll backward half screen	^U
Scroll forward one line	^E
Scroll backward one line	^Y
Move current line to top of screen and scroll	z ENTER
Move current line to center of screen and scroll	z.
Move current line to bottom of screen and scroll	z-
Redraw the screen	^L
Move to home—the top line of screen	H
Move to middle line of screen	M
Move to bottom line of screen	L
Move to first character of next line	ENTER
Move to first character of next line	+

Movement	Command
Move to first character of previous line	-
Move to first nonblank character of current line	^
Move to column *n* of current line	*n*|
Move to end of word	e
Move to end of word (ignore punctuation)	E
Move to beginning of current sentence	(
Move to beginning of next sentence	)
Move to beginning of current paragraph	{
Move to beginning of next paragraph	}
Move to beginning of current section	[[
Move to beginning of next section	]]
Search forward for pattern	/*pattern*
Search backward for pattern	?*pattern*
Repeat last search	n
Repeat last search in opposite direction	N
Repeat last search forward	/
Repeat last search backward	?
Move to next occurrence of *x* in current line	f*x*
Move to previous occurrence of *x* in current line	F*x*
Move to just before next occurrence of *x* in current line	t*x*
Move to just after previous occurrence of *x* in current line	T*x*
Repeat previous find command in same direction	;
Repeat previous find command in opposite direction	,
Go to given line *n*	*n*G
Go to end of file	G
Return to previous mark or context	``
Return to beginning of line containing previous mark	' '
Show current line (not a movement command)	^G

Beyond the Basics

You have already been introduced to the basic **vi** editing commands, **i**, **a**, **c**, **d**, and **y**. This chapter expands on what you already know about editing. It covers:

- Descriptions of additional editing facilities, with a review of the general command form
- Additional ways to enter **vi**
- Making use of buffers that store yanks and deletions
- Marking your place in a file

More Command Combinations

In Chapter 2, you learned the edit commands **c**, **d**, and **y**, as well as how to combine them with movements and numbers (such as **2cw** or **4dd**). In Chapter 3, you added many more movement commands to your repertoire. Although the fact that you can combine edit commands with movement is not a new concept to you, Table 4-1 gives you a feel for the many editing options you now have.

Table 4-1. More editing commands

Change	Delete	Copy	From cursor to...
cH	dH	yH	Top of screen
cL	dL	yL	Bottom of screen
c+	d+	y+	Next line
c5|	d5|	y5|	Column 5 of current line
2c)	2d)	2y)	Second sentence following
c{	d{	y{	Previous paragraph
c/pattern	d/pattern	y/pattern	*Pattern*
cn	dn	yn	Next *pattern*
cG	dG	yG	End of file
c13G	d13G	y13G	Line number 13

Notice how all of the sequences in Table 4-1 follow the general pattern:

(number)(command)(text object)

number is the optional numeric argument. *command* in this case is one of c, d, or y. *text object* is a movement command.

The general form of a vi command is discussed in Chapter 2. You may wish to review Tables 2-1 and 2-2 as well.

Options When Starting vi

So far, you have invoked the vi editor with the command:

```
$ vi file
```

There are other options to the vi command that can be helpful. You can open a file directly to a specific line number or pattern. You can also open a file in read-only mode. Another option recovers all changes to a file that you were editing when the system crashed.

Advancing to a Specific Place

When you begin editing an existing file, you can call the file in and then move to the first occurrence of a *pattern* or to a specific line number. You can also specify your first movement by search or by line number right on the command line:[*]

$ **vi** *+n file*
> Opens *file* at line number *n*.

$ **vi** *+ file*
> Opens *file* at last line.

$ **vi** *+/pattern file*
> Opens *file* at the first occurrence of *pattern*.

In the file practice, to open the file and advance directly to the line containing the word *Screen*, enter:

Keystrokes	Results
vi +/Screen practice	With a screen editor you can scroll the page, move the cursor, delete lines, and insert characters, while seeing the results of your edits as you make them. Screen editors are very popular, since they allow you to make changes as you read

---

[*] According to the POSIX standard, vi should use -c *command* instead of +*command* as shown here. Typically, for backward compatibility, both versions are accepted.

Keystrokes	Results
	Give the vi command with the option +/ *pattern* to go directly to the line containing *Screen*.

As you see in this example, your search pattern will not necessarily be positioned at the top of the screen. If you include spaces in the *pattern*, you must enclose the whole pattern within single or double quotes:[†]

    +/"you make"

or escape the space with a backslash:

    +/you\ make

In addition, if you want to use the general pattern-matching syntax described in Chapter 6, you may need to protect one or more special characters from interpretation by the shell with either single quotes or backslashes.

Using +/*pattern* is helpful if you have to leave an editing session before you're finished. You can mark your place by inserting a pattern such as ZZZ or HERE. Then, when you return to the file, all you have to remember is /ZZZ or /HERE.

 Normally, when you're editing in vi, the wrapscan option is enabled. If you've customized your environment so that wrapscan is always disabled (see "Repeating Searches" on page 40), you might not be able to use +/*pattern*. If you try to open a file this way, vi opens the file at the last line and displays the message, "Address search hit BOTTOM without matching pattern."

Read-Only Mode

There will be times when you want to look at a file but want to protect that file from inadvertent keystrokes and changes. (You might want to call in a lengthy file to practice vi movements, or you might want to scroll through a command file or program.) You can enter a file in read-only mode and use all the vi movement commands, but you won't be able to change the file.

To look at a file in read-only mode, enter either:

    $ vi -R *file*

or:

    $ view *file*

(The view command, like the vi command, can use any of the command-line options for advancing to a specific place in the file.[‡]) If you do decide to make some edits to

---

[†] It is the shell that imposes the quoting requirement, not vi.

[‡] Typically view is just a link to vi.

the file, you can override read-only mode by adding an exclamation point to the `write` command:

```
:w!
```

or:

```
:wq
```

If you have a problem writing out the file, see the problem checklists summarized in Appendix C.

Recovering a Buffer

Occasionally a system failure may happen while you are editing a file. Ordinarily, any edits made after your last write (save) are lost. However, there is an option, -r, which lets you recover the edited buffer at the time of a system crash.

On a traditional Unix system with the original vi, when you first log on after the system is running again, you will receive a mail message stating that your buffer has been saved. In addition, if you type the command:

```
$ ex -r
```

or:

```
$ vi -r
```

you will get a list of any files that the system has saved.

Use the -r option with a filename to recover the edited buffer. For example, to recover the edited buffer of the file **practice** after a system crash, enter:

```
$ vi -r practice
```

It is wise to recover the file immediately, lest you inadvertently make edits to the file and then have to resolve a version skew between the preserved buffer and the newly edited file.

You can force the system to preserve your buffer even when there is not a crash by using the command :pre (short for :preserve). You may find it useful if you have made edits to a file and then discover that you can't save your edits because you don't have write permission. (You could also just write out a copy of the file under another name or into a directory where you do have write permission. See "Problems Saving Files" on page 10.)

Recovery may work differently for the various clones and can change from version to version. It is best to check your local documentation. vile does not support any kind of recovery. The vile documentation recommends the use of the `autowrite` and `autosave` options. How to do this is described in "Customizing vi" on page 95.

Making Use of Buffers

You have seen that while you are editing, your last deletion (d or x) or yank (y) is saved in a buffer (a place in stored memory). You can access the contents of that buffer and put the saved text back in your file with the put command (p or P).

The last nine deletions are stored by vi in numbered buffers. You can access any of these numbered buffers to restore any (or all) of the last nine deletions. (Small deletions, of only parts of lines, are not saved in numbered buffers, however. These deletions can be recovered only by using the p or P command immediately after you've made the deletion.)

vi also allows you to place yanks (copied text) into buffers identified by letters. You can fill up to 26 (a–z) buffers with yanked text and restore that text with a put command at any time in your editing session.

Recovering Deletions

Being able to delete large blocks of text in a single bound is all very well and good, but what if you mistakenly delete 53 lines that you need? You can recover any of your past *nine* deletions, for they are saved in numbered buffers. The last delete is saved in buffer 1, the second-to-last in buffer 2, and so on.

To recover a deletion, type " (double quote), identify the buffered text by number, then give the put command. To recover your second-to-last deletion from buffer 2, type:

    "2p

The deletion in buffer 2 is placed after the cursor.

If you're not sure which buffer contains the deletion you want to restore, you don't have to keep typing "*n*p over and over again. If you use the repeat command (.) with p after u, it automatically increments the buffer number. As a result, you can search through the numbered buffers using:

    "1pu.u.u *etc.*

to put the contents of each succeeding buffer in the file one after the other. Each time you type u, the restored text is removed; when you type a dot (.), the contents of the *next* buffer is restored to your file. Keep typing u and . until you've recovered the text you're looking for.

Yanking to Named Buffers

You have seen that you must put (p or P) the contents of the unnamed buffer before you make any other edit, or the buffer will be overwritten. You can also use y and d with a set of 26 named buffers (a–z) that are specifically available for copying and moving text. If you name a buffer to store the yanked text, you can retrieve the contents of the named buffer at any time during your editing session.

To yank into a named buffer, precede the yank command with a double quote (") and the character for the name of the buffer you want to load. For example:

"dyy   *Yank current line into buffer d.*
"a7yy   *Yank next seven lines into buffer a.*

After loading the named buffers and moving to the new position, use p or P to put the text back:

"dP   *Put the contents of buffer d before cursor.*
"ap   *Put the contents of buffer a after cursor.*

There is no way to put part of a buffer into the text—it is all or nothing.

In the next chapter, you'll learn how to edit multiple files. Once you know how to travel between files without leaving vi, you can use named buffers to selectively transfer text between files. When using the multiple-window feature of the various clones, you can also use the unnamed buffer to transfer data between files.

You can also delete text into named buffers using much the same procedure:

"a5dd   *Delete five lines into buffer a.*

If you specify a buffer name with a capital letter, your yanked or deleted text will be *appended* to the current contents of that buffer. This allows you to be selective in what you move or copy. For example:

"zd)
> Delete from cursor to end of current sentence and save in buffer z.

2)
> Move two sentences further on.

"Zy)
> Add the next sentence to buffer z. You can continue adding more text to a named buffer for as long as you like, but be warned: if you forget once, and yank or delete to the buffer without specifying its name in capitalized form, you'll overwrite the buffer, losing whatever you had accumulated in it.

Marking Your Place

During a vi session, you can mark your place in the file with an invisible "bookmark," perform edits elsewhere, and then return to your marked place. In command mode:

m*x*
> Marks the current position with *x* (*x* can be any letter). (The original vi allows only lowercase letters. Vim distinguishes between uppercase and lowercase letters.)

'*x***

(Apostrophe.) Moves the cursor to the first character of the line marked by *x*.

`*x***

(Backquote.) Moves the cursor to the character marked by *x*.

` `

(Backquotes.) Returns to the exact position of the previous mark or context after a move.

' '

(Apostrophes.) Returns to the beginning of the line of the previous mark or context.

Place markers are set only during the current **vi** session; they are not stored in the file.

Other Advanced Edits

There are other advanced edits that you can execute with **vi**, but to use them you must first learn a bit more about the **ex** editor by reading the next chapter.

Review of vi Buffer and Marking Commands

Table 4-2 summarizes the command-line options common to all versions of **vi**. Tables 4-3 and 4-4 summarize the buffer and marking commands.

Table 4-2. Command-line options

Option	Meaning
+*n file*	Open *file* at line number *n*.
+ *file*	Open *file* at last line.
+/*pattern file*	Open *file* at first occurrence of *pattern* (traditional version of POSIX -c).
-c *command file*	Run *command* after opening *file*; usually a line number or search (POSIX version of +).
-R	Operate in read-only mode (same as using **view** instead of **vi**).
-r	Recover files after a crash.

Table 4-3. Buffer names

Buffer names	Buffer use
1–9	The last nine deletions, from most to least recent.
a–z	Named buffers for you to use as needed. Uppercase letters append to the buffer.

Table 4-4. Buffer and marking commands

Command	Meaning
"b command	Do *command* with buffer *b*.
mx	Mark current position with *x*.
'x	Move cursor to first character of line marked by *x*.
`x	Move cursor to character marked by *x*.
``	Return to exact position of previous mark or context.
' '	Return to beginning of the line of previous mark or context.

Introducing the ex Editor

If this is a book on **vi**, why would we include a chapter on another editor? Well, **ex** is not really another editor. **vi** is the visual mode of the more general, underlying line editor, which is **ex**. Some **ex** commands can be useful to you while you are working in **vi**, since they can save you a lot of editing time. Most of these commands can be used without ever leaving **vi**.[*]

You already know how to think of files as a sequence of numbered lines. **ex** gives you editing commands with greater mobility and scope. With **ex**, you can move easily between files and transfer text from one file to another in a variety of ways. You can quickly edit blocks of text larger than a single screen. And with global replacement you can make substitutions throughout a file for a given pattern.

This chapter introduces **ex** and its commands. You will learn how to:

- Move around a file by using line numbers
- Use **ex** commands to copy, move, and delete blocks of text
- Save files and parts of files
- Work with multiple files (reading in text or commands, traveling between files)

ex Commands

Long before **vi** or any other screen editor was invented, people communicated with computers on printing terminals, rather than on today's CRTs (or bitmapped screens with pointing devices and terminal emulation programs). Line numbers were a way to quickly identify a part of a file to be worked on, and line editors evolved to edit those files. A programmer or other computer user would typically print out a line (or lines) on the printing terminal, give the editing commands to change just that line, and then reprint to check the edited line.

[*] **vile** is different from the other clones in that many of the more advanced **ex** commands simply don't work. Instead of noting each command here, we provide more details in Chapter 18.

People don't edit files on printing terminals anymore, but some ex line editor commands are still useful to users of the more sophisticated visual editor built on top of ex. Although it is simpler to make most edits with vi, the line orientation of ex gives it an advantage when you want to make large-scale changes to more than one part of a file.

 Many of the commands we'll see in this chapter have filename arguments. Although it's possible, it is usually a very bad idea to have spaces in your files' names. ex will be confused to no end, and you will go to more trouble than it's worth trying to get the filenames to be accepted. Use underscores, dashes, or periods to separate the components of your filenames, and you'll be much happier.

Before you start off simply memorizing ex commands (or worse, ignoring them), let's first take some of the mystery out of line editors. Seeing how ex works when it is invoked directly will help make sense of the sometimes obscure command syntax.

Open a file that is familiar to you and try a few ex commands. Just as you can invoke the vi editor on a file, you can invoke the ex line editor on a file. If you invoke ex, you will see a message about the total number of lines in the file, and a colon command prompt. For example:

```
$ ex practice
"practice" 6 lines, 320 characters
:
```

You won't see any lines in the file unless you give an ex command that causes one or more lines to be displayed.

ex commands consist of a line address (which can simply be a line number) plus a command; they are finished with a carriage return (by hitting ENTER). One of the most basic commands is p for print (to the screen). So, for example, if you type 1p at the prompt, you will see the first line of the file:

```
:1p
With a screen editor you can
:
```

In fact, you can leave off the p, because a line number by itself is equivalent to a print command for that line. To print more than one line, you can specify a range of line numbers (for example, 1,3—two numbers separated by a comma, with or without spaces in between). For example:

```
:1,3
With a screen editor you can
scroll the page, move the cursor,
delete lines, insert characters, and more,
```

A command without a line number is assumed to affect the current line. So, for example, the substitute command (s), which allows you to substitute one word for another, could be entered like this:

```
:1
With a screen editor you can
:s/screen/line/
With a line editor you can
```

Notice that the changed line is reprinted after the command is issued. You could also make the same change like this:

```
:1s/screen/line/
With a line editor you can
```

Even though you will be invoking ex commands from vi and will not be using them directly, it is worthwhile to spend a few minutes in ex itself. You will get a feel for how you need to tell the editor which line (or lines) to work on, as well as which command to execute.

After you have given a few ex commands in your practice file, you should invoke vi on that same file, so that you can see it in the more familiar visual mode. The command :vi will get you from ex to vi.

To invoke an ex command from vi, you must type the special bottom-line character : (colon). Then type the command and press ENTER to execute it. So, for example, in the ex editor you move to a line simply by typing the number of the line at the colon prompt. To move to line 6 of a file using this command from within vi, enter:

```
:6
```

Press ENTER.

After the following exercise, we will discuss ex commands only as they are executed from vi.

Exercise: The ex Editor

At the Unix prompt, invoke the ex editor on a file called practice:	`ex practice`
A message appears:	`"practice" 6 lines, 320 charac ters`
Go to and print (display) the first line:	`:1`
Print (display) lines 1 through 3:	`:1,3`
Substitute *screen* for *line* on line 1:	`:1s/screen/line`
Invoke the vi editor on file:	`:vi`
Go to the first line:	`:1`

Problem Checklist

- *While editing in* vi, *you accidentally end up in the* ex *editor.*

  A Q in the command mode of vi invokes ex. Any time you are in ex, the command vi returns you to the vi editor.

Editing with ex

Many ex commands that perform normal editing operations have an equivalent in vi that does the job more simply. Obviously, you will use dw or dd to delete a single word or line rather than using the delete command in ex. However, when you want to make changes that affect numerous lines, you will find the ex commands more useful. They allow you to modify large blocks of text with a single command.

These ex commands are listed here, along with abbreviations for those commands. Remember that in vi, each ex command must be preceded with a colon. You can use the full command name or the abbreviation, whichever is easier to remember.

Full name	Abbreviation	Meaning
delete	d	Delete lines
move	m	Move lines
copy	co	Copy lines
	t	Copy lines (a synonym for co)

You can separate the different elements of an ex command with spaces, if you find the command easier to read that way. For example, you can separate line addresses, patterns, and commands in this way. You cannot, however, use a space as a separator inside a pattern or at the end of a substitute command.

Line Addresses

For each ex editing command, you have to tell ex which line number(s) to edit. And for the ex move and copy commands, you also need to tell ex where to move or copy the text to.

You can specify line addresses in several ways:

- With explicit line numbers
- With symbols that help you specify line numbers relative to your current position in the file
- With search patterns as *addresses* that identify the lines to be affected

Let's look at some examples.

Defining a Range of Lines

You can use line numbers to explicitly define a line or range of lines. Addresses that use explicit numbers are called *absolute* line addresses. For example:

:3,18d

Delete lines 3 through 18.

```
:160,224m23
```
Move lines 160 through 224 to follow line 23. (Like delete and put in **vi**.)
```
:23,29co100
```
Copy lines 23 through 29 and put after line 100. (Like yank and put in **vi**.)

To make editing with line numbers easier, you can also display all line numbers on the left of the screen. The command:
```
:set number
```
or its abbreviation:
```
:set nu
```
displays line numbers. The file **practice** then appears:

```
1  With a screen editor
2  you can scroll the page,
3  move the cursor, delete lines,
4  insert characters and more
```

The displayed line numbers are not saved when you write a file, and they do not print if you print the file. Line numbers are displayed either until you quit the **vi** session or until you disable the **set** option:
```
:set nonumber
```
or:
```
:set nonu
```
To temporarily display the line numbers for a set of lines, you can use the # sign. For example:
```
:1,10#
```
would display the line numbers from line 1 to line 10.

As described in Chapter 3, you can also use the CTRL-G command to display the current line number. You can thus identify the line numbers corresponding to the start and end of a block of text by moving to the start of the block, typing CTRL-G, and then moving to the end of the block and typing CTRL-G again.

Yet another way to identify line numbers is with the **ex** = command:
```
:=
```
Print the total number of lines.
```
:.=
```
Print the line number of the current line.
```
:/pattern/=
```
Print the line number of the first line that matches *pattern*.

Line Addressing Symbols

You can also use symbols for line addresses. A dot (.) stands for the current line; and $ stands for the last line of the file. % stands for every line in the file; it's the same as the combination 1,$. These symbols can also be combined with absolute line addresses. For example:

`:.,$d`
> Delete from current line to end of file.

`:20,.m$`
> Move from line 20 through the current line to the end of the file.

`:%d`
> Delete all the lines in a file.

`:%t$`
> Copy all lines and place them at the end of the file (making a consecutive duplicate).

In addition to an absolute line address, you can specify an address relative to the current line. The symbols + and - work like arithmetic operators. When placed before a number, these symbols add or subtract the value that follows. For example:

`:.,.+20d`
> Delete from current line through the next 20 lines.

`:226,$m.-2`
> Move lines 226 through the end of the file to two lines above the current line.

`:.,+20#`
> Display line numbers from the current line to 20 lines further on in the file.

In fact, you don't need to type the dot (.) when you use + or - because the current line is the assumed starting position.

Without a number following them, + and - are equivalent to +1 and −1, respectively.[†] Similarly, ++ and -- each extend the range by an additional line, and so on. The + and - can also be used with search patterns, as shown in the next section.

The number 0 stands for the top of the file (imaginary line 0). 0 is equivalent to 1-, and both allow you to move or copy lines to the very start of a file, before the first line of existing text. For example:

`:-,+t0`
> Copy three lines (the line above the cursor through the line below the cursor) and put them at the top of the file.

[†] In a relative address, you shouldn't separate the plus or minus symbol from the number that follows it. For example, +10 means "10 lines following," but + 10 means "11 lines following (1 + 10)," which is probably not what you mean (or want).

Search Patterns

Another way that ex can address lines is by using search patterns. For example:

`:/pattern/d`
> Delete the next line containing *pattern*.

`:/pattern/+d`
> Delete the line *below* the next line containing *pattern*. (You could also use +1 instead of + alone.)

`:/pattern1/,/pattern2/d`
> Delete from the first line containing *pattern1* through the first line containing *pattern2*.

`:.,/pattern/m23`
> Take the text from the current line (.) through the first line containing *pattern* and put it after line 23.

Note that a pattern is delimited by a slash both *before* and *after*.

If you make deletions by pattern with **vi** and **ex**, there is a difference in the way the two editors operate. Suppose your file **practice** contains the lines:

```
With a screen editor you can scroll the
page, move the cursor, delete lines, insert
characters and more, while seeing results
of your edits as you make them.
```

Keystrokes	Results
| d/while | ```
With a screen editor you can scroll the
page, move the cursor, while seeing results
of your edits as you make them.
``` |
| | The **vi** delete to *pattern* command deletes from the cursor up to the word *while*, but leaves the remainder of both lines. |
| :.,/while/d | ```
With a screen editor you can scroll the
of your edits as you make them.
``` |
| | The **ex** command deletes the entire range of addressed lines, in this case both the current line and the line containing the pattern. All lines are deleted in their entirety. |

Redefining the Current Line Position

Sometimes, using a relative line address in a command can give you unexpected results. For example, suppose the cursor is on line 1 and you want to print line 100 plus the five lines below it. If you type:

```
:100,+5 p
```

you'll get an error message saying, "First address exceeds second." The reason the command fails is that the second address is calculated relative to the current cursor position (line 1), so your command is really saying this:

    :100,6 p

What you need is some way to tell the command to think of line 100 as the "current line," even though the cursor is on line 1.

ex provides such a way. When you use a semicolon instead of a comma, the first line address is recalculated as the current line. For example, the command:

    :100;+5 p

prints the desired lines. The +5 is now calculated relative to line 100. A semicolon is useful with search patterns as well as absolute addresses. For example, to print the next line containing *pattern*, plus the 10 lines that follow it, enter the command:

    :/pattern/;+10 p

Global Searches

You already know how to use / (slash) in vi to search for patterns of characters in your files. ex has a global command, g, that lets you search for a pattern and display all lines containing the pattern when it finds them. The command :g! does the opposite of :g. Use :g! (or its synonym, :v) to search for all lines that do *not* contain *pattern*.

You can use the global command on all lines in the file, or you can use line addresses to limit a global search to specified lines or to a range of lines.

:g/*pattern*
> Finds (moves to) the last occurrence of *pattern* in the file.

:g/*pattern*/p
> Finds and displays all lines in the file containing *pattern*.

:g!/*pattern*/nu
> Finds and displays all lines in the file that don't contain *pattern*; also displays the line number for each line found.

:60,124g/*pattern*/p
> Finds and displays any lines between lines 60 and 124 containing *pattern*.

As you might expect, g can also be used for global replacements. We'll talk about that in Chapter 6.

Combining ex Commands

You don't always need to type a colon to begin a new ex command. In ex, the vertical bar (|) is a command separator, allowing you to combine multiple commands from the same ex prompt (in much the same way that a semicolon separates multiple commands at the Unix shell prompt). When you use the |, keep track of the line addresses you specify. If one command affects the order of lines in the file, the next command does its work using the new line positions. For example:

`:1,3d | s/thier/their/`
> Delete lines 1 through 3 (leaving you now on the top line of the file), and then make a substitution on the current line (which was line 4 before you invoked the ex prompt).

`:1,5 m 10 | g/pattern/nu`
> Move lines 1 through 5 after line 10, and then display all lines (with numbers) containing *pattern*.

Note the use of spaces to make the commands easier to read.

Saving and Exiting Files

You have learned the `vi` command `ZZ` to quit and write (save) your file. But you will frequently want to exit a file using `ex` commands, because these commands give you greater control. We've already mentioned some of these commands in passing. Now let's take a more formal look:

`:w`
> Writes (saves) the buffer to the file but does not exit. You can (and should) use `:w` throughout your editing session to protect your edits against system failure or a major editing error.

`:q`
> Quits the editor (and returns to the Unix prompt).

`:wq`
> Both writes the file and quits the editor. The write happens unconditionally, even if the file was not changed.

`:x`
> Both writes the file and quits (e**x**its) the editor. The file is written only if it has been modified.‡

`vi` protects existing files and your edits in the buffer. For example, if you want to write your buffer to an existing file, `vi` gives you a warning. Likewise, if you have invoked `vi` on a file, made edits, and want to quit *without* saving the edits, `vi` gives you an error message such as:

`No write since last change.`

---

‡ The difference between `:wq` and `:x` is important when editing source code and using `make`, which performs actions based upon file modification times.

These warnings can prevent costly mistakes, but sometimes you want to proceed with the command anyway. An exclamation point (!) after your command overrides the warning:

```
:w!
:q!
```

:w! can also be used to save edits in a file that was opened in read-only mode with vi -R or view (assuming you have write permission for the file).

:q! is an essential editing command that allows you to quit without affecting the original file, regardless of any changes you made in this session. The contents of the buffer are discarded.

Renaming the Buffer

You can also use :w to save the entire buffer (the copy of the file you are editing) under a new filename.

Suppose you have a file practice, which contains 600 lines. You open the file and make extensive edits. You want to quit but also save *both* the old version of practice and your new edits for comparison. To save the edited buffer in a file called practice.new, give the command:

```
:w practice.new
```

Your old version, in the file practice, remains unchanged (provided that you didn't previously use :w). You can now quit editing the new version by typing :q.

Saving Part of a File

While editing, you will sometimes want to save just part of your file as a separate, new file. For example, you might have entered formatting codes and text that you want to use as a header for several files.

You can combine ex line addressing with the write command, w, to save part of a file. For example, if you are in the file practice and want to save part of practice as the file *newfile*, you could enter:

:230,$w *newfile*
: Saves from line 230 to end of file in newfile.

:.,600w *newfile*
: Saves from the current line to line 600 in newfile.

Appending to a Saved File

You can use the Unix redirect and append operator (>>) with w to append all or part of the contents of the buffer to an existing file. For example, if you entered:

```
:1,10w newfile
```

and then:

```
:340,$w >>newfile
```

newfile would contain lines 1–10 and from line 340 to the end of the buffer.

Copying a File into Another File

Sometimes you want to copy text or data already entered on the system into the file you are editing. In **vi**, you can read in the contents of another file with the **ex** command:

```
:read filename
```

or its abbreviation:

```
:r filename
```

This command inserts the contents of *filename* starting on the line after the cursor position in the file. If you want to specify a line other than the one the cursor's on, simply type the line number (or other line address) you want before the **read** or **r** command.

Let's suppose you are editing the file **practice** and want to read in a file called **data** from another directory called **/home/tim**. Position the cursor one line above the line where you want the new data inserted, and enter:

```
:r /home/tim/data
```

The entire contents of **/home/tim/data** are read into **practice**, beginning below the line with the cursor.

To read in the same file and place it after line 185, you would enter:

```
:185r /home/tim/data
```

Here are other ways to read in a file:

`:$r /home/tim/data`
> Place the read-in file at the end of the current file.

`:0r /home/tim/data`
> Place the read-in file at the very beginning of the current file.

`:/pattern/r /home/tim/data`
> Place the read-in file in the current file, after the line containing *pattern*.

Editing Multiple Files

ex commands enable you to switch between multiple files. The advantage of editing multiple files is speed. If you are sharing the system with other users, it takes time to exit and reenter **vi** for each file you want to edit. Staying in the same editing session and traveling between files is not only faster for access, but you also save abbreviations and command sequences that you have defined (see Chapter 7), and you keep yank buffers so that you can copy text from one file to another.

Invoking vi on Multiple Files

When you first invoke vi, you can name more than one file to edit, and then use ex commands to travel between the files. For example:

    $ vi file1 file2

edits file1 first. After you have finished editing the first file, the ex command :w writes (saves) file1 and :n calls in the next file (file2).

Suppose you want to edit two files, practice and note:

Keystrokes	Results
vi practice note	```With a screen editor you can scroll the page, move the cursor, delete lines, insert characters, and more, while seeing```
	Open the two files practice and note. The first-named file, practice, appears on your screen. Perform any edits.
:w	```"practice" 6 lines, 328 characters```
	Save the edited file practice with the ex command w. Press ENTER.
:n	```Dear Mr. Henshaw: Thank you for the prompt . . .```
	Call in the next file, note, with the ex command n. Press ENTER. Perform any edits.
:x	```"note" 23 lines, 1343 characters```
	Save the second file, note, and quit the editing session.

Using the Argument List

ex actually lets you do more than just move to the next file in the argument list with :n. The :args command (abbreviated :ar) lists the files named on the command line, with the current file enclosed in brackets.

Keystrokes	Results
vi practice note	```With a screen editor you can scroll the page, move the cursor, delete lines, insert characters, and more, while seeing```
	Open the two files practice and note. The first-named file, practice, appears on your screen.
:args	```[practice] note```
	vi displays the argument list in the status line, with brackets around the current filename.

The `:rewind` (`:rew`) command resets the current file to be the first file named on the command line. `elvis` and Vim provide a corresponding `:last` command to move to the last file on the command line.

Calling in New Files

You don't have to call in multiple files at the beginning of your editing session. You can switch to another file at any time with the ex command `:e`. If you want to edit another file within `vi`, you first need to save your current file (`:w`), then give the command:

    :e filename

Suppose you are editing the file **practice** and want to edit the file **letter**, and then return to **practice**:

Keystrokes	Results
`:w`	`"practice" 6 lines, 328 characters`
	Save practice with w and press ENTER. practice is saved and remains on the screen. You can now switch to another file, because your edits are saved.
`:e letter`	`"letter" 23 lines, 1344 characters`
	Call in the file letter with e and press ENTER. Perform any edits.

`vi` "remembers" two filenames at a time as the current and alternate filenames. These can be referred to by the symbols `%` (current filename) and `#` (alternate filename). `#` is particularly useful with `:e`, since it allows you to switch easily back and forth between two files. In the example just given, you could return to the first file, **practice**, by typing the command `:e #`. You could also read the file **practice** into the current file by typing `:r #`.

If you have not first saved the current file, `vi` will not allow you to switch files with `:e` or `:n` unless you tell it imperatively to do so by adding an exclamation point after the command.

For example, if after making some edits to **letter**, you wanted to discard the edits and return to **practice**, you could type `:e! #`.

The following command is also useful. It discards your edits and returns to the last saved version of the current file:

    :e!

In contrast to the `#` symbol, `%` is useful mainly when writing out the contents of the current buffer to a new file. For example, in the earlier section "Renaming the Buffer" on page 64, we showed you how to save a second version of the file **practice** with the command:

    :w practice.new

Since % stands for the current filename, that line could also have been typed:

```
:w %.new
```

Switching Files from vi

CTRL **^** Since switching back to the previous file is something that you will tend to do a lot, you don't have to move to the **ex** command line to do it. The **vi** command ^^ (the Ctrl key with the caret key) will do this for you. Using this command is the same as typing :e #. As with the :e command, if the current buffer has not been saved, **vi** will not let you switch back to the previous file.

Edits Between Files

When you give a yank buffer a one-letter name, you have a convenient way to move text from one file to another. Named buffers are not cleared when a new file is loaded into the **vi** buffer with the :e command. Thus, by yanking or deleting text from one file (into multiple named buffers if necessary), calling in a new file with :e, and putting the named buffer(s) into the new file, you can transfer material between files.

The following example illustrates how to transfer text from one file to another:

Keystrokes	Results
"f4yy	With a **S**creen editor you can scroll the page, move the cursor, delete lines, insert characters, and more, while seeing the results of the edits as you make them
	Yank four lines into buffer f.
:w	"practice" 6 lines, 238 characters
	Save the file.
:e letter	Dear Mr. Henshaw: I thought that you would **b**e interested to know that: Yours truly,
	Enter the file letter with :e. Move the cursor to where the copied text will be placed.
"fp	Dear Mr. Henshaw: I thought that you would be interested to know that: **W**ith a screen editor you can scroll the page, move the cursor, delete lines, insert characters, and more, while seeing the results of the edits as you make them Yours truly,
	Place yanked text from named buffer f below the cursor.

Another way to move text from one file to another is to use the ex commands :ya (yank) and :pu (put). These commands work the same way as the equivalent vi commands y and p, but they are used with ex's line-addressing capability and named buffers.

For example:

```
:160,224ya  a
```

would yank (copy) lines 160 through 224 into buffer a. Next you would move with :e to the file where you want to put these lines. Place the cursor on the line where you want to put the yanked lines. Then type:

```
:pu a
```

to put the contents of buffer a after the current line.

Global Replacement

Sometimes, halfway through a document or at the end of a draft, you may recognize inconsistencies in the way that you refer to certain things. Or, in a manual, some product whose name appears throughout your file is suddenly renamed (marketing!). Often enough it happens that you have to go back and change what you've already written, and you need to make the changes in several places.

The way to make these changes is with a powerful change command called global replacement. With one command you can automatically replace a word (or a string of characters) wherever it occurs in the file.

In a global replacement, the **ex** editor checks each line of a file for a given pattern of characters. On all lines where the pattern is found, ex replaces the pattern with a *new string* of characters. For right now, we'll treat the search pattern as if it were a simple string; later in the chapter we'll look at the powerful pattern-matching language known as *regular expressions*.

Global replacement really uses two **ex** commands: :**g** (global) and :**s** (substitute). Since the syntax of global replacement commands can get fairly complex, let's look at it in stages.

The substitute command has the syntax:

> :s/*old*/*new*/

This changes the *first* occurrence of the pattern *old* to *new* on the current line. The / (slash) is the delimiter between the various parts of the command. (The slash is optional when it is the last character on the line.)

A substitute command with the syntax:

> :s/*old*/*new*/g

changes *every* occurrence of *old* to *new* on the current line, not just the first occurrence. The :**s** command allows options following the substitution string. The g option in the syntax above stands for *global*. (The g option affects each pattern on a line; don't confuse it with the :**g** command, which affects each line of a file.)

By prefixing the `:s` command with addresses, you can extend its range to more than one line. For example, this command will change every occurrence of *old* to *new* from line 50 to line 100:

```
:50,100s/old/new/g
```

This command will change every occurrence of *old* to *new* within the entire file:

```
:1,$s/old/new/g
```

You can also use `%` instead of `1,$` to specify every line in a file. Thus, the last command could also be given like this:

```
:%s/old/new/g
```

Global replacement is much faster than finding each instance of a string and replacing it individually. Because the command can be used to make many different kinds of changes, and because it is so powerful, we will first illustrate simple replacements and then build up to complex, context-sensitive replacements.

Confirming Substitutions

It makes sense to be overly careful when using a search and replace command. It sometimes happens that what you get is not what you expect. You can undo any search and replacement command by entering `u`, provided that the command was the most recent edit you made. But you don't always catch undesired changes until it is too late to undo them. Another way to protect your edited file is to save the file with `:w` before performing a global replacement. Then at least you can quit the file without saving your edits and can go back to where you were before the change was made. You can also read the previous version of the buffer back in with `:e!`.

It's wise to be cautious and know exactly what is going to be changed in your file. If you'd like to see what the search turns up and confirm each replacement before it is made, add the `c` option (for confirm) at the end of the substitute command:

```
:1,30s/his/the/gc
```

ex will display the entire line where the string has been located, and the string will be marked by a series of carets (`^^^^`):

```
copyists at his school
          ^^^
```

If you want to make the replacement, you must enter `y` (for yes) and press ENTER. If you don't want to make a change, simply press ENTER.

```
this can be used for invitations, signs, and menus.
     ^^^
```

The combination of the vi commands n (repeat last search) and dot (`.`) (repeat last command) is also an extraordinarily useful and quick way to page through a file and make repetitive changes that you may not want to make globally. So, for example, if your editor has told you that you're using *which* when you should be using *that*, you can spot-check every occurrence of *which*, changing only those that are incorrect:

/which	Search for *which*
cwthat ESC	Change to *that*
n	Repeat search
n	Repeat search, skip a change
.	Repeat change (if appropriate)
	(Etc.)

Context-Sensitive Replacement

The simplest global replacements substitute one word (or a phrase) for another. If you have typed a file with several misspellings (*editer* for *editor*), you can do the global replacement:

    :%s/editer/editor/g

This substitutes *editor* for every occurrence of *editer* throughout the file.

There is a second, slightly more complex syntax for global replacement. This syntax lets you search for a pattern, and then, once you find the line with the pattern, make a substitution on a string different from the pattern. You can think of this as context-sensitive replacement.

The syntax is as follows:

    :g/pattern/s/old/new/g

The first **g** tells the command to operate on all lines of a file. *pattern* identifies the lines on which a substitution is to take place. On those lines containing *pattern*, **ex** is to substitute (**s**) for *old* the characters in *new*. The last **g** indicates that the substitution is to occur globally *on that line*.

For example, as we write this book, the XML directives **<keycap>** and **</keycap>** place a box around ESC to show the Escape key. You want ESC to be all in caps, but you don't want to change any instances of *Escape* that might be in the text. To change instances of *Esc* to *ESC* only when *Esc* is on a line that contains the **<keycap>** directive, you could enter:

    :g/<keycap>/s/Esc/ESC/g

If the pattern being used to find the line is the same as the one you want to change, you don't have to repeat it. The command:

    :g/string/s//new/g

would search for lines containing *string* and substitute for that same *string*.

Note that:

```
:g/editer/s//editor/g
```

has the same effect as:

```
:%s/editer/editor/g
```

You can save some typing by using the second form. It is also possible to combine the :g command with :d, :mo, :co, and other ex commands besides :s. As we'll show, you can thus make global deletions, moves, and copies.

Pattern-Matching Rules

In making global replacements, Unix editors such as vi allow you to search not just for fixed strings of characters, but also for variable patterns of words, referred to as *regular expressions*.

When you specify a literal string of characters, the search might turn up other occurrences that you didn't want to match. The problem with searching for words in a file is that a word can be used in different ways. Regular expressions help you conduct a search for words in context. Note that regular expressions can be used with the vi search commands / and ?, as well as in the ex commands :g and :s.

For the most part, the same regular expressions work with other Unix programs, such as grep, sed, and awk.[*]

Regular expressions are made up by combining normal characters with a number of special characters called *metacharacters*.[†] The metacharacters and their uses are listed next.

Metacharacters Used in Search Patterns

. *(period, dot)*

   Matches any *single* character except a newline. Remember that spaces are treated as characters. For example, p.p matches character strings such as *pep*, *pip*, and *pcp*.

*

   Matches zero or more (as many as there are) of the single character that immediately precedes it. For example, bugs* will match *bugs* (one *s*) or *bug* (no *s*). (It will also match *bugss*, *bugsss*, and so on.)

---

[*] Much more information on regular expressions can be found in the two O'Reilly books *sed & awk*, by Dale Dougherty and Arnold Robbins, and *Mastering Regular Expressions*, by Jeffrey E.F. Friedl.

[†] Technically speaking, we should probably call these *metasequences*, since sometimes two characters together have special meaning, and not just single characters. Nevertheless, the term *metacharacters* is in common use in Unix literature, so we follow that convention here.

The * can follow a metacharacter. For example, since . (dot) means any character, .* means "match any number of any character."

Here's a specific example of this: the command :s/End.*/End/ removes all characters after *End* (it replaces the remainder of the line with nothing).

^

When used at the start of a regular expression, requires that the following regular expression be found at the beginning of the line. For example, ^Part matches *Part* when it occurs at the beginning of a line, and ^... matches the first three characters of a line. When not at the beginning of a regular expression, ^ stands for itself.

$

When used at the end of a regular expression, requires that the preceding regular expression be found at the end of the line; for example, here:$ matches only when *here:* occurs at the end of a line. When not at the end of a regular expression, $ stands for itself.

****

Treats the following special character as an ordinary character. For example, \. matches an actual period instead of "any single character," and * matches an actual asterisk instead of "any number of a character." The \ (backslash) prevents the interpretation of a special character. This prevention is called "escaping the character." (Use \\ to get a literal backslash.)

[ ]

Matches any *one* of the characters enclosed between the brackets. For example, [AB] matches either *A* or *B*, and p[aeiou]t matches *pat*, *pet*, *pit*, *pot*, or *put*. A range of consecutive characters can be specified by separating the first and last characters in the range with a hyphen. For example, [A-Z] will match any uppercase letter from *A* to *Z*, and [0-9] will match any digit from *0* to *9*.

You can include more than one range inside brackets, and you can specify a mix of ranges and separate characters. For example, [:;A-Za-z( )] will match four different punctuation marks, plus all letters.

 When regular expressions and vi were first developed, they were meant to work only with the ASCII character set. In today's global market, modern systems support *locales*, which provide different interpretations of the characters that lie between a and z. To get accurate results, you should use POSIX bracket expressions (discussed shortly) in your regular expressions, and avoid ranges of the form a-z.

Most metacharacters lose their special meaning inside brackets, so you don't need to escape them if you want to use them as ordinary characters. Within brackets, the three metacharacters you still need to escape are \ -]. The hyphen (-) acquires meaning as a range specifier; to use an actual hyphen, you can also place it as the first character inside the brackets.

A caret (^) has special meaning only when it is the first character inside the brackets, but in this case the meaning differs from that of the normal ^ metacharacter. As the first character within brackets, a ^ reverses their sense: the brackets will match any one character *not* in the list. For example, [^0-9] matches any character that is not a digit.

\(\)

Saves the pattern enclosed between \(and \) into a special holding space, or a "hold buffer." Up to nine patterns can be saved in this way on a single line. For example, the pattern:

    \(That\) or \(this\)

saves *That* in hold buffer number 1 and saves *this* in hold buffer number 2. The patterns held can be "replayed" in substitutions by the sequences \1 to \9. For example, to rephrase *That or this* to read *this or That*, you could enter:

    :%s/\(That\) or \(this\)/\2 or \1/

You can also use the \n notation within a search or substitute string. For example:

    :s/\(abcd\)\1/alphabet-soup/

changes *abcdabcd* into *alphabet-soup*.‡

\< \>

Matches characters at the beginning (\<) or at the end (\>) of a word. The end or beginning of a word is determined either by a punctuation mark or by a space. For example, the expression \<ac will match only words that begin with *ac*, such as *action*. The expression ac\> will match only words that end with *ac*, such as *maniac*. Neither expression will match *react*. Note that unlike \(...\), these do not have to be used in matched pairs.

~

Matches whatever regular expression was used in the *last* search. For example, if you searched for *The*, you could search for *Then* with /~n. Note that you can use this pattern only in a regular search (with /).§ It won't work as the pattern in a substitute command. It does, however, have a similar meaning in the replacement portion of a substitute command.

All of the clones support optional, extended regular expression syntaxes. See the section "Extended Regular Expressions" on page 128 for more information.

---

‡ This works with vi, nvi, and Vim, but not with elvis or vile.

§ This is a rather flaky feature of the original vi. After using it, the saved search pattern is set to the *new* text typed after the ~, *not* the combined new pattern, as one might expect. Also, none of the clones behave this way. So, while this feature exists, it has little to recommend its use.

POSIX Bracket Expressions

We have just described the use of brackets for matching any one of the enclosed characters, such as [a-z]. The POSIX standard introduced additional facilities for matching characters that are not in the English alphabet. For example, the French è is an alphabetic character, but the typical character class [a-z] would not match it. Additionally, the standard provides for sequences of characters that should be treated as a single unit when matching and collating (sorting) string data.

POSIX also formalizes the terminology. Groups of characters within brackets are called "bracket expressions" in the POSIX standard. Within bracket expressions, beside literal characters such as *a*, *!*, and so on, you can have additional components. These *components* are:

Character classes
> A POSIX character class consists of keywords bracketed by [: and :]. The keywords describe different classes of characters, such as alphabetic characters, control characters, and so on (see Table 6-1).

Collating symbols
> A collating symbol is a multicharacter sequence that should be treated as a unit. It consists of the characters bracketed by [. and .].

Equivalence classes
> An equivalence class lists a set of characters that should be considered equivalent, such as *e* and *è*. It consists of a named element from the locale, bracketed by [= and =].

All three of these constructs *must* appear inside the square brackets of a bracket expression. For example, [[:alpha:]!] matches any single alphabetic character or the exclamation point, [[.ch.]] matches the collating element *ch*, but does not match just the letter *c* or the letter *h*. In a French locale, [[=e=]] might match any of *e*, *è*, or *é*. Classes and matching characters are shown in Table 6-1.

Table 6-1. POSIX character classes

Class	Matching characters
[:alnum:]	Alphanumeric characters
[:alpha:]	Alphabetic characters
[:blank:]	Space and tab characters
[:cntrl:]	Control characters
[:digit:]	Numeric characters
[:graph:]	Printable and visible (nonspace) characters
[:lower:]	Lowercase characters
[:print:]	Printable characters (includes whitespace)
[:punct:]	Punctuation characters
[:space:]	Whitespace characters

Class	Matching characters
[:upper:]	Uppercase characters
[:xdigit:]	Hexadecimal digits

vi on HP-UX 9.x (and newer) systems support POSIX bracket expressions, as does /usr/xpg4/bin/vi on Solaris (but not /usr/bin/vi). This facility is also available in nvi, elvis, Vim, and vile. Current GNU/Linux systems, in particular, are sensitive to the locale chosen at installation time, and you can expect to get reasonable results, particularly when trying to match only lowercase or uppercase letters, just by using the POSIX bracket expressions.

Metacharacters Used in Replacement Strings

When you make global replacements, the regular expression metacharacters discussed earlier carry their special meanings only within the search portion (the first part) of the command.

For example, when you type this:

    :%s/1\. Start/2. Next, start with $100/

note that the replacement string treats the characters . and $ literally, without your having to escape them. By the same token, let's say you enter:

    :%s/[ABC]/[abc]/g

If you're hoping to replace *A* with *a*, *B* with *b*, and *C* with *c*, you'll be surprised. Since brackets behave like ordinary characters in a replacement string, this command will change every occurrence of *A*, *B*, or *C* to the five-character string *[abc]*.

To solve problems like this, you need a way to specify variable replacement strings. Fortunately, there are additional metacharacters that have special meaning in a *replacement* string.

\n

Is replaced with the text matched by the *n*th pattern previously saved by \(and \), where *n* is a number from 1 to 9, and previously saved patterns (kept in hold buffers) are counted from the left on the line. See the explanation for \(and \) in the earlier section "Metacharacters Used in Search Patterns" on page 74.

\

Treats the following special character as an ordinary character. Backslashes are metacharacters in replacement strings as well as in search patterns. To specify a real backslash, type two in a row (\\).

&

Is replaced with the entire text matched by the search pattern when used in a replacement string. This is useful when you want to avoid retyping text:

```
:%s/Yazstremski/&, Carl/
```

The replacement will say *Yazstremski, Carl*. The & can also replace a variable pattern (as specified by a regular expression). For example, to surround each line from 1 to 10 with parentheses, type:

```
:1,10s/.*/(&)/
```

The search pattern matches the whole line, and the & "replays" the line, included within your text.

~

Has a similar meaning as when it is used in a search pattern: the string found is replaced with the replacement text specified in the last substitute command. This is useful for repeating an edit. For example, you could say `:s/thier/their/` on one line and repeat the change on another with `:s/thier/~/`. The search pattern doesn't need to be the same, though.

For example, you could say `:s/his/their/` on one line and repeat the replacement on another with `:s/her/~/`.[||]

\u *or* \l

Causes the next character in the replacement string to be changed to uppercase or lowercase, respectively. For example, to change *yes, doctor* into *Yes, Doctor*, you could say:

```
:%s/yes, doctor/\uyes, \udoctor/
```

This is a pointless example, though, since it's easier just to type the replacement string with initial caps in the first place. As with any regular expression, \u and \l are most useful with a variable string. Take, for example, the command we used earlier:

```
:%s/\(That\) or \(this\)/\2 or \1/
```

The result is *this or That*, but we need to adjust the cases. We'll use \u to uppercase the first letter in *this* (currently saved in hold buffer 2); we'll use \l to lowercase the first letter in *That* (currently saved in hold buffer 1):

```
:s/\(That\) or \(this\)/\u\2 or \l\1/
```

The result is *This or that*. (Don't confuse the number one with the lowercase l; the one comes after.)

\U *or* \L *and* \e *or* \E

\U and \L are similar to \u or \l, but all following characters are converted to uppercase or lowercase until the end of the replacement string or until \e or \E is reached. If there is no \e or \E, all characters of the replacement text are affected by the \U or \L. For example, to uppercase *Fortran*, you could say:

[||] Modern versions of the **ed** editor use **%** as the sole character in the replacement text to mean "the replacement text of the last substitute command."

```
:%s/Fortran/\UFortran/
```

or, using the & character to repeat the search string:

```
:%s/Fortran/\U&/
```

All pattern searches are case-sensitive. That is, a search for *the* will not find *The*. You can get around this by specifying both uppercase and lowercase in the pattern:

```
/[Tt]he
```

You can also instruct **vi** to ignore case by typing `:set ic`. See Chapter 7 for additional details.

More Substitution Tricks

You should know some additional important facts about the substitute command:

- A simple `:s` is the same as `:s//~/`. In other words, repeat the last substitution. This can save enormous amounts of time and typing when you are working your way through a document making the same change repeatedly but you don't want to use a global substitution.

- If you think of the & as meaning "the same thing" (as in, what was just matched), this command is relatively mnemonic. You can follow the & with a g, to make the substitution globally on the line, and even use it with a line range:

  `:%&g`   *Repeat the last substitution everywhere*

- The ⟨&⟩ key can be used as a **vi** command to perform the `:&` command, i.e., to repeat the last substitution. This can save even more typing than `:s` ⟨ENTER⟩—one keystroke versus three.

- The `:~` command is similar to the `:&` command but with a subtle difference. The search pattern used is the last regular expression used in *any* command, not necessarily the one used in the last substitute command.

  For example,[#] in the sequence:

  ```
  :s/red/blue/
  :/green
  :~
  ```

  the `:~` is equivalent to `:s/green/blue/`.

- Besides the / character, you may use any nonalphanumeric, nonwhitespace character as your delimiter, except backslash, double quotes, and the vertical bar (\, ", and |). This is particularly handy when you have to make a change to a pathname.

  ```
  :%s;/user1/tim;/home/tim;g
  ```

- When the `edcompatible` option is enabled, **vi** remembers the flags (g for global and c for confirmation) used on the last substitution and applies them to the next one.

[#] Thanks to Keith Bostic, in the **nvi** documentation, for this example.

This is most useful when you are moving through a file and you wish to make global substitutions. You can make the first change:

```
:s/old/new/g
:set edcompatible
```

and after that, subsequent substitute commands will be global.

Despite the name, no known version of Unix ed actually works this way.

Pattern-Matching Examples

Unless you are already familiar with regular expressions, the preceding discussion of special characters probably looks forbiddingly complex. A few more examples should make things clearer. In the examples that follow, a square (□) is used to mark a space; it is not a special character.

Let's work through how you might use some special characters in a replacement. Suppose that you have a long file and that you want to substitute the word *child* with the word *children* throughout that file. You first save the edited buffer with :w, then try the global replacement:

```
:%s/child/children/g
```

When you continue editing, you notice occurrences of words such as *childrenish*. You have unintentionally matched the word *childish*. Returning to the last saved buffer with :e!, you now try:

```
:%s/child□/children□/g
```

(Note that there is a space after *child*.) But this command misses the occurrences *child.*, *child,*, *child:* and so on. After some thought, you remember that brackets allow you to specify one character from among a list, so you realize a solution:

```
:%s/child[□,.;:!?]/children[□,.;:!?]/g
```

This searches for *child* followed by either a space (indicated by □) or any one of the punctuation characters , . ; : ! ?. You expect to replace this with *children* followed by the corresponding space or punctuation mark, but you've ended up with a bunch of punctuation marks after every occurrence of *children*. You need to save the space and punctuation marks inside a \(and \). Then you can "replay" them with a \1. Here's the next attempt:

```
:%s/child\([□,.;:!?]\)/children\1/g
```

When the search matches a character inside the \(and \), the \1 on the righthand side restores the same character. The syntax may seem awfully complicated, but this command sequence can save you a lot of work. *Any time you spend learning regular expression syntax will be repaid a thousandfold!*

The command is still not perfect, though. You've noticed that occurrences of *Fairchild* have been changed, so you need a way to match *child* when it isn't part of another word.

As it turns out, vi (but not all other programs that use regular expressions) has a special syntax for saying "only if the pattern is a complete word." The character sequence \< requires the pattern to match at the beginning of a word, whereas \> requires the pattern to match at the end of a word. Using both will restrict the match to a whole word. So, in the example task, \<child\> will find all instances of the word *child*, whether followed by punctuation or spaces. Here's the substitution command you should use:

```
:%s/\<child\>/children/g
```

Search for General Class of Words

Suppose your subroutine names begin with the prefixes *mgi*, *mgr*, and *mga*:

```
mgibox routine,
mgrbox routine,
mgabox routine,
```

If you want to save the prefixes, but want to change the name *box* to *square*, either of the following replacement commands will do the trick. The first example illustrates how \(and \) can be used to save whatever pattern was actually matched. The second example shows how you can search for one pattern but change another:

```
:g/mg\([ira]\)box/s//mg\1square/g
```

```
mgisquare routine,
mgrsquare routine,
mgasquare routine,
```

The global replacement keeps track of whether an *i*, *r*, or *a* is saved. In that way, *box* is changed to *square* only when *box* is part of the routine's name.

```
:g/mg[ira]box/s/box/square/g
```

```
mgisquare routine,
mgrsquare routine,
mgasquare routine,
```

This has the same effect as the previous command, but it is a little less safe since it could change other instances of *box* on the same line, not just those within the routine names.

Block Move by Patterns

You can also move blocks of text delimited by patterns. For example, assume you have a 150-page reference manual written in troff. Each page is organized into three paragraphs with the same three headings: SYNTAX, DESCRIPTION, and PARAMETERS. A sample of one reference page follows:

```
.Rh 0 "Get status of named file" "STAT"
.Rh "SYNTAX"
.nf
integer*4 stat, retval
integer*4 status(11)
character*123 filename
...
retval = stat (filename, status)
.fi
.Rh "DESCRIPTION"
Writes the fields of a system data structure into the
status array.
These fields contain (among other
things) information about the file's location, access
privileges, owner, and time of last modification.
.Rh "PARAMETERS"
.IP "\fBfilename\fR" 15n
A character string variable or constant containing
the Unix pathname for the file whose status you want
to retrieve.
You can give the ...
```

Suppose that you decide to move DESCRIPTION above the SYNTAX paragraph. With pattern matching, you can move blocks of text on all 150 pages with one command!

```
:g /SYNTAX/.,/DESCRIPTION/-1 move /PARAMETERS/-1
```

This command works as follows. First, **ex** finds and marks each line that matches the first pattern (i.e., that contains the word *SYNTAX*). Second, for each marked line, it sets **.** (dot, the current line) to that line, and executes the command. Using the move command, the command moves the block of lines from the current line (dot) to the line before the one containing the word *DESCRIPTION* (`/DESCRIPTION/-1`) to just before the line containing *PARAMETERS* (`/PARAMETERS/-1`).

Note that **ex** can place text only below the line specified. To tell **ex** to place text above a line, you first subtract one with **-1**, and then **ex** places your text below the previous line. In a case like this, one command saves literally hours of work. (This is a real-life example—we once used a pattern match like this to rearrange a reference manual containing hundreds of pages.)

Block definition by patterns can be used equally well with other **ex** commands. For example, if you wanted to delete all DESCRIPTION paragraphs in the reference chapter, you could enter:

```
:g/DESCRIPTION/,/PARAMETERS/-1d
```

This very powerful kind of change is implicit in **ex**'s line addressing syntax, but it is not readily apparent even to experienced users. For this reason, whenever you are faced with a complex, repetitive editing task, take the time to analyze the problem and find out if you can apply pattern-matching tools to get the job done.

More Examples

Since the best way to learn pattern matching is by example, here is a list of pattern-matching examples, with explanations. Study the syntax carefully, so that you understand the principles at work. You should then be able to adapt these examples to your own situation:

1. Put `troff` italicization codes around the word *ENTER*:

   ```
   :%s/ENTER/\\fI&\\fP/g
   ```

   Notice that two backslashes (\\) are needed in the replacement, because the backslash in the `troff` italicization code will be interpreted as a special character. (`\fI` alone would be interpreted as *fI*; you must type `\\fI` to get \fI.)

2. Modify a list of pathnames in a file:

   ```
   :%s/\/home\/tim/\/home\/linda/g
   ```

   A slash (used as a delimiter in the global replacement sequence) must be escaped with a backslash when it is part of the pattern or replacement; use \/ to get /. An alternate way to achieve this same effect is to use a different character as the pattern delimiter. For example, you could make the previous replacement using colons as delimiters. (The delimiter colons and the `ex` command colon are separate entities.) Thus:

   ```
   :%s:/home/tim:/home/linda:g
   ```

   This is much more readable.

3. Put HTML italicization codes around the word *ENTER*:

   ```
   :%s:ENTER:<I>&</I>:g
   ```

   Notice here the use of & to represent the text that was actually matched, and, as just described, the use of colons as delimiters instead of slashes.

4. Change all periods to semicolons in lines 1 to 10:

   ```
   :1,10s/\./;/g
   ```

   A dot has special meaning in regular expression syntax and must be escaped with a backslash (\.).

5. Change all occurrences of the word *help* (or *Help*) to *HELP*:

   ```
   :%s/[Hh]elp/HELP/g
   ```

   or:

   ```
   :%s/[Hh]elp/\U&/g
   ```

   The \U changes the pattern that follows to all uppercase. The pattern that follows is the repeated search pattern, which is either *help* or *Help*.

6. Replace *one or more* spaces with a single space:

```
:%s/□□*/□/g
```

Make sure you understand how the asterisk works as a special character. An asterisk following any character (or following any regular expression that matches a single character, such as . or [[:lower:]]) matches *zero or more* instances of that character. Therefore, you must specify *two* spaces followed by an asterisk to match one or more spaces (one space, plus zero or more spaces).

7. Replace one or more spaces following a colon with two spaces:

```
:%s/:□□*/:□□/g
```

8. Replace one or more spaces following a period *or* a colon with two spaces:

```
:%s/\([:.]\)□□*/\1□□/g
```

Either of the two characters within brackets can be matched. This character is saved into a hold buffer, using \(and \), and restored on the righthand side by the \1. Note that within brackets a special character such as a dot does not need to be escaped.

9. Standardize various uses of a word or heading:

```
:%s/^Note[□:s]*/Notes:□/g
```

The brackets enclose three characters: a space, a colon, and the letter *s*. Therefore, the pattern Note[□s:] will match *Note*□, *Notes*, or *Note:*. An asterisk is added to the pattern so that it also matches *Note* (with zero spaces after it) and *Notes:* (the already correct spelling). Without the asterisk, *Note* would be missed entirely and *Notes:* would be incorrectly changed to *Notes:*□:.

10. Delete all blank lines:

```
:g/^$/d
```

What you are actually matching here is the beginning of the line (^) followed by the end of the line ($), with nothing in between.

11. Delete all blank lines, plus any lines that contain only whitespace:

```
:g/^[□tab]*$/d
```

(In the example, a tab is shown as *tab*.) A line may appear to be blank, but may in fact contain spaces or tabs. The previous example will not delete such a line. This example, like the previous one, searches for the beginning and end of the line. But instead of having nothing in between, the pattern tries to find any number of spaces or tabs. If no spaces or tabs are matched, the line is blank. To delete lines that contain whitespace but that *aren't* empty, you would have to match lines with *at least* one space or tab:

```
:g/^[□tab][□tab]*$/d
```

12. Delete all leading spaces on every line:

```
:%s/^□□*\(.*\)/\1/
```

Use `^`□□`*` to search for one or more spaces at the beginning of each line; then use `\(.*\)` to save the rest of the line into the first hold buffer. Restore the line without leading spaces, using `\1`.

13. Delete all spaces at the end of every line:

    `:%s/\(.*\)`□□`*$/\1/`

    For each line, use `\(.*\)` to save all the text on the line, but only up until one or more spaces at the end of the line. Restore the saved text without the spaces.

    The substitutions in this example and the previous one will happen only once on any given line, so the **g** option doesn't need to follow the replacement string.

14. Insert a `>`□□ at the start of every line in a file:

    `:%s/^/>`□□`/`

    What we're really doing here is "replacing" the start of the line with `>`□□. Of course, the start of the line (being a logical construct, not an actual character) isn't really replaced!

    This command is useful when replying to mail or Usenet news postings. Frequently, it is desirable to include part of the original message in your reply. By convention, the inclusion is distinguished from your reply by setting off the included text with a right angle bracket and a couple of spaces at the start of the line. This can be done easily, as shown in the example. (Typically, only part of the original message will be included. Unneeded text can be deleted either before or after the replacement.) Advanced mail systems do this automatically. However, if you're using **vi** to edit your mail, you can do it with this command.

15. Add a period to the end of the next six lines:

    `:.,+5s/$/./`

    The line address indicates the current line plus five lines. The `$` indicates the end of line. As in the previous example, the `$` is a logical construct. You aren't really replacing the end of the line.

16. Reverse the order of all hyphen-separated items in a list:

    `:%s/\(.*\)`□`-`□`\(.*\)/\2`□`-`□`\1/`

    Use `\(.*\)` to save text on the line into the first hold buffer, but only until you find □`-`□. Then use `\(.*\)` to save the rest of the line into the second hold buffer. Restore the saved portions of the line, reversing the order of the two hold buffers. The effect of this command on several items is shown here:

    ```
    more - display files
    ```

    becomes:

    ```
    display files - more
    ```

and:

```
lp - print files
```

becomes:

```
print files - lp
```

17. Change every letter in a file to uppercase:

    ```
    :%s/.*/\U&/
    ```

    or:

    ```
    :%s/./\U&/g
    ```

    The \U flag at the start of the replacement string tells vi to change the replacement to uppercase. The & character replays the text matched by the search pattern as the replacement. These two commands are equivalent; however, the first form is considerably faster, since it results in only one substitution per line (.* matches the entire line, once per line), whereas the second form results in repeated substitutions on each line (. matches only a single character, with the replacement repeated on account of the trailing g).

18. Reverse the order of lines in a file:[*]

    ```
    :g/.*/mo0
    ```

    The search pattern matches all lines (a line contains zero or more characters). Each line is moved, one by one, to the top of the file (that is, moved after imaginary line 0). As each matched line is placed at the top, it pushes the previously moved lines down, one by one, until the last line is on top. Since all lines have a beginning, the same result can be achieved more succinctly:

    ```
    :g/^/mo0
    ```

19. In a text-file database, on all lines not marked *Paid in full*, append the phrase *Overdue*:

    ```
    :g!/Paid in full/s/$/ Overdue/
    ```

    or the equivalent:

    ```
    :v/Paid in full/s/$/ Overdue/
    ```

    To affect all lines *except* those matching your pattern, add a ! to the g command, or simply use the v command.

20. For any line that doesn't begin with a number, move the line to the end of the file:

    ```
    :g!/^[[:digit:]]/m$
    ```

    or:

    ```
    :g/^[^[:digit:]]/m$
    ```

---

[*] From an article by Walter Zintz in *Unix World*, May 1990.

As the first character within brackets, a caret negates the sense, so the two commands have the same effect. The first one says, "Don't match lines that begin with a number," and the second one says, "Match lines that don't begin with a number."

21. Change manually numbered section heads (e.g., 1.1, 1.2, etc.) to a `troff` macro (e.g., `.Ah` for an A-level heading):

    `:%s/^[1-9]\.[1-9]/.Ah/`

    The search string matches a digit other than zero, followed by a period, followed by another nonzero digit. Notice that the period doesn't need to be escaped in the replacement (though a \ would have no effect, either). The command just shown won't find chapter numbers containing two or more digits. To do so, modify the command like this:

    `:%s/^[1-9][0-9]*\.[1-9]/.Ah/`

    Now it will match chapters 10 to 99 (digits 1 to 9, followed by a digit), 100 to 999 (digits 1 to 9, followed by two digits), etc. The command still finds chapters 1 to 9 (digits 1 to 9, followed by no digit).

22. Remove numbering from section headings in a document. You want to change the sample lines:

    ```
    2.1 Introduction
    10.3.8 New Functions
    ```

    into the lines:

    ```
    Introduction
    New Functions
    ```

    Here's the command to do this:

    `:%s/^[1-9][0-9]*\.[1-9][0-9.]*□//`

    The search pattern resembles the one in the previous example, but now the numbers vary in length. At a minimum, the headings contain *number, period, number,* so you start with the search pattern from the previous example:

    `[1-9][0-9]*\.[1-9]`

    But in this example, the heading may continue with any number of digits or periods:

    `[0-9.]*`

23. Change the word *Fortran* to the phrase *FORTRAN (acronym of FORmula TRANslation)*:

    `:%s/\(For\)\(tran\)/\U\1\2\E□(acronym□of□\U\1\Emula□\U\2\Eslation)/g`

    First, since we notice that the words *FORmula* and *TRANslation* use portions of the original words, we decide to save the search pattern in two pieces: `\(For\)` and `\(tran\)`. The first time we restore it, we use both pieces together, converting all characters to uppercase: `\U\1\2`. Next, we undo the uppercase with `\E`; otherwise, the remaining replacement text would all be uppercase. The replacement continues with actual typed words, and then we restore the first hold buffer. This buffer still contains *For*, so again we convert to uppercase first: `\U\1`. Immediately after, we lowercase the rest of the word: `\Emula`. Finally, we restore the second hold buffer. This contains *tran*, so we precede the "replay" with uppercase, follow it with lowercase, and type out the rest of the word: `\U\2\Eslation)`.

A Final Look at Pattern Matching

We conclude this chapter by presenting sample tasks that involve complex pattern-matching concepts. Rather than solve the problems right away, we'll work toward the solutions step by step.

Deleting an Unknown Block of Text

Suppose you have a few lines with this general form:

```
the best of times; the worst of times:  moving
The coolest of times; the worst of times:  moving
```

The lines that you're concerned with always end with *moving*, but you never know what the first two words might be. You want to change any line that ends with *moving* to read:

```
The greatest of times; the worst of times:  moving
```

Since the changes must occur on certain lines, you need to specify a context-sensitive global replacement. Using `:g/moving$/` will match lines that end with *moving*. Next, you realize that your search pattern could be any number of any character, so the metacharacters `.*` come to mind. But these will match the whole line unless you somehow restrict the match. Here's your first attempt:

```
:g/moving$/s/.*of/The␣greatest␣of/
```

This search string, you decide, will match from the beginning of the line to the first *of*. Since you needed to specify the word *of* to restrict the search, you simply repeat it in the replacement. Here's the resulting line:

```
The greatest of times:  moving
```

Something went wrong. The replacement gobbled the line up to the second *of* instead of the first. Here's why: when given a choice, the action of "match any number of any character" will match *as much text as possible*. In this case, since the word *of* appears twice, your search string finds:

```
the best of times; the worst of
```

rather than:

```
the best of
```

Your search pattern needs to be more restrictive:

```
:g/moving$/s/.*of times;/The greatest of times;/
```

Now the .* will match all characters up to the instance of the phrase *of times;*. Since there's only one instance, it has to be the first.

There are cases, though, when it is inconvenient, or even incorrect, to use the .* metacharacters. For example, you might find yourself typing many words to restrict your search pattern, or you might be unable to restrict the pattern by specific words (if the text in the lines varies widely). The next section presents such a case.

Switching Items in a Textual Database

Suppose you want to switch the order of all last names and first names in a (text) database. The lines look like this:

```
Name: Feld, Ray; Areas: PC, Unix; Phone: 123-4567
Name: Joy, Susan S.; Areas: Graphics; Phone: 999-3333
```

The name of each field ends with a colon, and each field is separated by a semicolon. Using the top line as an example, you want to change *Feld, Ray* to *Ray Feld*. We'll present some commands that look promising but don't work. After each command, we show you the line the way it looked before the change and after the change.

```
:%s/: \(.*\), \(.*\);/: \2 \1;/
```

```
Name: Feld, Ray; Areas: PC, Unix; Phone: 123-4567      Before
Name: Unix Feld, Ray; Areas: PC; Phone: 123-4567       After
```

We've highlighted the contents of the first hold buffer in **bold** and the contents of the second hold buffer in *italic*. Note that the first hold buffer contains more than you want. Since it was not sufficiently restricted by the pattern that follows it, the hold buffer was able to save up to the second comma. Now you try to restrict the contents of the first hold buffer:

```
:%s/: \(....\), \(.*\);/: \2 \1;/
```

```
Name: Feld, Ray; Areas: PC, Unix; Phone: 123-4567      Before
Name: Ray; Areas: PC, Unix Feld; Phone: 123-4567       After
```

Here you've managed to save the last name in the first hold buffer, but now the second hold buffer will save anything up to the last semicolon on the line. Now you restrict the second hold buffer, too:

```
:%s/: \(....\), \(...\);/: \2 \1;/
```

```
Name: Feld, Ray; Areas: PC, Unix; Phone: 123-4567      Before
Name: Ray Feld; Areas: PC, Unix; Phone: 123-4567       After
```

This gives you what you want, but only in the specific case of a four-letter last name and a three-letter first name. (The previous attempt included the same mistake.) Why not just return to the first attempt, but this time be more selective about the end of the search pattern?

```
:%s/: \(.*\), \(.*\); Area/: \2 \1; Area/
```

```
Name: Feld, Ray; Areas: PC, Unix; Phone: 123-4567      Before
Name: Ray Feld; Areas: PC, Unix; Phone: 123-4567       After
```

This works, but we'll continue the discussion by introducing an additional concern. Suppose that the *Area* field isn't always present or isn't always the second field. The command just shown won't work on such lines.

We introduce this problem to make a point. Whenever you rethink a pattern match, it's usually better to work toward refining the variables (the metacharacters), rather than using specific text to restrict patterns. The more variables you use in your patterns, the more powerful your commands will be.

In the current example, think again about the patterns you want to switch. Each word starts with an uppercase letter and is followed by any number of lowercase letters, so you can match the names like this:

```
[[:upper:]][[:lower:]]*
```

A last name might also have more than one uppercase letter (*McFly*, for example), so you'd want to search for this possibility in the second and succeeding letters:

```
[[:upper:]][[:alpha:]]*
```

It doesn't hurt to use this for the first name, too (you never know when *McGeorge Bundy* will turn up). Your command now becomes:

```
:%s/: \([[:upper:]][[:alpha:]]*\), \([[:upper:]][[:alpha:]]*\);/: \2 \1;/
```

Quite forbidding, isn't it? It still doesn't cover the case of a name like *Joy, Susan S.* Since the first-name field might include a middle initial, you need to add a space and a period within the second pair of brackets. But enough is enough. Sometimes, specifying exactly what you want is more difficult than specifying what you *don't* want. In your sample database, the last names end with a comma, so a last-name field can be thought of as a string of characters that are *not* commas:

```
[^,]*
```

This pattern matches characters up until the first comma. Similarly, the first-name field is a string of characters that are *not* semicolons:

```
[^;]*
```

Putting these more efficient patterns back into your previous command, you get:

```
:%s/: \([^,]*\), \([^;]*\);/: \2 \1;/
```

The same command could also be entered as a context-sensitive replacement. If all lines begin with *Name*, you can say:

```
:g/^Name/s/: \([^,]*\), \([^;]*\);/: \2 \1;/
```

You can also add an asterisk after the first space, in order to match a colon that has extra spaces (or no spaces) after it:

```
:g/^Name/s/: *\([^,]*\), \([^;]*\);/: \2 \1;/
```

Using :g to Repeat a Command

In the usual way we've seen the :g command used, it selects lines that are typically then edited by subsequent commands on the same line—for example, we select lines with g, and then make substitutions on them, or select them and delete them:

```
:g/mg[ira]box/s/box/square/g
:g/^$/d
```

However, in his two-part tutorial in *Unix World*,[†] Walter Zintz makes an interesting point about the g command. This command selects lines, but the associated editing commands need not actually affect the lines that are selected.

Instead, he demonstrates a technique by which you can repeat **ex** commands some arbitrary number of times. For example, suppose you want to place 10 copies of lines 12 through 17 of your file at the end of your current file. You could type:

```
:1,10g/^/ 12,17t$
```

This is a very unexpected use of g, but it works! The g command selects line 1, executes the specified t command, then goes on to line 2 to execute the next copy command. When line 10 is reached, **ex** will have made 10 copies.

Collecting Lines

Here's another advanced g example, again building on suggestions provided in Zintz's article. Suppose you're editing a document that consists of several parts. Part 2 of this file is shown here, using ellipses to show omitted text and displaying line numbers for reference:

```
301  Part 2
302  Capability Reference
303  .LP
304  Chapter 7
305  Introduction to the Capabilities
306  This and the next three chapters ...

400  ... and a complete index at the end.
401  .LP
402  Chapter 8
403  Screen Dimensions
404  Before you can do anything useful
405  on the screen, you need to know ...
```

[†] Part one, "vi Tips for Power Users," appears in the April 1990 issue of *UNIX World*. Part two, "Using vi to Automate Complex Edits," appears in the May 1990 issue. The examples presented are from Part 2.

```
555  .LP
556  Chapter 9
557  Editing the Screen
558  This chapter discusses ...

821  .LP
822  Part 3:
823  Advanced Features
824  .LP
825  Chapter 10
```

The chapter numbers appear on one line, their titles appear on the line below, and the chapter text (marked in **bold** for emphasis) begins on the line below that. The first thing you'd like to do is copy the beginning line of each chapter, sending it to an already existing file called `begin`.

Here's the command that does this:

```
:g /^Chapter/ .+2w >> begin
```

You must be at the top of your file before issuing this command. First, you search for *Chapter* at the start of a line, but then you want to run the command on the beginning line of each chapter—the second line below *Chapter*. Because a line beginning with *Chapter* is now selected as the current line, the line address `.+2` will indicate the second line below it. The equivalent line addresses `+2` or `++` work as well. You want to write these lines to an existing file named `begin`, so you issue the `w` command with the append operator `>>`.

Suppose you want to send the beginnings of chapters that are only within Part 2. You need to restrict the lines selected by `g`, so you change your command to this:

```
:/^Part 2/,/^Part 3/g /^Chapter/ .+2w >> begin
```

Here, the `g` command selects the lines that begin with *Chapter*, but it searches only that portion of the file from a line starting with *Part 2* through a line starting with *Part 3*. If you issue the command just shown, the last lines of the file `begin` will read as follows:

```
This and the next three chapters ...
Before you can do anything useful
This chapter discusses ...
```

These are the lines that begin Chapters 7, 8, and 9.

In addition to the lines you've just sent, you'd like to copy chapter titles to the end of the document, in preparation for making a table of contents. You can use the vertical bar to tack on a second command after your first command, like so:

```
:/^Part 2/,/^Part 3/g /^Chapter/ .+2w >> begin | +t$
```

Remember that with any subsequent command, line addresses are relative to the previous command. The first command has marked lines (within Part 2) that start with *Chapter*, and the chapter titles appear on a line below such lines. Therefore, to access chapter titles in the second command, the line address is + (or the equivalents +1 or .+1). Then, use t$ to copy the chapter titles to the end of the file.

As these examples illustrate, thought and experimentation may lead you to some un- usual editing solutions. Don't be afraid to try things. Just be sure to back up your file first! (Of course, with the infinite "undo" facilities in the clones, you may not even need to save a backup copy.)

Advanced Editing

This chapter introduces you to some of the more advanced capabilities of the **vi** and **ex** editors. You should be reasonably familiar with the material presented in the earlier chapters of this book before you start working with the concepts presented here.

We have divided this chapter into five parts. The first part discusses a number of ways to set options that allow you to customize your editing environment. You'll learn how to use the **set** command and how to create a number of different editing environments using `.exrc` files.

The second part discusses how you can execute Unix commands from within **vi**, and how you can use **vi** to filter text through Unix commands.

The third part discusses various ways to save long sequences of commands by reducing them to abbreviations, or even to commands that use only one keystroke (this is called *mapping* keys). It also includes a section on @-functions, which allow you to store command sequences in a buffer.

The fourth part discusses the use of **ex** scripts from the Unix command line or from within shell scripts. Scripting provides a powerful way to make repetitive edits.

The fifth part discusses some features of **vi** that are especially useful to programmers. **vi** has options that control line indentation and an option to display invisible characters (specifically tabs and newlines). There are search commands that are useful with program code blocks or with C functions.

Customizing vi

vi operates differently on various terminals. On modern Unix systems, **vi** gets operating instructions about your terminal type from the `terminfo` terminal database. (On older systems, **vi** uses the original `termcap` database.)[*]

---

[*] The location of these two databases varies from vendor to vendor. Try the commands `man terminfo` and `man termcap` to get more information about your specific system.

There are also a number of options that you can set from within `vi` that affect how it operates. For example, you can set a right margin that will cause `vi` to wrap lines automatically, so you don't need to hit ENTER.

You can change options from within `vi` by using the `ex` command `:set`. In addition, whenever `vi` is started up, it reads a file in your home directory called `.exrc` for further operating instructions. By placing `:set` commands in this file, you can modify the way `vi` acts whenever you use it.

You can also set up `.exrc` files in local directories to initialize various options that you want to use in different environments. For example, you might define one set of options for editing English text, but another set for editing source programs. The `.exrc` file in your home directory will be executed first, and then the one in your current directory.

Finally, any commands stored in the environment variable `EXINIT` will be executed by `vi` on startup. The settings in `EXINIT` take precedence over those in the home directory `.exrc` file.

The :set Command

There are two types of options that can be changed with the `:set` command: toggle options, which are either on or off, and options that take a numeric or string value (such as the location of a margin or the name of a file).

Toggle options may be on or off by default. To turn a toggle option on, the command is:

    :set option

To turn a toggle option off, the command is:

    :set nooption

For example, to specify that pattern searches should ignore case, type:

    :set ic

If you want `vi` to return to being case-sensitive in searches, give the command:

    :set noic

Some options have a value assigned to them. For example, the `window` option sets the number of lines shown in the screen's "window." You set values for these options with an equals sign (=):

    :set window=20

During a `vi` session, you can check which options `vi` is using. The command:

    :set all

displays the complete list of options, including options that you have set and defaults that `vi` has "chosen."

The display should look something like this:[†]

autoindent	nomodelines	noshowmode
autoprint	nonumber	noslowopen
noautowrite	nonovice	tabstop=8
beautify	nooptimize	taglength=0
directory=/var/tmp	paragraphs=IPLPPPQPP LIpplpipnpbp	tags=tags /usr/lib/tags
noedcompatible	prompt	tagstack
errorbells	noreadonly	term=vt102
noexrc	redraw	noterse
flash	remap	timeout
hardtabs=8	report=5	ttytype=vt102
noignorecase	scroll=11	warn
nolisp	sections=NHSHH HUuhsh+c	window=23
nolist	shell=/bin/ksh	wrapscan
magic	shiftwidth=8	wrapmargin=0
nomesg	showmatch	nowriteany

You can find out the current value of any individual option by name, using the command:

```
:set option?
```

The command:

```
:set
```

shows options that you have specifically changed, or set, either in your .exrc file or during the current session.

For example, the display might look like this:

```
number sect=AhBhChDh window=20 wrapmargin=10
```

The .exrc File

The .exrc file that controls your own vi environment is in your home directory (the directory you are in when you first log on). You can modify the .exrc file with the vi editor, just as you can any other text file.

If you don't yet have an .exrc file, simply use vi to create one. Enter into this file the set, ab, and map commands that you want to have in effect whenever you use vi or ex. (ab and map are discussed later in this chapter.) A sample .exrc file might look like this:

```
set nowrapscan wrapmargin=7
set sections=SeAhBhChDh nomesg
map q :w^M:n^M
map v dwElp
ab ORA O'Reilly Media, Inc.
```

[†] The result of :set all depends very much on the version of vi you have. This particular display is typical of Unix vi; what comes out of the various clones will be different. The order is alphabetical going down the columns, ignoring any leading no.

Since the file is actually read by ex before it enters visual mode (vi), commands in .exrc need not have a preceding colon.

Alternate Environments

In addition to reading the .exrc file in your home directory, you can allow vi to read a file called .exrc in the current directory. This lets you set options that are appropriate to a particular project.

In all modern versions of vi, you have to first set the exrc option in your home directory's .exrc file before vi will read the .exrc file in the current directory:

```
set exrc
```

This mechanism prevents other people from placing, in your working directory, an .exrc file whose commands might jeopardize the security of your system.[‡]

For example, you might want to have one set of options in a directory mainly used for programming:

```
set number autoindent sw=4 terse
set tags=/usr/lib/tags
```

and another set of options in a directory used for text editing:

```
set wrapmargin=15 ignorecase
```

Note that you can set certain options in the .exrc file in your home directory and unset them in a local directory.

You can also define alternate vi environments by saving option settings in a file other than .exrc and reading in that file with the :so command. (so is short for source.)

For example:

```
:so .progoptions
```

Local .exrc files are also useful for defining abbreviations and key mappings (described later in this chapter). When we write a book or manual, we save all abbreviations to be used in that book in an .exrc file in the directory in which the book is being created.

Some Useful Options

As you can see when you type :set all, there are an awful lot of options that can be set. Many of them are used internally by vi and aren't usually changed. Others are important in certain cases but not in others (for example, noredraw and window can be useful over a cross-continental ssh session). Table B-1 in the section "Solaris vi Options" on page 415 contains a brief description of each option. We recommend that you take

---

[‡] The original versions of vi automatically read both files, if they existed. The exrc option closes a potential security hole.

---

some time to play with setting options. If an option looks interesting, try setting it (or unsetting it) and watch what happens while you edit. You may find some surprisingly useful tools.

As discussed earlier in the section "Movement Within a Line" on page 16, one option, `wrapmargin`, is essential for editing nonprogram text. `wrapmargin` specifies the size of the right margin that will be used to autowrap text as you type. (This saves manually typing carriage returns.) A typical value is 7 to 15:

    :set wrapmargin=10

Three other options control how `vi` acts when conducting a search. Normally, a search differentiates between uppercase and lowercase (*foo* does not match *Foo*), wraps around to the beginning of the file (meaning that you can begin your search anywhere in the file and still find all occurrences), and recognizes wildcard characters when pattern matching. The default settings that control these options are `noignorecase`, `wrapscan`, and `magic`, respectively. To change any of these defaults, you would set the opposite toggle options: `ignorecase`, `nowrapscan`, and `nomagic`.

Options that may be of particular interest to programmers include `autoindent`, `showmatch`, `tabstop`, `shiftwidth`, `number`, and `list`, as well as their opposite toggle options.

Finally, consider using the `autowrite` option. When set, `vi` will automatically write out the contents of a changed buffer when you issue the `:n` (next) command to move to the next file to be edited, and before running a shell command with `:!`.

Executing Unix Commands

You can display or read in the results of any Unix command while you are editing in `vi`. An exclamation mark (!) tells `ex` to create a shell and to regard what follows as a Unix command:

    :!command

So if you are editing and you want to check the time or date without exiting `vi`, you can enter:

    :!date

The time and date will appear on your screen; press ENTER to continue editing at the same place in your file.

If you want to give several Unix commands in a row without returning to `vi` editing in between, you can create a shell with the `ex` command:

    :sh

When you want to exit the shell and return to `vi`, press CTRL-D.

You can combine :read with a call to Unix, to read the results of a Unix command into your file. As a very simple example:

```
:r !date
```

will read in the system's date information into the text of your file. By preceding the :r command with a line address, you can read the result of the command in at any desired point in your file. By default, it will appear after the current line.

Suppose you are editing a file and want to read in four phone numbers from a file called phone, but in alphabetical order. phone reads:

```
Willing, Sue   333-4444
Walsh, Linda   555-6666
Quercia, Valerie   777-8888
Dougherty, Nancy   999-0000
```

The command:

```
:r !sort phone
```

reads in the contents of phone after they have been passed through the sort filter:

```
Dougherty, Nancy   999-0000
Quercia, Valerie   777-8888
Walsh, Linda   555-6666
Willing, Sue   333-4444
```

Suppose you are editing a file and want to insert text from another file in the directory, but you can't remember the new file's name. You *could* perform this task the long way: exit your file, give the ls command, note the correct filename, reenter your file, and search for your place.

Or you could do the task in fewer steps:

Keystrokes	Results
:!ls	file1 file2 letter newfile practice
	Display a list of files in the current directory. Note the correct filename. Press ENTER to continue editing.
:r newfile	"newfile" 35 lines, 949 characters
	Read in the new file.

Filtering Text Through a Command

You can also send a block of text as standard input to a Unix command. The output from this command replaces the block of text in the buffer. You can filter text through a command from either **ex** or **vi**. The main difference between the two methods is that you indicate the block of text with line addresses in **ex** and with text objects (movement commands) in **vi**.

Filtering text with ex

The first example demonstrates how to filter text with **ex**. Assume that the list of names in the preceding example, instead of being contained in a separate file called phone, is already contained in the current file on lines 96 through 99. You simply type the addresses of the lines you want to filter, followed by an exclamation mark and the Unix command to be executed. For example, the command:

    :96,99!sort

will pass lines 96 through 99 through the **sort** filter and replace those lines with the output of **sort**.

Filtering text with vi

In **vi**, text is filtered through a Unix command by typing an exclamation mark followed by any of **vi**'s movement keystrokes that indicate a block of text, and then by the Unix command line to be executed. For example:

    !)command

will pass the next sentence through *command*.

There are a few unusual aspects of the way **vi** acts when you use this feature:

- The exclamation mark doesn't appear on your screen right away. When you type the keystroke(s) for the text object you want to filter, the exclamation mark appears at the bottom of the screen, *but the character you type to reference the object does not.*

- Text blocks must be more than one line, so you can use only the keystrokes that would move more than one line (G, { }, ( ), [[ ]], +, -). To repeat the effect, a number may precede either the exclamation mark or the text object. (For example, both !10+ and 10!+ would indicate the next 10 lines.) Objects such as w do not work unless enough of them are specified so as to exceed a single line. You can also use a slash (/) followed by a *pattern* and a carriage return to specify the object. This takes the text up to the pattern as input to the command.

- Entire lines are affected. For example, if your cursor is in the middle of a line and you issue a command to go to the end of the next sentence, the entire lines containing the beginning and end of the sentence will be changed, not just the sentence itself.§

- There is a special text object that can be used only with this command syntax: you can specify the current line by entering a second exclamation mark:

    !!command

---

§ Of course, there's always an exception. In this example, Vim changes only the current line.

Remember that either the entire sequence or the text object can be preceded by a number to repeat the effect. For instance, to change lines 96 through 99 as in the previous example, you could position the cursor on line 96 and enter either:

```
4!!sort
```

or:

```
!4!sort
```

As another example, assume you have a portion of text in a file that you want to change from lowercase to uppercase letters. You could process that portion with the **tr** command to change the case. In this example, the second sentence is the block of text that will be filtered through the command:

```
One sentence before.
With a screen editor you can scroll the page
move the cursor, delete lines, insert characters,
and more, while seeing the results of your edits
as you make them.
One sentence after.
```

Keystrokes	Results
| !) | ```
One sentence after.
~
~
~
!
``` |
| | An exclamation mark appears on the last line to prompt you for the Unix command. The) indicates that a sentence is the unit of text to be filtered. |
| tr '[:lower:]' '[:upper:]' | ```
One sentence before.
WITH A SCREEN EDITOR YOU CAN SCROLL THE PAGE
MOVE THE CURSOR, DELETE LINES, INSERT CHARACTERS,
AND MORE, WHILE SEEING THE RESULTS OF YOUR EDITS
AS YOU MAKE THEM.
One sentence after.
``` |
| | Enter the Unix command and press ENTER. The input is replaced by the output. |

To repeat the previous command, the syntax is:

```
! object !
```

It is sometimes useful to send sections of a coded document to **nroff** to be replaced by formatted output. (Or, when editing electronic mail, you might use the **fmt** program to "beautify" your text before sending the message.) Remember that the "original" input is replaced by the output. Fortunately, if there is a mistake—such as an error message being sent instead of the expected output—you can undo the command and restore the lines.

Saving Commands

Often you type the same long phrases over and over in a file. **vi** and **ex** have a number of different ways of saving long sequences of commands, both in command mode and in insert mode. When you call up one of these saved sequences to execute it, all you do is type a few characters (or even only one), and the entire sequence is executed as if you had entered the whole sequence of commands one by one.

Word Abbreviation

You can define abbreviations that **vi** will automatically expand into the full text whenever you type the abbreviation in insert mode. To define an abbreviation, use this **ex** command:

    :ab *abbr phrase*

abbr is an abbreviation for the specified *phrase*. The sequence of characters that make up the abbreviation will be expanded in insert mode only if you type it as a full word; *abbr* will not be expanded within a word.

Suppose in the file **practice** you want to enter text that contains a frequently recurring phrase, such as a difficult product or company name. The command:

    :ab imrc International Materials Research Center

abbreviates *International Materials Research Center* to the initials *imrc*. Now whenever you type *imrc* in insert mode, *imrc* expands to the full text.

Keystrokes	Results
ithe imrc	the International Materials Research Center

Abbreviations expand as soon as you press a nonalphanumeric character (e.g., punctuation), a space, a carriage return, or ESC (returning to command mode). When you are choosing abbreviations, choose combinations of characters that don't ordinarily occur while you are typing text. If you create an abbreviation that ends up expanding in places where you don't want it to, you can disable the abbreviation by typing:

    :unab *abbr*

To list your currently defined abbreviations, type:

    :ab

The characters that compose your abbreviation cannot also appear at the end of your phrase. For example, if you issue the command:

    :ab PG This movie is rated PG

you'll get the message "No tail recursion," and the abbreviation won't be set. The message means that you have tried to define something that will expand itself repeatedly, creating an infinite loop. If you issue the command:

```
:ab PG the PG rating system
```

you may or may not produce an infinite loop, but in either case you won't get a warning message. For example, when the above command was tested on a System V version of Unix, the expansion worked. Circa 1990 on a Berkeley version, the abbreviation expanded repeatedly, like this:

```
the the the the the ...
```

until a memory error occurred and **vi** quit.

When tested, we obtained the following results on these **vi** versions:

Solaris **vi**

> The tail recursive version is not allowed, while the version with the name in the middle of the expansion expands only once.

nvi *1.79*

> Both versions exceed an internal expansion limit, the expansion stops, and **nvi** produces an error message.

elvis, *Vim, and* **vile**

> Both forms are detected and expand only once.

If you are using Unix **vi** or **nvi**, we recommend that you avoid repeating your abbreviation as part of the defined phrase.

Using the map Command

While you're editing, you may find that you are using a command sequence frequently, or that you occasionally use a very complex command sequence. To save yourself keystrokes, or the time that it takes to remember the sequence, you can assign the sequence to an unused key by using the **map** command.

The **map** command acts a lot like **ab** except that you define a macro for **vi**'s command mode instead of for insert mode:

`:map x sequence`

> Define character *x* as a *sequence* of editing commands.

`:unmap x`

> Disable the *sequence* defined for *x*.

`:map`

> List the characters that are currently mapped.

Before you can start creating your own maps, you need to know the keys not used in command mode that are available for user-defined commands:

Letters
  g, K, q, V, and v
Control keys
  ^A, ^K, ^O, ^W, and ^X
Symbols
  _, *, \, and =

 The = is used by vi if Lisp mode is set, and to do text formatting by several of the clones. In many modern versions of vi, the _ is equivalent to the ^ command, and elvis and Vim have a "visual mode" that uses the v, V, and ^V keys. The moral is to test your version carefully.

Depending on your terminal, you may also be able to associate map sequences with special function keys.

With maps, you can create simple or complex command sequences. As a simple example, you could define a command to reverse the order of words. In vi, with the cursor as shown:

```
you can ▊he scroll page
```

the sequence to put *the* after *scroll* would be dwelp: delete word, dw; move to the end of next word, e; move one space to the right, l; put the deleted word there, p. Saving this sequence:

```
:map v dwelp
```

enables you to reverse the order of two words at any time in the editing session with the single keystroke v.

Protecting Keys from Interpretation by ex

Note that when defining a map, you cannot simply type certain keys, such as ENTER, ESC, BACKSPACE, and DELETE, as part of the command to be mapped, because these keys already have meaning within ex. If you want to include one of these keys as part of the command sequence, you must escape the normal meaning by preceding the key with CTRL-V. The keystroke ^V appears in the map as the ^ character. Characters following the ^V also do not appear as you expect. For example, a carriage return appears as ^M, escape as ^[, backspace as ^H, and so on.

On the other hand, if you want to use a control character as the character to be mapped, in most cases all you have to do is hold down the CTRL key and press the letter key at the same time. So, for example, all you need to do in order to map ^A is to type:

```
:map CTRL-A sequence
```

There are, however, three control characters that must be escaped with a ^V. They are ^T, ^W, and ^X. So, for example, if you want to map ^T, you must type:

```
:map CTRL-V CTRL-T sequence
```

The use of CTRL-V applies to any ex command, not just a map command. This means that you can type a carriage return in an abbreviation or a substitution command. For example, the abbreviation:

```
:ab 123 one^Mtwo^Mthree
```

expands to this:

```
one
two
three
```

(Here we show the sequence CTRL-V ENTER as ^M, the way it would appear on your screen.)

You can also globally add lines at certain locations. The command:

```
:g/^Section/s//As you recall, in^M&/
```

inserts, before all lines beginning with the word *Section*, a phrase on a separate line. The & restores the search pattern.

Unfortunately, one character always has special meaning in ex commands, even if you try to quote it with CTRL-V. Recall that the vertical bar (|) has special meaning as a separator of multiple ex commands. You cannot use a vertical bar in insert mode maps.

Now that you've seen how to use CTRL-V to protect certain keys inside ex commands, you're ready to define some powerful map sequences.

A Complex Mapping Example

Assume that you have a glossary with entries like this:

```
map - an ex command which allows you to associate
a complex command sequence with a single key.
```

You would like to convert this glossary list to troff format, so that it looks like this:

```
.IP "map" 10n
An ex command...
```

The best way to define a complex map is to do the edit once manually, writing down each keystroke that you have to type. Then recreate these keystrokes as a map. You want to:

1. Insert the MS macro for an indented paragraph at the beginning of the line. Insert the first quotation mark as well (I.IP ").
2. Press ESC to terminate insert mode.

3. Move to the end of the first word (e) and add a second quotation mark, followed by a space and the size of the indent (a" 10n).

4. Press ENTER to insert a new line.

5. Press ESC to terminate insert mode.

6. Remove the hyphen and two surrounding spaces (3x) and capitalize the next word (~).

That will be quite an editing chore if you have to repeat it more than just a few times.

With :map you can save the entire sequence so that it can be reexecuted with a single keystroke:

```
:map g I.IP "^[ea" 10n^M^[3x~
```

Note that you have to "quote" both the ESC and the ENTER characters with CTRL-V. ^[is the sequence that appears when you type CTRL-V followed by ESC. ^M is the sequence shown when you type CTRL-V ENTER.

Now, simply typing g will perform the entire series of edits. On a slow connection you can actually see the edits happening individually. On a fast one it will seem to happen by magic.

Don't be discouraged if your first attempt at key mapping fails. A small error in defining the map can give very different results from the ones you expect. Type u to undo the edit, and try again.

More Examples of Mapping Keys

The following examples will give you an idea of the clever shortcuts possible when defining keyboard maps:

1. Add text whenever you move to the end of a word:

```
:map e ea
```

Most of the time, the only reason you want to move to the end of a word is to add text. This map sequence puts you in insert mode automatically. Note that the mapped key, e, has meaning in vi. You're allowed to map a key that is already used by vi, but the key's normal function will be unavailable as long as the map is in effect. This isn't so bad in this case, since the E command is often identical to e.

2. Transpose two words:

```
:map K dwElp
```

We discussed this sequence earlier in the chapter, but now you need to use E (assume here, and in the remaining examples, that the e command is mapped to ea). Remember that the cursor begins on the first of the two words. Unfortunately, because of the l command, this sequence (and the earlier version) doesn't work if the two words are at the end of a line: during the sequence, the cursor ends up at the end of the line, and l cannot move further right. Here's a better solution:

```
:map K dwwP
```

You could also use W instead of w.

3. Save a file and edit the next one in a series:

```
:map q :w^M:n^M
```

Notice that you can map keys to **ex** commands, but be sure to finish each **ex** command with a carriage return. This sequence makes it easy to move from one file to the next and is useful when you've opened many short files with one **vi** command. Mapping the letter q helps you remember that the sequence is similar to a "quit."

4. Put **troff** emboldening codes around a word:

```
:map v i\fB^[e\fP^[
```

This sequence assumes that the cursor is at the beginning of the word. First, you enter insert mode, then you type the code for the bold font. In map commands, you don't need to type two backslashes to produce one backslash. Next, you return to command mode by typing a "quoted" ESC. Finally, you append the closing **troff** code at the end of the word, and you return to command mode. Notice that when we appended to the end of the word, we didn't need to use **ea**, since this sequence is itself mapped to the single letter **e**. This shows you that map sequences are allowed to contain other mapped commands. (The ability to use nested map sequences is controlled by **vi**'s **remap** option, which is normally enabled.)

5. Put HTML emboldening codes around a word, even when the cursor is not at the beginning of the word:

```
:map V lbi<B>^[e</B>^[
```

This sequence is similar the previous one; besides using HTML instead of **troff**, it uses **lb** to handle the additional task of positioning the cursor at the beginning of the word. The cursor might be in the middle of the word, so you want to move to the beginning with the **b** command. But if the cursor were already at the beginning of the word, the **b** command would move the cursor to the previous word instead. To guard against that case, type an l before moving back with **b**, so that the cursor never starts on the first letter of the word. You can define variations of this sequence by replacing the **b** with **B** and the **e** with **Ea**. In all cases, though, the l command prevents this sequence from working if the cursor is at the end of a line. (You could append a space to get around this.)

6. Repeatedly find and remove parentheses from around a word or phrase: ‖

```
:map = xf)xn
```

‖ From the article by Walter Zintz, in *Unix World*, April 1990.

This sequence assumes that you first found an open parenthesis, by typing /(followed by ENTER.

If you choose to remove the parentheses, use the map command: delete the open parenthesis with x, find the closing one with f), delete it with x, and then repeat your search for an open parenthesis with n.

If you don't want to remove the parentheses (for example, if they're being used correctly), don't use the mapped command: press n instead to find the next open parenthesis.

You could also modify the map sequence in this example to handle matching pairs of quotes.

7. Place C/C++ comments around an entire line:

```
:map g I/* ^[A */^[
```

This sequence inserts /* at the line's beginning and appends */ at the line's end. You could also map a substitute command to do the same thing:

```
:map g :s;.*;/* & */;^M
```

Here, you match the entire line (with .*), and when you replay it (with &), you surround the line with the comment symbols. Note the use of semicolon delimiters, to avoid having to escape the / in the comment.

8. Safely repeat a long insertion:

```
:map ^J :set wm=0^M.:set wm=10^M
```

We mentioned in Chapter 2 that vi occasionally has difficulty repeating long insertions of text when wrapmargin is set. This map command is a useful workaround. It temporarily turns off the wrapmargin (by setting it to 0), gives the repeat command, and then restores the wrapmargin. Note that a map sequence can combine ex and vi commands.

In the previous example, even though ^J is a vi command (it moves the cursor down a line), this key is safe to map because it's really the same as the j command. There are many keys that either perform the same tasks as other keys or are rarely used. However, you should be familiar with the vi commands before you boldly disable their normal use by using them in map definitions.

Mapping Keys for Insert Mode

Normally, maps apply only to command mode—after all, in insert mode, keys stand for themselves and shouldn't be mapped as commands. However, by adding an exclamation mark (!) to the map command, you can force it to override the ordinary meaning of a key and produce the map in insert mode. This feature is useful when you find yourself in insert mode but need to escape briefly to command mode, run a command, and then return to insert mode.

For example, suppose you just typed a word but forgot to italicize it (or place quotes around it, etc.). You can define this map:

```
:map! + ^[bi<I>^[ea</I>
```

Now, when you type a + at the end of a word, you will surround the word with HTML italicization codes. The + won't show up in the text.

The sequence just shown escapes to command mode (^[), backs up to insert the first code (bi<I>), escapes again (^[), and moves ahead to append the second code (ea</I>). Since the map sequence begins and ends in insert mode, you can continue entering text after marking the word.

Here's another example. Suppose that you've been typing your text, and you realize that the previous line should have ended with a colon. You can correct that by defining this map sequence:#

```
:map! % ^[kA:^[jA
```

Now, if you type a % anywhere along your current line, you'll append a colon to the end of the previous line. This command escapes to command mode, moves up a line, and appends the colon (^[kA:). The command then escapes again, moves down to the line you were on, and leaves you in insert mode (^[jA).

Note that we wanted to use uncommon characters (% and +) for the previous map commands. When a character is mapped for insert mode, you can no longer type that character as text.

To reinstate a character for normal typing, use the command:

```
:unmap! x
```

where *x* is the character that was previously mapped for insert mode. (Although **vi** will expand *x* on the command line as you type it, making it look like you are unmapping the expanded text, it will correctly unmap the character.)

Insert-mode mapping is often more appropriate for tying character strings to special keys that you wouldn't otherwise use. It is especially useful with programmable function keys.

Mapping Function Keys

Many terminals have programmable function keys (which are faithfully emulated by today's terminal emulators on bitmapped workstations). You can usually set up these keys to print whatever character or characters you want using a special setup mode on the terminal. However, keys programmed using a terminal's setup mode work only on that terminal; they may also limit the action of programs that want to set up those function keys themselves.

From an article by Walter Zintz, in *Unix World*, April 1990.

---

ex allows you to map function keys by number, using the syntax:

```
:map #1 commands
```

for function key number 1, and so on. (It can do this because the editor has access to the entry for that terminal found in either the `terminfo` or `termcap` database and knows the escape sequence normally put out by the function key.)

As with other keys, maps apply by default to command mode, but by using the `map!` commands as well, you can define two separate values for a function key—one to be used in command mode, the other in insert mode. For example, if you are an HTML user, you might want to put font-switch codes on function keys. For example:

```
:map #1 i<I>^[
:map! #1 <I>
```

If you are in command mode, the first function key will enter insert mode, type in the three characters `<I>`, and return to command mode. If you are already in insert mode, the key will simply type the three-character HTML code.

If the sequence contains `^M`, which is a carriage return, press CTRL-M. For instance, in order to have function key 1 available for mapping, the terminal database entry for your terminal must have a definition of `k1`, such as:

```
k1=^A@^M
```

In turn, the definition:

```
^A@^M
```

must be what is output when you press that key.

To see what the function key puts out, use the `od` (octal dump) command with the `-c` option (show each character). You will need to press ENTER after the function key, and then CTRL-D to get `od` to print the information. For example:

```
$ od -c
^[[A
^D
0000000 033   [   [   A  \n
0000005
```

Here, the function key sent Escape, two left brackets, and an A.

Mapping Other Special Keys

Many keyboards have special keys, such as HOME, END, PAGE UP, and PAGE DOWN, that duplicate commands in `vi`. If the terminal's `terminfo` or `termcap` description is complete, `vi` will be able to recognize these keys. But if it isn't, you can use the `map` command to make them available to `vi`. These keys generally send an escape sequence to the computer—an Escape character followed by a string of one or more other characters. To trap the Escape, you should press `^V` before pressing the special key in the map. For example, to map the HOME key on the keyboard of an IBM PC to a reasonable **vi** equivalent, you might define the following map:

```
:map CTRL-V HOME 1G
```

This appears on your screen as:

```
:map ^[[H 1G
```

Similar map commands display as follows:

`:map CTRL-V END G`	*displays*	`:map ^[[Y G`	
`:map CTRL-V PAGE UP ^F`	*displays*	`:map ^[[V ^F`	
`:map CTRL-V PAGE DOWN ^B`	*displays*	`:map ^[[U ^B`	

You'll probably want to place these maps in your **.exrc** file. Note that if a special key generates a long escape sequence (containing multiple nonprinting characters), ^V quotes only the initial escape character, and the map doesn't work. You will have to find the entire escape sequence (perhaps from the terminal manual) and type it in manually, quoting at the appropriate points, rather than simply pressing ^V and then the key.

If you use different kinds of terminals (such as both the console of a PC and an **xterm**), you cannot expect that mappings like those just presented will always work. For this reason, Vim provides a portable way to describe such key mappings:

```
:map <Home> 1G          Enter six characters: < H o m e > (Vim)
```

Mapping Multiple Input Keys

Mapping multiple keystrokes is not restricted just to function keys. You can also map sequences of regular keystrokes. This can help make it easier to enter certain kinds of text, such as XML or HTML.

Here are some **:map** commands, thanks to Jerry Peek, coauthor of O'Reilly's *Learning the Unix Operating System*, that make it easier to enter XML markup. (The lines beginning with a double quote are comments. This is discussed later in the section "Comments in ex Scripts" on page 119.)

```
" ADR: need this
:set noremap
" bold:
map! =b </emphasis>^[F<i<emphasis role="bold">
map =B i<emphasis role="bold">>^[
map =b a</emphasis>^[
" Move to end of next tag:
map! =e ^[f>a
map =e f>
" footnote (tacks opening tag directly after cursor in text-input mode):
map! =f <footnote>^M<para>^M</para>^M</footnote>^[kO
" Italics ("emphasis"):
map! =i </emphasis>^[F<i<emphasis>
map =I i<emphasis>^[
map =i a</emphasis>^[
```

```
" paragraphs:
map! =p ^[jo<para>^M</para>^[0
map =P O<para>^[
map =p o</para>^[
" less-than:
map! *l &lt;
...
```

Using these commands, to enter a footnote you would enter insert mode and type =f.
vi would then insert the opening and closing tags, and leave you in insert mode between
them:

```
All the world's a stage.<footnote>
<para>
█
</para>
</footnote>
```

Needless to say, these macros proved quite useful during the development of this book.

@-Functions

Named buffers provide yet another way to create "macros"—complex command sequences that you can repeat with only a few keystrokes.

If you type a command line in your text (either a vi sequence or an ex command *preceded
by a colon*), and then delete it into a named buffer, you can execute the contents of that
buffer with the @ command. For example, open a new line and enter:

cwgadfly CTRL-V ESC

This will appear as:

```
cwgadfly^[
```

on your screen. Press ESC again to exit insert mode, then delete the line into buffer g
by typing "gdd. Now whenever you place the cursor at the beginning of a word and type
@g, that word in your text will be changed to *gadfly*.

Since @ is interpreted as a vi command, a dot (.) will repeat the entire sequence, even
if the buffer contains an ex command. @@ repeats the last @, and u or U can be used to
undo the effect of @.

This is a simple example. @-functions are useful because they can be adapted to very
specific commands. They are especially useful when you are editing between files, because you can store the commands in their named buffers and access them from any
file you edit. @-functions are also useful in combination with the global replacement
commands discussed in Chapter 6.

Executing Buffers from ex

You can also execute text saved in a buffer from **ex** mode. In this case, you would enter an **ex** command, delete it into a named buffer, and then use the **@** command from the **ex** colon prompt. For example, enter the following text:

```
ORA publishes great books.
ORA is my favorite publisher.
1,$s/ORA/O'Reilly Media/g
```

With your cursor on the last line, delete the command into the **g** buffer: **"gdd**. Move your cursor to the first line: **kk**. Then, execute the buffer from the colon command line: **:@g** ENTER. Your screen should now look like this:

```
O'Reilly Media publishes great books.
O'Reilly Media is my favorite publisher.
```

Some versions of **vi** treat * identically to **@** when used from the **ex** command line. In addition, if the buffer character supplied after the **@** or * command is *, the command will be taken from the default (unnamed) buffer.

Using ex Scripts

Certain **ex** commands you use only within **vi**, such as maps, abbreviations, and so on. If you store these commands in your `.exrc` file, the commands will automatically be executed when you invoke **vi**. Any file that contains commands to execute is called a *script*.

The commands in a typical `.exrc` script are of no use outside **vi**. However, you can save other **ex** commands in a script, and then execute the script on a file or on multiple files. Mostly you'll use substitute commands in these external scripts.

For a writer, a useful application of **ex** scripts is to ensure consistency of terminology —or even of spelling—across a document set. For example, let's assume that you've run the Unix **spell** command on two files and that the command has printed out the following list of misspellings:

```
$ spell sect1 sect2
chmod
ditroff
myfile
thier
writeable
```

As is often the case, **spell** has flagged a few technical terms and special cases it doesn't recognize, but it has also identified two genuine spelling errors.

Because we checked two files at once, we don't know which files the errors occurred in or where they are in the files. Although there are ways to find this out, and the job wouldn't be too hard for only two errors in two files, you can easily imagine how time-consuming the job could grow to be for a poor speller or for a typist proofing many files at once.

To make the job easier, you could write an ex script containing the following commands:

```
%s/thier/their/g
%s/writeable/writable/g
wq
```

Assume you've saved these lines in a file named exscript. The script could be executed from within vi with the command:

```
:so exscript
```

or the script can be applied to a file right from the command line. Then you could edit the files sect1 and sect2 as follows:

```
$ ex -s sect1 < exscript
$ ex -s sect2 < exscript
```

The -s following the invocation of ex is the POSIX way to tell the editor to suppress the normal terminal messages.[*]

If the script were longer than the one in our simple example, we would already have saved a fair amount of time. However, you might wonder if there isn't some way to avoid repeating the process for each file to be edited. Sure enough, we can write a shell script that includes—but generalizes—the invocation of ex, so that it can be used on any number of files.

Looping in a Shell Script

You may know that the shell is a programming language as well as a command-line interpreter. To invoke ex on a number of files, we use a simple type of shell script command called the for loop. A for loop allows you to apply a sequence of commands for each argument given to the script. (The for loop is probably the single most useful piece of shell programming for beginners. You'll want to remember it even if you don't write any other shell programs.)

Here's the syntax of a for loop:

```
for variable in list
do
    command(s)
done
```

For example:

```
for file in $*
do
```

---

[*] Traditionally, ex used a single minus sign for this purpose. Typically, for backward compatibility, both versions are accepted.

```
        ex - $file < exscript
done
```

(The command doesn't need to be indented; we indented it for clarity.) After we create this shell script, we save it in a file called **correct** and make it executable with the **chmod** command. (If you aren't familiar with the **chmod** command and the procedures for adding a command to your Unix search path, see *Learning the Unix Operating System*, published by O'Reilly.) Now type:

```
$ correct sect1 sect2
```

The **for** loop in **correct** will assign each argument (each file in the list specified by **$***, which stands for *all arguments*) to the variable **file** and execute the **ex** script on the contents of that variable.

It may be easier to grasp how the **for** loop works with an example whose output is more visible. Let's look at a script to rename files:

```
for file in $*
do
    mv $file $file.x
done
```

Assuming this script is in an executable file called **move**, here's what we can do:

```
$ ls
ch01 ch02 ch03 move
$ move ch??              Just the chapter files
$ ls                     Check the results
ch01.x ch02.x ch03.x move
```

With creativity, you could rewrite the script to rename the files more specifically:

```
for nn in $*
do
    mv ch$nn sect$nn
done
```

With the script written this way, you'd specify numbers instead of filenames on the command line:

```
$ ls
ch01 ch02 ch03 move
$ move 01 02 03
$ ls
sect01 sect02 sect03 move
```

The **for** loop need not take **$*** (all arguments) as the list of values to be substituted. You can specify an explicit list as well. For example:

```
for variable in a b c d
```

assigns *variable* to *a, b, c,* and *d* in turn. Or you can substitute the output of a command. For example:

```
for variable in `grep -l "Alcuin" *`
```

---

assigns *variable* in turn to the name of each file in which **grep** finds the string *Alcuin*. (**grep -l** prints the filenames whose contents match the pattern, without printing the actual matching lines.)

If no list is specified:

```
for variable
```

the variable is assigned to each command-line argument in turn, much as it was in our initial example. This is actually not equivalent to:

```
for variable in $*
```

but to:

```
for variable in "$@"
```

which has a slightly different meaning. The symbol $* expands to $1, $2, $3, etc., but the four-character sequence "$@" expands to "$1", "$2", "$3", etc. Quotation marks prevent further interpretation of special characters.

Let's return to our main point and our original script:

```
for file in $*
do
     ex - $file < exscript
done
```

It may seem a little inelegant to have to use two scripts—the shell script and the **ex** script. And in fact, the shell does provide a way to include an editing script inside a shell script.

Here Documents

In a shell script, the operator << means to take the following lines, up to a specified string, as input to a command. (This is often called a *here document*.) Using this syntax, we could include our editing commands in **correct** like this:

```
for file in $*
do
ex - $file << end-of-script
g/thier/s//their/g
g/writeable/s//writable/g
wq
end-of-script
done
```

The string `end-of-script` is entirely arbitrary—it just needs to be a string that won't otherwise appear in the input and can be used by the shell to recognize when the here document is finished. It also *must* be placed at the start of the line. By convention, many users specify the end of a here document with the string `EOF`, or `E_O_F`, to indicate the end of the file.

There are advantages and disadvantages to each approach shown. If you want to make a one-time series of edits and don't mind rewriting the script each time, the here document provides an effective way to do the job.

However, it's more flexible to write the editing commands in a separate file from the shell script. For example, you could establish the convention that you will always put editing commands in a file called **exscript**. Then you only need to write the **correct** script once. You can store it away in your personal "tools" directory (which you've added to your search path) and use it whenever you like.

Sorting Text Blocks: A Sample ex Script

Suppose you want to alphabetize a file of **troff**-encoded glossary definitions. Each term begins with an .IP macro. In addition, each entry is surrounded by the .KS/.KE macro pair. (This ensures that the term and its definition will print as a block and will not be split across a new page.) The glossary file looks something like this:

```
.KS
.IP "TTY_ARGV" 2n
The command, specified as an argument vector,
that the TTY subwindow executes.
.KE
.KS
.IP "ICON_IMAGE" 2n
Sets or gets the remote image for icon's image.
.KE
.KS
.IP "XV_LABEL" 2n
Specifies a frame's header or an icon's label.
.KE
.KS
.IP "SERVER_SYNC" 2n
Synchronizes with the server once.
Does not set synchronous mode.
.KE
```

You can alphabetize a file by running the lines through the Unix **sort** command, but you don't really want to sort every line. You want to sort only the glossary terms, moving each definition—untouched—along with its corresponding term. As it turns out, you can treat each text block as a unit by joining the block into one line. Here's the first version of your **ex** script:

```
g/^\.KS/,/^\.KE/j
%!sort
```

Each glossary entry is found between a .KS and .KE macro. j is the **ex** command to join a line (the equivalent in **vi** is J). So, the first command joins every glossary entry into one "line." The second command then sorts the file, producing lines like this:

```
.KS .IP "ICON_IMAGE" 2n Sets or gets ... image.    .KE
.KS .IP "SERVER_SYNC" 2n Synchronizes with ... mode.    .KE
```

```
.KS .IP "TTY_ARGV" 2n The command, ... executes.   .KE
.KS .IP "XV_LABEL" 2n Specifies a ... icon's label.   .KE
```

The lines are now sorted by glossary entry; unfortunately, each line also has macros and text mixed in (we've used ellipses [...] to show omitted text). Somehow, you need to insert newlines to "un-join" the lines. You can do this by modifying your **ex** script: mark the joining points of the text blocks *before* you join them, and then replace the markers with newlines. Here's the expanded **ex** script:

```
g/^\.KS/,/^\.KE/-1s/$/@@/
g/^\.KS/,/^\.KE/j
%!sort
%s/@@ /^M/g
```

The first three commands produce lines like this:

```
.KS@@ .IP "ICON_IMAGE" 2nn@@ Sets or gets ... image. @@ .KE
.KS@@ .IP "SERVER_SYNC" 2nn@@ Synchronizes with ... mode. @@ .KE
.KS@@ .IP "TTY_ARGV" 2nn@@ The ... vector, @@ that ... .@@ .KE
.KS@@ .IP "XV_LABEL" 2nn@@ Specifies a ... icon's label. @@ .KE
```

Note the extra space following the @@. The spaces result from the j command, because it converts each newline into a space.

The first command marks the original line breaks with @@. You don't need to mark the end of the block (after the .KE), so the first command uses a -1 to move back up one line at the end of each block. The fourth command restores the line breaks by replacing the markers (plus the extra space) with newlines. Now your file is sorted by blocks.

Comments in ex Scripts

You may want to reuse such a script, adapting it to a new situation. With a complex script like this, it is wise to add comments so that it's easier for someone else (or even yourself!) to reconstruct how it works. In **ex** scripts, anything following a double quote is ignored during execution, so a double quote can mark the beginning of a comment. Comments can go on their own line. They can also go at the end of any command that doesn't interpret a quote as part of the command. (For example, a quote has meaning to map commands and shell escapes, so you can't end such lines with a comment.)

Besides using comments, you can specify a command by its full name, something that would ordinarily be too time-consuming from within **vi**. Finally, if you add spaces, the **ex** script shown previously becomes this more readable one:

```
" Mark lines between each KS/KE block
global /^\.KS/,/^\.KE/-1 s /$/@@/
" Now join the blocks into one line
global /^\.KS/,/^\.KE/ join
" Sort each block--now really one line each
%!sort
" Restore the joined lines to original blocks
% s /@@ /^M/g
```

Surprisingly, the `substitute` command does not work in `ex`, even though the full names for the other commands do.

Beyond ex

If this discussion has whetted your appetite for even more editing power, you should be aware that Unix provides editors even more powerful than `ex`: the `sed` stream editor and the `awk` data manipulation language. There is also the extremely popular `perl` programming language. For information on these programs, see the O'Reilly books *sed & awk*, *Effective awk Programming*, *Learning Perl*, and *Programming Perl*.

Editing Program Source Code

All of the features discussed so far are of interest whether you are editing regular text or program source code. However, there are a number of additional features that are of interest chiefly to programmers. These include indentation control, searching for the beginning and end of procedures, and using `ctags`.

The following discussion is adapted from documentation provided by Mortice Kern Systems with their excellent implementation of **vi** for DOS and Windows-based systems, available as a part of the MKS Toolkit or separately as MKS Vi. It is reprinted by permission of Mortice Kern Systems.

Indentation Control

The source code for a program differs from ordinary text in a number of ways. One of the most important of these is the way in which source code uses indentation. Indentation shows the logical structure of the program: the way in which statements are grouped into blocks. **vi** provides automatic indentation control. To use it, issue the command:

```
:set autoindent
```

Now, when you indent a line with spaces or tabs, the following lines will automatically be indented by the same amount. When you press ENTER after typing the first indented line, the cursor goes to the next line and automatically indents the same distance as the previous line.

As a programmer, you will find this saves you quite a bit of work getting the indentation right, especially when you have several levels of indentation.

When you are entering code with autoindent enabled, typing CTRL-T at the start of a line gives you another level of indentation, and typing CTRL-D takes one away.

We should point out that CTRL-T and CTRL-D are typed while you are in insert mode, unlike most other commands, which are typed in command mode.

There are two additional variants of the CTRL-D command:[†]

^ ^D

> When you type ^ ^D (^ CTRL-D), vi shifts the cursor back to the beginning of the line, but only for the current line. The next line you enter will start at the current autoindent level. This is particularly useful for entering C preprocessor commands while typing in C/C++ source code.

0 ^D

> When you type 0 ^D, vi shifts the cursor back to the beginning of the line. In addition, the current autoindent level is reset to zero; the next line you enter will not be autoindented.[‡]

Try using the `autoindent` option when you are entering source code. It simplifies the job of getting indentation correct. It can even sometimes help you avoid bugs—e.g., in C source code, where you usually need one closing curly brace (}) for every level of indentation you go backward.

The << and >> commands are also helpful when indenting source code. By default, >> shifts a line right eight spaces (i.e., adds eight spaces of indentation) and << shifts a line left eight spaces. For example, move the cursor to the beginning of a line and press > twice (>>). You will see the line move right. If you now press < twice (<<), the line will move back again.

You can shift a number of lines by typing the number followed by >> or <<. For example, move the cursor to the first line of a good-sized paragraph and type 5>>. You will shift the first five lines in the paragraph.

The default shift is eight spaces (right or left). This default can be changed with a command such as:

```
:set shiftwidth=4
```

You will find it convenient to have a `shiftwidth` that is the same size as the width between tab stops.

vi attempts to be smart when doing indenting. Usually, when you see text indented by eight spaces at a time, vi will actually insert tab characters into the file, since tabs usually expand to eight spaces. This is the Unix default; it is most noticeable when you type a tab during normal input and when files are sent to a printer—Unix expands them with a tab stop of eight spaces.

If you wish, you can change how vi represents tabs on your screen, by changing the `tabstop` option. For example, if you have something that is deeply indented, you might

---

[†] These do not work in `elvis`.

[‡] The `nvi` 1.79 documentation has these two commands switched, but the program actually behaves as described here.

wish to have use a tab stop setting of every four characters, so that the lines will not wrap. The following command will make this change:

```
:set tabstop=4
```

 Changing your tab stops is not recommended. Although **vi** will display the file using an arbitrary tab stop setting, the tab characters in your files will still be expanded using an eight-character tab stop by every other Unix program.

Even worse: mixing tabs, spaces, and unusal tab stops will make your file completely unreadable when viewed outside the editor, with a pager such as **more**, or when printed. Eight-character tab stops are one of the facts of life on Unix, and you should just get used to them.

Sometimes indentation won't work the way you expect, because what you believe to be a tab character is actually one or more spaces. Normally, your screen displays both a tab and a space as whitespace, making the two indistinguishable. You can, however, issue the command:

```
:set list
```

This alters your display so that a tab appears as the control character ^I and an end-of-line appears as a $. This way, you can spot a true space, and you can see extra spaces at the end of a line. A temporary equivalent is the :l command. For example, the command:

```
:5,20 l
```

displays lines 5 through 20, showing tab characters and end-of-line characters.

A Special Search Command

The characters (, [, {, and < can all be called opening brackets. When the cursor is resting on one of these characters, pressing the % key moves the cursor from the opening bracket forward to the corresponding closing bracket—),], }, or >—keeping in mind the usual rules for nesting brackets.§ For example, if you were to move the cursor to the first (in:

```
if ( cos(a[i]) == sin(b[i]+c[i]) )
{
    printf("cos and sin equal!\n");
}
```

and press %, you would see that the cursor jumps to the parenthesis at the end of the line. This is the closing parenthesis that matches the opening one.

---

§ Of the versions tested, only **nvi** supported matching < and > with %. **vile** lets you set an option with the sets of pairs of characters that match for %.

Similarly, if the cursor is on one of the closing bracket characters, pressing % will move the cursor backward to the corresponding opening bracket character. For example, move the cursor to the closing brace after the printf line just shown and press %.

vi is even smart enough to find a bracket character for you. If the cursor is not on a bracket character, when you press %, vi will search forward on the current line to the first open or close bracket character it finds, and then it will move to the matching bracket! For instance, with the cursor on the > in the first line of the example just shown, % will find the open parenthesis and then move to the close parenthesis.

Not only does this search character help you move forward and backward through a program in long jumps, it lets you check the nesting of brackets and parentheses in source code. For example, if you put the cursor on the first { at the beginning of a C function, pressing % should move you to the } that (you think) ends the function. If it's the wrong one, something has gone wrong somewhere. If there is no matching } in the file, vi will beep at you.

Another technique for finding matching brackets is to turn on the following option:

```
:set showmatch
```

Unlike %, setting showmatch (or its abbreviation sm) helps you while you're in insert mode. When you type a) or a },‖ the cursor will briefly move back to the matching (or { before returning to your current position. If the match doesn't exist, the terminal beeps. If the match is merely off-screen, vi silently keeps going. Vim 7.0 and later can highlight the matching parenthesis or brace, using the matchparen plugin, which is loaded by default.

Using Tags

The source code for a large C or C++ program will usually be spread over several files. Sometimes, it is difficult to keep track of which file contains which function definitions. To simplify matters, a Unix command called ctags can be used together with the :tag command of vi.

Unix versions of ctags handle the C language and often Pascal and Fortran 77. Sometimes they even handle assembly language. Almost universally, however, they do not handle C++. Other versions are available that can generate tags files for C++ and for other languages and file types. For more information, see "Enhanced Tags" on page 129.

‖ In elvis, Vim, and vile, showmatch also shows you matching square brackets ([and]).

You issue the `ctags` command at the Unix command line. Its purpose is to create an information file that `vi` can use later to determine which files define which functions. By default, this file is called `tags`. From within `vi`, a command of the form:

```
:!ctags file.c
```

creates a file named `tags` in your current directory that contains information on the functions defined in `file.c`. A command such as:

```
:!ctags *.c
```

creates a `tags` file describing all the C source files in the directory.

Now suppose your `tags` file contains information on all the source files that make up a C program. Also suppose that you want to look at or edit a function in the program, but you do not know where the function is. From within `vi`, the command:

```
:tag name
```

looks at the `tags` file to find out which file contains the definition of the function *name*. It then reads in the file and positions the cursor on the line where the name is defined. In this way, you don't have to know which file you have to edit; you only have to decide which function you want to edit.

You can use the tag facility from `vi`'s command mode as well. Place the cursor on the identifier you wish to look up, and then type ^]. `vi` will perform the tag lookup and move to the file that defines the identifier. Be careful where you place the cursor; `vi` uses the "word" under the cursor starting at the current cursor position, not the entire word containing the cursor.

If you try to use the `:tag` command to read in a new file and you haven't saved your current text since the last time you changed it, `vi` will not let you go to the new file. You must either write out your current file with the `:w` command and then issue `:tag`, or else type:

```
:tag! name
```

to override `vi`'s reluctance to discard edits.

The Solaris version of `vi` actually supports tag *stacks*. It appears, however, to be completely undocumented in the Solaris manpages. Because many, if not most, versions of Unix `vi` don't do tag stacking, in this book we have moved the discussion of this feature to "Tag Stacks" on page 131 where tag stacking is introduced.

Introduction to the vi Clones

And These Are My Brothers, Darrell, Darrell, and Darrell

There are a number of freely available "clones" of the vi editor. Appendix D provides a pointer to a web site that lists all known vi clones, and Part II covers Vim in great detail. Part III covers an additional three of the more popular clones. They are:

- Version 1.79 of Keith Bostic's nvi (Chapter 16)
- Version 2.2.0 of Steve Kirkendall's elvis (Chapter 17)
- Version 9.6.4 of vile, by Kevin Buettner, Tom Dickey, Paul Fox, and Clark Morgan (Chapter 18)

All the clones were written either because the source code for vi was not freely available —making it impossible to port vi to a non-Unix environment or to study the code— or because Unix vi (or another clone!) did not provide desired functionality. For example, Unix vi often has limits on the maximum length of a line, and it cannot edit binary files. (The chapters on the various programs present more information about each one's history.)

Each program provides a large number of extensions to Unix vi; often, several of the clones provide the same extensions, although usually not in an identical way. Instead of repeating the treatment of each common feature in each program's chapter, we have centralized the discussion here. You can think of this chapter as presenting "what the clones do," with each clone's own chapter presenting "how the clone does it."

The order in which topics are presented in this chapter is used in an expanded fashion in Part II on Vim, and in a much more compact fashion in the chapters in Part III. This chapter covers the following:

Multiwindow editing

This is the ability to split the (terminal) screen into multiple "windows," and/or the ability to use multiple windows within a GUI environment. You can edit a different file in each window or have several views into the same file. This is perhaps the single most important extension over regular vi.

GUI interfaces

All of the clones except nvi can be compiled to support an X Window interface. If you have a system running X, use of the GUI version may be preferable to splitting the screen of an xterm (or other terminal emulator); the GUI versions generally provide such nice features as scrollbars and multiple fonts. The native GUIs of other operating systems may also be supported.

Extended regular expressions

All of the clones make it possible to match text using regular expressions that are similar or identical to those provided by the Unix egrep command.

Enhanced tags

As described earlier in "Using Tags" on page 123, you can use the ctags program to build up a searchable database of your files. The clones make it possible to "stack" tags by saving your current location when you do a tag search. You can then return to that location. Multiple locations can be saved in a "last in, first out" (LIFO) order, producing a stack of locations.

Several of the vi clone authors and the author of at least one ctags clone have gotten together to define a standard form for an enhanced version of the ctags format. In particular, it is now easier to use the tag functionality with programs written in C++, which allows overloaded function names.

Improved editing facilities

All of the clones provide the ability to edit the ex command line, an "infinite undo" capability, arbitrary length lines and 8-bit data, incremental searching, an option to scroll the screen left to right for long lines instead of wrapping long lines, and mode indicators, as well as other features.

Programming assistance

Several of the editors provide features that allow you to stay within the editor during the typical "edit-compile-debug" cycle of software development.

Syntax highlighting

In elvis, Vim, and vile, you can arrange to display different parts of a file in different colors and fonts. This is particularly useful for editing program source code.

Multiwindow Editing

Perhaps the single most important feature that the clones offer over standard vi is the ability to edit files in multiple "windows." This makes it possible to easily work on more than one file at the same time, and to "cut and paste" text from one file to another via yanking and putting.

 In the clones, you need not split the screen to yank and put between files; only the original vi discards the cut buffers when switching between files.

There are two fundamental concepts underlying each editor's multiwindow implementation: buffers and windows.

A *buffer* holds text to be edited. The text may come from a file, or it may be brand new text to be eventually written to a file. Any given file has only one buffer associated with it.

A *window* provides a view into a buffer, allowing you to see and modify the text in the buffer. There may be multiple windows associated with the same buffer. Changes made to the buffer in one window are reflected in any other windows open on the same buffer. A buffer may also have no windows associated with it. In that case, you can't do a whole lot with the buffer, although you can open a window on it later. Closing the last window open on a buffer effectively "hides" the file. If the buffer has been modified but not written to disk, the editor may or may not let you close the last window that's open on it.

When you create a new window, the editor splits the current screen. For most of the editors, this new window shows another view on the file you're currently editing. You then switch to the window where you wish to edit the next file, and instruct the editor to start editing the file there. Each editor provides **vi** and **ex** commands to switch back and forth between windows, as well as the ability to change the window size and hide and restore windows.

Chapter 11 is devoted to multiwindow editing in Vim. In each of the other editors' chapters in Part III, we show a sample split screen (editing the same two files), and describe how to split the screen and move between windows.

GUI Interfaces

elvis, Vim, and **vile** provide graphical user interface (GUI) versions that can take advantage of a bitmapped display and mouse. Besides supporting X Windows under Unix, support for Microsoft Windows or other windowing systems may also be available. Table 8-1 summarizes the available GUIs for the different clones.

Table 8-1. Available GUIs

Editor	Terminal	X11	Microsoft Windows	OS/2	BeOS	Macintosh	Amiga	QNX	OpenVMS
Vim	•	•	•	•	•	•	•		
nvi	•								
elvis	•	•	•	•					
vile	•	•	•	•	•			•	•

Extended Regular Expressions

The metacharacters available in `vi`'s search and substitution regular expressions are described back in Chapter 6 in the section "Metacharacters Used in Search Patterns" on page 74. Each of the clones provides some form of extended regular expressions, which are either optional or always available. Typically, these are the same (or almost the same) as those provided by `egrep`. Unfortunately, each clone's extended flavor is slightly different from the others'.

To give you a feel for what extended regular expressions can do, we present them in the context of `nvi`. The section "Extended Regular Expressions" on page 169 describes Vim's extended regular expressions, and each clone's chapter in Part III describes that editor's extended syntax, without repeating the examples.

`nvi`'s extended regular expressions are the Extended Regular Expressions (EREs) as defined by the POSIX standard. To enable this feature, use `set extended` from either your `.nexrc` file or from the `ex` colon prompt.

Besides the standard metacharacters described in Chapter 6 and the POSIX bracket expressions mentioned in "POSIX Bracket Expressions" on page 77 in the same chapter, the following metacharacters are available:

`|`

> Indicates alternation. For example, a|b matches either *a* or *b*. However, this construct is not limited to single characters: house|home matches either of the strings *house* or *home*.

`(...)`

> Used for grouping, to allow the application of additional regular expression operators. For example, house|home can be shortened (if not simplified) to ho(use|me). The * operator can be applied to text in parentheses: (house|home)* matches *home*, *homehouse*, *househomehousehouse*, and so on.
>
> When `extended` is set, text grouped with parentheses acts like text grouped in \(...\) in regular `vi`: the actual text matched can be retrieved in the replacement part of a substitute command with \1, \2, etc. In this case, \(represents a literal left parenthesis.

`+`

> Matches *one* or more of the preceding regular expressions. This is either a single character or a group of characters enclosed in parentheses. Note the difference between + and *. The * is allowed to match nothing, but with + there must be at least one match. For example, ho(use|me)* matches *ho* as well as *home* and *house*, but ho(use|me)+ will not match *ho*.

`?`

> Matches zero or one occurrence of the preceding regular expression. This indicates "optional" text that is either present or not present. For example, free?d will match either *fred* or *freed*, but nothing else.

{...}

Defines an *interval expression*. Interval expressions describe counted numbers of repetitions. In the following descriptions, *n* and *m* represent integer constants:

{n}

Matches exactly *n* repetitions of the previous regular expression. For example, (home|house){2} matches *homehome*, *homehouse*, *househome*, and *house-house*, but nothing else.

{n,}

Matches *n* or more repetitions of the previous regular expression. Think of it as "as least *n*" repetitions.

{n,m}

Matches *n* to *m* repetitions. The bounding is important, since it controls how much text would be replaced during a substitute command.[*]

When extended is not set, nvi provides the same functionality with \{ and \}.

Enhanced Tags

The "Exuberant ctags" program is a ctags clone that is considerably more capable than Unix ctags. It produces an extended tags file format that makes the tag searching and matching process more flexible and powerful. We describe the Exuberant version first, since it is supported by most of the vi clones.

This section also describes tag stacks: the ability to save multiple locations visited with the :tag or ^] commands. All of the clones support tag stacking.

Exuberant ctags

The Exuberant ctags program was written by Darren Hiebert, and, as of this writing, the current version is 5.7. Its home page is *http://ctags.sourceforget.net/*. The following list of the program's features is adapted from the README file in the ctags distribution:

- It is capable of generating tags for *all* types of C and C++ language tags, including class names, macro definitions, enum names, enumerators (values inside an enumeration), function (method) definitions, function (method) prototypes/declarations, structure members and class data members, struct names, typedefs, union names, and variables. (Whew!)

- It supports both C and C++ code.

- Twenty-nine other languages are also supported, including C# and Java.

---

[*] The *, +, and ? operators can be reduced to {0,}, {1,}, and {0,1} respectively, but the former are much more convenient to use. Also, interval expressions were developed later in the history of Unix regular expressions.

- It is very robust in parsing code and is far less easily fooled by code containing #if preprocessor conditional constructs.
- It can be used to print out a human-readable list of selected objects found in source files.
- It supports generation of GNU Emacs-style tag files (etags).
- It works on Amiga, Cray, MS-DOS, Macintosh, OS/2, QDOS, QNX, RISC OS, Unix, VMS, and Windows 95 through XP. Some precompiled binaries are available on the web site.

Exuberant ctags produces tags files in the form described next.

The New tags Format

Traditionally, a tags file has three tab-separated fields: the tag name (typically an identifier); the source file containing the tag; and an indication of where to find the identifier. This indication is either a simple line number or a nomagic search pattern enclosed either in slashes or question marks. Furthermore, the tags file is always sorted.

This is the format generated by the Unix ctags program. In fact, many versions of vi allowed *any* command in the search pattern field (a rather gaping security hole). Furthermore, due to an undocumented implementation quirk, if the line ended with a semicolon and then a double quote (;"), anything following those two characters would be ignored. (The double quote starts a comment, as it does in .exrc files.)

The new format is backward compatible with the traditional one. The first three fields are the same: tag, filename, and search pattern. Exuberant ctags only generates search patterns, not arbitrary commands. Extended attributes are placed after a separating ;". Each attribute is separated from the next by a tab character, and consists of two colon-separated subfields. The first subfield is a keyword describing the attribute; the second is the actual value. Table 8-2 lists the supported keywords.

Table 8-2. Extended ctags keywords

Keyword	Meaning
kind	The value is a single letter that indicates the tag's lexical type. It can be f for a function, v for a variable, and so on. Since the default attribute name is kind, a solitary letter can denote the tag's type (e.g., f for a function).
file	For tags that are "static," i.e., local to the file. The value should be the name of the file.
	If the value is given as an empty string (just file:), it is understood to be the same as the filename field; this special case was added partly for the sake of compactness, and partly to provide an easy way to handle tags files that aren't in the current directory. The value of the filename field is always relative to the directory in which the tags file itself resides.
function	For local tags. The value is the name of function in which they're defined.
struct	For fields in a struct. The value is the name of the structure.
enum	For values in an enum data type. The value is the name of the enum type.
class	For C++ member functions and variables. The value is the name of the class.

Keyword	Meaning
scope	Intended mostly for C++ class member functions. It will usually be `private` for private members or omitted for public members, so users can restrict tag searches to only public members.
arity	For functions. Defines the number of arguments.

If the field does not contain a colon, it is assumed to be of type kind. Here are some examples:

```
ARRAYMAXED      awk.h     427;"   d
AVG_CHAIN_MAX   array.c   38;"    d       file:
array.c         array.c   1;"     F
```

ARRAYMAXED is a C `#define` macro defined in `awk.h`. AVG_CHAIN_MAX is also a C macro, but it is used only in `array.c`. The third line is a bit different: it is a tag for the actual source file! This is generated with the `-i F` option to Exuberant `ctags`, and allows you to give the command `:tag array.c`. More usefully, you can put the cursor over a filename and use the `^]` command to go to that file (for example, if you're editing a `Makefile` and wish to go to a particular source file).

Within the value part of each attribute, the backslash, tab, carriage return, and newline characters should be encoded as \\, \t, \r, and \n, respectively.

Extended `tags` files may have some number of initial tags that begin with `!_TAG_`. These tags usually sort to the front of the file and are useful for identifying which program created the file. Here is what Exuberant `ctags` generates:

```
!_TAG_FILE_FORMAT      2    /extended format; --format=1 will not append ;" to lines/
!_TAG_FILE_SORTED      1    /0=unsorted, 1=sorted, 2=foldcase/
!_TAG_PROGRAM_AUTHOR   Darren Hiebert  /dhiebert@users.sourceforge.net/
!_TAG_PROGRAM_NAME     Exuberant Ctags //
!_TAG_PROGRAM_URL      http://ctags.sourceforge.net    /official site/
!_TAG_PROGRAM_VERSION  5.7    //
```

Editors can take advantage of these special tags to implement special features. For example, Vim pays attention to the `!_TAG_FILE_SORTED` tag and will use a binary search to search the `tags` file instead of a linear search if the file is indeed sorted.

If you use `tags` files, we recommend that you get and install Exuberant `ctags`.

Tag Stacks

The ex command `:tag` and the vi mode `^]` command provide a limited means of finding identifiers, based on the information provided in a `tags` file. Each of the clones extends this ability by maintaining a *stack* of tag locations. Each time you issue the ex command `:tag`, or use the vi mode `^]` command, the editor saves the current location before searching for the specified tag. You may then return to a saved location using (usually) the vi command `^T` or an ex command.

Solaris **vi** tag stacking and an example are presented next. Vim's tag stacking is described in the section "Tag Stacking" on page 268. The ways the other clones handle tag stacking is described in each editor's respective chapter in Part III.

Solaris vi

Surprisingly enough, the Solaris version of **vi** supports tag stacking. Perhaps not so surprisingly, this feature is completely undocumented in the Solaris *ex*(1) and *vi*(1) manual pages. For completeness, we summarize Solaris **vi** tag stacking in Tables 8-3, 8-4, and 8-5. Tag stacking in Solaris **vi** is quite simple.[†]

Table 8-3. Solaris vi tag commands

Command	Function
ta[g][!] *tagstring*	Edit the file containing *tagstring* as defined in the **tags** file. The ! forces **vi** to switch to the new file if the current buffer has been modified but not saved.
po[p][!]	Pop the tag stack by one element.

Table 8-4. Solaris vi command mode tag commands

Command	Function
^]	Look up the location of the identifier under the cursor in the **tags** file, and move to that location. If tag stacking is enabled, the current location is automatically pushed onto the tag stack.
^T	Return to the previous location in the tag stack, i.e., pop off one element.

Table 8-5. Solaris vi options for tag management

Option	Function
taglength, tl	Controls the number of significant characters in a tag that is to be looked up. The default value of zero indicates that all characters are significant.
tags, tagpath	The value is a list of filenames in which to look for tags. The default value is "**tags / usr/lib/tags**".
tagstack	When set to true, **vi** stacks each location on the tag stack. Use :**set notagstack** to disable tag stacking.

Exuberant ctags and Vim

To give you a feel for using tag stacks, we present a short example that uses Exuberant **ctags** and Vim.

Suppose you are working with a program that uses the GNU **getopt_long** function, and you need to understand more about it.

GNU **getopt** consists of three files: **getopt.h**, **getopt.c**, and **getopt1.c**.

---

† This information was discovered based on experimentation. YMMV (your mileage may vary).

First, you create the **tags** file, and then you start by editing the main program, found in `main.c`:

```
$ ctags *.[ch]
$ ls
Makefile  getopt.c  getopt.h  getopt1.c  main.c  tags
$ vim main.c
```

Keystrokes	Results
/getopt_	```/* option processing. ready, set, go! */
for (optopt = 0, old_optind = 1;
(c = getopt_long(argc, argv, optlist, optab, NULL)) != EOF;
optopt = 0, old_optind = optind) {
if (do_posix)
opterr = TRUE;```
	Edit main.c and move to the call to getopt_long.
^]	```int
getopt_long (int argc, char *const *argv, const char *options,
             const struct option *long_options, int *opt_index)
{
  return _getopt_internal (argc, argv, options, long_options, opt_index, 0);
}

"getopt1.c" 192L, 4781C``` |
| | Do a tag lookup on getopt_long. Vim moves to getopt1.c, placing the cursor on the definition of getopt_long. |

It turns out that **getopt_long** is a "wrapper" function for **_getopt_internal**. You place the cursor on **_getopt_internal** and do another tag search.

Keystrokes	Results
3jf_ ^]	```int
_getopt_internal (int argc, char *const *argv, const char *optstring,
                  const struct option *longopts, int *longind, int long_only)
{
  int result;

  getopt_data.optind = optind;
  getopt_data.opterr = opterr;

  result = _getopt_internal_r (argc, argv, optstring, longopts,
                               longind, long_only, &getopt_data);

  optind = getopt_data.optind;
"getopt.c" 1225L, 33298C``` |
| | You have now moved to getopt.c. To find out more about struct option, move the cursor to option and do another tag search. |
| jfo; ^] | ```one). For long options that have a zero `flag' field, `getopt'
returns the contents of the `val' field. */

struct option
{
  const char *name;
  /* has_arg can't be an enum because some compilers complain about
     type mismatches in all the code that assumes it is an int. */
  int has_arg;
  int *flag;
  int val;``` |

Keystrokes	Results

	`};`
	
	`/* Names for the values of the `has_arg' field of `struct option'.  */`
	
	`"getopt.h" 177L, 6130C`

The editor moves to the definition of struct option in getopt.h. You may now look over the comments that explain how it's used.

Keystrokes	Results

:tags	`# TO tag        FROM line  in file/text`
	`1  1 getopt_long        310  main.c`
	`2  1 _getopt_internal    67  getopt1.c`
	`3  1 option            1129  getopt.c`

The :tags command in Vim displays the tag stack.

Typing ^T three times would move you back to main.c, where you started. The tag facilities make it easy to move around as you edit source code.

Improved Facilities

All of the clones provide additional features that make simple text editing easier and more powerful:

Editing the ex command line
> The ability to edit ex mode commands as you type them, possibly including a saved history of ex commands. Also, the ability to complete filenames and possibly other things, such as commands and options.

No line length limit
> The ability to edit lines of essentially arbitrary length. Also, the ability to edit files containing any 8-bit character.

Infinite undo
> The ability to successively undo all of the changes you've made to a file.

Incremental searching
> The ability to search for text while you are typing the search pattern.

Left/right scrolling
> The ability to let long lines trail off the edge of the screen instead of wrapping.

Visual mode
> The ability to select arbitrary contiguous chunks of texts upon which some operation will be done.

Mode indicators
> A visible indication of insert mode versus command mode, as well as indicators of the current line and column.

Command-Line History and Completion

Users of the csh, tcsh, ksh, zsh, and bash shells have known for years that being able to recall previous commands, edit them slightly, and resubmit them makes them more productive.

This is no less true for editor users than it is for shell users; unfortunately, Unix vi does not have any facility to save and recall ex commands.

This lack is remedied in each of the clones. Although each one provides a different way of saving and recalling the command history, each one's mechanism is usable and useful.

In addition to a command history, all of the editors can do some kind of *completion*. This is where you type the beginning of, for example, a filename. You then type a special character (such as tab), and the editor completes the filename for you. All of the editors can do filename completion, and some of them can complete other things as well. Details for Vim are found in the section "Keyword and Dictionary Word Completion" on page 259. Details for the other editors are provided in each editor's chapter in Part III.

Arbitrary Length Lines and Binary Data

All the clones can handle lines of any length.‡ Historic versions of vi often had limits of around 1,000 characters per line; longer lines would be truncated.

All are also 8-bit clean, meaning that they can edit files containing any 8-bit character. It is even possible to edit binary and executable files, if necessary. This can be really useful at times. You may or may not have to tell each editor that a file is binary:

nvi
Automatically handles binary data. No special command-line or ex options are required.

elvis
Under Unix, does not treat a binary file differently from any other file. On other systems, it uses the elvis.brf file to set the binary option, to avoid newline translation issues. (The elvis.brf file and hex display modes are described in the section "Interesting Features" on page 335.)

Vim
Does not limit the length of a line. When binary is not set, Vim is like nvi and automatically handles binary data. However, when editing a binary file, you should either use the -b command-line option or :set binary. These set several other Vim options that make it easier to edit binary files.

---

‡ Well, up to the maximum value of a C long, 2,147,483,647 (on a 32-bit computer).

`vile`

> Automatically handles binary data. No special command-line or **ex** options are required.

Finally, there is one tricky detail. Traditional **vi** always writes the file with a final new-line appended. When editing a binary file, this might add one character to the file and cause problems. **nvi** and Vim are compatible with **vi** by default and add that newline. In Vim you can set the `binary` option so this doesn't happen. `elvis` and `vile` never append the extra newline.

Infinite Undo

Unix **vi** allows you to undo only your last change, or to restore the current line to the state it was in before you started making any changes. All of the clones provide "infinite undo," the ability to keep undoing your changes, all the way back to the state the file was in before you started *any* editing.

Incremental Searching

When *incremental searching* is used, the editor moves the cursor through the file, matching text *as you type* the search pattern. When you finally type ENTER , the search is finished.[§] If you've never seen it before, it is rather disconcerting at first. However, after a while you get used to it, and eventually you come to wonder how you ever did without it.

nvi, Vim, and `elvis` enable incremental searching with an option, and `vile` uses two special **vi** mode commands. `vile` can be compiled with incremental searching disabled, but it is enabled by default. Table 8-6 shows the options each editor provides.

Table 8-6. Incremental searching

Editor	Option	Command	Action
nvi	searchincr		The cursor moves through the file as you type, always being placed on the first character of the text that matches.
Vim	incsearch		The cursor moves through the file as you type. Vim highlights the text that matches what you've typed so far.
elvis	incsearch		The cursor moves through the file as you type. `elvis` highlights the text that matches what you've typed so far.
vile		^X S, ^X R	The cursor moves through the file as you type, always being placed on the first character of the text that matches. ^X S incrementally searches forward through the file, while ^X R incrementally searches backward.

[§] Emacs has always had incremental searching.

Left-Right Scrolling

By default, `vi` and most of the clones wrap long lines around the screen. Thus, a single logical line of the file may occupy multiple physical lines on your screen.

There are times when it might be preferable for a long line to simply disappear off the righthand edge of the screen instead of wrapping. Moving onto that line and then moving to the right would "scroll" the screen sideways. This feature is available in all of the clones. Typically, a numeric option controls how much to scroll the screen, and a Boolean option controls whether lines wrap or disappear off the edge of the screen. `vile` also has command keys to perform sideways scrolling of the entire screen. Table 8-7 shows how to use horizontal scrolling with each editor.

Table 8-7. Sideways scrolling

Editor	Scroll amount	Option	Action
nvi	sidescroll = 16	leftright	Off by default. When set, long lines simply go off the edge of the screen. The screen scrolls left or right by 16 characters at a time.
elvis	sidescroll = 8	wrap	Off by default. When set, long lines simply go off the edge of the screen. The screen scrolls left or right by eight characters at a time.
Vim	sidescroll = 0	wrap	Off by default. When set, long lines simply go off the edge of the screen. With `sidescroll` set to zero, each scroll puts the cursor in the middle of the screen. Otherwise, the screen scrolls by the desired number of characters.
vile	sideways = 0	linewrap	Off by default. When set, long lines wrap. Thus, the default is to have long lines go off the edge of the screen. Long lines are marked at the left and right edges with ‹ and ›. With `sideways` set to zero, each scroll moves the screen by ⅓. Otherwise, the screen scrolls by the desired number of characters.
		horizscroll	On by default. When set, moving the cursor along a long line offscreen shifts the whole screen. When not set, only the current line shifts; this may be desirable on slower displays.

`vile` has two additional commands, `^X ^R` and `^X ^L`. These two commands scroll the screen right and left, respectively, leaving the cursor in its current location on the line. You cannot scroll so far that the cursor position would go off the screen.

Visual Mode

Typically, operations in `vi` apply to units of text—such as lines, words, or characters—or to sections of text from the current cursor position to a position specified by a search command. For example, `d/^}` deletes up to the next line that starts with a right brace. `elvis` and `vile` provide a mechanism to explicitly select a region of text to which an operation will apply. In particular, it is possible to select a rectangular block of text and apply an operation to all the text within the rectangle. See the section "Visual Mode

Motion" on page 168 for details on Vim. For details on the other editors, see each editor's respective chapter in Part III.

Mode Indicators

As you know by now, vi has two modes—command mode and insert mode. Usually, you can't tell by looking at the screen which mode you're in. Furthermore, it's often useful to know where in the file you are, without having to use the ^G or ex := commands.

Two options address these issues: showmode and ruler. All the clones agree on the option names and meanings, and even Solaris vi has the showmode option.

Table 8-8 lists the special features in each editor.

Table 8-8. Position and mode indicators

Editor	With ruler, displays	With showmode, displays
nvi	Row and column	Insert, change, replace, and command mode indicators
elvis	Row and column	Input and command mode indicators
Vim	Row and column	Insert, replace, and visual mode indicators
vile	Row, column, and percent of file	Insert, replace, and overwrite mode indicators
vi	N/A	Separate mode indicators for open, input, insert, append, change, replace, replace one character, and substitute modes

The GUI version of elvis changes the cursor shape depending on the current mode.

Programming Assistance

vi was developed primarily as a programmer's editor. It has features that make things especially easy for the traditional-style Unix programmer—someone writing C programs and troff documentation. (Real programmers write real documentation in troff.) Several of the clones are proud bearers of this tradition, adding a number of features that make them even more usable and capable for the "power user."‖

Two features (among many) most deserve discussion:

Edit-compile speedup
    elvis, Vim, and vile allow you to easily invoke make, capture the errors from your compiler, and automatically move to the lines containing the errors. You can then fix the errors and rerun make, all from within the editor.

‖ In contrast to the What You See Is What You Get (WYSIWYG) philosophy, Unix is the You Asked For It, You Got It operating system. (With thanks to Scott Lee.)

Syntax highlighting

elvis, Vim, and vile have the ability to highlight and/or change the color of different syntactic elements in different kinds of files.

Edit-Compile Speedup

Programming often consists of an "edit-compile-debug" cycle. You make changes, compile the new code, and then test and debug it. When learning a new language, syntax errors are especially common, and it is frustrating to be constantly stopping and restarting (or suspending and resuming) the editor in between compiles.

elvis, Vim, and vile all provide facilities that allow you to stay within the editor while compiling your program. Furthermore, they capture the compiler's output and use it to automatically go to each line that contains an error.[#] Consistent use of this capability can save time and improve programmer productivity.

Here is an example, using elvis. You are beginning to learn C++, so you start out with the obligatory first program:

Keystrokes	Results

:w hello.C	```
	#include <iostream>
	
	int main()
	{
	        std::cout << "hello, world!\n ;
	        return 0;
	}
	``
	You enter the program, forgetting the closing quote, and then write the program to hello.C.

:make hello	```
	g++ hello.C -o hello
	hello.C:5: error: missing terminating " character
	hello.C: In function 'int main()':
	hello.C:6: error: expected primary-expression before 'return'
	hello.C:6: error: expected `;' before 'return'
	make: *** [hello] Error 1
	``
	You type the :make command to run make, which in turn runs the C++ compiler. (In this case, g++.) The output from g++ describes each error.
	``
	#include <iostream>
	
	int main()
	{
	        ▌std::cout << "hello, world\n ;
	        return 0;
	}
	~
	line 5: missing terminating " character 5,8 Command
	``
	The make output disappears quickly, and elvis replaces the status line with the first error message, positioning the cursor on the line that needs to be fixed.

[#] Yet another feature that Emacs users are accustomed to comes to vi.

You can fix the error, resave the file, rerun `:make`, and eventually compile your program without errors.

All of the editors have similar facilities. They will all compensate for changes in the file, correctly moving you to subsequent lines with errors. See the section "Compiling and Checking Errors with Vim" on page 279 for details on Vim. For details on the other editors, see each editor's respective chapter in Part III.

Syntax Highlighting

`elvis`, Vim, and `vile` all provide some form of syntax highlighting. All three also provide syntax coloring, which changes the color of different parts of the file on displays that can do so (such as under X11 or the Linux console). See the section "Syntax Highlighting" on page 270 for more information on syntax highlighting in Vim. For information on the other editors, see each editor's chapter in Part III.

Editor Comparison Summary

Most of the clones support most or all of the features described earlier in this chapter. Table 8-9 summarizes what each editor supports. Of course, the table does not tell the full story; the details are provided in the rest of the book.

Table 8-9. Feature summary chart

Feature	nvi	elvis	vim	vile
Multiwindow editing	•	•	•	•
GUI		•	•	•
Extended regular expressions	•	•	•	•
Enhanced tags		•	•	•
Tag stacks	•	•	•	•
Arbitrary length lines	•	•	•	•
8-bit data	•	•	•	•
Infinite undo	•	•	•	•
Incremental searching	•	•	•	•
Left-right scrolling	•	•	•	•
Mode indicators	•	•	•	•
Visual mode		•	•	•
Edit-compile speedup		•	•	•
Syntax highlighting		•	•	•
Multiple OS support		•	•	•

Nothing Like the Original

For many, many years, the source code to the original vi was unavailable without a Unix source code license. Although educational institutions were able to get licenses at a relatively low cost, commercial licenses were always expensive. This fact prompted the creation of all of the vi clones described in this book.

In January 2002, the source code for V7 and 32V UNIX was made available under an open source-style license.[*] This opened up access to almost all of the code developed for BSD Unix, including ex and vi.

The original code does not compile "out of the box" on modern systems, such as GNU/Linux, and porting it is difficult.[†] Fortunately, the work has already been done. If you would like to use the original, "real" vi, you can download the source code and build it yourself. See *http://ex-vi.sourceforge.net/* for more information.

A Look Ahead

Part II covers Vim in excruciating detail. Seven full chapters cover the topics listed here, as well as the important subject of writing scripts for Vim, which provide much of the power and usefulness that come "out of the box" with that editor.

The three chapters in Part III cover nvi, elvis, and vile, in that order. Each chapter has the following outline:

1. Who wrote the editor, and why.
2. Important command-line arguments.
3. Online help and other documentation.
4. Initialization—what files and environment variables the program reads, and in what order.
5. Multiwindow editing.
6. GUI interface(s), if any.
7. Extended regular expressions.
8. Improved editing facilities (tag stacks, infinite undo, etc.).
9. Programming assistance (edit-compile speedup, syntax highlighting).
10. Interesting features unique to the program.
11. Where to get the sources, and what operating systems the editor runs on.

---

[*] For more information about this, see the Unix Historical Society web site at *http://www.tuhs.org*.

[†] We know. We tried.

All of the distributions are compressed with gzip, GNU zip. If you don't already have it, you can get gzip from *ftp://ftp.gnu.org//gnu/gzip/gzip-1.3.12.tar*.‡ The untar.c program available from the elvis FTP site is a very portable, simple program for unpacking gziped tar files on non-Unix systems.

Because each of the programs discussed in Part III continues to undergo development, we have not attempted an exhaustive treatment of each one's features. Such an approach would quickly become outdated. Instead, we have "hit the highlights," covering the features that you are most likely to need and that are least likely to change as the program evolves. You should supplement this book with each program's online documentation if you need to know how to use every last feature of your editor.

---

‡ This is current as of this writing. You may find a newer version.

Vim

Part II describes the most popular vi clone, named Vim (which stands for "vi improved"). This part contains the following chapters:

Vim (vi Improved): An Introduction

This part of the book describes Vim, the other vi. We briefly introduce Vim and the most noteworthy of its many technical advances over vi, along with a bit of history. We'll finish this chapter with some pointers to special Vim modes and teaching tools for new users. The following chapters cover:

- Editing enhancements over vi
- Multiwindow editing
- Vim scripts
- The Vim graphical user interface (GUI)
- Programming enhancements
- Editing patterns
- Other cool stuff

Vim stands for "vi improved." It was written and is maintained by Bram Moolenaar. Today, Vim is perhaps the most widely used vi clone, and there exists a separate Internet domain (*vim.org*) dedicated to it. The current version is 7.1.

Unconstrained by standards or committees, Vim continues to grow in functionality. An entire community has grown up around it. Collectively, they decide what new features to add and what existing features to modify, by nominating and voting for suggestions during development cycles.

Inspired by Bram's dedicated energy and the voting system, Vim enjoys a strong following. It maintains its value by growing and changing with the computing industry and, correspondingly, with editing needs. For instance, its context-specific language editing started with C and has grown to encompass C++, Java, and now C#.

Vim includes many new features that facilitate the editing of code in many new languages. In fact, many features promised at the release of this book's previous edition are now fully implemented. The computing landscape has changed dramatically and dynamically these last 10 years, and Vim has matched it stride for stride.

Today Vim is so ubiquitous, especially among Unix and its variants (e.g., BSD and GNU/Linux), that for many users Vim has become synonymous with vi. Indeed, many distributions of GNU/Linux come with a default installation of Vim as the /bin/vi binary!

Vim provides features not in vi that are considered essential in modern-day text editors, such as ease of use, graphical terminal support, color, syntax highlighting and formatting, as well as extended customization.

Overview

Author and History[*]

Bram started work on Vim after buying an Amiga computer. As a Unix user he'd been using the vi-like editor called stevie, one he considered far from perfect. Fortunately, it came with the source code, and he began by making the editor more compatible with vi and fixing bugs. After a while the program became quite usable, and Vim version 1.14 was published on Fred Fish disk 591 (a collection of free software for the Amiga).

Other people began to use the program, liked it, and started helping with its development. A port to Unix was followed by ports to MS-DOS and other systems, and subsequently Vim became one of the most widely available vi clones. More features were added gradually: multilevel undo, multiwindowing, etc. Some features were unique to Vim, but many were inspired by other vi clones. The goal has always been to provide the best features to the user.

Today Vim is one of the most full-featured of the vi-style editors anywhere. The online help is extensive.

One of the more obscure features of Vim is its support for typing from right to left, which is useful for languages such as Hebrew and Farsi and illustrates Vim's versatility. Being a rock-stable editor on which professional software developers can rely is another of Vim's design goals. Vim crashes are rare, and when they happen you can recover your changes.

Development on Vim continues. The group of people helping to add features and port Vim to more platforms is growing, and the quality of the ports to different computer systems is increasing. The Microsoft Windows version has dialogs and a file-selector, which opens up the hard-to-learn vi commands to a large group of users.

---

[*] This section is adapted from material supplied by Bram Moolenaar, Vim's author. We thank him.

Why Vim?

Vim so dramatically extends the traditional vi functionality that one might more easily ask, "Why *not* Vim?" vi introduced the standard from which others borrowed (vile, elvis, nvi), and Vim took the baton and ran with it. Vim dared to radically extend features, sometimes pushing processors to the edge of their ability to perform Vim's work with adequate response time. We don't know whether it was an article of faith by Bram that processor and memory speeds would improve enough to catch up with Vim's demands, but fortunately, modern processors and computers handle even the toughest Vim tasks well.

Compare and Contrast with vi

Vim is more universally available than vi. There is at least some version of Vim available on virtually all operating systems, whereas vi is available only on Unix or Unix work-alike systems.

vi is the original and has changed little over the years. It is the POSIX standard-bearer and fulfills its role well. Vim starts where vi leaves off, providing all of vi's functionality and then extending that to add graphical interfaces and features such as complex options and scripting that go far beyond vi's original capabilities.

Vim ships with its own built-in documentation in the form of a directory of specialized text files. A casual inspection of this directory (using the standard Unix word count tool, wc -c *.txt) shows 129 files comprising almost 122,000 lines of documentation! This is the first hint at the scope of Vim's features. Vim accesses these files via its internal "help" command, another feature not available in vi. We look more closely at Vim's help system later and offer tips and tricks to maximize your learning experience.

One way to contrast Vim's features with vi's is to look more closely at the included directory of help files. Vim flags options, commands, and functions in these files with an annotation of "not in vi" or "not available in vi". A nonscientific scan of the help files (using a quick grep -i 'not.. *in vi') yields over 700 hits. Even if these hits were redundant by a factor of two, it's clear Vim has many features vi does not.

The following chapters cover some of the more interesting Vim features. From extensions of the historic Vim to new functionality, we describe the best and most popular productivity features. We cover topics universally recognized as useful enhancements, such as syntax color highlighting. We also look at some more obscure features that are useful for added productivity. For example, we show a way to customize the Vim status line to show a real-time update of the date and time each time you move the cursor.

Categories of Features

Vim's features span the range of activities common to virtually any text-editing task. Some features just extend what users wanted the original vi to do; others are completely new and not in **vi**. And if you need something that's *not* there, Vim offers built-in scripting for unlimited extensibility and customization. Some categories of Vim features include:

Syntax extensions

Vim lets you control indentation and syntax-based color coding of your text. And you have many options to define this automatic format. If you don't like the color highlighting, you can change it. If you need a certain style of indentation, Vim provides it, or if you have a specialized need, it lets you customize your environment.

Programmer assistance

Although Vim doesn't try to provide all programming needs, it offers many features normally found in Integrated Development Environments (IDEs). From quick edit-compile-debug cycles to autocompletion of keywords, Vim has specialized features to let you do more than edit quickly—it helps you program.

Graphical user interface (GUI) features

Vim extends usability to a more general population by allowing point-and-click editing, like many modern easy-to-use editors. All of the power-user functionality gets the boost of simple GUI accessibility for lighter and simpler editing tasks.

Scripting and plug-ins

You can write your own Vim extensions or download plug-ins from the Internet. You can even contribute to the Vim community by publishing your extensions for others to use.

Initialization

Vim, like **vi**, uses configuration files to define sessions at startup time, but Vim has a vastly expanded repertoire of definable behaviors. You can keep it as simple as setting a few options, as you would in **vi**, or you can write an entire suite of customizations that define your session based on any context you define. For example, you can script your initialization files to precompile code based on which directory you're editing files in, or you can retrieve information from some real-time source and incorporate it into your text at startup.

Session context

Vim keeps session information in a file, `.viminfo`. Ever wonder "Where was I?" when revisiting and editing a file? This fixes that! You can define how much and what kind of information to sustain across sessions. For example, you can define how many "recent documents" or last-edited files to track, how many edits (deletions, changes) to remember per file, how many commands to remember from the command history, and how many buffers and lines to keep from previous edit actions ("puts," "deletes," etc.). Not only does Vim remember edits in your last session for a file, it remembers basic things *between* files. This is handy for editing activities such as grabbing a sequence of lines in one file (with **y** [yank], or **d** [delete]) and "putting" them in another. Whatever is in the unnamed buffer is remembered and available from one file to the next. Also, Vim remembers the last search pattern, so you can simply use the command n (find next occurrence) when beginning a session to find the last-used search pattern.

Vim also remembers which line you were on for each of your most recently edited files. If you exit your edit session with the cursor on line 25, it repositions you on line 25 the next time you edit that file.

Postprocessing

In addition to performing presession functions, Vim lets you define what to do *after* you've edited a file. You can write cleanup routines to delete temporary files accumulated from compiles, or do real-time edits to the file before it's written back to storage. You have complete control to customize any postedit activities

Transitions

Vim manages state transitions. When you move within a session from buffer to buffer or window to window (usually the same thing), Vim automatically does pre- and post- housekeeping.

Transparent editing

Vim detects and automatically unbundles archived or compressed files. For example, you can directly edit a zipped file such as `myfile.tar.gz`. You can even edit directories. Vim lets you navigate a directory and select files to edit using familiar Vim navigation commands.

Meta-information

Vim offers four handy read-only registers from which the user may extract meta-information for "puts": the current filename (%), the alternate filename (#), the last command-line command executed (:), and the last inserted text (., a period).

The black-hole register

This is an obscure but useful extension of editing registers. Normally, text deletions put this text into buffers using a rotation scheme, which is useful for cycling through old deletes to get back old and deleted text. Vim provides the "black-hole" register as a place to throw deleted text away, without affecting the rotation of deleted text in the normal registers. If you're a Unix user, this register is Vim's version of `/dev/null.`

Keyword completion

Vim lets you complete partially typed words with context-sensitive completion rules. For example, Vim can look up words in a dictionary or in a file containing keywords specific to a language.

Vim also lets you drop back to a `vi`-compatible mode with its `compatible` option (`:set compatible`). Most of the time you'll probably want Vim's extra features, but it's a thoughtful touch to provide for backward compatibility if you need it.

Philosophy

Vim's philosophy aligns closely with vi's. Both provide power and elegance in editing. Both rely on modality (command mode versus input mode). And both bring editing to the keyboard: that is, users can perform all of their editing work quickly and efficiently and never touch a mouse (or a ^X ^C). We like to think of this as "touch editing," which is analogous to "touch typing," reflecting the corresponding increase in speed and efficiency that both bring to their respective tasks.

Vim extends that philosophy by permitting and providing features for less experienced users (GUI, visual highlight mode) and power options for the power users (scripting, extended regular expressions, configurable syntax, and configurable indenting).

And for the super power users who like to code, Vim comes with source code. Users are free (even encouraged) to improve on the improvements. Philosophically, Vim strikes a balance for *all* users' needs.

Where to Get Vim

If your environment is some variant of Unix—including Mac OS X—you may be in luck and already have Vim installed. If it's available and executable in your predefined PATH environment variable, you should be able to type vim at the shell command line and open a Vim window. If you get the following typical Unix error message:

```
sh: command not found: vim
```

try vi and see whether a Vim welcome message appears. Your installation may actually substitute Vim for vi.

On many systems you'll find old versions of Vim. This section may therefore be useful to help you install the latest version, even if you have Vim already. Once you are in the editor, check not only that you are running Vim but also the version with the :version command. Vim will provide a screen resembling this:

```
:version
VIM - Vi IMproved 7.0 (2006 May 7, compiled Aug 30 2006 21:54:03)
Included patches: 1-76
Compiled by corinna@cathi
Huge version without GUI.  Features included (+) or not (-):
+arabic +autocmd -balloon_eval -browse ++builtin_terms +byte_offset +cindent
-clientserver -clipboard +cmdline_compl +cmdline_hist +cmdline_info +comments
+cryptv +cscope +cursorshape
 ...
 +profile -python +quickfix +reltime +rightleft -ruby +scrollbind +signs
+smartindent -sniff +statusline -sun_workshop +syntax +tag_binary +tag_old_static
-tag_any_white -tcl +terminfo +termresponse +textobjects +title -toolbar
+user_commands +vertsplit +virtualedit +visual +visualextra +viminfo +vreplace
+wildignore +wildmenu +windows +writebackup -X11 -xfontset -xim -xsmp
-xterm_clipboard -xterm_save
    system vimrc file: "$VIM/vimrc"
```

```
      user vimrc file: "$HOME/.vimrc"
       user exrc file: "$HOME/.exrc"
    fall-back for $VIM: "/usr/share/vim"
    Compilation: gcc -c -I. -Iproto -DHAVE_CONFIG_H    -g -O2
    Linking: gcc    -L/usr/local/lib -o vim.exe       -lncurses  -liconv -lint
```

Some of this output is discussed in Chapter 10 in the context of helping you compile Vim with customizations.

> Interestingly, on one of the authors' Mac Mini, with OS X version 10.4.10 installed, not only does a vi command invoke Vim but the documentation (the "manpage") documents Vim!

If you haven't found Vim so far, here are a few common directories you may want to search before you try to download and install it. If you find the executable, add its directory as part of your PATH and you're ready to go:

/usr/bin (this should be in PATH anyway)
/bin (so should this)
/opt/local/bin
/usr/local/bin

If none of those work, you probably don't have Vim. Happily, Vim is available in many forms for many platforms and is (usually and relatively) easy to retrieve and install. The following sections guide you to getting Vim for your platform. We discuss how to install Vim for these platforms, in order:

- Unix and variants, including GNU/Linux
- Windows XP, 2000, Vista
- Macintosh

Getting Vim for Unix and GNU/Linux

Many modern Unix environments already come with some version of Vim. Most GNU/Linux distributions simply link the default vi location /bin/vi to a Vim executable. Most Unix users won't ever need to install it.

Because there are so many variants of Unix and so many flavors of some variants (e.g., Sun Solaris HP-UX, *BSD, all the distributions of GNU/Linux), the most straightforward and recommended way to get Vim is to download its source, compile it, and install it.

The installation procedure described here requires a development environment capable of compiling source code. Although most Unix variants provide compilers and related tools, some (notably current releases of the Ubuntu GNU/Linux distribution) require you to download and install additional packages before you can experience the pleasures of compiling code.

The Vim home page refers to a new installation procedure it recommends, called aap. It provides a link and brief introduction. Because aap is new and the old method of installing by downloading and compiling works well, we are not recommending aap as the installation procedure of choice. By the time you read this book, use of aap may be well established.

There are also prepackaged Vim bundles offering easy standard installations for GNU/Linux (Red Hat RPMs, Debian pkgs), IRIX (SoftwareManager), Sun Solaris (Companion Software), and HP-UX. The Vim home page provides links for all of these systems.

Vim source code is available from the Vim home page, *http://www.vim.org*. Source code is bundled in tarballs compressed in either GZIP (`.gz`) or BZIP2 (`.bz2`) format. Virtually all operating systems recognize and handle GZIP files nowadays, and most Unix variants have the utilities to handle BZIP2 as well. Download the source and unpack the compressed file as follows, substituting the name of the file you downloaded if you are installing a different version:

`.gz` *file*

```
$ gunzip vim-7.1.tar.gz
```

`.bz2` *file*

```
$ bunzip2 vim-7.1.tar.gz
```

After the command completes, the file `vim-7.1.tar` (or a comparable file reflecting the version you downloaded) remains. Now untar the tar file:

```
$ tar xvf vim-7.1.tar
vim71
vim71/README.txt
vim71/runtime
vim71/README_unix.txt
vim71/README_lang.txt
vim71/src
vim71/Makefile
vim71/Filelist
vim71/README_src.txt
   ...
vim71/runtime/doc/vimtutor-ru.1
vim71/runtime/doc/xxd-ru.1
vim71/runtime/doc/evim-ru.UTF-8.1
vim71/runtime/doc/vim-ru.UTF-8.1
```

```
vim71/runtime/doc/vimdiff-ru.UTF-8.1
vim71/runtime/doc/vimtutor-ru.UTF-8.1
vim71/runtime/doc/xxd-ru.UTF-8.1
```

You can now remove the `vim-7.1.tar` file. Change directories to the Vim directory created by the `tar` command:

$ cd vim71

The `configure` file is a script that configures the compilation parameters. Most configuration work should be left to the script, which examines the host environment and turns on and off features according to software installed on the system.

You can decide at this point whether to use the defaults or selectively choose (or not choose) features. For example, you may want to compile with the `perl` interface turned on where the `configure` script otherwise would not have done so, anticipating future installation of `perl` scripting tools:

```
$ ./configure --enable-perlinterp
```

Or, you may decide you have no use for a `perl` interface and turn that feature off with the `configure` options:

```
$ ./configure --disable-perlinterp
```

Current versions of Vim offer slightly different ways to customize your installation. Instead of putting all of the `--disable-XXX` and `--enable-XXX` options in `configure` options, the `INSTALL` file points you to making changes in the `feature.h` file. Unless you have compelling reasons to make changes in that file, we recommend you compile with available options (described in `README.txt`) and customize your editing needs in Vim configuration files.

The normal `configure` output (default, with no options) looks something like:

```
$ configure
/home/ehannah/Desktop/vim/vim71/src
configure: loading cache auto/config.cache
checking whether make sets $(MAKE)... (cached) yes
checking for gcc... (cached) gcc
checking for C compiler default output file name... a.out
checking whether the C compiler works... yes
checking whether we are cross compiling... no
checking for suffix of executables...
...
checking for NLS... no "po/Makefile" - disabled
checking for dlfcn.h... (cached) yes
checking for dlopen()... no
checking for dlopen() in -ldl... yes
checking for dlsym()... yes
checking for setjmp.h... (cached) yes
checking for GCC 3 or later... yes
configure: creating auto/config.status
```

```
config.status: creating auto/config.mk
config.status: creating auto/config.h
config.status: auto/config.h is unchanged
```

Now build Vim with the make utility:

```
$ make
Starting make in the src directory.
If there are problems, cd to the src directory and run make there
cd src && /usr/local/lib/cw/make first
/home/ehannah/Desktop/vim/vim71/src
make[1]: Entering directory `/home/ehannah/Desktop/vim/vim71/src'
gcc -c -I. -Iproto -DHAVE_CONFIG_H       -g -O2        -o objects/
    charset.o charset.c
gcc -c -I. -Iproto -DHAVE_CONFIG_H       -g -O2        -o objects/
    diff.o diff.c
gcc -c -I. -Iproto -DHAVE_CONFIG_H       -g -O2        -o objects/
    digraph.o digraph.c
gcc -c -I. -Iproto -DHAVE_CONFIG_H       -g -O2        -o objects/
    edit.o edit.c


    ...


make[2]: Entering directory `/home/ehannah/Desktop/vim/vim71/src'
creating auto/pathdef.c
gcc -c -I. -Iproto -DHAVE_CONFIG_H       -g -O2        -o objects/
    pathdef.o auto/
    pathdef.c
make[2]: Leaving directory `/home/ehannah/Desktop/vim/vim71/src'
link.sh: Using auto/link.sed file to remove a few libraries
  gcc      -o vim objects/buffer.o objects/charset.o objects/diff.o
  objects/digraph.o objects/edit.o objects/eval.o objects/ex_cmds.o
  objects/ex_cmds2.o objects/ex_docmd.o objects/ex_eval.o
  objects/ex_getln.o objects/fileio.o objects/fold.o objects/getchar.o
  objects/hardcopy.o objects/hashtab.o  objects/if_cscope.o
  objects/if_xcmdsrv.o objects/main.o objects/mark.o objects/memfile.o
  objects/memline.o objects/menu.o objects/message.o objects/misc1.o
  objects/misc2.o objects/move.o objects/mbyte.o objects/normal.o
  objects/ops.o objects/option.o objects/os_unix.o objects/pathdef.o
  objects/popupmnu.o objects/quickfix.o objects/regexp.o objects/screen.o
  objects/search.o objects/spell.o objects/syntax.o  objects/tag.o
  objects/term.o objects/ui.o objects/undo.o objects/window.o
  objects/netbeans.o  objects/version.o        -lncurses -lgpm -ldl
link.sh: Linked fine with a few libraries removed
cd xxd; CC="gcc" CFLAGS=" -g -O2" \
    /usr/local/lib/cw/make -f Makefile
/home/ehannah/Desktop/vim/vim71/src/xxd
make[2]: Entering directory `/home/ehannah/Desktop/vim/vim71/src/xxd'
gcc  -g -O2  -DUNIX -o xxd xxd.c
make[2]: Leaving directory `/home/ehannah/Desktop/vim/vim71/src/xxd'
make[1]: Leaving directory `/home/ehannah/Desktop/vim/vim71/src'
```

If all has gone well, you now have an executable Vim binary in the src directory. Vim is now ready for use, but you have to either invoke it by specifying a full pathname or add the directory in which Vim was placed to each user's executable path. If you can't install programs as an administrator, this will have to do.

To finish installing Vim as a general resource to all users of the machine, you must have administrator (**root**) privileges. If you do, become **root** and enter:

```
# make install
Starting make in the src directory.
If there are problems, cd to the src directory and run make there
cd src && make install
/home/ehannah/Desktop/vim/vim71/src
make[1]: Entering directory `/home/ehannah/Desktop/vim/vim71/src'
if test -f /usr/local/bin/vim; then \
  mv -f /usr/local/bin/vim /usr/local/bin/vim.rm; \
  rm -f /usr/local/bin/vim.rm; \
fi
cp vim /usr/local/bin
strip /usr/local/bin/vim
chmod 755 /usr/local/bin/vim
cp vimtutor /usr/local/bin/vimtutor
chmod 755 /usr/local/bin/vimtutor
/bin/sh ./installman.sh install /usr/local/man/man1 "" /usr/local/
    share/vim /usr/local/share/vim/vim71 /usr/local/share/vim ../
    runtime/doc 644 vim vimdiff evim
installing /usr/local/man/man1/vim.1
installing /usr/local/man/man1/vimtutor.1
installing /usr/local/man/man1/vimdiff.1


  ...


if test -d /usr/local/share/icons/hicolor/48x48/apps -a -w /usr/
    local/share/icons/hicolor/48x48/apps \
   -a ! -f /usr/local/share/icons/hicolor/48x48/apps/gvim.png; then \
    cp ../runtime/vim48x48.png /usr/local/share/icons/hicolor/48x48/
        apps/gvim.png; \
fi
if test -d /usr/local/share/icons/locolor/32x32/apps -a -w /usr/
    local/share/icons/locolor/32x32/apps \
   -a ! -f /usr/local/share/icons/locolor/32x32/apps/gvim.png; then \
    cp ../runtime/vim32x32.png /usr/local/share/icons/locolor/32x32/
        apps/gvim.png; \
fi
if test -d /usr/local/share/icons/locolor/16x16/apps -a -w /usr/
    local/share/icons/locolor/16x16/apps \
   -a ! -f /usr/local/share/icons/locolor/16x16/apps/gvim.png; then \
    cp ../runtime/vim16x16.png /usr/local/share/icons/locolor/16x16/
        apps/gvim.png; \
fi
make[1]: Leaving directory `/home/ehannah/Desktop/vim/vim71/src'
```

Installation is complete; as long as users' PATH variables are set correctly, they should all have access to Vim.

Getting Vim for Windows Environments

There are two main options for Microsoft Windows. The first is the self-installing executable, `gvim.exe`, available from the Vim home page. Download and run this, and it should do the rest. We have installed Vim using this executable on different Windows machines, and it's always worked cleanly. The binary should install correctly on Windows XP, 2000, NT, ME, 98, and 95.

 At one point in the install process, a DOS window pops up and gives a warning about something not being verifiable. We have never seen this become a problem.

Another option for Windows users is to install Cygwin (*http://www.cygwin.com/*), a suite of common GNU tools ported to the Windows platform. It's an amazingly full implementation of virtually all mainstream software used on Unix platforms. Vim is part of the standard Cygwin installation and can run from a Cygwin shell window.

Using Vim with Cygwin

The text-based console Vim works fine in Cygwin, but Cygwin's `gvim` expects an X Window System server to be running and will degrade gracefully into running text-based Vim if started without this server.

To get Cygwin's `gvim` working (assuming you wish to run it on a local screen), start Cygwin's X server from the command line in a Cygwin shell as follows:

```
$ X -multiwindow &
```

The `-multiwindow` option tells the X server to let Windows manage the Cygwin applications. There are many other ways to use Cygwin's X server, but that discussion is outside the scope of this book. Installation of Cygwin's X server is also outside the scope; if it is not installed, see the Cygwin home page for further information. A graphical "X" icon should appear in the Windows systray. This assures that the X server is in fact running.

It is confusing to have both Cygwin's Vim and *www.vim.org*'s Vim installed at the same time. Some of the configuration files referenced for Vim configuration may reside in different places, thus resulting in seemingly identical versions of Vim that start up with completely different options. For instance, Cygwin and Windows may have different notions of what is the home directory.

Getting Vim for the Macintosh Environment

Mac OS X comes with Vim 6.2 installed, but not with any GUI version. Users can download `.tar.bz2` files to compile versions 6.4 and 7.1 with a GUI.

When downloading the source, however, the maintainer recommends downloading from CVS (a source control system) to ensure up-to-date source code along with the most recent patches. This isn't difficult, but the idea of downloading via command line may seem a bit foreign to newer users.

Once files are downloaded, the procedure for installation is very similar to the Unix compilation and installation procedure described earlier in the section "Getting Vim for Unix and GNU/Linux" on page 151.

Other Operating Systems

Vim's home page lists more environments for which Vim ostensibly works, but it offers the caveat to use them at your own risk. These other Vims are for:

- QNX, a real-time operating system (RTOS)
- Agenda
- Sharp Zaurus, a Linux-based handheld device
- HP Jornada, a Linux-based handheld device
- Windows CE, a Windows version for handheld devices
- Compaq Tru64 Unix on Alpha
- Open VMS, Digital's VMS with POSIX
- Amiga
- OS/2
- RISC OS, an OS-based on a reduced instruction set CPU (RISC)
- MorphOS, an OS-based on the Amiga OS built on top of the Quark kernel

Aids and Easy Modes for New Users

Recognizing that both `vi` and Vim make some learning demands on new users, Vim provides several features that make it easier to use for some:

Graphical Vim (`gvim`)
When the user invokes the `gvim` command, a rich graphical window is displayed, offering Vim with some of the point-and-click features made popular by modern GUI programs. In many environments, `gvim` is a different binary file created by compiling Vim with all of the GUI options turned on. It can also be invoked through `vim -g`.

"Easy" Vim (evim)

The evim command substitutes some simple behaviors for standard vi features, which some users who are unfamiliar with vi might find to be a more intuitive way to edit files. Expert users probably won't find this mode easy, because they're already used to standard vi behavior. It can also be invoked through vim -e.

vimtutor

Vim comes with vimtutor, a separate command that essentially starts Vim with a special help file. This invocation of Vim gives users another starting point for learning the editor. vimtutor takes about 30 minutes to complete.

Summary

vi is still the standard text-editing tool on Unix. vi was almost revolutionary in its time, with its dual mode and touch-edit philosophy. Vim continues where vi stops, and it is the next evolutionary step for powerful editing and text management:

- Vim extends vi, building on the excellent standard set by the older editor. Although other editors have also built upon the original, Vim has emerged as the most popular and widely used vi clone.

- Vim offers far more than vi, enough more to become the new standard.

- Vim is for beginners *and* for power users. For beginners, it offers various learning tools and "easy" modes, whereas for experts it offers powerful extensions to vi, along with a platform on which power users can enhance and tune Vim to their exact needs.

- Vim runs everywhere. As discussed earlier, in environments where Vim wasn't available, others stepped in and ported it to most useful OS platforms. Vim may not literally be everywhere, but it's close!

- Vim is free. Furthermore, as mentioned in the previous release of this book, Vim is charityware. The work Bram Moolenaar has done creating, improving, maintaining, and sustaining Vim is one of the truly remarkable feats in the free software market. If you like *his* work, Bram invites you to learn about his favorite cause, helping children in Uganda. More information is available at the web site, *http://iccf-holland.org/*, or simply use Vim's built-in help command, topic "uganda" (:help uganda).

Major Vim Improvements over vi

Vim's improvements over vi are myriad, ranging from multiple color syntax definitions to full-blown scripting. If vi is excellent (it is), Vim is amazing. In this chapter we discuss how Vim fills in many features that users have complained were missing from vi. Some of these include:

- Built-in help
- Startup and initialization options
- New motion commands
- Extended regular expressions
- Extended undo
- Customizing the executable

Built-in Help

As mentioned in the previous chapter, Vim comes with more than 100,000 lines of documentation. Almost all of this is immediately available to you from Vim's built-in help facility. In its simplest form, you invoke the :help command. (This is interesting because it exposes users to their first example of Vim's multiple window editing.)

While this is nice, it presents a bit of a chicken-and-egg conundrum because the built-in help requires a modicum of understanding of vi navigation techniques; for it to be really effective, users must know how to jump back and forth in tags. We'll give an overview of help screen navigation here.

The :help command brings up something similar to:

```
    *help.txt*      For Vim version 7.0.  Last change: 2006 May 07

                        VIM - main help file
                                                                    k
        Move around: Use the cursor keys, or "h" to go left,     h     l
                     "j" to go down, "k" to go up, "l" to go right.   j
    Close this window: Use ":q[Enter]".
```

```
          Get out of Vim:  Use ":qa![Enter]" (careful, all changes are lost!).

      Jump to a subject:  Position the cursor on a tag (e.g. |bars|) and hit CTRL-].
          With the mouse:  ":set mouse=a" to enable the mouse (in xterm or GUI).
                           Double-click the left mouse button on a tag, e.g. |bars|.
              Jump back:  Type CTRL-T or CTRL-O (repeat to go further back).

      Get specific help:  It is possible to go directly to whatever you want help
                           on, by giving an argument to the |:help| command.
                           It is possible to further specify the context:
                                                          *help-context*
                        WHAT                     PREPEND    EXAMPLE       ~
                        Normal mode command      (nothing)  :help x
```

Thankfully, Vim accommodates the potential navigation problem for beginners and considerably opens with basic guidelines for navigation, and even tells you how to exit the help screen. We recommend this as a starting point and urge you to spend time exploring the help.

Once you are familiar with help, you can branch out by using tab completion in Vim's command line. For any command at the command prompt (:), pressing the Tab key results in context-sensitive command-line completion. For example, the following:

```
:e /etc/termc[TAB]
```

on any Unix system would expand to:

```
:e /etc/termcap
```

The :e command implies that the command argument is a file, so command completion looks for files that match the partial filename to complete the input.

But :help has its own context, covering the help topics. The partial topic string you type is matched by a substring in any available Vim help topic. We strongly encourage you to learn and use this feature. It saves time and reveals new and interesting features you probably didn't know about.

For example, suppose you want to know how to split a screen. Start with:

```
:help split
```

and press the Tab key. In the current session, the help command cycles through: split( ); :split; :split_f; splitview; splitfind; 'splitright'; 'splitbelow'; g:netrw_browse_split; :dsplit; :vsplit; :isplit; :diffsplit; +vertsplit; and more. To see help for any topic, press the ENTER key when that topic is highlighted. You'll not only see what you're probably looking for (:split), but you will also discover things you didn't realize you could do, such as :vsplit, the "vertical split" command.

Startup and Initialization Options

Vim uses different mechanisms to set up its environment at startup. It inspects command-line options. It self-inspects (how was it invoked, and by what name?). There are different compiled binaries to serve different needs (GUI versus text window). Vim also uses a sequence of initialization files in which uncountable combinations of behaviors can be defined and modified. There are too many options to cover completely; we will touch on some of the interesting ones. In the next sections, we discuss Vim's starting sequence along the following lines:

- Command-line options
- Behaviors associated to command name
- Configuration files (system-wide and per-user)
- Environment variables

This section introduces you to *some* of the ways to start Vim. For a more detailed discussion of many more options, use the help command:

```
:help startup
```

Command-Line Options

Vim's command-line options provide flexibility and power. Some options invoke extra features, whereas others override and suppress default behavior. We will discuss the command-line syntax as it would be used in a typical Unix environment. Single-letter options begin with - (one hyphen), as in -b, which allows editing of binary files. Word-length options begin with -- (two hyphens), as in --noplugin, which overrides the default behavior of loading plugins. A command-line argument of two hyphens by themselves tells Vim that the rest of the command line contains no options (this is a standard Unix behavior).

Following the command-line options, you can optionally list one or more filenames to be edited. (Actually, there is an interesting case where a filename can be a single "-", telling Vim that input comes from the standard input, *stdin*. This will be covered later, but you are encouraged to look at uses for this on your own.)

The following is a partial list of Vim command-line options not available in vi (all vi options are available in Vim):

-b

Edit in binary mode. This is self-explanatory and very cool. Editing binary files is an acquired taste, but this is a powerful way to edit files not touchable by most other tools. Users should read Vim's help section on editing binary files.

-c *command*

command will be executed as an ex command. vi has this same option, but Vim allows up to 10 -c instances in one command.

-C

Run Vim in compatible (vi) mode. For obvious reasons, this option would never be in vi.

-cmd *command*

> *command* executes before `vimrc` files. This is the long form of the `-c` option.

-d

> Start in diff mode. Vim performs a diff on two, three, or four files and sets options making inspection of files differences simple (scrollbind, foldcolumn, etc.).
>
> Vim uses the OS-available diff command, which is `diff` on Unix systems. The Windows version offers a downloadable executable with which Vim can perform the diff.

-E

> Start in improved `ex` mode. For example, improved `ex` mode would use extended regular expressions.

-F *or* -A

> Farsi or Arabic modes, respectively. These require key and character maps to be useful and draw the screen from right to left.

-g

> Start `gvim` (GUI).

-m

> Turn off the write option. Buffers will not be modifiable.

-o

> Open all files in a separate window. Optionally an integer can specify the number of windows to open. Files named on the command line fill that number of windows only (the rest are in Vim buffers). If the specified number of windows exceeds the listed files, Vim opens empty windows to satisfy the request count of windows.

-O

> Like -o, but opens vertically split windows.

-y

> Run Vim in easy mode. This sets options to a more intuitive behavior for beginners. While "easy" may help the uninitiated, seasoned users will find this mode confusing and irritating.

-z

> Run in restricted mode. This basically turns off all external interfaces and prevents access to the system features. For example, users can't use `!G!sort` to sort from the current line in the buffer to end-of-file; the filter `sort` will not be available.

The following is a series of related options to use a remote instance of a server Vim. `remote` commands tell a remote Vim (which may or may not be executing on the same machine) to edit a file or evaluate an expression in that remote server. The server commands tell Vim which server to send to or can declare itself as a server. `serverlist` simply lists available servers:

> -remote *file*
> -remote-silent *file*

```
-remote-wait file
-remote-send file
-servername name
-remote-expr expr
-remote-wait-silent file
-remote-tab
-remote-send keys
-remote-wait-silent file
-serverlist
```

For a more complete discussion of all command-line options, including the complete vi set, refer to the section "Command-Line Syntax" on page 377.

Behaviors Associated to Command Name

Vim comes in two main flavors, graphical (using the X Window System under Unix variants and native GUIs in other operating systems) and text, each of which can start up with subsets of characteristics. Unix users simply use one of the commands in the following list to get the desired behavior:

vim

> Start the text-based Vim.

gvim

> Start Vim in graphical mode. In many environments, gvim is a different binary file of Vim with all of the GUI options turned on during compilation. Same as vim -g. (In Unix environments, gvim requires the X Window System.)

view, gview

> Start Vim or gvim in read-only mode. Same as vim -R.

rvim

> Start Vim in restrictive mode. All external access to shell commands is disabled, as well as the ability to suspend the edit session with the ^Z command.

rgvim

> Same as rvim but for the graphical version.

rview

> Analogous to view, but start in restricted mode. In restricted mode, users do not have access to filters, outside enviroments, or OS features. Same as vim -Z (the -R option invokes just the read-only effect described previously).

rgview

> Same as rview but for the graphical version.

evim, eview

> Use "easy" mode for editing or read-only viewing. Vim sets options and features so it behaves in a more intuitive way for those who are not familiar with the Vim

paradigm. Same as vim -y. Expert users probably won't find this mode easy because they're already used to standard vi behavior.

Note there is no analogous *gXXX* version of these commands, because gvim is ostensibly thought to be already easy, or at least intuitive to learn, with predictable point-and-click behavior.

vimdiff, gvimdiff

Start in "diff" mode and perform a diff on the input files. This is covered in depth later in the section "What's the Difference?" on page 294.

ex, gex

Use the old line-editing ex mode. Useful in scripts. Same as vim -e.

Windows users can access a similar choice of Vim versions in the program list (Start menu).

System and User Configuration Files

Vim looks for initialization cues in a special sequence. It executes the first set of instructions it finds (either in the form of an environment variable or in a file) and begins editing. So, the first element of the following list that is encountered is the only element of the list that is executed. The sequence follows:

1. VIMINIT. This is an environment variable. If it is nonempty, Vim executes its content as an ex command.

2. User vimrc files. The vimrc (Vim resource) initialization file is a cross-platform concept, but because of subtle operating system and platform differences, Vim looks for it in different places in the following order:

   $HOME/.vimrc (Unix, OS/2, and Mac OS X)
   s:.vimrc (Amiga)
   home:.vimrc (Amiga)
   $VIM/.vimrc (OS/2 and Amiga)
   $HOME/_vimrc (DOS and Windows)
   $VIM/_vimrc (DOS and Windows)

3. exrc option. If the Vim exrc option is set, Vim looks for the three additional config files: [._]vimrc; [._]vimrc; and [._]exrc.

The vimrc file is a good place to configure Vim's editing characteristics. Virtually any Vim option can be set or unset in this file, and it is particularly suited to setting up global variables and defining functions, abbreviations, key mappings, etc. Here are a few things to know about the vimrc file:

- Comments begin with a double quote ("), and the double quote can be anywhere in the line. All text after and including the double quote is ignored.

- ex commands can be specified with or without a colon. For example, set autoindent is identical to :set autoindent.

- The file is much more manageable if you break large sets of option definitions into separate lines. For example:

```
set terse sw=1 ai ic wm=15 sm nows ruler wc=<Tab> more
```

is equivalent to:

```
set terse       " short error and info messages
set shiftwidth=1
set autoindent
set ignorecase
set wrapmargin=15
set nowrapscan  " don't scan past end or top of file in searches
set ruler
set wildchar=<TAB>
set more
```

Notice how much more readable the second set of commands is. The second method is also much easier to maintain through deletions, insertions, and temporarily commenting out lines when debugging settings in the configuration file. For example, should you want to temporarily disable line numbering in the startup configuration, you simply insert the double quote (") at the beginning of the **set number** line in your configuration file.

Environment Variables

Many environment variables affect Vim's startup behavior and even some edit-session behavior. These are mostly transparent and handled with defaults if not configured.

How to set environment variables

The command environment you have when you log in (called the *shell* in Unix) sets variables to reflect or control its behavior. Environment variables are especially powerful because they affect programs invoked within the command environment. The following instructions are not specific to Vim; they can be used to set any environment variables you want set in the command environment.

Windows

To set an environment variable:

1. Bring up the control panel.

2. Double-click System.

3. Click the Advanced tab.

4. Click the Environment Variables button.

The result is a window divided into two environment variable areas, User and System. Novices shouldn't modify the System environment variables. In the User area, you can set environment variables related to Vim and make them persist across login sessions.

Unix/Linux Bash and other Bourne shells

Edit the appropriate shell configuration file (such as `.bashrc` for Bash users) and insert lines resembling:

```
VARABC=somevalue
VARXYZ=someothervalue
MYVIMRC=myfavoritevimrcfile
export VARABC VARXYZ MYVIMRC
```

The order of these lines is irrelevant. The `export` statement just makes variables visible to programs that run in the shell, and thus turns them into environment variables. The value of exported variables can be set before or after exporting them.

Unix/Linux C shells

Edit the appropriate shell configuration file (such as `.cshrc`) and insert lines resembling the following:

```
setenv VARABC somevalue
setenv VARXYZ someothervalue
setenv MYVIMRC myfavoritevimrcfile
```

Environment variables relevant to Vim

The following list shows most of Vim's environment variables and their effects.

The Vim -u command-line option overrides Vim's environment variables and goes directly to the specified initialization file. The -u does *not* override non-Vim environment variables:

SHELL

Specifies which shell or external command interpreter Vim uses for shell commands (!!, :!, etc.). In MS-DOS, if SHELL is not set, the COMSPEC environment variable is used instead.

TERM

Sets Vim's internal `term` option. This is somewhat unnecessary, because the editor sets its terminal itself as it deems appropriate. In other words, Vim probably knows what the terminal is better than a predefined variable.

MYVIMRC

Overrides Vim's search for initialization files. If MYVIMRC has a value when starting, Vim assumes the value is the name of an initialization file and, if the file exists, takes initial settings from it. No other file is consulted (see the search sequence in the previous section).

VIMINIT

Specifies `ex` commands to execute when Vim starts. Define multiple commands by separating them with vertical bars (|).

EXINIT

Same as VIMINIT.

VIM

Contains the path of a system directory where standard Vim installation information is found (for information only and not used by Vim).

> If more than one version of Vim exists on a machine, VIM will likely reflect different values depending upon which version the user started. For example, on one author's machine, the Cygwin version sets the VIM environment variable to /usr/share/vim, whereas the vim.org package sets it to C:\Program Files\Vim.
>
> This is important to know if you are making changes to Vim files, as changes may not take effect if you edit the wrong files!

VIMRUNTIME

Points to Vim support files, such as online documentation, syntax definitions, and plug-in directories. Vim typically figures this out on its own. If the user sets the variable—for example, in the vimrc file—it can cause errors if a newer version of Vim is installed because the user's personal VIMRUNTIME variable may point to an old, nonexistent, or invalid location.

New Motion Commands

Vim provides all vi movement or motion commands, most of which are listed in Chapter 3, and adds several others, summarized in Table 10-1.

Table 10-1. Motion commands in Vim

Command	Description
<C-End>	Go to the end of the file, i.e., the last character of the last line of the file. If a *count* is given, go to the last character of the line *count*.
<C-Home>	Go to the first nonwhitespace character of the first line of the file. This differs from <C-End> because <C-Home> does not move the cursor to whitespace.
count%	Go to the line *count* percent into the file, putting the cursor on the first nonblank line. It's important to note that Vim bases its calculation on the number of lines in the file, not the total character count. This may not seem important, but consider an example of a file containing 200 lines, of which the first 195 contain 5 characters (for example, prices such as $4.98), and the last four lines contain 1,000 characters. In Unix, accounting for the newline character, the file would contain approximately: (195 * (5 + 1)) *(The number of characters in the first 5-character lines)* + 2 + (4 * (1000 + 1)) *(The number of characters in the 1,000-character lines)* or 5,200 characters. A true 50% count would place the cursor on line 96, and Vim's 50% motion command would place the cursor on line 100.
:go n	Go to the nth byte in the buffer. All characters, including end-of-line characters, are counted.
n go	

Visual Mode Motion

Vim lets users define selections visually and perform editing commands on the visual selection. This is similar to what many users see in graphical editors where they highlight areas by clicking and dragging the mouse. What Vim offers with its visual mode is the convenience of seeing the selection on which work is done *and* all of the powerful Vim commands with which to do work on the visually selected text. This lets you do much more sophisticated work on highlighted text than the traditional cut and paste actions in less sophisticated editors.

You can select a visual area in Vim in the same manner as other editors, by clicking and dragging the mouse. But Vim also lets you use its powerful motion commands and some special visual mode commands to define the visual selection.

For example, you can type v in normal mode to start visual mode. Once you are in visual mode, any motion commands move the cursor *and* highlight text as the cursor moves to a new position. So, the "next word" command (w) in visual mode moves the cursor to the next word and highlights the selected text. Additional movements extend the selected region appropriately.

In visual mode, Vim uses some specialized commands with which you conveniently extend the selected text by selecting the text object around the cursor. For example, the cursor can be within a "word," and at the same time be within a "sentence," and also be within a "paragraph." Vim lets you add to the visual selection with commands that extend the highlighted region to a text object. To visually select a word, you can use aw (when in visual mode).

Vim uses the following motion commands by taking advantage of "visual mode," which highlights lines and characters in the buffer in order to provide visual cues about what text will be targeted by subsequent Vim actions. You can highlight visual areas of the buffer in several ways. In text-based mode, simply type v to toggle visual mode on and off. When on, visual mode selects and highlights the buffer as the cursor moves. In gvim, just click and drag the mouse across the desired region. This sets Vim's visual flag.

Table 10-2 shows some of Vim's visual mode motion commands.

Table 10-2. Visual mode motion commands in Vim

Command	Description
countaw, countaW	Select *count* words. Intervening whitespace is included. This is slightly different from iw (see next entry). Lowercase w looks for punctuation-delimited words, whereas uppercase W looks for whitespace-delimited words.
countiw, countiW	Select *count* words. Add words but not whitespace. Lowercase w looks for punctuation-delimited words, whereas uppercase W looks for whitespace-delimited words.
as, is	Add sentence, or inner sentence.
ap, ip	Add paragraph, or inner paragraph.

For a more detailed discussion of text objects and how they are used in visual mode, use the help command:

```
:help text-objects
```

Extended Regular Expressions

Of all the clones, Vim provides the richest set of regular expression matching facilities. Much of the descriptive text in the following list is borrowed from the Vim documentation:

\|
> Indicates alternation, house\|home.

\+
> Matches one or more of the preceding regular expression.

\=
> Matches zero or one of the preceding regular expression.

\{*n,m*}
> Matches *n* to *m* of the preceding regular expression, as much as possible. *n* and *m* are numbers between 0 and 32,000. Vim requires only the left brace to be preceded by a backslash, not the right brace.

\{*n*}
> Matches *n* of the preceding regular expression.

\{*n,*}
> Matches at least *n* of the preceding regular expression, as much as possible.

\{*,m*}
> Matches 0 to *m* of the preceding regular expression, as much as possible.

\{}
> Matches 0 or more of the preceding regular expression, as much as possible (same as *).

\{-*n,m*}
> Matches *n* to *m* of the preceding regular expression, as few as possible.

\{-*n*}
> Matches *n* of the preceding regular expression.

\{-*n,*}
> Matches at least *n* of the preceding regular expression, as few as possible.

\{-*,m*}
> Matches 0 to *m* of the preceding regular expression, as few as possible.

\i
> Matches any identifier character, as defined by the isident option.

\I

Like \i, but excluding digits.

\k

Matches any keyword character, as defined by the iskeyword option.

\K

Like \k, but excluding digits.

\f

Matches any filename character, as defined by the isfname option.

\F

Like \f, but excluding digits.

\p

Matches any printable character, as defined by the isprint option.

\P

Like \p, but excluding digits.

\s

Matches a whitespace character (exactly a space or a tab).

\S

Matches anything that isn't a space or a tab.

\b

Backspace.

\e

Escape.

\r

Carriage return.

\t

Tab.

\n

Reserved for future use. Eventually, it will be used for matching multiline patterns. See the Vim documentation for more details.

~

Matches the last given substitute (i.e., replacement) string.

\(...\)

Provides grouping for *, \+, and \=, as well as making matched subtexts available in the replacement part of a substitute command (\1, \2, etc.).

\1

Matches the same string that was matched by the first subexpression in \(and \). For example, \([a-z]\).\1 matches *ata*, *ehe*, *tot*, etc. \2, \3, and so on may be used to represent the second, third, and so on subexpressions.

The `isident`, `iskeyword`, `isfname`, and `isprint` options define the characters that appear in identifiers, keywords, and filenames, and that are printable. Use of these options makes regular expression matching very flexible.

Customizing the Executable

For most users, the default Vim suffices nicely. Today's computers provide enough processing power (memory and processing cycles) for the full-featured Vim executable. You get all of Vim's extended features with the confidence of good performance. However, in some instances, environment or circumstance may dictate a more stripped down Vim.

Users may need Vim to take up a minimal footprint, for example, on a handheld device running Linux that has limited memory. Users may also have no use for compiled-in features such as spellcheck (because they may be programmers with no interest in features that mimic word processing) or `perl` (because `perl` may not be installed on their machines).

It's much easier to live with the available features than to reconfigure, recompile, and reinstall Vim with all new options, just to add missing features.

Multiple Windows in Vim

By default, Vim edits all its files in a single window, showing just one buffer at a time as you move between files or to different parts of a single file. But Vim also offers multi-window editing, which can make complex editing tasks easier. This is different from starting multiple instances of Vim on a graphical terminal. This chapter covers the use of multiple windows in a single instance of a running Vim process (which we'll call a *session*).

You can initiate your editing session with multiple windows or create new windows after a session starts. You can add windows to your edit session up to the limit imposed by sanity, and you can delete them back to a single edit window.

Here are some examples where multiple windows make your life easier:

- Editing a number of files that need to be formatted the same way, where you would like to compare them visually as you go along
- Cutting and pasting text quickly and repeatedly among multiple files or multiple parts of a single file
- Displaying one part of a file for reference, to facilitate work elsewhere in the same file
- Comparing two versions of a file

Vim offers many window-managing convenience features, including the ability to:

- Split windows horizontally or vertically
- Navigate from one window to another and back again quickly
- Copy and move text to and from multiple windows
- Move and reposition windows
- Work with buffers, including hidden buffers (to be described later)
- Use external tools such as the `diff` command with multiple windows

In this chapter, we guide you through the multiwindow experience. We show you how to start a multiwindow session, discuss features and tips for the edit session, and describe how to exit your work and ensure that all your work is properly saved (or abandoned, if you wish!). The following topics are covered:

- Initializing or starting multiwindow editing
- Multiwindow :ex commands
- Moving the cursor from window to window
- Moving windows around the display
- Resizing windows
- Buffers and their interaction with windows
- Tabbed editing (like the tabs offered by modern Internet browsers and dialog boxes)
- Closing and quitting windows

Initiating Multiwindow Editing

You can initiate multiwindow editing when you start Vim, or you can split windows within your editing session. Multiwindow editing is dynamic in Vim, allowing you to open, close, and navigate among multiple windows at any point, from most contexts.

Multiwindow Initiation from the Command Line (Shell)

By default, Vim opens only one window for a session, even if you specify more than one file. While we don't know for sure why Vim would not open multiple windows for multiple files, it may be because using just a single window is consistent with vi behavior. Multiple files occupy multiple buffers, with each file in its own buffer. (Buffers are discussed shortly.)

To open multiple windows from the command line, use Vim's -o option. For example:

```
$ Vim -o file1 file2
```

This opens the edit session with the display horizontally split into two equal-sized windows, one for each file (see Figure 11-1). For each file named on the command line, Vim tries to open a window for editing. If Vim cannot split the screen into enough windows for the files, the first files listed in the command-line arguments get windows, while the remaining files are loaded into buffers not visible (but still available) to the user.

Another form of the command line preallocates the windows by appending a number *n* to -o:

```
$ Vim -o5 file1 file2
```

This opens a session with the display horizontally split into five equal-sized windows, the topmost of which contains file1 and the second of which contains file2 (see Figure 11-2).

```
1
2
3    XX      X      XX                  X
4    X              X              XXX
5    X              X                  X
6    XXXX    XXX    X      XXXXX        X
7    X       X      X      X    X       X
8    X       X      █      X    XXXXXXX X
9    X       X      X      X    X       X
10   X       X      X      X    X     X X
11   XXXX    XXXXX  XXXXX  XXXXX  XXXXX
12
13
file1[+]   (1 of 2) 2/10/2008 11:48:19 AM          0x20  line:8,  col:16 All NONE
1
2
3    XX      X      XX              XXX
4    X              X              X   X
5    X              X                  X
6    XXXX    XXX    X      XXXXX        X
7    X       X      X      X    X       X
8    X       X      X      XXXXXXX      X
9    X       X      X      X            X
10   X       X      X      X    X     X X
11   XXXX    XXXXX  XXXXX  XXXXX  XXXXX
12
13
~
file2[+]   (2 of 2) 2/10/2008 11:48:16 AM          0x20  line:1,  col:40 All NONE
```

Figure 11-1. Results of "Vim -o5 file1 file2"

When Vim creates more than one window, its default behavior is to create a status line for each window (whereas the default behavior for a single window is not to display any status line). You can control this behavior with Vim's `laststatus` option, e.g.:

`:set laststatus=1`

Set `laststatus` to 2 to always see a status line for each window, even in single window mode. (It is best to set this in your `.vimrc` file.)

Because window size affects readability and usability, you may want to control Vim's limits for window sizes. Use Vim's `winheight` and `winwidth` options to define reasonable limits for the current window (other windows may be resized to accommodate it).

Multiwindow Editing Inside Vim

You can initiate and modify the window configuration from within Vim. Create a new window with the `:split` command. This breaks the current window in half, showing the same buffer in both halves. Now you can navigate independently in each window on the same file.

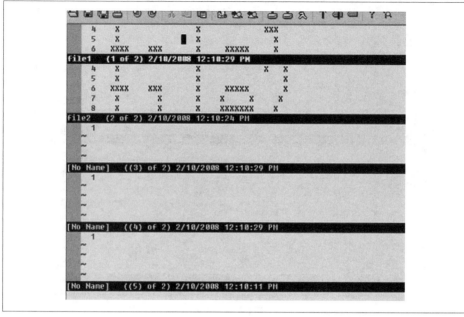

Figure 11-2. Results of "Vim -o5 file1 file2"

There are convenience key sequences for many of the commands in this chapter. In this case, for instance, ^Ws splits a window. (All Vim window-related commands begin with ^W, with the "W" being mnemonic for "window.") For the purposes of discussion, we show only the command-line methods because they provide the added power of optional parameters that customize the default behavior. If you find yourself using commands routinely, you can easily find the corresponding key sequence in the Vim documentation, as described in "Built-in Help" on page 159.

Similarly, you can create a new, vertically separated edit window with the :vsplit command (see Figure 11-3).

For each of these methods, Vim splits the window (horizontally or vertically), and since no file was specified on the :split command line, you end up editing the same file with two views or windows.

Don't believe you're editing the same file at the same time? Split the edit window and scroll each window so that each shows the same area of the file. Make changes. Watch the other window. Magic.

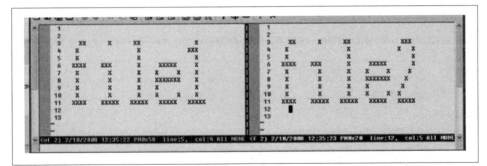

Figure 11-3. Vertically split window

Why or how is this useful? One common use by this author, when writing shell scripts or C programs, is to code a block of text that describes the program's usage. (Typically, the program will display the block when passed a --help option.) I split the display so that one window displays the usage text, and I use this as a template to edit the code in the other window that parses all the options and command-line arguments described in the usage text. Often (almost always) this code is complex and ends up far enough from the usage text that I can't display everything I want in a single window.

If you want to edit or browse another file without losing your place in your current file, provide the new file as an argument to your :split command. For instance:

```
:split otherfile
```

The next section describes splitting and unsplitting windows in more detail.

Opening Windows

This section goes into depth about how to get the precise behavior you want when you split your window.

New Windows

As discussed previously, the simplest way to open a new window is to issue :split (for a horizontal division) or :vsplit (for a vertical division). A more in-depth discussion of the many commands and variations follows. We also include a command synopsis for quick reference.

Options During Splits

The full :split command to open a new horizontal window is:

```
:[n]split [++opt] [+cmd] [file]
```

where:

n

Tells Vim how many lines to display in the new window, which goes at the top.

opt

Passes Vim option information to the new window session (note that it must be preceded by two plus signs).

cmd

Passes a command for execution in the new window (note that it must be preceded by a single plus sign).

file

Specifies a file to edit in the new window.

For example, suppose you are editing a file and want to split the window to edit another file named `otherfile`. You want to ensure that the session uses a `fileformat` of `unix` (which ensures the use of a line feed to end each line instead of a carriage return and line feed combination). Finally, you want the window to be 15 lines tall. Enter:

```
:15split ++fileformat=unix otherfile
```

To simply split the screen, showing the same file in both windows and using all the current defaults, you can use the key commands `^Ws`, `^WS`, or `^W^S`.

 If you want windows to always split equally, set the `equalalways` option, preferably putting it in your `.vimrc` to make it persistent over sessions. By default, setting `equalalways` splits both horizontal and vertical windows equally. Add the `eadirection` option (`hor`, `ver`, `both`, for horizontal, vertical, or both, respectively) to control which direction splits equally.

The following form of the `:split` command opens a new horizontal window as before, but with a slight nuance:

```
:[n]new [++opt] [+cmd] [file]
```

In addition to creating the new window, the `WinLeave`, `WinEnter`, `BufLeave`, and `BufEnter` autocommands execute. (For more information on autocommands, see the section "Autocommands" on page 206.)

Along with the horizontal split commands, Vim offers analogous vertical ones. So, for example, to split a vertical window, instead of `:split` or `:new`, use `:vsplit` and `:vnew` respectively. The same optional parameters are available as for the horizontal split commands.

There are two horizontal split commands without vertical cousins:

`:sview` *filename*

Splits the screen horizontally to open a new window and sets the `readonly` for that buffer. `:sview` requires the filename argument.

`:sfind [++opt] [+cmd]` *filename*

Works like `:split`, but looks for the *filename* in the `path`. If Vim does not find the file, it doesn't split the window.

Conditional Split Commands

Vim lets you specify a command that causes a window to open if a new file is found. `:topleft` *cmd* tells Vim to execute *cmd* and display a new window with the cursor at the top left if *cmd* opens a new file. The command can produce three different results:

- *cmd* splits the window horizontally, and the new window spans the top of the Vim window.

- *cmd* splits the window vertically, and the new window spans the left side of the Vim window.

- *cmd* causes no split but instead positions the cursor at the top left of the current window.

Window Command Summary

Table 11-1 summarizes the commands for splitting windows.

Table 11-1. Summary of window commands

ex command	vi command	Description
`:[n]split [++opt] [+cmd] [file]`	`^Ws` `^WS` `^W^S`	Split the current window into two from side to side, placing the cursor in the new window. The optional *file* argument places that file in the newly created window. The windows are created as equal in size as possible, determined by free window space.
`:[n]new [++opt] [+cmd]`	`^Wn` `^W^N`	Same as `:split`, but start the new window editing an empty file. Note that the buffer will have no name until one is assigned.
`:[n]sview [++opt] [+cmd] [file]`		Read-only version of `:split`.
`:[n]sfind [++opt] [+cmd] [file]`		Split window and open *file* (if specified) in the new window. Look for *file* in the `path`.
`:[n]vsplit [++opt] [+cmd] [file]`	`^Wv` `^W^V`	Split current window into two from top to bottom and open *file* (if specified) in the new window.
`:[n]vnew [++opt] [+cmd]`		Vertical version of `:new`.

Moving Around Windows (Getting Your Cursor from Here to There)

It's easy to move from window to window with a mouse in both gvim and Vim. gvim supports clicking with the mouse by default, whereas in Vim you can enable the behavior with the mouse option. A good default setting for Vim is :set mouse=a, to activate the mouse for all uses: command line, input, and navigation.

If you don't have a mouse, or prefer to control your session from the keyboard, Vim provides a full set of navigation commands to move quickly and accurately among session windows. Happily, Vim uses the mnemonic prefix keystroke ^W consistently for window navigation. The keystroke that follows defines the motion or other action, and should be familiar to experienced vi and Vim users because they map closely to the same motion commands for editing.

Rather than describe each command and its behavior, we will consider an example. The command-synopsis table should then be self-explanatory.

To move from the current Vim window to the next one, type CTRL-W j (or CTRL-W <down> or CTRL-W CTRL-J). The CTRL-W is the mnemonic for "window" command, and the j is analogous to Vim's j command, which moves the cursor to the next line.

Table 11-2 summarizes the window navigation commands.

 As with many Vim and vi commands, these can be multiply executed by prefixing them with a count. For example, 3^Wj tells Vim to jump to the third window down from the current window.

Table 11-2. Window navigation commands

Command	Description
CTRL-W <DOWN> CTRL-W CTRL-J CTRL-W j	Move to the next window down. Note that this command does not cycle through the windows; it simply moves down to the next window below the current window. If the cursor is in a window at the bottom of the screen, this command has no effect. Also, this command bypasses adjacent windows on its "way down"; for example, if there is a window to the right of the current window, the command does not jump across to the adjacent window. (Use CTRL-W CTRL-W to cycle through windows.)
CTRL-W <UP> CTRL-W CTRL-K CTRL-W k	Move to the next window up. This is the opposite-direction counterpart to the CTRL-W j command.
CTRL-W <LEFT> CTRL-W CTRL-H	Move to the window to the left of the current window.

Command	Description
CTRL-W h CTRL-W \<BS> CTRL-W \<RIGHT> CTRL-W CTRL-L CTRL-W l	Move to the window to the right of the current window.
CTRL-W w CTRL-W CTRL-W	Move to the next window below or to the right. Note that this command, unlike CTRL-W j, will cycle through all of the Vim windows. When the lowermost window is reached, Vim restarts the cycle and moves to the top leftmost window.
CTRL-W	Move to next window above or to the left. This is the upward counterpart to the CTRL-W w command.
CTRL-W t CTRL-W CTRL-T	Move cursor to the top leftmost window.
CTRL-W b CTRL-W CTRL-B	Move cursor to the bottom rightmost window.
CTRL-W p CTRL-W CTRL-P	Move to the previous (last accessed) window.

Mnemonic Tips

t and b are mnemonic for *top* and *bottom* windows.

In keeping with the convention that lowercase and uppercase implement opposites, CTRL-W w moves you through the windows in the opposite direction from CTRL-W W.

The Control characters do not distinguish between uppercase and lowercase; in other words, pressing the Shift key while pressing a CTRL- key itself has no effect. However, an upper/lowercase distinction *is* recognized for the regular keyboard key you press afterward.

Moving Windows Around

You can move windows two ways in Vim. One way simply swaps the windows on the screen. The other way changes the actual window layouts. In the first case, window sizes remain constant while windows change position on the screen. In the second case, windows not only move but are resized to fill the position to which they've moved.

Moving Windows (Rotate or Exchange)

Three commands move windows without modifying layout. Two of these rotate the windows positionally in one direction (to the right or down) or the other (to the left or up), and the other one exchanges the position of two possibly nonadjacent windows. These commands operate *only* on the row or column in which the current window lives.

CTRL-W r rotates windows to the right or down. Its complement is CTRL-W R, which rotates windows in the opposite direction.

An easier way to imagine how these work is to think of a row or column of Vim windows as a one-dimensional array. CTRL-W r would shift each element of the array one position to the right, and move the last element into the vacated first position. CTRL-W R simply moves the elements the other direction.

If there are no windows in a column or row that aligns with the current window, this command does nothing.

After Vim rotates the windows, the cursor remains in the window from which the rotate command executed; thus, the cursor moves with the window.

CTRL-W x and CTRL-W CTRL-X let you exchange two windows in a row or column of windows. By default, Vim exchanges the current window with the next window, and if there is no next window, Vim tries to exchange with the previous window. You can exchange with the nth next window by prepending a count before the command. For example, to switch the current window with the third next window, use the command 3^Wx.

As with the two previous commands, the cursor stays in the window from which the exchange command executes.

Moving Windows and Changing Their Layout

Five commands move and reflow the windows: two move the current window to a full-width top or bottom window, two move the current window to a full-height left or right window, and the fifth moves the current window to another existing tab. (See the section "Tabbed Editing" on page 191.) The first four commands bear familiar mnemonic relationships to other Vim commands; for instance, CTRL-W K maps to the traditional notion of k as "up." Table 11-3 summarizes these commands.

Table 11-3. Commands to move and reflow windows

Command	Description
^WK	Move the current window to the top of the screen, using the full width of the screen.
^WJ	Move the current window to the bottom of the screen, using the full width of the screen.
^WH	Move the current window to the left of the screen, using the full height of the screen.
^WL	Move the current window to the right of the screen, using the full height of the screen.
^WT	Move the current window to a new existing tab.

It is difficult to describe the exact behavior of these layout commands. After the move and expansion of the window to the full height or width of the screen, Vim reflows the windows in a reasonable way. The behavior of the reflow can also be influenced by some of the windows options settings.

Window Move Commands: Synopsis

Tables 11-4 and 11-5 summarize the commands introduced in this section.

Table 11-4. Commands to rotate window positions

Command	Description
^Wr	Rotate windows down or to the right.
^W^R	
^WR	Rotate windows up or to the left.
^Wx	Swap positions with the next window, or if issued with a count n, swap with n^{th} next window.
^W^X	

Table 11-5. Commands to change position and layout

Command	Description
^WK	Move window to top of screen and use full width. The cursor stays with the moved window.
^WJ	Move window to bottom of screen and use full width. The cursor stays with the moved window.
^WH	Move window to left of screen and use full height. The cursor stays with the moved window.
^WL	Move window to right of screen and use full height. The cursor stays with the moved window.
^WT	Move window to new tab. The cursor stays with the moved window. If the current window is the only window in the current tab, no action is taken.

Resizing Windows

Now that you're more familiar with Vim's multiwindowing features, you need a little more control over them. This section addresses how you can change the size of the current window, with, of course, effects on other windows in the screen. Vim provides options to control window sizes and window sizing behavior when opening new windows with split commands.

If you'd rather control window sizes *sans* commands, use `gvim` and let the mouse do the work for you. Simply click and drag window boundaries with the mouse to resize. For vertically separated windows, click the mouse on the vertical separator of | characters. Horizontal windows are separated by their status lines.

Window Resize Commands

As you'd expect, Vim has vertical and horizontal resize commands. Like the other window commands, these all begin with CTRL-W and map nicely to mnemonic devices, making them easy to learn and remember.

CTRL-W = tries to resize all windows to equal size. (This is also influenced by the current values of winheight and windwidth, discussed in the following section.) If the available screen real estate doesn't divide equally, Vim sizes the windows to be as close to equal as possible.

CTRL-W - decreases the current window height by one line. Vim also has an ex command that lets you decrease the window size explicitly. For example, the command resize -4 decreases the current window by four lines and gives those lines to the window below it.

> It's interesting to note that Vim obediently decreases your window size even if you are not in a multiple window edit session. While it may seem counterintuitive at first, the side effect is that Vim decreases the window as requested and the vacated screen real estate is allocated to the command-line window. Typically, the command-line window always uses a single line, but there are reasons to use a command-line window larger than one line high. (The most common reason we know of is to provide enough space to let Vim display complete command-line status and feedback without intermediate prompts.) That said, it's best to use the :resize command to resize your current window, and to use the winheight option to size your command window.

CTRL-W + increases the current window by one line. The :resize +n command increases the current window size by n lines. Once the window's maximum height is reached, further use of this command has no effect.

> One of the authors' favorite ways to use the CTRL-W + and CTRL-W - commands is by mapping each to keys, both keys adjacent. The + key is a convenient choice. Though it is already the Vim "up" command, that behavior is redundant and little used by veteran Vim users (who use the k command instead). Therefore, this key is a good candidate to map to something else, in this case CTRL-W +. Immediately to that key's left (on most standard keyboards) is the -. But since it is unshifted and the + is shifted, map the shifted key, ⎵, to CTRL-W -. Now you have two convenient side-by-side keys to easily and quickly expand and contract your current window horizontally.

:resize n sets the horizontal size of the current window to n lines. It sets an absolute size, in contrast to the previously described commands that make a relative change.

zn sets the current window height to *n* lines. Note that *n* is *not* optional! Omitting it results in the vi/Vim command z, which moves the cursor to the top of the screen.

CTRL-W < and CTRL-W > decrease and increase the window width, respectively. Think of the mnemonic device of "shift left" (<<) and "shift right" (>>) to associate these commands to their function.

Finally, CTRL-W | resizes the current window to the widest size possible (by default). You can also specify explicitly how to change the window width with vertical resize *n*. The *n* defines the window's new width.

Window Sizing Options

Several Vim options influence the behavior of the resize commands described in the previous section.

winheight and winwidth define the minimal window height and width, respectively, when a window becomes active. For example, if the screen accommodates two equal-sized windows of 45 lines, the default Vim behavior is to split them equally. If you were to set winheight to a value larger than 45—say, 60—Vim will resize the window to which you move each time to 60 lines, and will resize the other window to 30. This is handy for editing two files simultaneously; you automatically increase the allocated window size for maximum context when you switch from window to window and from file to file.

equalalways tells Vim to always resize windows equally after splitting or closing a window. This is a good option to set in order to ensure equitable allocation of windows as you add and delete them.

eadirection defines directional jurisdiction for equalalways. The possible values hor, ver, and both tell Vim to make windows of equal size *horizontally*, *vertically*, or *both*, respectively. The resizing applies each time you split or delete a window.

cmdheight sets the command line height. As described previously, decreasing a window's height when there is only one window increases the command-line height. You can keep the command line the height you want using this option.

Finally, winminwidth and winminheight tell Vim the *minimum* width and height to size windows. Vim considers these to be hard values, meaning that windows will never be allowed to get smaller than these values.

Resizing Command Synopsis

Table 11-6 summarizes the ways to resize windows. Options are set with the :set command.

Table 11-6. Window resizing commands

Command or option	Description
^W=	Resize all windows equally. The current window honors the settings of the winheight and winwidth options.
:resize -n ^W-	Decrease the current window size. The default amount is one line.
:resize +n ^W+	Increase the current window size. The default amount is one line.
:resize n ^W^_ ^W_	Set the current window height. The default is to maximize window height (unless *n* is specified).
zn <ENTER>	Set the current window height to *n*.
^W<	Increase the current window width. The default amount is one column.
^W>	Decrease the current window width. The default amount is one column.
:vertical resize n ^W|	Set the current window width to *n*. The default is to make window as wide as possible.
winheight option	When entering or creating a window, set its height to at least the specified value.
winwidth option	When entering or creating a window, set its width to at least the specified value.
equalalways option	When the number of windows changes, either by splitting or closing windows, resize them to be the same size.
eadirection option	Define whether Vim resizes windows equally vertically, horizontally, or both.
cmdheight option	Set the command line height.
winminheight option	Define the minimum window height, which applies to all windows created.
winminwidth option	Define the minimum window width, which applies to all windows created.

Buffers and Their Interaction with Windows

Vim uses *buffers* as containers for work. Understanding buffers completely is an acquired skill; there are many commands for manipulating and navigating them. However, it is worthwhile to familiarize yourself with some of the buffer basics and understand how and why they exist throughout a Vim session.

A good starting point is to open up a few windows editing different files. For example, start Vim by opening file1. Then, within the session, issue :split file2 and then :split file3. You should now have three open files in three separate Vim windows.

Now use the commands :ls, :files, or :buffers to list the buffers. You should see three lines, each numbered and including the filenames, along with additional information. These are Vim's buffers for this session. There is one buffer for each file and each buffer has a unique, nonchanging associated number. In this example, file1 is in buffer 1, file2 is in buffer 2, etc.

Additional information on each buffer can be displayed if you append an exclamation point (!) after any of the commands.

To the right of each buffer number are status flags. These flags describe the buffers as shown in Table 11-7.

Table 11-7. Status flags describing buffers

Code	Description
u	Unlisted buffer. This buffer is not listed unless you use the ! modifier. To see an example of an unlisted buffer, type :help. Vim splits the current window to include a new window in which the built-in help appears. The plain :ls command will not show the help buffer, but :ls! includes it.
% or (mutually exclusive) #	% is the buffer for the current window. # is the buffer to which you would switch with the :edit # command.
a or (mutually exclusive) h	a indicates an active buffer. That means the buffer is loaded and visible. h indicates a hidden buffer. The hidden buffer exists but is not visible in any window.
- or (mutually exclusive) =	- means that a buffer has the modifiable option turned off. The file is read-only. = is a read-only buffer that cannot be made modifiable (for instance, because you don't have filesystem privileges to write to the file).
+ or (mutually exclusive) x	+ indicates a modified buffer. x is a buffer with read errors.

The u flag is an interesting way to know what help file you are viewing in Vim. For example, had you issued :help split followed by :ls!, you would see that the unlisted buffer refers to the built-in Vim help file, windows.txt.

Now that you can list Vim buffers, we can talk about them and their various uses.

Vim's Special Buffers

Vim uses some buffers for its own purposes, called *special* buffers. For instance, the help buffers described in the previous section are special. Typically, these buffers cannot be edited or modified.

Here are four examples of Vim special buffers:

quickfix
> Contains the list of errors created by your commands (which can be viewed with :cwindow) or the location list (which can be viewed with the :lwindow command). Do not edit the contents of this buffer! It helps programmers iterate through the edit-compile-debug cycle. See Chapter 14.

help
> Contains Vim help files, described earlier in the section "Built-in Help" on page 159. :help loads these text files into this special buffer.

directory

> Contain directory contents, that is, a list of files for a directory (and some helpful extra command hints). This is a handy tool within Vim that lets you move around in this buffer as you would in a regular text file and select files under the cursor for editing by pressing ENTER .

scratch

> These buffers contain text for general purposes. This text is expendable and can be deleted at any time.

Hidden Buffers

Hidden buffers are Vim buffers that are not currently displayed in any window. This makes it easier to edit multiple files, considering the limited screen real estate for multiple windows, without constantly retrieving and rewriting files. For example, imagine you are editing the `myfile` file but wish to momentarily edit some other file, `myOtherfile`. If the `hidden` option is set, you can edit `myOtherfile` through `:edit myOtherfile`, causing Vim to hide the `myfile` buffer and display `myOtherfile` in its place. You can verify this with `:ls` and see both buffers listed with `myfile` flagged as *hidden*.

Buffer Commands

There are almost 50 commands that specifically target buffers. Many are useful but are for the most part outside the scope of this discussion. Vim manages buffers automatically as you open and close multiple files and windows. The suite of buffer commands allows you to do almost anything with buffers. Often they are used within scripts to handle such tasks as unloading, deleting, and modifying buffers.

Two buffer commands are worth knowing for general use because of their power to do lots of work across many files:

`windo` *cmd*

> Short for "window do" (at least we think it's a decent mnemonic), this pseudo-buffer command (actually it's a window command) executes the command *cmd* in each window. It acts as if you go to the top of the screen (^Wt), and cycles through each window to execute the specified command as `:cmd` in that window. It acts only within the current tab and stops at any window where `:cmd` generates an error. The window in which the error occurs becomes the new current window.
>
> `cmd` is not permitted to change the state of the windows; that is, it cannot delete, add, or change the order of the windows.

cmd can concatenate multiple commands with the pipe (|) symbol. *Do not confuse this notation with the Unix shell convention of piping commands!* The commands are executed in sequence, with the first command executed sequentially through all windows, then the second command in all windows, etc.

As an example of :windo in action, suppose you are editing a suite of Java files and for some reason you have a class name that is improperly capitalized. You need to repair this by changing every occurrence of myPoorlyCapitalizedClass to MyPoorly CapitalizedClass. With :windo you can do that with:

```
:windo %s/myPoorlyCapitalizedClass/MyPoorlyCapitalizedClass/g
```

Pretty cool!

bufdo[!] *cmd*

This is analogous to windo but operates on all of the buffers in your editing session, not just visible buffers in the current tab. bufdo stops at the first error encountered, just like windo, and leaves the cursor in the buffer where the command fails.

The following example changes all buffers to Unix file format:

```
:bufdo set fileformat=unix
```

Buffer Command Synopsis

Table 11-8 makes no attempt to describe all the commands related to buffers; instead it summarizes the ones described in this section and some other popular commands.

Table 11-8. Summary of buffer commands

Command	Description
:ls[!] :files[!] :buffers[!]	List buffers and file names. Include unlisted buffers if ! modifier is included.
:ball :sball	Edit all args or buffers. (sball opens them in new windows.)
:unhide :sunhide	Edit all *loaded* buffers. (sunhide opens them in new windows.)
:badd file	Add file to list.
:bunload[!]	Unload buffer from memory. The ! modifier forces a modified buffer to be unloaded without being saved.
:bdelete[!]	Unload buffer and delete it from the buffer list. The ! modifier forces a modified buffer to be unloaded without being saved.
:buffer [n] :sbuffer [n]	Move to buffer *n*. (sbuffer opens a new window.)
:bnext [n] :sbnext [n]	Move to next n^{th} buffer. (sbnext opens a new window.)
:bNext [n] :sbNext [n] :bprevious [n]	Move to n^{th} next or previous buffer. (sbNext and sbprevious open a new window.)

Command	Description
:sbprevious [n]	
:bfirst :sbfirst	Move to first buffer (sbfirst opens a new window).
:bfirst :sbfirst	Move to last buffer (sblast opens a new window).
:bmod [n] :sbmod [n]	Move to nth modified buffer (sbmod opens a new window).

Playing Tag with Windows

Vim extends the vi tag functionality into windows by offering the same tag traversal mechanisms through multiple windows. Following a tag can also open a file in the associated place in a new window.

The tag windowing commands split the current window and follow a tag either to a file matching the tag or to the file matching the filename under the cursor.

:stag[!] *tag* splits the window to display the location for the tag found. The new file containing the matched tag becomes the current window, and the cursor is placed over the matched tag. If no tag is found, the command fails and no new window is created.

 As you become more familiar with Vim's help system, you can use this :stag command to split your way through the help system rather than jumping from file to file in the same window.

^WJ or ^W^J splits the window and opens a window above the current window. The new window becomes the current window, and the cursor is placed on the matching tag. If there is no match on the tag, the command fails.

^Wg] splits the window and creates a new window above the current window. In the new window, Vim performs the command :tselect *tag*, where *tag* was the tag identifier under the cursor. If no matching tag exists, the command fails. The cursor is placed in the new window, and that new window becomes the current window.

^Wg^J works exactly like ^Wg], except that instead of performing :tselect, it performs :tjump.

^Wf (or ^W^F) splits the window and edits the filename underneath the cursor. Vim will look sequentially through the files set in the option variable path to find the file. If the file doesn't exist in any of the path directories, the command fails and does not create a new window.

^WF splits the window and edits the filename under the cursor. The cursor is placed in the new window editing that file and positioned at the line number matching the number following the filename in the first window.

^Wgf opens the file under the cursor in a new tab. If the file doesn't exist, the new tab is not created.

^Wgf opens the file under the cursor in a new tab and positions the cursor on the line specified by the number following the filename in the first window. If the file doesn't exist, the new tab is not created.

Tabbed Editing

Did you know that in addition to editing in multiple windows, you can create multiple *tabs*? Vim lets you create new tabs, each of which behaves independently. In each tab you can split the screen, edit multiple files—virtually anything you would normally do in a single window, but now all of your work is easily managed in one window with tabs.

Many Firefox users are very familiar with and dependent on tabbed browsing and will recognize what this feature brings to power editing. For the uninitiated, it's worth trying.

You can use tabs in both regular Vim and gvim, but gvim is much nicer and easier. Some of the more important ways to create and manage tabs include:

:tabnew *filename*
  Open a new tab and edit a file (optional). If no file is specified Vim opens a new tab with an empty buffer.

:tabclose
  Close the current tab.

:tabonly
  Close all other tabs. If other tabs have modified files, they are not removed unless the autowrite option is set, in which case all modified files are written before the other tabs are closed.

In gvim you can activate any tab simply by clicking the tab at the top of the screen. You can also activate tabs in character-based terminals with the mouse if the mouse is configured (see the mouse option). Also, it's easy to move right and left from tab to tab with CTRL PAGE DOWN (move one tab to the right) and CTRL PAGE UP (move one tab to the left). If you are in the leftmost or rightmost tabs and you try to move left or right respectively, Vim moves to the far right or far left tab.

gvim offers right-click pop-up menus for the tab, from which you can open a new tab (with or without a new file to edit) and close a tab.

Figure 11-4 is an example of a set of tabs (notice the tab pop-up menu).

Figure 11-4. Example of gvim tabs and tabbed editing

Closing and Quitting Windows

There are four different ways to close a window that are specific to window editing: *quit*, *close*, *hide*, and *close all others*.

^Wq (or ^W^Q, or :quit) is really just a window version of the :quit command. In its simplest form (i.e., a single session edit with only one window), it behaves exactly like vi's :quit command. If the hidden option is set and the current window is the last window on the screen referencing that file, the window is closed but the file buffer is retained (it can be retrieved) and hidden. In other words, Vim is still storing the file and you can return to editing it later. If hidden is *not* set, the window is the last one referencing that file, and there are unsaved changes in the current window buffer, the command fails in order to avoid losing your changes. But if some other window displays the file, the current window closes.

^Wc (or :close[!]) closes the current window. If the hidden option is set and this is the last window referencing this file, Vim closes the window and the buffer is hidden. If this window is on a tab page and is the last window for that tab page, the window *and* the tab page are closed. As long as you don't use the ! modifier, this command will not abandon any file with unsaved changes. The ! modifier tells Vim to close the current window unconditionally.

> Note that this command does not use ^W^C, because Vim uses ^C to *cancel* commands. Therefore, if you try to use ^W^C, the ^C simply cancels the command.
>
> Similarly, while the ^W commands are used in combination with ^S and ^Q, *some* users may find their terminals frozen because some interpret ^S and ^Q as control characters to stop and start displaying information to the screen. If you find your screen freezing mysteriously when using these combinations, try the other listed combinations instead.

^Wo, ^W^O, and :only[!] close all windows except the current window. If the hidden option is set, all closed windows hide their buffers. If it's not set, any window referencing a file with unsaved changes remains on the screen, unless you included the ! modifier, in which case all windows are closed and the files are abandoned. The behavior of this command can be affected by the `autowrite` option: if it's set, all windows are closed, but windows containing unsaved changes are written to the files on disk before being exited.

`:hide [cmd]` quits the current window and hides the buffer if no other window references it. If the optional *cmd* is supplied, the buffer is hidden and the command is executed.

Table 11-9 provides a summary of these commands.

Table 11-9. Commands for closing and quitting windows

Command	Description

`:quit[!]`
`^Wq`
 	
`^W^Q`
	Quit the current window.

`:close[!]` `^Wc`	Close the current window.

`:only[!]`
`^Wo`
 	
`^W^O`
	Make the current window the only window.

Summary

As you now appreciate, Vim ramps up the editing horsepower with its many windowing features. Vim lets you create and delete windows easily and on the fly. Additionally, Vim provides the under-the-hood power of the raw buffer commands, buffers being the underlying file management infrastructure with which Vim manages window editing. This is once again a perfect example of how Vim brings multiwindow editing to beginners while simultaneously giving power users the tools they need to tune their windowing experience.

Vim Scripts

Sometimes customization alone isn't enough for your editing environment. Vim lets you define all of your favorite settings in your `.vimrc` file, but maybe you want more dynamic or "just in time" configuration. Vim scripts let you do that.

From inspecting buffer contents to handling unanticipated external factors, Vim's scripting language lets you complete complex tasks and make decisions based on *your* needs.

If you have a Vim configuration file (`.vimrc`, `.gvimrc`, or both), you are already scripting in Vim; you just don't know it. All of the Vim commands and options are valid inputs to scripts. And, as you'd expect, Vim provides all of the standard flow control (`if...then...else`, `while`, etc.), variables, and functions typical in any language.

In this chapter, we'll walk through an example and incrementally build up a script. We'll look at simple constructs, use some of Vim's built-in functions, and examine rules you must consider in order to write well-behaved and predictable Vim scripts.

What's Your Favorite Color (Scheme)?

Let's begin with the simplest of configurations. We'll customize our environment to a color scheme *we* prefer. This is simple, and uses one of the basics of Vim scripts, the simple Vim command.

Vim ships with 17 customized color schemes. You can choose and activate a color scheme by putting the `colorscheme` command in your `.vimrc` or `.gvimrc` file. A favorite "understated" color scheme of one author is the desert scheme:

```
colorscheme desert
```

Put a `colorscheme` like that in your configuration file, and now every time you edit with Vim you will see your favorite colors.

So our first script is trivial. What if your tastes for your color scheme are more complex? What if you like more than one color scheme? What if the time of day correlates to your preferences? Vim scripts easily let you do this.

Choosing an alternate color scheme depending on the time of day may seem trite, but maybe not as much as you may think. Even Google changes the colors and tone of your *iGoogle* home page throughout the day.

Conditional Execution

One of the authors likes to divide the day into four partitions, each with its own dedicated color scheme:

darkblue
> Midnight to 6 a.m.

morning
> 6 a.m. to noon

shine
> Noon to 6 p.m.

evening
> 6 p.m. to midnight

We'll build a nested `if...then...else...` block of code for this purpose. There are a couple of different syntaxes you can use for this block. One is more traditional, with an explicitly laid out syntax:

```
if cond expr
  line of vim code
  another line of vim code
  ...
elseif some secondary cond expr
  code for this case
else
  code that runs if none of the cases apply
endif
```

The `elseif` and `else` blocks are optional, and you can include multiple `elseif` blocks. Vim also allows the more terse and C-like construct:

```
cond ? expr 1 : expr 2
```

Vim checks the condition *cond*. If it's true, *expr 1* executes; otherwise, *expr 2* executes.

Using the strftime( ) function

Now that we can conditionally execute code, we need to figure out what part of the day it is. Vim has built-in *functions* that return this kind of information. In our case, we use the `strftime( )` function. `strftime` accepts two parameters, the first of which defines the output format of a time string. (This format is system dependent, and not portable, so you must pay due care when choosing a format. Fortunately, most mainstream formats are common across systems.) The second optional parameter is a time measured in seconds since Jan 1, 1970 (standard C time representation). This optional parameter defaults to the current time. For our example, we can use the time format %H, producing `strftime("%H")`, because the hour of the day is all we need to decide on our color scheme.

Now that we know how to use conditional code, we have the Vim built-in function to give us the information about the time of day with which we choose our matching color scheme. Put this code into your `.vimrc` file:

```
" progressively check higher values... falls out on first "true"
" (note addition of zero ... this guarantees return from function is numeric
if strftime("%H") < 6 + 0
  colorscheme darkblue
  echo "setting colorscheme to darkblue"
elseif strftime("%H") < 12 + 0
  colorscheme morning
  echo "setting colorscheme to morning"
elseif strftime("%H") < 18 + 0
  colorscheme shine
  echo "setting colorscheme to shine"
else
  colorscheme evening
  echo "setting colorscheme to evening"
endif
```

Notice that we introduce another Vim script command, `echo`. As a convenience, we add this to echo the current scheme to ourselves; it also lets us check that the code actually ran and produced the desired result. The message should appear in Vim's command status window or as a pop up, depending on where in the startup sequence the `echo` command is encountered.

When we issue the command `colorscheme`, we use the name of the scheme (e.g., `desert`) *without* surrounding quotes, but when we use the `echo` command, we *do* quote the name (`"desert"`). This is an important distinction!

In the case of the `colorscheme` command in our script, we are issuing a direct Vim command, and the parameter for this command is a literal. If we include surrounding quotes, the quotes are interpreted as part of the name of the color scheme by the `colorscheme`. This is an error because none of the schemes include quotes in their names.

On the other hand, the `echo` command interpolates words without quotes as expressions (calculations that return values) or functions. Therefore, we need to quote the name of the color scheme we choose.

Variables

If you are a programmer, you probably see a problem with the script we just presented. While it's unlikely to be a big concern in what we are trying to do, we are executing a conditional check of the hour of the day by invoking the `strftime( )` function at each conditional point. Technically, we are conditionally checking one thing, but we are evaluating it as an expression multiple times, potentially making a conditional decision on something that changes value mid-execution.

Instead of executing the function each time, let's evaluate it once and store the results in a Vim script *variable*. We can then use the variable as often as we want in our conditional, without incurring the overhead of a function call.

Vim variables are fairly straightforward, but there are a few things to know and manage. Specifically, we must manage our variable's *scope*. Vim defines a variable's scope through a convention that depends on the name's prefix. The prefixes include:

`b:`
> A variable recognized in a single Vim buffer

`w:`
> A variable recognized in a single Vim window

`t:`
> A variable recognized in a single Vim tab

`g:`
> A variable recognized globally—i.e., it can be referenced *anywhere*

`l:`
> A variable recognized within the function (a local variable)

`s:`
> A variable recognized within the sourced Vim script

`a:`
> A function argument

`v:`
> A Vim variable—one controlled by Vim (these are also global variables)

 If you do not define a Vim variable's scope with a prefix, it defaults to a global (g:) variable when defined outside a function, and to a local (l:) variable when defined within a function.

You assign a value to a variable with the `let` command:

```
:let var = "value"
```

For our purposes, we can define our variable any way we want (context allowing) because we use it only once (though this will change later). For now, we use no prefix and let Vim treat it as global by default. Let's call our variable `currentHour`. By assigning the result from `strftime( )` only once, we now have a more efficient script:

```
" progressively check higher values... falls out on first "true"
" (note addition of zero ... this guarantees return from function is numeric)
```

```
let currentHour = strftime ("%H")
echo "currentHour is " currentHour
if currentHour < 6 + 0
  colorscheme darkblue
  echo "setting colorscheme to darkblue"
elseif currentHour < 12 + 0
  colorscheme morning
  echo "setting colorscheme to morning"
elseif currentHour < 18 + 0
  colorscheme shine
  echo "setting colorscheme to shine"
else
  colorscheme evening
  echo "setting colorscheme to evening"
endif
```

We can clean up the code a little more and get rid of a few lines by introducing a variable named colorScheme. This variable holds the value of the color scheme that we determine by time of day. We've added a capital "S" to distinguish the variable from the name of the colorscheme command, but we could use the exact same letters and it wouldn't matter: Vim can determine from the context what is a command and what is a variable.

Notice the use of the dot (.) notation with the echo command. This operator concatenates expressions into one string, which echo ultimately displays. In this case we concatenate a literal string, "setting color scheme to ", and the value assigned to the variable colorScheme.

```
" progressively check higher values... falls out on first "true"
" (note addition of zero ... this guarantees return from function is numeric
let currentHour = strftime("%H")
echo "currentHour is " . currentHour
if currentHour < 6 + 0
  let colorScheme ="darkblue"
elseif currentHour < 12 + 0
  let colorScheme = "morning"
elseif currentHour < 18 + 0
  let colorScheme = "shine"
else
  let colorScheme = "evening"
endif
echo "setting color scheme to" . colorScheme
colorscheme colorScheme
```

We made an incorrect assumption about executing commands within this script. If you coded along with the example, you already know this. We correct the error in the next section.

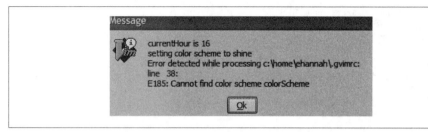

Figure 12-1. colorscheme colorScheme error

The execute Command

So far we have improved how we pick our color scheme, but our last change introduced a slight twist. Initially, we decided to execute a color scheme discretely based on time of day. Our last improvement looks correct, but after defining a variable (color Scheme) to hold the value of our color scheme, we find that the command:

```
colorscheme colorScheme
```

results in the error shown in Figure 12-1.

We need a way to execute a Vim command that refers to a variable instead of a literal string such as darkblue. Vim gives us the execute command for this purpose. When passed a command, it evaluates variables and expressions and substitutes their values into the command. We can exploit this feature along with the concatenation shown in the previous section to pass the value of our variable to the colorscheme command:

```
execute "colorscheme " . colorScheme
```

The exact syntax used here (particularly the quotation marks) may be confusing. The execute command expects variables or expressions, but colorscheme is just a plain string, not a variable or expression. We don't want execute to evaluate colorscheme; we just want it to accept the name as is. So we turn the name of the command into a literal string by enclosing it in quotation marks. While we're at it, we add a blank space to the end, before the final quotation mark. This is important because we need a space between the command and the value.

Our variable colorScheme must be *outside* the quotation marks so that it's evaluated by execute. Think of execute's behavior this way:

- Plain words are evaluated as variables or expressions, and execute substitutes their values.

- Quotation marks enclosing strings are taken literally; execute does not try to evaluate them to return a value.

Using execute fixes our error, and Vim now loads the color scheme as expected.

After loading Vim, you can verify that you loaded the proper color scheme. The colorscheme command sets its own variable, colors_name. In addition to echoing values of the variables you set in your script, you can manually execute the echo command

and examine the `colors_name` variable to see whether our script has in fact executed the correct `colorscheme` command based on the time of day:

```
echo colors_name
```

Defining Functions

So far we've created a script that works nicely for us. Now let's create code we can execute at any time during a session, not just when Vim starts. We will give an example of this soon, but first we need to create a *function* containing the code of our script.

Vim lets you define your own functions with `function...endfunction` statements. Here is a sample skeleton of a user-defined function:

```
function myFunction (arg1, arg2...)
  line of code
  another line of code
endfunction
```

We can easily turn our script into a function. Notice that we don't need to pass in any arguments, so the parentheses in the function definition are empty:

```
function SetTimeOfDayColors()
  " progressively check higher values... falls out on first "true"
  " (note addition of zero ... this guarantees return from function is numeric)
  let currentHour = strftime("%H")
  echo "currentHour is " . currentHour
  if currentHour < 6 + 0
    let colorScheme = "darkblue"
  elseif currentHour < 12 + 0
    let colorScheme = "morning"
  elseif currentHour < 18 + 0
    let colorScheme = "shine"
  else
    let colorScheme = "evening"
  endif
  echo "setting color scheme to" . colorScheme
  execute "colorscheme " . colorScheme
endfunction
```

 Vim user-defined function names must begin with a capital letter.

Now we have a function defined in our `.gvimrc` file. But if we don't call it, the code will never execute. You call a function with Vim's `call` statement. In our example it would look like:

```
call SetTimeOfDayColors()
```

Now we can set our color scheme at any time, anywhere within a Vim session. One option is just to put the previous `call` line in our `.gvimrc`. The results are the same as our earlier example, where we ran the code without using a function. But in the next section, we'll see a neat Vim trick that calls our function repeatedly so that our color scheme gets set regularly throughout our session, thus changing dynamically throughout the day! Of course, this introduces other problems that we must address.

A Nice Vim Piggybacking Trick

In the previous section we defined a Vim function, `SetTimeOfDayColors( )`, which we call once to define our color scheme. What if we want to repeatedly check the time of day and change the color scheme accordingly? Obviously the one-time call in `.gvimrc` doesn't accomplish this. To fix this, we introduce a neat Vim trick using the `status line` option.

Most Vim users take the Vim status line for granted. By default, `statusline` has no value, but you can define it to display virtually any information available to Vim in the status line. And because the status line can display dynamic information, such as the current line and column, Vim recalculates and redisplays `statusline` any time the edit status changes. Almost any action in Vim triggers a `statusline` redraw. So we'll use this as a trick to call our color scheme function and change the color scheme dynamically. As we will soon see, this is an imperfect approach.

The `statusline` accepts an expression, evaluates it, and displays it in the status line. This includes functions. We use this feature to call our `SetTimeOfDayColors( )` every time the status line is updated, which is often. Because this feature overrides the default status line and we don't want to lose the valuable information we get by default, let's incorporate a wealth of information in the following initial definition of our status line:

```
set statusline=%<%t%h%m%r\ \ %a\ %{strftime(\"%c\")}%=0x%B\
    \\ line:%l,\ \ col:%c%V\ %P
```

 The definition for `statusline` is split across two lines. Vim considers any line with an initial nonblank character of backslash (\) to be a continuation of the previous line, and it ignores all whitespace up to the backslash. So if you use our definition, make sure it is copied and entered exactly. If you can't get it to work, you can revert to starting with an undefined `statusline`.

You can look up the meaning of the various characters preceded by percent signs in the Vim documentation. The definition produces a status line like the following:

```
ch12.xml   Wed 13 Feb 2008 06:24:25 PM EST        0x3C line:1,  col:1 Top
```

Our focus in this chapter is not on what the status line can display, but on exploiting the `statusline` option to evaluate a function.

Now we add our `SetTimeOfDayColors( )` function to the `statusline`. By using `+=` instead of a plain equals sign, we add something to the end instead of replacing what we defined earlier:

```
set statusline += \ %{SetTimeOfDayColors()}
```

Now our function is part of the status line. Even though it doesn't contribute interesting information to the status line, it now checks the time of day and potentially updates our color scheme as the hour of the day progresses. Can you see a problem with this?

We now have a Vim script function that inspects the hour of the day each time the Vim status line gets updated. In an earlier section we put some effort into eliminating a few calls to `strftime( )` for the sake of efficiency, but now we've added so many calls to our session that the number is dizzying.

When our session happens to evaluate the `statusline` at the proper hour of the day, it does what we want and changes the color scheme. But as we've defined it, it checks the time and resets the color scheme regardless of whether there's a change. In the next section, we examine more efficient means to this end by using global variables outside of our function.

Tuning a Vim Script with Global Variables

As we discovered with our last modification to our Vim script, we *almost* have the desired behavior. Our function is called every time the Vim status line is updated, but because that happens quite often, it's problematic on several levels.

First, because it's called so often, we might be concerned about the load it creates on the computer's processor. Fortunately, with today's computers this is unlikely to be of much concern, but it's still probably bad form to redefine the color scheme over and over so often. If this were the only issue, we might consider our script complete and not bother tuning it further. However, it is not.

If you've coded along with the examples, you already know the problem. The constant reestablishment of the color scheme while you move around in the edit session creates a noticeable and annoying flicker, because each definition of the color scheme, even if it's the same as the current color scheme, requires Vim to reread the color scheme definition script, reinterpret the text, and reapply all of the color syntax highlight rules. Even computers with extremely high computing power are unlikely to provide enough graphics processing power to render the constant updating flicker-free. We need to fix this.

We can define our color scheme once, and then, within a conditional block, determine each time whether the color scheme changes and consequently needs to be defined and drawn. We do this by taking advantage of the global variable set by the `colorscheme` command: `colors_name`. Let's recast our function to take this into consideration:

```
function SetTimeOfDayColors()
  " progressively check higher values... falls out on first "true"
```

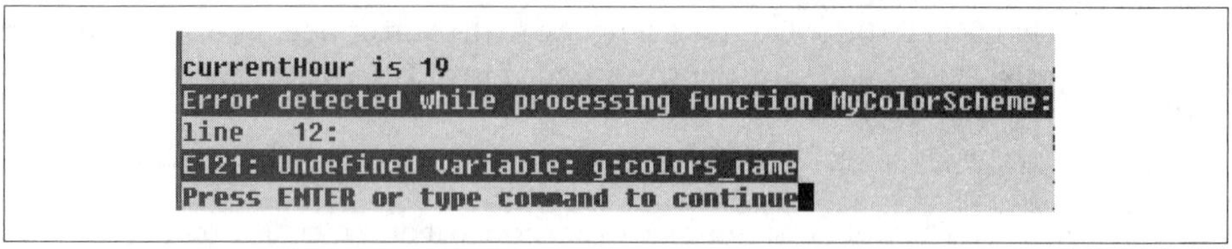

```
currentHour is 19
Error detected while processing function MyColorScheme:
line    12:
E121: Undefined variable: g:colors_name
Press ENTER or type command to continue
```

Figure 12-2. Undefined variable

```
    " (note addition of zero ... this guarantees return from function is numeric)
    let currentHour = strftime("%H")
      if currentHour < 6 + 0
      let colorScheme = "darkblue"
    elseif currentHour < 12 + 0
      let colorScheme = "morning"
    elseif currentHour < 18 + 0
      let colorScheme = "shine"
    else
      let colorScheme = "evening"
    endif

    " if our calculated value is different, call the colorscheme command.
    if g:colors_name !~ colorScheme
      echo "setting color scheme to " . colorScheme
      execute "colorscheme " . colorScheme
    endif
  endfunction
```

This would seem to solve our problem, but now we have a different one. We now get the error shown in Figure 12-2.

It turns out that Vim takes a very stern attitude when we try to refer to a variable that hasn't yet been defined. But what's wrong with the `colors_name` variable? We know that `colorscheme` sets it. We've even taken the precaution of using the `g:` prefix to indicate that it's a global variable. But the first time this function executes, `g:colors_name` has no value and hasn't even been defined, because the `colorscheme` command hasn't executed. Only after the command runs can we safely check `g:colors_name`.

This is simple to fix, and we can do it one of two ways. Insert either:

```
    let g:colors_name = "xyzzy"
```

or:

```
    colorscheme default
```

in your *.gvimrc* file. Either statement defines the global variable as soon as your session starts, so the comparison in our function will always be valid. Now we have a dynamic and efficient function. We will make one last improvement in the following section.

Arrays

It would be nice if somehow we could just extract our color scheme value without the extended `if...then...else` block. With Vim arrays, we can improve the script and make it eminently more readable.

Vim arrays are created by defining a variable's value as a comma-separated list of values within square brackets. We introduce an array named `Favcolorschemes` for our function. We could define it within the scope of the function, but to leave open the possibility of accessing the array elsewhere in our session, we'll define the array outside of the function as a global array:

```
let g:Favcolorschemes = ["darkblue", "morning", "shine", "evening"]
```

This line should go in your `.gvimrc` file. Now we can reference any value within the array variable `g:Favcolorschemes` by its subscript, starting with element zero. For example, `g:Favcolorschemes[2]` is equal to the string `"shine"`.

Taking advantage of Vim's treatment of math functions, where results of integer division are integers (the remainder gets truncated), we can now quickly and easily get our preferred color scheme based on the hour of the day. Let's look at a final version of our function:

```
function SetTimeOfDayColors()
  " currentHour will be 0, 1, 2, or 3
  let g:CurrentHour = (strftime("%H") + 0) / 6
  if g:colors_name !~ g:Favcolorschemes[g:CurrentHour]
    execute "colorscheme " . g:Favcolorschemes[g:CurrentHour]
    echo "execute " "colorscheme " . g:Favcolorschemes[g:CurrentHour]
    redraw
  endif
endfunction
```

Congratulations! You have built a complete Vim script that takes into consideration many of the factors needed to build any useful script you may want.

Dynamic File Type Configuration Through Scripting

Let's look at another nifty script example. Normally, when editing a new file, the only clue Vim gets in order to determine and set `filetype` is the file's extension. For example, `.c` means the file is C code. Vim easily determines this and loads the correct behavior to make it easy to edit a C program.

But not all files require an extension. For example, while it's become common convention to create shell scripts with a `.sh` extension, this author doesn't like or abide by this convention, especially having created thousands of scripts before a notion of this convention arose. Vim is actually sufficiently well-trained to recognize a shell script without the crutch of a file extension, by looking at the text inside the file. However, it can do so only on the second edit, when the file provides some context for determining the type. Vim scripts can fix that!

Autocommands

In our first script example, we relied on Vim's habit of updating the status line constantly and "hid" our function in the status line to set the color scheme by time of day. Our script to determine the file type dynamically relies on a bit more formal Vim convention, *autocommands*.

Autocommands include any valid Vim commands. Vim uses *events* to execute commands. Some examples of Vim events include:

BufNewFile
> Triggers an associated command when Vim begins editing a new file

BufReadPre
> Triggers an associated command *before* Vim moves to a new buffer

BufRead, BufReadPost
> Trigger an associated command when editing a new buffer, but *after* reading the file

BufWrite, BufWritePre
> Trigger an associated command before writing a buffer to a file

FileType
> Triggers an associated command after setting the `filetype`

VimResized
> Triggers an associated command after a Vim window size has changed

WinEnter, WinLeave
> Trigger an associated command upon entering or leaving a Vim window, respectively

CursorMoved, CursorMovedI
> Trigger an associated command every time the cursor moves in *normal* mode or in *insert* mode, respectively

Altogether there are almost 80 Vim events. For any of these events, you can define an automatic `autocmd` that executes when that event occurs. The `autocmd` format is:

```
autocmd [group] event pattern [nested] command
```

The elements of this format are:

group
> An optional command group (described later)

event
> The event that will trigger *command*

pattern
> The pattern matching the filename for which *command* should execute

---

nested
> If present, allows this autocommand to be nested within others

command
> The Vim command, function, or user-defined script to execute when the event occurs

For our example, our goal is to identify the file type for any new file we open, so we use * for *pattern*.

The next decision is which event to use to trigger our script. Because we want to try to identify our file type as early as possible, two good candidates suggest themselves: `CursorMovedI` and `CursorMoved`.

`CursorMoved` triggers an event when the cursor moves, which seems wasteful because merely moving the cursor is not likely to provide more information about a file's type. `CursorMovedI`, in contrast, fires when text is input, and therefore seems like the best candidate.

We must write a function to do the work each time. Let's call it `CheckFileType`. We now have enough information to define our `autocmd` command. It looks like this:

```
autocmd CursorMovedI * call CheckFileType()
```

Checking Options

In our `CheckFileType` function, we need to inspect the value of the `filetype` option. Vim scripts use special variables to extract values from options, by prefixing the option name (`filetype` in our case) with an ampersand (&) character. Hence we will use the variable `&filetype` in our function.

We start with a simple version of our `CheckFileType` function:

```
function CheckFileType()
  if &filetype == ""
    filetype detect
  endif
endfunction
```

The Vim command `filetype detect` is a Vim script installed in the `$VIMRUNTIME` directory. It runs through many criteria and tries to assign a file type to your file. Normally this occurs once, so if the file is new and `filetype` cannot determine a file type, the edit session cannot assign syntax formatting.

There is a problem: we call our function each time the cursor moves during input mode, continually trying to detect the file type. We first check to see whether the file already has a file type, which would mean that our function succeeded in its previous execution and therefore does not need to do it anymore. We won't worry about anomalies, such as a mistaken identification or a file that we start in one programming language and then decide to change to another.

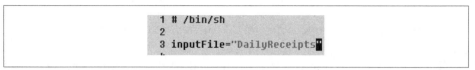

Figure 12-3. File type of new file detected

Figure 12-4. conf file type detected

Let's edit a new shell script file and see the results:

```
$ vim ScriptWithoutSuffix
```

Input the following:

```
#! /bin/sh

inputFile="DailyReceipts"
```

By now, Vim turns on color syntax, as shown in Figure 12-3.

You can tell from the picture that Vim is using gray for the string, but the black-and-white image does not show that # /bin/sh is blue, inputFile= is black, and "DailyReceipts" is purple. Unfortunately, these aren't the colors for shell syntax highlighting. A quick check of the filetype option through the command set file type displays the message shown in Figure 12-4.

Vim assigned file type conf to our file, which is not what we want. What went wrong?

If you try this example, you will see that Vim assigned the file type immediately when you entered the first character, #, at the first CursorMovedI event. Configuration files for Unix utilities and daemons typically use the # character to start a comment, so Vim's heuristics assume that a # at the beginning of the line is the beginning of a comment in a configuration file. We have to teach Vim to be more patient.

Let's change our function to allow for more context. Instead of trying to detect the file type at the first available opportunity, let's allow the user to enter about 20 characters first.

Buffer Variables

We need to introduce a variable into our function to tell Vim to hold off and *not* try to detect the file type until the CursorMovedI autocommand calls the function more than 20 times. Our notion of what is a new file, as well as the number of characters we want to enter into that file, are specific to a buffer. In other words, cursor movement in other

Figure 12-5. b:countCheck generates an "undefined" error

buffers of the edit session should not count against the check. Therefore, we use a buffer variable and call it `b:countCheck`.

Next, we revise the function to check for at least 20 moves of the cursor in input mode (implying approximately 20 characters entered), along with checking whether a file type has already been assigned:

```
function CheckFileType()

let b:countCheck += 1

" Don't start detecting until approx. 20 chars.
 if &filetype == "" && b:countCheck > 20
   filetype detect
 endif
 endfunction
```

But now we get the error shown in Figure 12-5.

That's a familiar error. As before, we had the gall to check a variable before it was defined. And this time, it's all our fault because our script is responsible for defining `b:countCheck`. We'll handle this subtlety in the next section.

The exists( ) Function

It's important to know how to manage all of your variables and functions: Vim requires you to define each one so it already *exists* before any type of evaluation references it.

We can easily resolve our script error by checking for `b:countCheck`'s existence and assigning it a value with the `:let` command shown earlier:

```
function CheckFileType()

 if exists("b:countCheck") == 0
  let b:countCheck = 0
 endif

let b:countCheck += 1

 " Don't start detecting until approx. 20 chars.
 if &filetype == "" && b:countCheck > 20
   filetype detect
 endif
 endfunction
```

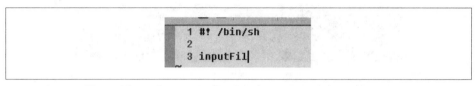

Figure 12-6. No file type detected yet

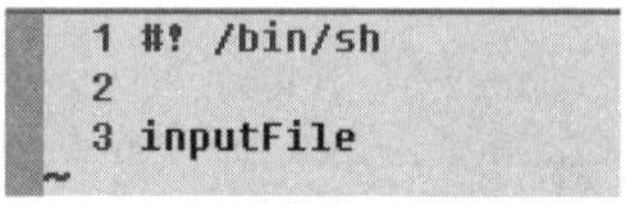

```
1 #! /bin/sh
2
3 inputFile
~
```

Figure 12-7. File type detected

```
ScriptWithoutSuffix[+]
  filetype=sh
```

Figure 12-8. Correct detection

Now test the code. Figure 12-6 shows the moment before the 20-character limit is reached, and Figure 12-7 shows the effect of entering the 21st character.

The /bin/sh text suddenly has syntax color highlighting. A quick check with set filetype verifies that Vim has made the correct assignment, as shown in Figure 12-8.

For all practical purposes, we have a complete and satisfactory solution, but for good form we add another check to stop Vim from trying to detect a file type after approximately 200 characters have been entered:

```
function CheckFileType()

if exists("b:countCheck") == 0
  let b:countCheck = 0
endif

let b:countCheck += 1

  " Don't start detecting until approx. 20 chars.
  if &filetype == "" && b:countCheck > 20 && b:countCheck < 200
    filetype detect
  endif
endfunction
```

Now, even though our function CheckFileType is called each time Vim's cursor moves, we incur little overhead because the initial checks exit the function once a file type is detected or the threshold of 200 characters is exceeded. Although this is probably all we need for reasonable functionality and minimal processing overhead, we'll continue to look at more mechanisms to give us a more complete and satisfactory solution that not only incurs minimal overhead, but actually "goes away" when we don't need it any more.

 You may have noticed we have been slightly vague about the exact meaning of our threshold count of 20 characters. This ambiguity is intentional. Because we are counting cursor movements, in input mode it's reasonable to assume each movement of the cursor corresponds to a new character, adding to the "sufficient" context text from which CheckFileType( ) will determine the file type. However, *all* cursor movement in input mode counts, so any backspacing to correct typing errors also counts against the threshold counter. To confirm this, try our example, type #, and backspace over it and retype it 10 times. The 11th time should reveal a color-coded #, and the file type should now be (incorrectly) set to conf.

Autocommands and Groups

Our script so far ignores any side effects introduced by calling our function for every movement of the cursor. We minimized overhead through reasonableness checks that avoid calling the heavy filetype detect command unnecessarily. But what if even minimal code for our function is expensive? We need a way to stop calling code when we don't need it. For this we leverage Vim's notion of autocommand *groups* and their ability to remove commands based on their group association.

We modify our example by first associating our function called by the CursorMovedI event with a group. Vim provides an augroup command to do this. Its syntax is:

```
augroup groupname
```

All subsequent autocmd definitions become associated with group *groupname* until the statement:

```
augroup END
```

(There's also a default group for commands not entered within an augroup block.)

Now we associate our previous autocmd command with our own group.

```
augroup newFileDetection
autocmd CursorMovedI * call CheckFileType()
augroup END
```

Our CursorMovedI-triggered function is part of the autocommand group new FileDetection. We will explore the usefulness of this in the next section.

Deleting Autocommands

To implement our function as cleanly as possible, we strive to have it remain effective only as long as necessary. We want to undefine its reference once it has exceeded its useful life (that is, as soon as we've either detected a file type or decided we can't). Vim

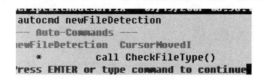

Figure 12-9. Response to autocmd newFileDetection command

lets you delete an autocommand simply by referencing the event, the pattern that filenames must match, or its group.

```
autocmd! [group] [event] [pattern]
```

The usual Vim "force" character—an exclamation point (!)—follows the autocmd keyword to indicate that commands associated with the group, event, or pattern are to be
removed.

Because we previously associated our function with our user-defined group new
FileDetection, we now have control over it and can remove it by referencing the group
in the autocommand remove syntax. We do so with:

```
autocmd! newFileDetection
```

This deletes all autocommands associated with the group newFileDetection, which in
our case is only our function.

We verify both the definition and removal of our autocommand by querying Vim at
startup (when creating the new file) with the command:

```
autocmd newFileDetection
```

Vim responds as shown in Figure 12-9.

After a file type has been detected and assigned *or* the threshold of 200 characters has
been exceeded, we no longer want the autocommand definition. So, we add the final
touch to our code. Combining the definition of our augroup, our autocmd command,
and our function, the lines in our .vimrc look like:

```
augroup newFileDetection
autocmd CursorMovedI * call CheckFileType()
augroup END

function CheckFileType()

  if exists("b:countCheck") == 0
    let b:countCheck = 0
  endif

  let b:countCheck += 1

  " Don't start detecting until approx. 20 chars.
  if &filetype == "" && b:countCheck > 20 && b:countCheck < 200
    filetype detect
```

Figure 12-10. After the deletion criteria have been met for our autocommand group

```
" If we've exceeded the count threshold (200), OR a filetype has been detected
" delete the autocmd!
elseif b:countCheck >= 200 || &filetype != ""
  autocmd! newFileDetection
endif
endfunction
```

After the syntax color highlighting begins, we can verify that our function deletes itself by entering the same command as when we entered the buffer:

```
autocmd newFileDetection
```

Vim's response is shown in Figure 12-10.

Notice now that no autocommands are defined for the `newFileDetection` group. You can delete the auto group as follows:

```
augroup! groupname
```

but doing so does *not* delete the associated autocommands, and Vim will create an error condition each time those autocommands are referenced. Therefore, make sure to delete the autocommands within a group before deleting the group.

 Do not confuse deleting autocommands with deleting auto groups.

Congratulations! You have completed your second Vim script. This script extends your Vim knowledge and gives you a peek at the different features accessible with scripting.

Some Additional Thoughts About Vim Scripting

We've covered only a small corner of the entire Vim scripting universe, but we hope you get the sense of Vim's power. Virtually everything you can do interactively using Vim can be coded in a script.

In this section we look at a nice example included in the built-in Vim documentation, discuss in more detail concepts we touched on earlier, and look at a few new features.

A Useful Vim Script Example

Vim's built-in documentation includes a handy script we think you'll want to use. It specifically addresses keeping a current timestamp in the `meta` line of an HTML file, but it could easily be used for many other types of files where it is useful to have the most recent modification time of the file within the text of that file.

Here is the example essentially intact (we have modified it slightly):

```
autocmd BufWritePre,FileWritePre *.html    mark s|call LastMod()|'s
fun LastMod()
  " if there are more than 20 lines, set our max to 20, otherwise, scan
  " entire file.
  if line("$") > 20
    let lastModifiedline = 20
  else
    let lastModifiedline = line("$")
  endif
  exe "1," . lastModifiedline . "g/Last modified: /s/Last modified:
      .*/Last modified: " .
  \ strftime("%Y %b %d")
endfun
```

Here's a brief breakdown of the `autocmd` command:

`BufWritePre, FileWritePre`

These are the events for which the command is triggered. In this case, Vim executes the autocommand *before* the file or buffer gets written to the storage device.

`*.html`

Execute this autocommand for any file whose name ends in `.html`.

`mark s`

We changed this for readability from the original. Instead of `ks`, we used the equivalent but more obvious command `mark s`. This simply creates a marked position named `s` in the file so we can return to this point later.

`|`

Pipe characters separate multiple Vim commands that are executed within an autocommand definition. These are simple separators with no relationship to Unix shell pipes.

`call LastMod( )`

This calls our user-defined `LastMod` function.

`|`

Same as previous.

`'s`

Return to the line we marked with the name `s`.

It's worth verifying this script by editing a `.html` file, adding the line "Last modified: " ", and issuing the `w` command.

This example is useful, but it's not canonically correct in relation to its stated goal of substituting the HTML `meta` statement. More appropriately, if indeed it were meant to address a `meta` statement, the substitution should look for the `content=...` part of the `meta` statement. Still, this example is a good start toward solving that problem and is a useful example for other file types.

More About Variables

We now discuss in more detail what makes up Vim variables and how they're used. Vim has five variable types:

Number
> A signed 32-bit number. This number can be represented in decimal, hexadecimal (e.g., `0xffff`), or octal (e.g., `0177`).

String
> A string of characters.

Funcref
> A reference to a function.

List
> This is Vim's version of an array. It is an ordered "list" of values and can contain any mix of Vim values as elements.

Dictionary
> This is Vim's version of a *hash*, often also referred to as an *associative array*. It is an unordered collection of value-pairs, the first being a *key* that can be used to retrieve an associated *value*.

Vim performs convenience conversions of variables where context allows, most notably back and forth between strings and numbers. To be safe (as we were in our first script example), when using a string as a number, ensure conversion by adding 0 to it:

```
if strftime("%H") < 6 + 0
```

Expressions

Vim evaluates expressions in a fairly straightforward way. An expression can be as simple as a number or literal string, or it can be as complex as a compound statement, itself composed of expressions.

It is important to note that Vim's math functions work with integers only. If you want floating-point and precision, you need to use extensions, such as system calls to external math-capable routines.

Extensions

Vim offers a number of extensions and interfaces to other scripting languages. Notably, these include `perl`, Python, and Ruby, three of the most popular scripting languages. See Vim's built-in documentation for details on usage.

A Few More Comments About autocmd

In our earlier example in the section "Dynamic File Type Configuration Through Scripting" on page 205, we used Vim's `autocmd` command to key on events from which our user-defined functions are called. This is very powerful, but do not discount simpler uses of `autocmd`. For example, you can use `autocmd` to tune specific Vim options for different file types.

A good example might be to change the `shiftwidth` option for different file types. File types with copious indentation and nesting levels may benefit from more modest indentation. You may want to define your `shiftwidth` as 2 for HTML in order to prevent code from "walking" off the right side of the screen, but use a `shiftwidth` of 4 for C programs. To accomplish this distinction, include these lines in your `.vimrc` or `.gvimrc` file:

```
autocmd BufRead,BufNewFile *.html set shiftwidth=2
autocmd BufRead,BufNewFile *.c,*.h set shiftwidth=4
```

Internal Functions

In addition to all the Vim commands, you have access to about 200 built-in functions. It is beyond the scope of this discussion to identify and document all of these functions, but it is useful to know what categories or types of functions are available. The following categories are taken from the Vim built-in help file, `usr_41.txt`:

String manipulation
All of the standard string functions that programmers expect are included in these functions, from conversion routines to substring routines and more.

List functions
This is an entire array of array functions. They mirror closely the array functions found in `perl`.

Dictionary (associative array) functions
These functions include extraction, manipulation, verification, and other types of functions. Again, these closely resemble `perl` hash functions.

Variable functions
These functions are "getters" and "setters" to move variables around in Vim windows and buffers. There is also a `type` to determine variable types.

Cursor and position functions
These functions allow moving around in files and buffers, and creating marks so that positions can be remembered and returned to. There are also functions that give positional information (e.g., cursor line and column).

Text in current buffer functions
These functions manipulate text within buffers, for example, changing a line, retrieving a line, etc. There are also search functions.

System and file manipulation functions
These include functions to navigate the operating system on which Vim is running, for example, finding files within paths, determining the current working directory, creating and deleting files, etc. This group includes the system( ) function, which passes commands to the operating system for external execution.

Date and time functions
These do a wide variety of manipulations of date and time formats.

Buffer, window, and argument list functions
These functions provide mechanisms to gather information about buffers, and the arguments for each one.

Command-line functions
These functions get command-line position, the command line, and the command-line type, and set the cursor position within the command line.

Quick fix and location lists functions
These functions retrieve and modify the quick fix lists.

Insert mode completion functions
These functions are used for command and insertion completion features.

Folding functions
These functions give information for folds, and expand text displayed for closed folds.

Syntax and highlighting functions
These functions retrieve information about syntax highlighting groups and syntax IDs.

Spelling functions
These functions find suspected misspelled words and offer suggested correct spellings.

History functions
These functions get, add, and delete history items.

Interactive functions
These functions provide an interface to the user for activities such as file selection.

GUI functions
There are three simple functions here to get the name of the current font, get the GUI window *x* coordinate, and get the GUI window *y* coordinate.

Vim server functions
These functions communicate with a (possibly) remote Vim server.

Window size and position functions
These functions get window information and allow for saving and restoring window "views."

Various functions
These are the miscellaneous "other" functions that don't fit nicely in the previous categories. They include functions such as `exists`, which checks for the existence of a Vim item, and `has`, which checks to see whether Vim supports a certain feature.

Resources

We hope we've piqued enough interest and provided enough information to get you started with Vim scripts. An entire book could be devoted to the subject of Vim scripting. Luckily, there are other resources to turn to for help.

A good starting point is to go to the source of Vim itself and visit the pages specifically dedicated to scripting: *http://www.vim.org/scripts/index.php*. Here you will find over 2,000 scripts available for download. The entire body of work is searchable and you are invited to participate by rating scripts and even contributing your own.

We also remind you that the built-in Vim help is invaluable. The most productive help topics we recommend are:

```
help autocmd
help scripts
help variables
help functions
help usr_41.txt
```

And don't forget the myriad Vim scripts in the Vim runtime directories. All of the files with the suffix `.vim` are scripts, and these provide an excellent and fertile playground for learning how to code by example.

Go play. It's the best way to learn.

Graphical Vim (gvim)

A longtime complaint about **vi** and its clones was the lack of a graphical user interface (GUI). Especially for those caught up in the Emacs versus **vi** religious wars, **vi**'s lack of a GUI was the ultimate trump card to argue that **vi** was a nonstarter when discussing editors.

Eventually, the **vi** clones and "work-alikes" created their own GUI versions. Graphical Vim is called **gvim**. Like the other **vi** clones, **gvim** offers robust and extensible GUI functions and features. We'll cover the most useful ones in this chapter.

Some of **gvim**'s graphical functionality wraps commonly used Vim features, whereas others introduce the point-and-click convenience functionality most computer users now expect. Although some veteran Vim users (this author included!) may cringe at the thought of grafting a GUI onto their workhorse editor, **gvim** is thoughtfully conceived and implemented. **gvim** offers functionality and features spanning the range of its users' abilities, softening Vim's steep learning curve for beginners and transparently bringing expert users extra editing power. This strikes a nice compromise.

gvim for MS Windows comes with a menu entry labeled "easy **gvim**." This is indeed valuable to people who have never used Vim, but, ironically, it is anything *but* easy for expert users.

In this chapter we first discuss the general **gvim** GUI concepts and features, with a brief introductory section about mouse interaction. Additionally, we refine the discussion around differences and things you should know for different **gvim** environments. Specifically, we focus on MS Windows and the X Window System, the two main graphical platforms. We touch briefly on other platforms and guide you to appropriate resources for more complete information. We also provide a brief list of GUI options with synopses.

General Introduction to gvim

gvim brings all the functionality, power, and features of Vim while adding the convenience and intuitive nature of a GUI environment. From traditional menus to visual highlighting editing, gvim provides the GUI experience today's users expect. For veteran, console-based, text-environment vi users, gvim still gives the familiar core power and doesn't dumb down the paradigm that garnered vi its reputation as a power editor.

Starting gvim

When Vim is compiled with GUI support, you can invoke it by issuing a gvim command or a Vim command with an added -g option. On Windows, the self-installing executable adds one interesting feature that many discover only accidentally after installation: a new Windows Explorer menu item labeled "Edit with Vim." This provides quick and easy access to gvim by integrating it into the Windows environment. It is worth trying on files you maybe wouldn't have considered before, especially unusual files such as binaries. However, it *is* potentially dangerous to edit binary files, and we caution you to use extreme care when editing these files.

The configuration files and options recognized by gvim are slightly different from those used by Vim. gvim reads and executes two startup files: .vimrc, followed by .gvimrc. Although you can put gvim-specific options and definitions in .vimrc, it's better to define them in .gvimrc. This provides a nice separation of regular Vim and gvim customization. It also assures proper behavior on startup. For example, :set columns=100 isn't valid in Vim and will generate an error when Vim is started.

If a system gvimrc exists (usually in $VIM/gvimrc), it is executed. Administrators can use this system-wide configuration file to set common options for their users. This provides a baseline configuration so that users will share a common editing experience.

More experienced Vim users can add their own favorite custom settings and features. After gvim reads the optional system configuration, it looks in four places for additional configuration information, in the following order, and stops searching after finding any one of these:

- An exrc command stored in the $GVIMINIT environment variable.
- A user's gvimrc file, usually stored in $HOME/.gvimrc. If it is found, it is *sourced*.
- In a Windows environment, if $HOME is not set, gvim looks in $VIM/_gvimrc. (This is the normal situation for Windows users, but it's an important distinction for users who have Unix work-alikes installed and are likely to have the $HOME variable set. One example would be the popular Cygwin suite of Unix tools.)
- If a _gvimrc isn't found, gvim finally looks again for .gvimrc.

If gvim finds a nonempty file to execute, that file's name is stored in the $MYGVIMRC variable and further initialization stops.

There is one more option for customization. If, in the cascading sequence of initialization just described, the option **exrc** is set:

```
set exrc
```

gvim will additionally look in the current directory for **.gvimrc**, **.exrc**, or **.vimrc** and *source* that file if it isn't one of the previously listed files (i.e., it hasn't already been discovered as an initialization file and already executed).

 In a Unix environment, there are security issues around local directories containing configuration files (both **.gvimrc** *and* **.vimrc** files), and gvim defaults to enforcing some restrictions on what can be executed from these files by setting the **secure** option if the file is not owned by the user. This helps prevent malicious code from being malicious. If you want to be sure, set the **secure** option explicitly in your **.vimrc** or **.gvimrc** file.

Using the Mouse

The mouse in gvim does something useful in every editing mode. Let's look at the standard Vim editing modes and how gvim treats the mouse in each:

Command mode

You enter this mode when you open the command buffer at the bottom of the window by typing a colon (:). If the window is in command mode, you can use the mouse to reposition the cursor anywhere in the command line. This is enabled by default or when you include the **c** flag in your **mouse** option.

Insert mode

This is the mode for entering text. If you click in a buffer that's in insert mode, the mouse repositions the cursor and lets you immediately start entering text at that position. This mode is enabled by default or when you include the **i** flag in your **mouse** option.

The mouse's behavior in insert mode provides easy and intuitive point-and-click positioning. In particular, it bypasses the need to exit insert mode, navigate with the mouse, motion commands, or other methods, and then reenter insert mode.

Superficially, this seems like a great idea, but in practice it will appeal to only a subset of users. It may be more annoying than helpful to experienced Vim users.

Consider what happens when you are in insert mode and leave gvim for some other application. When you click back into the gvim window, the point you click is now the insertion point for text, and probably not the one you want. In a single-window gvim session, you could land in a different spot from where you were originally working; in a multiple-window gvim screen, you could end up with the mouse in a completely different window. You might end up entering text into the wrong file!

Normal mode

This includes any time you're not in insert mode or on the command line. Clicking the mouse in the screen simply leaves the cursor on the character where you clicked. This mode is enabled by default or when you include the n flag in your mouse option.

Normal mode provides a straightforward and easy method to position the cursor, but it offers only clunky support for moving beyond the top or bottom of the visible window. Click and hold the mouse and slide to the top or bottom of a window; gvim will scroll up and down correspondingly. If scrolling stops, move the mouse back and forth sideways to make it resume. (It's not clear why normal mode acts this way.)

Another drawback to normal mode is that users, especially beginners, can come to rely on point and click as the positioning method of choice. This can hold back their motivation to learn Vim's navigation commands, and hence its power-editing methods. Finally, it creates the same potential confusion as insert mode.

Additionally, gvim offers *visual* mode, also known as *select* mode. This mode is enabled by default, or when you include the v flag in your mouse option. Visual is the most versatile mode, because it lets you select text by dragging the mouse, which highlights the selection. It can be used in combination with command, insert, and normal modes.

Any combination of flags can be specified in the mouse option. The syntax to use is illustrated by the following commands:

`:set mouse=""`
Disable all mouse behavior.

`:set mouse=a`
Enable all mouse behavior (the default).

`:set mouse+=v`
Enable visual mode (v). This example uses the += syntax to add a flag to the current mouse setting.

`:set mouse-=c`
Disable mouse behavior in command mode (c). This example uses the -= syntax to remove a flag from the current mouse setting.

Beginners may prefer more "on" settings, whereas experts may turn the mouse off completely (as the author of this chapter does).

If you use the mouse, we recommend choosing a familiar behavior through gvim's :behave command, which accepts either mswin or xterm as an argument. As suggested by the names of the arguments, mswin will set options to closely mimic Windows behavior, whereas xterm mimics a window on the X Window System.

Vim has a number of other mouse options, including mousefocus, mousehide, mousemodel, and selectmode. For more information, refer to the Vim built-in documentation for these options.

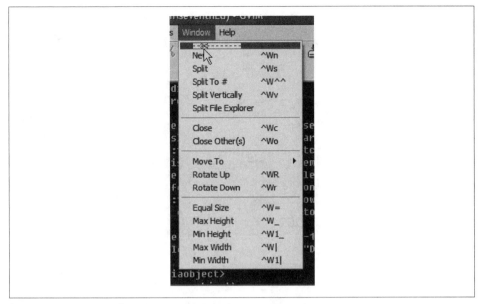

Figure 13-1. gvim Window menu

If you have a mouse with a scroll wheel, `gvim` handles it well by default, scrolling the screen or window up and down predictably, regardless of how you set the `mouse` option.

Useful Menus

One nice touch `gvim` brings to the GUI environment is menu actions that simplify some of Vim's more esoteric commands. There are two worth mentioning.

gvim's Window menu

`gvim`'s *Window* menu contains many of the most useful and common Vim window management commands: commands that split a single GUI window into multiple display areas. You may find it worth "tearing off" this menu, as shown in Figure 13-1, so that you can conveniently open and bounce around among windows. The result is shown in Figure 13-2.

gvim's right-click pop-up menu

`gvim` pops up the menu shown in Figure 13-3 when you right-click within a buffer you're editing.

If any text is selected (highlighted), another menu pops up when you right-click, as shown in Figure 13-4.

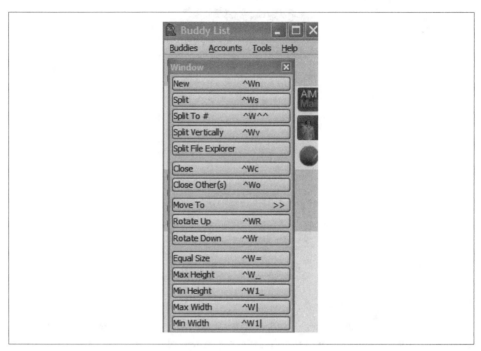

Figure 13-2. gvim Window menu, torn off and floating

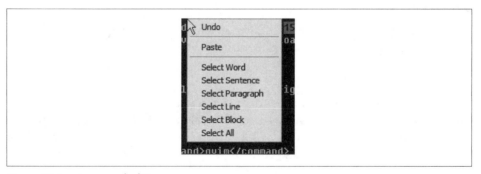

Figure 13-3. gvim general editing menu

Notice how the menu in Figure 13-3 is moved and floats over completely unrelated application. This is a nice way to have an often-used menu conveniently available but out of the way of the editing. Both of these are handy for common select, cut, copy, delete, and paste operations. Users of other GUI editors employ this kind of feature all the time, but this is useful even for long-time Vim users. It is especially useful in that it interacts with the Windows clipboard in a predictable way.

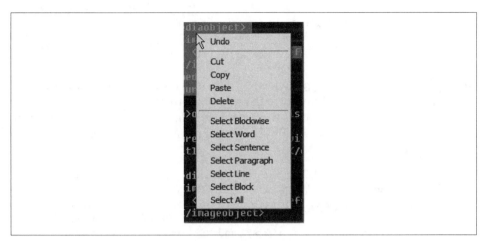

Figure 13-4. gvim editing menu when text is selected

Figure 13-5. Top of gvim window

Customizing Scrollbars, Menus, and Toolbars

gvim provides the usual GUI widgets, such as scrollbars, menus, and toolbars. Like most modern GUI applications, these widgets are customizable.

The gvim window, by default, shows several menus and a toolbar at the top, as illustrated by Figure 13-5.

Scrollbars

Scrollbars, which let you navigate up and down or right and left quickly through a file, are optional in gvim. You can display or hide them with the guioptions option, described at the end of this chapter in "GUI Options and Command Synopsis" on page 237.

Because Vim's standard behavior is to show all text in the file (wrapping lines in the window if necessary), it's interesting to note that the horizontal scrollbar serves no purpose in typically configured gvim sessions.

Turn the left and right scrollbars on and off by including or excluding r or l in the guioptions option. l makes sure the screen always has a left scrollbar, whereas r makes it always have a right scrollbar. The uppercase variants L and R tell gvim to show left or right scrollbars only when there is a vertically split window.

The horizontal scrollbar is controlled by including or excluding b in the guioptions option.

And yes, you *can* scroll the right and left scrollbars at the same time! More precisely, scrolling either one causes the other to move in the corresponding direction. It can be pretty convenient to have scrollbars configured on both sides. Depending upon where your mouse is positioned, you simply click and drag the nearest scrollbar.

Many options, including guioptions, control many behaviors, and thus can include many flags by default. New flags could even be added in future versions of gvim. Hence, it is important to use the += and -= syntax in the :set guioptions command, to avoid deleting desirable behaviors. For example, :set guioptions+=l adds the "scrollbar always on left" option to gvim, leaving the other components in the guioptions string intact.

Menus

gvim has a fully customizable menu feature. In this section we describe the default menu characteristics, which appeared earlier in Figure 13-5, and show how you can control the menu layout.

Figure 13-6 shows one example of using a menu. In this case we're choosing Global Settings from the Edit menu.

It's interesting to note these menu options are merely wrappers for Vim commands. In fact, that is exactly how you can create and customize your own menu entries, which we discuss shortly.

Notice that if you pay attention to the menus, including the keystrokes or commands shown on the right side, you can learn Vim commands over time. For example, in Figure 13-6, although it's handy for beginners to find the familiar Undo command in the Edit menu, where it appears in other popular applications, it is *much* faster and easier to use the Vim u keystroke, which is shown in the menu.

As shown in Figure 13-6, each menu starts with a dashed line containing a picture of scissors. Clicking this line "tears off" the menu to create a free-standing window in which that submenu's options are available without going to the menu bar. If you clicked the dashed line above the Toggle Pattern Highlight menu in Figure 13-6, you would see something like Figure 13-7. You can position the free-floating menu any-where on your desktop.

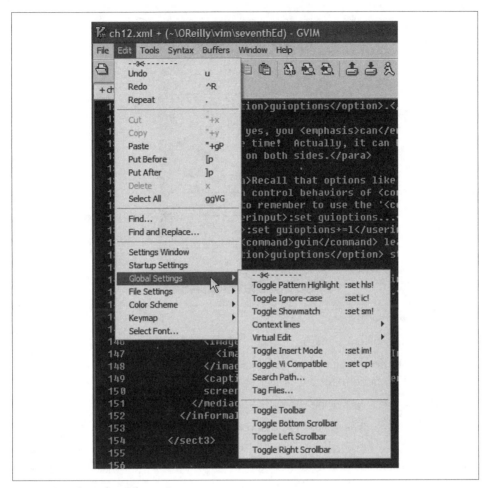

Figure 13-6. Cascading Edit menu

Now, all of the commands on this submenu are immediately available with just one click in the submenu's window. Each menu selection is mapped to a button. If a menu selection itself is a submenu, it is represented by a button with greater-than signs (which look like rightward-pointing arrows) at the right side of the button. Clicking these arrows expands the submenu.

Basic menu customization

gvim stores menu definitions in a file named $VIMRUNTIME/menu.vim.

Defining menu items is similar to mapping. As you saw in the section "Using the map Command" on page 104, you can map a key like this:

```
:map <F12> :set syntax=html<CR>
```

Figure 13-7. Tearing off a menu

Menus are handled very similarly.

Suppose that, rather than map F12 to set the syntax to `html`, we want a special "HTML" entry on our File menu to do this task. Use the `:amenu` command:

```
:amenu File.HTML :set syntax=html<CR>
```

The four characters `<CR>` are to be typed as shown, and are part of the command.

Now look at your file menu. You should see a new HTML entry, as shown in Figure 13-8. By using `amenu` instead of `menu`, we ensure that the entry is available in all modes (command, insert, and normal).

> The `menu` command adds the entry to the menu only in command mode; the entry does not appear in insert and normal modes.

The location for a menu entry is specified by a series of cascading menu entries separated by periods (`.`). In our example, `File.HTML` added the menu entry "HTML" to the File menu. The last entry in the series is the one you want to add. Here we've added it to an existing menu, but we'll soon see that we can just as easily create a whole cascading series of new menus.

Be sure to test your new menu selection. For example, we started editing a file that Vim treats as an XML file, as can be seen in the status line in Figure 13-9. We've customized

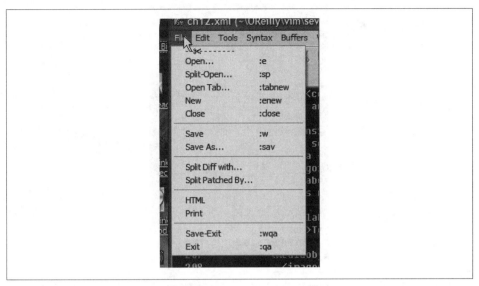

Figure 13-8. HTML menu item under File menu

Figure 13-9. Status line showing XML syntax before new menu action

Figure 13-10. Status line showing HTML syntax after new menu action

the status line so that Vim and **gvim** display the currently active syntax on the far right. (See "A Nice Vim Piggybacking Trick" on page 202.)

After invoking our new HTML menu item, the Vim status line verifies that the menu item worked and that the syntax is now HTML. See Figure 13-10.

Notice that the HTML menu item we added doesn't have a shortcut or command on the righthand side. So let's redo the menu addition and include this nice enhancement.

First, delete the existing entry:

```
:aunmenu File.HTML
```

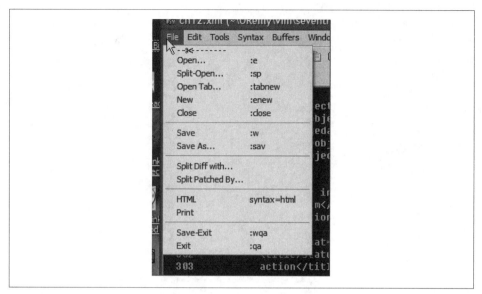

Figure 13-11. HTML menu item, displaying associated command

If you add a menu entry for command mode only using the menu command, you can remove it using unmenu.

Next, add a new HTML menu item that displays the command you associated to the item:

```
:amenu File.HTML<TAB>syntax=html<CR> :set syntax=html<CR>
```

The specification of the menu entry is now followed by <TAB> (typed literally) and syntax=html<CR>. In general, to display text on the righthand side of the menu, place it after the string <TAB> and terminate it with <CR>. Figure 13-11 shows the resulting File menu.

If you want spaces in the descriptive text of the menu item (or in the menu name itself), quote the spaces with backslashes (\). If you don't, Vim uses everything after the first space character for the definition of the menu action. In the previous example, if we wanted :set syntax=html instead of just syntax=html for the descriptive text, the :amenu command would have to be:

```
:amenu File.HTML<TAB>set\ syntax=html<CR> :set syntax=html<CR>
```

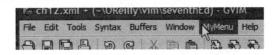

Figure 13-12. Menu bar with "MyMenu" menu added

In most cases, it's probably best not to modify the default menu definitions, but instead to create separate and independent entries. This requires defining a new menu at the root level, but this is just as simple as adding an entry to an existing menu.

Continuing our example, let's create a new menu tree called MyMenu on the menu bar, and then add an HTML menu item to it. First, remove the HTML item from the File menu:

```
:aunmenu File.HTML
```

Next, enter the command:

```
:amenu MyMenu.HTML<TAB>syntax=html :set syntax=html<CR>
```

Figure 13-12 shows how your menu bar may appear.

The menu commands offer more subtle control over where the menus appear and their behavior, such as whether the command indicates any activity, or even whether the menu item is visible. We discuss these possibilities further in the following section.

More menu customization

Now that we see how easy it is to modify and extend gvim's menus, let's look at more examples of customization and control.

Our previous example didn't specify where to put the new MyMenu menu, and gvim arbitrarily placed it on the menu bar between Window and Help. gvim lets us control the position with its notion of *priority*, which is simply a numerical value assigned to each menu to determine where it goes on the menu bar. The higher this value is, the further to the right the menu appears. Unfortunately, the way users think of priority is the opposite of how it's defined by gvim. To get priority straight, look back at the order of menus in Figure 13-5 and compare it to gvim's default menu priorities, as listed in Table 13-1.

Table 13-1. gvim's default menu priorities

Menu	Priority
File	10
Edit	20
Tools	40
Syntax	50
Buffers	60
Window	70

Menu	Priority
Help	9999

Most users would consider File a higher priority than Help (which is why File is on the left and Help on the right), but the priority of Help is higher. So, just think of the priority value as an indication of how far to the right a menu appears.

You can define a menu's priority by prepending its numeric value to the menu command. If no value is specified, a default value of 500 is assigned, which explains why MyMenu ended up where it did in our earlier example: it landed between Window (priority 70) and Help (priority 9999).

Assume we want our new menu to be between the File and Edit menus. We need to assign MyMenu a numeric priority greater than 10 and less than 20. The following command assigns a priority of 15, leading to the desired effect:

```
:15amenu MyMenu.HTML<TAB>syntax=html :set syntax=html<CR>
```

> Once a menu exists, its position is fixed for an entire editing session and does not change in response to additional commands that affect the menu. For example, you cannot change a menu's position by adding a new item to it and prefixing the command with a different priority value.

To add some more confusion to priorities and menu placement, you can also control item placement *within* a menu by specifying a priority. Higher-priority menu items appear further down in the menu than lower-priority items, but the syntax is different from priority definitions for menus.

We'll extend one of our earlier menu examples here by assigning a very high value (9999) to the HTML menu item, so that it appears at the bottom of the File menu:

```
:amenu File.HTML .9999 <TAB>syntax=html<CR> :set syntax=html<CR>
```

Why is there a period before 9999? You need to specify two priorities here, separated by a period: one for File and one for HTML. We are leaving the File priority blank because it's a pre-existing menu and can't be changed.

In general, priorities for a menu item appear between the item's menu placement and the item's definition. For every level in the menu hierarchy, you must specify a priority, or include a period to indicate that you're leaving it blank. Thus, if you add an item deep in the menu hierarchy—such as under Edit → Global Settings → Context lines→ Display—and you want to assign the priority 30 to the last item (Display), you would specify the priority as ...30, and the placement together with the priority would look like:

```
Edit.Global\ Settings.Context\ lines.Display ...30
```

As with menu priorities, menu item priorities are fixed once they are assigned.

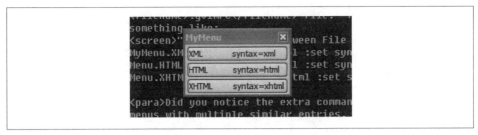

Figure 13-13. Personalized floating tearoff menu

Finally, you can control menu "whitespace" with **gvim**'s menu separators. Use the same definition as you would to add a menu item, but instead of a command named "...", place a hyphen (-) before and after it.

Putting it all together

Now we know how to create, place, and customize menus. Let's make our example a permanent part of our **gvim** environment by adding the commands we discussed to the **.gvimrc** file. The sequence of lines should look something like:

```
" add HTML menu between File and Edit menus
❶15amenu MyMenu.XML<TAB>syntax=xml :set syntax=xml<CR>
❷amenu ❸.600 MyMenu.-Sep- :
❹amenu ❺.650 MyMenu.HTML<TAB>syntax=html :set syntax=html<CR>
❻amenu ❼.700 MyMenu.XHTML<TAB>syntax=xhtml :set syntax=xhtml<CR>
```

We now have a top-level, personalized menu with three favorite syntax commands quickly available to us. There are a few important things to note in this example:

- The first command (❶) uses the prefix **15**, telling **gvim** to use priority **15**. For an uncustomized environment, this places the new menu between the File and Edit menus.

- The subsequent commands (❷, ❹, and ❻) do *not* specify the priority, because once a priority is determined, no other values are used.

- We've used the submenu priority syntax (❸, ❺, and ❼) after the first command to ensure the correct order for each new item. Notice we started with the first definition of **.600**. This assures that the submenu item is placed behind the first one we defined, because we didn't assign *that* priority and it therefore defaulted to **500**.

For even handier access, click on the "scissors" tear-off line to have your personalized floating menu, as shown in Figure 13-13.

Toolbars

Toolbars are long strips of icons that allow quick access to program functions. On Windows, for instance, **gvim** displays the toolbar shown in Figure 13-14 at the top of the window.

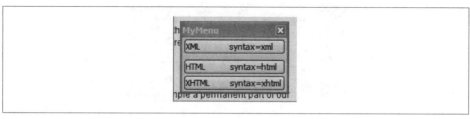

Figure 13-14. gvim's toolbar

Table 13-2 shows the toolbar icons and their meanings.

Table 13-2. gvim toolbar icons and their meanings

Icon	Description	Icon	Description
	Open file dialog		Find next occurence of search pattern
	Save current file		Find previous occurence of search pattern
	Save all files		Choose saved edit session to load
	Print buffer		Save current edit session
	Undo last change		Choose Vim script to run
	Redo last action		Make current project with make command
	Cut selection to clipboard		Build tags for current directory tree
	Copy selection to clipboard		Jump to tag under cursor
	Paste clipboard into buffer		Open help
	Find and replace		Search help

If these icons are not familiar or intuitive, you can make the toolbar show both text and icons. Issue this command:

```
:set toolbar="text,icons"
```

As with many advanced features, Vim requires toolbar features to be turned on during compilation so people who don't want them can save memory by not including them. The toolbar does not exist unless one of the +GUI_GTK, +GUI_Athena, +GUI_Motif, or +GUI_Photon features is compiled into your version of gvim. Chapter 9 explains how to recompile Vim, during which the link to the gvim executable is created.

We modify the toolbar very much like we do menus. As a matter of fact, we use the same :menu command, but with extra syntax to specify graphics. Although an algorithm exists to help gvim find the icon associated with each command, we recommend explicitly pointing to the icon graphic.

gvim treats the toolbar as a one-dimensional menu. And, just as you control the right-to-left position of new menus, you can control the position of new toolbar entries by prefixing the menu command with a number that determines its positional *priority*. Unlike menus, there is no notion of creating a new toolbar. All new toolbar definitions appear on the single toolbar. The syntax for adding a toolbar selection is:

```
:amenu icon=/some/icon/image.bmp ToolBar.NewToolBarSelection    Action
```

where */some/icon/image.bmp* is the path of the file containing the toolbar button or image (usually an icon) to display in the toolbar, *NewToolBarSelection* is the new entry for the toolbar button, and *Action* defines what the button does.

For example, let's define a new toolbar selection that, when clicked or selected, brings up a DOS window in Windows. Assuming the Windows path is set up correctly (it should be), we will define our toolbar selection to start a DOS window from within gvim by executing the following (this is its *Action*):

```
:!cmd
```

For the new selection's toolbar button, or image, we use an icon showing a DOS command prompt, shown in Figure 13-15, which on our system is stored in $HOME/dos.bmp.

Figure 13-15. DOS icon

Execute the command:

```
:amenu icon="c:$HOME/dos.bmp" ToolBar.DOSWindow :!cmd<CR>
```

This creates a toolbar entry and adds our icon at the end of the toolbar. The toolbar should now look like Figure 13-16. The new icon appears on the rightmost end of the toolbar.

Figure 13-16. Toolbar with added DOS command

Tooltips

gvim lets you define tooltips for both menu entries and toolbar icons. Menu tooltips display in the gvim command-line area when the mouse is over that menu selection. Toolbar tooltips pop up graphically when the mouse hovers over a toolbar icon. For example, Figure 13-17 shows the tooltip that pops up when we put the mouse over the toolbar's Find Previous button.

Figure 13-17. Tooltip for the Find Previous icon

The `:tmenu` command defines tooltips for both menus and toolbar items. The syntax is:

```
:tmenu TopMenu.NextLevelMenu.MenuItem tool tip text
```

where *TopMenu.NextLevellMenu.MenuItem* defines the menu as it cascades from the top level all the way to the menu item for which you wish to define a tooltip. So, for example, a tooltip for the Open menu item under the File menu would be defined with the command:

```
:tmenu File.Open Open a file
```

Use `ToolBar` for the top-level "menu" if you are defining a toolbar item (there is no real top-level menu for a toolbar).

Let's define a pop-up tooltip for the DOS toolbar icon we created in the previous section. Enter the command:

```
:tmenu ToolBar.DOSWindow Open up a DOS window
```

Now when you hover over the newly added toolbar icon, you can see the tooltip, as shown in Figure 13-18.

Figure 13-18. Toolbar with added DOS command and its new tooltip

gvim in Microsoft Windows

gvim is increasingly popular among Windows users. Veteran vi and Vim users will find the Windows version excellent, and it is probably the most current version across all operating systems.

The self-installing executable should automatically and seamlessly integrate Vim into the Windows environment. If it doesn't, consult the `gui-w32.txt` help file in the Vim runtime directory for `regedit` instructions. Because this involves editing the Windows Registry, do *not* try it if it's a procedure with which you are the slightest bit uncomfortable. You may be able to find someone with more expertise to help you. It is a common but nontrivial exercise.

Long-time Windows users are familiar with the *clipboard*, a storage area where text and other information is kept to facilitate copy, cut, and paste operations. Vim supports interaction with the Windows clipboard. Simply highlight text in visual mode and click the Copy or Cut menu item to store Vim text in the Windows clipboard. You can then paste that text into other Windows applications.

gvim in the X Window System

Users familiar with the X environment can define and use many of the tunable X features. For example, you can define many resources with the standard class definitions typically defined in the `.Xdefaults` file.

 Note that these standard X resources are useful only for the Motif or Athena versions of the GUI. Obviously, the Windows version has no understanding of X resources. Not so obviously, X resources are not picked up by KDE or GNOME either.

A full discussion of X and how you configure and customize it has been exhaustively documented elsewhere and is beyond the scope of this book. For a brief (or not so brief) introduction to X, we suggest the X manpage.

GUI Options and Command Synopsis

Table 13-3 summarizes the commands and options specially associated with `gvim`. These are added to Vim when it is compiled with GUI support, and they take effect when it is invoked as `gvim` or `vim -g`.

Table 13-3. gvim-specific options

Command or option	Type	Description
guicursor	Option	Settings for cursor shape and blinking
guifont	Option	Names of single-byte fonts to be used
guifontset	Option	Names of multi-byte fonts to be used
guifontwide	Option	List of font names for double-wide characters
guiheadroom	Option	Number of pixels to leave for window decorations

Command or option	Type	Description
`guioptions`	Option	Which components and options are used
`guipty`	Option	Use a pseudo-tty for ":!" commands
`guitablabel`	Option	Custom label for a tab page
`guitabtooltip`	Option	Custom tooltip for a tab page
`toolbar`	Option	Items to show in the toolbar
`-g`	Option	Start the GUI (which also allows the other options)
`-U gvimrc`	Option	Use `gvim` startup file, named `gvimrc` or something similar, when starting the GUI
`:gui`	Command	Start the GUI (on Unix-like systems only)
`:gui filename...`	Command	Start the GUI and edit the specified files
`:menu`	Command	List all menus
`:menu menupath`	Command	List menus starting with *menupath*
`:menu menupath action`	Command	Add menu *menupath*, to perform action *action*
`:menu n menupath action`	Command	Add menu *menupath* with positional priority of *n*
`:menu ToolBar.toolbarname action`	Command	Add toolbar item *toolbarname* to perform action *action*
`:tmenu menupath text`	Command	Create tooltip for menu item *menupath* with text of *text*
`:unmenu menupath`	Command	Remove menu *menupath*

Vim Enhancements for Programmers

Text editing is only one of Vim's strong suits. Good programmers demand powerful tools to ensure efficient and proficient work. A good editor is only a start and, by itself, isn't enough. Many modern programming environments attempt to provide comprehensive solutions when all that is really necessary is a strong editor with some extra smarts.

Programming tools offer extra features ranging from editors with syntax coloring, auto indentation and formatting, keyword completion, and so on, to full-blown *Integrated Development Environments* (IDEs) with sophisticated integration that build up complete development ecosystems. These IDEs can be expensive (e.g., Visual Studio) or free (Eclipse), but their disk and memory requirements are large, their learning curves steep, and their demand for resources immense.

Programmers' tasks vary, and so do their technology requirements. Small development tasks are easily completed with simple editors that offer little more than text editing capabilities. Large, multicomponent, multiplatform, and multistaff efforts *almost* demand the heavy lifting IDEs provide. But from anecdotal experience, many veteran programmers feel that IDEs offer little more than extra complexity with no higher probability of success.

Vim strikes a nice compromise between simple editors and monolithic IDEs. It has features that until recently were available only in expensive IDEs. It lets you do quick and simple programming tasks without the overhead and learning curve of an IDE.

The many options, features, commands, and functions especially suited to making the programmer's life easier range from folding lines of code into one line, to syntax coloring, to automatic formatting. Vim affords programmers many tools that can be fully appreciated only by using them. At the high end, it offers a sort of mini-IDE called Quickfix, but it also has convenience features specific to various programming tasks. We present the following topics in this chapter:

- Folding
- Auto and smart indenting

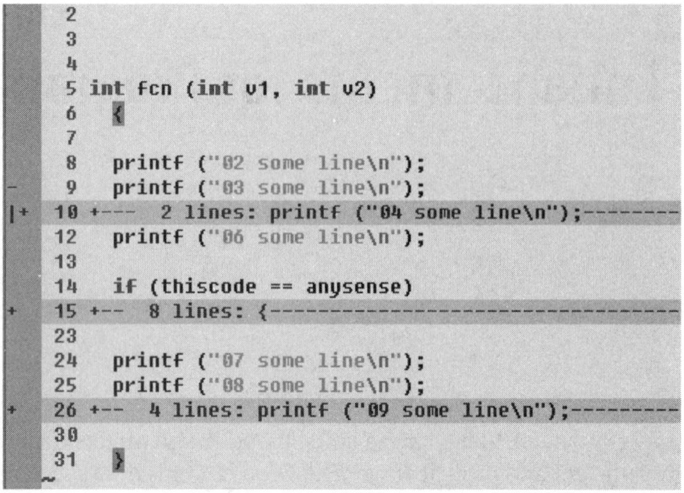

```
      2
      3
      4
      5  int fcn (int v1, int v2)
      6  {
      7
      8      printf ("02 some line\n");
      9      printf ("03 some line\n");
|+   10  +---   2 lines: printf ("04 some line\n");---------
     12      printf ("06 some line\n");
     13
     14      if (thiscode == anysense)
+    15  +--   8 lines: {----------------------------------
     23
     24      printf ("07 some line\n");
     25      printf ("08 some line\n");
+    26  +--   4 lines: printf ("09 some line\n");---------
     30
     31  }
~
```

Figure 14-1. Example of Vim folds

- Keyword and dictionary word completion
- Tags and extended tags
- Syntax highlighting
- Syntax highlight authoring (roll your own)
- Quickfix, Vim's mini-IDE

Folding and Outlining (Outline Mode)

Folding lets you define what parts of the file you see. For instance, in a block of code you can hide anything within curly braces, or hide all comments. Folding is a two-stage process. First, using any of several *fold methods* (we'll talk more about these later), you define what constitutes a block of text to fold. Then, when you use a fold command, Vim hides the designated text and leaves in its place a one-line placeholder. Figure 14-1 shows what folds look like in Vim. You can manage the lines hidden by the fold with the fold placeholder.

In the example, line 11 is hidden by a two-line fold starting with line 10. An eight-line fold starting at line 15 hides lines 16 through 22. And a four-line fold starting at line 26 hides lines 27 through 29.

There are virtually no limits on how many folds you can create. You can even create nested folds (folds within folds).

Several options control how Vim creates and displays folds. Also, if you've taken the time to create many folds, Vim provides the convenience commands `:mkview` and `:loadview` to preserve folds between sessions so you don't have to create them again.

Folds require some effort to learn but, when mastered, add a powerful way to control what to display and when. Do not underestimate the power this brings. Correct and maintainable programs require robust design at several levels, so good programming often requires looking at the forest rather than the trees—in other words, ignoring details of implementation in order to see the overall structure of a file.

For power users, Vim offers six different ways to define, create, and manipulate folds. This flexibility lets you create and manage folds in different contexts. Ultimately, once created, folds open and close and behave similarly for the whole suite of fold commands.

The six methods of creating folds are:

manual
> Define the span of a fold with standard Vim constructs, such as motion commands.

indent
> Folds and fold levels correspond to the indentation of text and the value of the option `shiftwidth`.

expr
> Regular expressions define folds.

syntax
> Folds correspond to the semantics of a file's language (e.g., a C program's function blocks could fold).

diff
> The differences between two files define folds.

marker
> Predefined (but also user-definable) markers in the file specify fold boundaries.

The manipulation of folds (opening and closing, deleting, etc.) is the same for all methods. We'll examine manual folds and discuss Vim fold commands in detail. We address some details for the other methods, but they are complex, specialized, and beyond the scope of this introduction. We hope our coverage will prompt you to explore the richness of these other methods.

So, let's take a brief look at the important fold commands and go through a short example of what folds look like.

The Fold Commands

Fold commands all begin with z. As a mnemonic to remember this, think of the side view of a folded piece of paper (when folded correctly) and how it looks like the letter "z."

There are about 20 z fold commands. With these commands you create and delete folds, open and close folds (hide and expose text belonging to folds), and toggle the expose/hide state of the folds. Here are short descriptions:

zA

> Toggle the state of folds, recursively.

zC

> Close folds, recursively.

zD

> Delete folds, recursively.

zE

> Eliminate *all* folds.

zf

> Create a fold from the current line to the one where the following motion command takes the cursor.

*count*zF

> Create a fold covering *count* lines, starting with the current line.

zM

> Set option `foldlevel` to 0.

zN, zn

> Set (zN) or reset (zn) the `foldenable` option.

zO

> Open folds, recursively.

za

> Toggle the state of one fold.

zc

> Close one fold.

zd

> Delete one fold.

zi

> Toggle the value of the `foldenable` option.

zj, zk

> Move cursor to the start (zj) of the next fold or to the end (zk) of the previous fold. (Note the mnemonic of the j ("jump") and k motion commands and how they are analogous to motions within the context of folds.)

zm, zr

> Decrement (zm) or increment (zr) the value of the `foldlevel` option by one.

zo

> Open one fold.

Don't confuse *delete fold* with the *delete* command. Use the *delete fold* command to remove, or undefine, a fold. A deleted fold has no effect on the text contained in that fold.

zA, zC, zD, and zO are called *recursive* because they operate on all folds nested within the one where you issue the commands.

Manual Folding

If you know Vim motion commands, you already know half of what you must learn to be proficient with manual fold commands.

For example, to hide three lines in a fold, enter either of the following:

```
3zF
2zfj
```

3zf executes the zF folding command over three lines, starting with the current one. 2zfj executes the zf folding command from the current line to the line where j moves the cursor (two lines down).

Let's try a more sophisticated command of use to C programmers. To fold a block of C code, position the cursor over the beginning or ending brace ({ or }) of a block of code and type zf%. (Remember that % moves to the matching brace.)

Create a fold from the cursor to the beginning of file by typing zfgg. (gg goes to the beginning of the file.)

It is easier to understand folds by seeing an example. We'll take a simple file, create and manipulate folds, and watch the behavior. We'll also see some of the enhanced visual folding cues that Vim provides.

First consider the example file in Figure 14-2, which contains some (meaningless) lines of C code. Initially, there are no folds.

There are a few things to note in this picture. First, Vim displays line numbers on the left side of the screen. We recommend that you always turn them on (using the number option) for added visual information about file location, and in this context the information becomes more valuable when you fold lines out of view. Vim tells you how many lines are not displayed, and the line numbers confirm and reinforce that information.

Also notice the gray columns to the left of the line numbers. These columns are reserved for more folding visual cues. As we create and use folds, we will see the visual cues Vim inserts into these columns.

In Figure 14-2, notice that the cursor is on line 18. Let's fold that line and the two following lines into one fold. We type zf2j. Figure 14-3 shows the result.

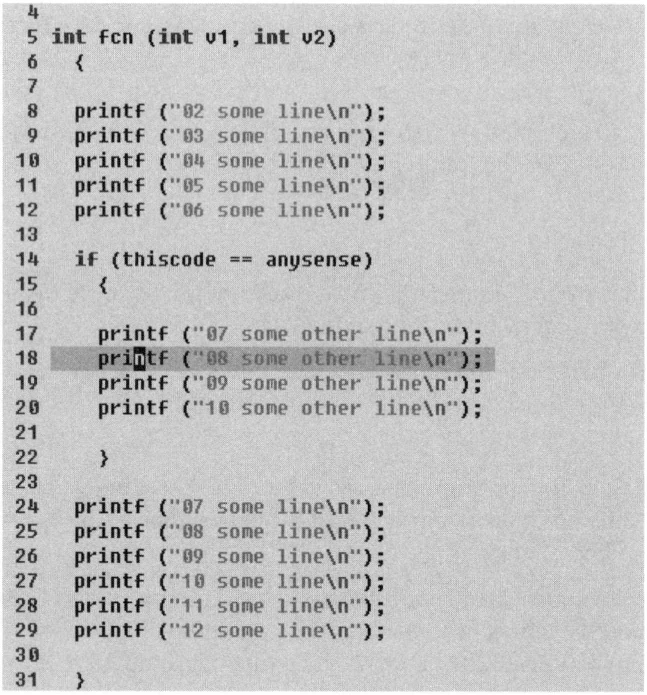

```
 4
 5 int fcn (int v1, int v2)
 6 {
 7
 8   printf ("02 some line\n");
 9   printf ("03 some line\n");
10   printf ("04 some line\n");
11   printf ("05 some line\n");
12   printf ("06 some line\n");
13
14   if (thiscode == anysense)
15     {
16
17       printf ("07 some other line\n");
18       printf ("08 some other line\n");
19       printf ("09 some other line\n");
20       printf ("10 some other line\n");
21
22     }
23
24   printf ("07 some line\n");
25   printf ("08 some line\n");
26   printf ("09 some line\n");
27   printf ("10 some line\n");
28   printf ("11 some line\n");
29   printf ("12 some line\n");
30
31 }
```

Figure 14-2. Sample file with no folds

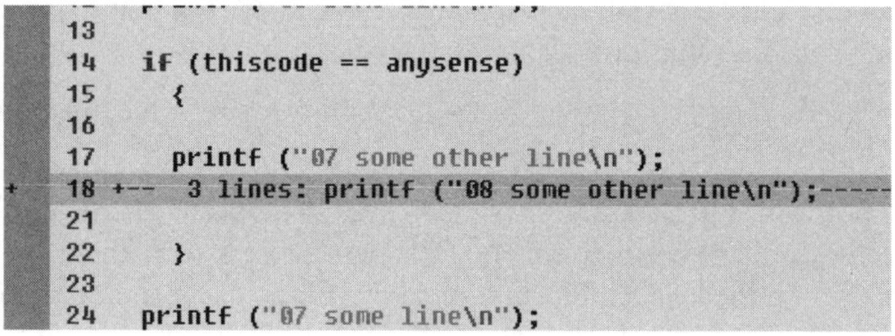

```
13
14   if (thiscode == anysense)
15     {
16
17       printf ("07 some other line\n");
+  18 +--  3 lines: printf ("08 some other line\n");-----
21
22     }
23
24   printf ("07 some line\n");
```

Figure 14-3. Three lines folded at line 18

Notice how Vim creates an easily identified marker with the +-- as a prefix, and how it displays text from the first folded line in the *fold* placeholder. Now notice the far left side of the screen where Vim inserted the +. This is another visual cue.

In the same file, we'll next fold the block of code between and including the braces after the if statement. Position the cursor on either one of the braces and type zf%. The file now appears as in Figure 14-4.

```
   8    printf ("02 some line\n");
   9    printf ("03 some line\n");
  10    printf ("04 some line\n");
  11    printf ("05 some line\n");
  12    printf ("06 some line\n");
  13
  14    if (thiscode == anysense)
+ 15 +--   8 lines: {---------------------------
  23
  24    printf ("07 some line\n");
  25    printf ("08 some line\n");
  26    printf ("09 some line\n");
```

Figure 14-4. Block of code folded following an if statement

```
   3
   4
+  5 +-- 21 lines: int fcn (int v1, int v2)--------
  26    printf ("09 some line\n");
  27    printf ("10 some line\n");
  28    printf ("11 some line\n");
  29    printf ("12 some line\n");
  30
  31    }
~
```

Figure 14-5. Folding to the beginning of a function

Now there are eight lines of code folded, three of which are contained in a fold already created. This is called a *nested* fold. Note there is no indication of the nested fold.

Our next experiment is to position the cursor on line 25 and fold all lines up to and including the function declaration for fcn. This time we use the Vim *search* motion. We initiate the fold command with zf, search backward to the beginning of the fcn function using ?int fcn (the backward search command in Vim), and press the ENTER key. The screen now looks like Figure 14-5.

If you count lines and create a fold that spans another fold (for example, 3zf), all lines contained in the spanned fold count as one line. For example, if the cursor is on line 30, and lines 31–35 are hidden in a fold on the next screen line, so that the next line on the screen displays line 36, 3zf creates a new fold containing three lines as they appear on the screen: the text line 30, the five lines contained in the fold holding lines 31–35, and the text line 36 displayed in the next line on the screen. Confusing? A little. You might say that the zf command counts lines in accordance with the rule, "What you see is what you fold."

```
       3
       4
 -     5  int fcn (int v1, int v2)
 |     6  {
 |     7
 |     8    printf ("02 some line\n");
 |     9    printf ("03 some line\n");
 |    10    printf ("04 some line\n");
 |    11    printf ("05 some line\n");
 |    12    printf ("06 some line\n");
 |    13
 |    14    if (thiscode == anysense)
 |-   15      {
 ||   16
 ||   17        printf ("07 some other line\n");
 ||-  18        printf ("08 some other line\n");
 |||  19        printf ("09 some other line\n");
 |||  20        printf ("10 some other line\n");
 ||   21
 ||   22      }
 |    23
 |    24    printf ("07 some line\n");
 |    25    printf ("08 some line\n");
```

Figure 14-6. All folds opened

Let's try some other features. First, open all the folds with the command z0 (that's z followed by the letter O, not z followed by a zero). Now we start seeing some visual cues in the left margin about the folds we made, as shown in Figure 14-6. Each of the columns in this margin is called a *foldcolumn*.

In this figure, the first line of each fold is marked with a minus sign (-), and all the other lines of the fold are marked by a vertical bar or pipe character (|). The largest (outermost) fold is in the leftmost column, and the innermost fold is in the rightmost column. As you see in our picture, lines 5–25 represent the lowest fold level (in this case, 1), lines 15–22 represent the next fold level (2), and lines 18–20 represent the highest fold level.

By default, this helpful visual metaphor is turned off (we don't know why; perhaps because it uses up screen space). Turn it on and define its width with the following command:

> `:set foldcolumns=n`

> where *n* is the number of columns to use (maximum is 12, default is 0). In the figure, we use `foldcolumn=5`. (For those paying close attention, yes, the earlier figures had `foldcolumn` set to 3. We changed the value for a better visual presentation.)

Now create more folds to observe their effects.

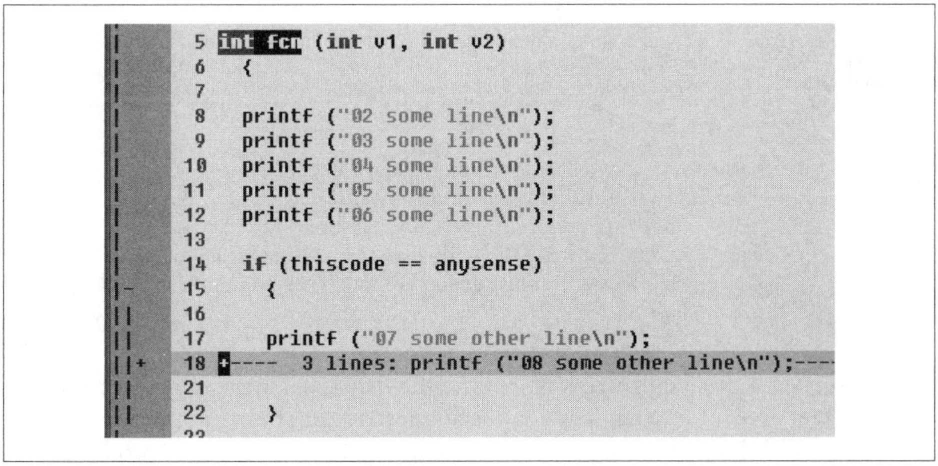

```
 5  int fcn (int v1, int v2)
 6  {
 7
 8      printf ("02 some line\n");
 9      printf ("03 some line\n");
10      printf ("04 some line\n");
11      printf ("05 some line\n");
12      printf ("06 some line\n");
13
14      if (thiscode == anysense)
15          {
16
17          printf ("07 some other line\n");
18 +----    3 lines: printf ("08 some other line\n");----
21
22          }
```

Figure 14-7. After refolding lines 18–20

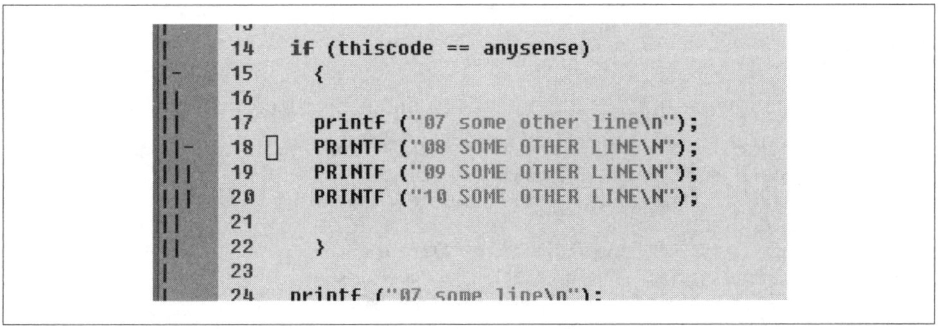

```
13
14      if (thiscode == anysense)
15          {
16
17          printf ("07 some other line\n");
18          PRINTF ("08 SOME OTHER LINE\N");
19          PRINTF ("09 SOME OTHER LINE\N");
20          PRINTF ("10 SOME OTHER LINE\N");
21
22          }
23
24      printf ("07 some line\n");
```

Figure 14-8. Case change applied to a fold

First, refold the deepest fold, which covers lines 18–20, by positioning the cursor on any line within the range of that fold and typing zc (close fold). Figure 14-7 shows the result.

See the change in the gray margin? Vim maintains the visual cues, making visualization and management of your folds easy.

Now let's see what a typical "one line" command does to a fold. Position the cursor on the folded line (18). Type ~~ (toggle case for all characters in the current line). Remember that in Vim, ~ is an object operator (unless the compatible option is set) and therefore should toggle the case of all the characters in the line for this example. Next, open the fold by typing zo (open fold). The code now looks like Figure 14-8.

This is a powerful feature. Line commands or operators act on the entire text represented by a fold line! Admittedly this may seem like a contrived example, but it illustrates nicely the potential of this technique.

Any action on a fold affects the whole fold. For instance, in Figure 14-7, if you position the cursor over line 18—a fold hiding lines 18 through 20—and type dd (delete line), all three lines are deleted and the fold is removed.

It's also important to note that Vim manages all edit actions as if there were no folds, so any undos will undo an entire edit's action. So, if we typed u (undo) after the previous change, all three lines that had been deleted would be restored. The undo feature is separate from the "one line" actions discussed in this section, although sometimes they seem to act similarly.

Now is a good time to familiarize yourself with the visual cues in the foldcolumn margin. They make it easy to see what fold you are about to act on. For example, the zc (close fold) command closes the innermost fold containing the line the cursor is on. You can see how large this fold is through the vertical bars in the foldcolumns. Once mastered, actions such as opening, closing, and deleting folds become second nature.

Outlining

Consider the following simple (and contrived) file using tabs for indentation:

```
1. This is Headline ONE with NO indentation and NO fold level.
    1.1 This is sub-headline ONE under headline ONE
        This is a paragraph under the headline.  Its fold
        level is 2.
    1.2 This is sub-headline TWO under headline ONE.
2. This is Headline TWO.  No indentation, so no folds!
    2.1 This is sub-headline ONE under headline TWO.
        Like the indented paragraph above, this has fold level 2.
            - Here is a bullet at fold level 3.
                A paragraph at fold level 4.
            - Here is the next bullet, again back at fold level 3.
        And, another set of bullets:
            - Bullet one.
            - Bullet two.
    2.2 This is heading TWO under Headline TWO.
3. This is Headline THREE.
```

You can use Vim folds to look at your file as a pseudo-outline. Define your folding method as indent:

```
:set foldmethod=indent
```

In our file we define the shiftwidth (the indentation level for tabs) to be 4. Now we can open and close folds based on indentation of lines. For each shiftwidth (a multiple of four columns in this case) to a line that is indented, its fold level increases by 1. For example, the subheadlines in our file are indented one shiftwidth, or four columns, and hence have a fold level of 1. Lines indented eight columns (two shiftwidths) have a fold level of 2, etc.

Figure 14-9. fold level = 0

Figure 14-10. fold level = 2

You can control the level of folds you see with the `foldlevel` command. It takes an integer as its argument and displays only lines whose fold levels are *less than or equal to* the argument. In our file we can ask to view only the highest-level headings with:

```
:set foldlevel=0
```

and our screen now looks like Figure 14-9.

Display everything up to and including the bullets by setting `foldlevel` to 2. Everything with a fold level *greater than or equal to* 2 is then displayed, as in Figure 14-10.

Using this technique to inspect your file, you can quickly expand and collapse the level of detail you see with Vim's fold increment (`zr`) and decrement (`zm`) commands.

A Few Words About the Other Fold Methods

We don't have time to cover all of the other fold methods, but to whet your appetite, we invite you to take a quick peek at the *syntax* folding method.

We use the same C file as before, but this time we let Vim decide what to fold based on C syntax. The rules governing folding within C are complex, but this simple snippet of code suffices to demonstrate Vim's automatic capabilities.

First, make sure to get rid of all folds by typing `zD` (delete all folds). The screen now displays all code with no visual markers in the fold column.

```
  2
  3
  4
  5 int fcn (int v1, int v2)
  6 +-- 26 lines: {------------------------------
  ~
  ~
  ~
```

Figure 14-11. After the command set foldmethod=syntax

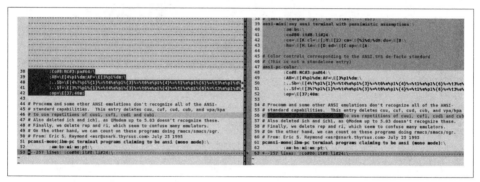

Figure 14-12. Vim diff feature and its use of folds

Make sure folding is turned on with the command:

```
:set foldenable
```

(You didn't need to do this before for *manual* folding, because `foldenable` was automatically set when `foldmethod` was set to `manual`.) Now type the command:

```
:set foldmethod=syntax
```

The folds appear as in Figure 14-11.

Vim folded all bracketed blocks of code, because those are logical semantic blocks in C. If you type `zo` on line 6 of this example, Vim expands the fold and reveals the inner fold.

Each fold method uses different rules to define folds. We encourage you to roll up (fold up?) your sleeves and read more on these powerful methods in the Vim documentation.

The Vim diff mode (also invoked through the `vimdiff` command) is a powerful combination of folding, windowing, and syntax highlighting, a feature we discuss later. As illustrated in Figure 14-12, the mode shows the differences between files, usually between two versions of the same file.

Auto and Smart Indenting

Vim offers four increasingly complex and powerful methods to automatically indent text. In its simplest form, Vim behaves almost identically to `vi`'s `autoindent` option, and indeed it uses the same name to describe the behavior.

You can choose the indentation method simply by specifying it in a `:set` command, such as:

```
:set cindent
```

Vim offers the following methods, listed in order of increasing sophistication:

`autoindent`

   Auto indentation closely mimics `vi`'s `autoindent`. It differs subtly as to where the cursor is placed after indentation is deleted.

`smartindent`

   Slightly more powerful than `autoindent`, but it recognizes some basic C syntax primitives for defining indentation levels.

`cindent`

   As its name implies, `cindent` embodies a much richer awareness of C syntax and introduces sophisticated customization beyond simple indentation levels. For example, `cindent` can be configured to match your (or your boss's) favorite coding style rules, including but not limited to how braces ({}) indent, where braces are placed, whether either or both braces are indented, and even how indentation matches included text.

`indentexpr`

   Lets you define your own expression, which Vim evaluates in the context of each new line you begin. With this feature, you write your own rules. We refer you to the discussions of scripting and functions in this book and to the Vim documentation for details. If the other three options don't give you enough flexibility for automatic indentation, `indentexpr` certainly will.

Vim autoindent Extensions to vi's autoindent

`autoindent` for Vim behaves almost like `vi`'s and can be made identical by setting the `compatible` option. One nice extension to `vi`'s `autoindent` is Vim's ability to recognize a file's "type" and insert appropriate comment characters when comment lines in a file wrap to a new line. This feature works cooperatively with either the `wrapmargin` (text wraps within `wrapmargin` columns of the right margin) or `textwidth` (text wraps when characters in a line exceed `textwidth` characters) options. Figure 14-13 shows the results of identical inputs, one using Vim's `autoindent` and the other using `vi`.

Notice that in the second block of text (line 16 and beyond) there is no leading comment character. Also, with the `compatible` option set (to mimic `vi`'s behavior), the

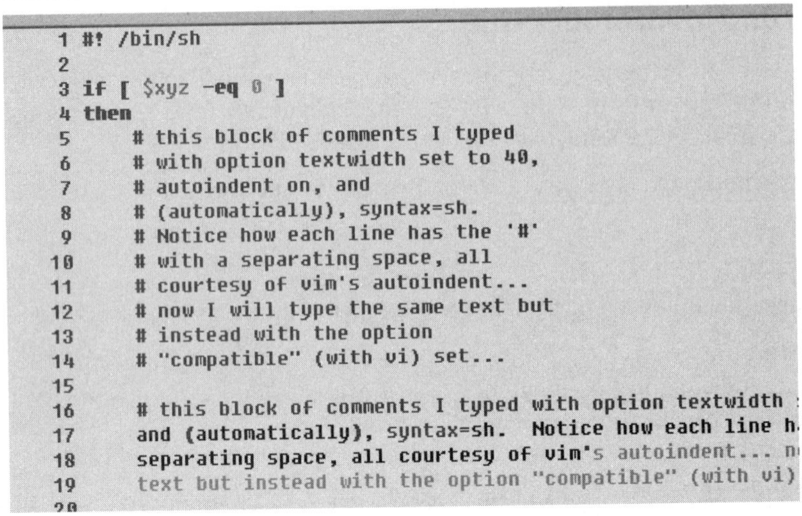

```
 1  #! /bin/sh
 2
 3  if [ $xyz -eq 0 ]
 4  then
 5       # this block of comments I typed
 6       # with option textwidth set to 40,
 7       # autoindent on, and
 8       # (automatically), syntax=sh.
 9       # Notice how each line has the '#'
10       # with a separating space, all
11       # courtesy of vim's autoindent...
12       # now I will type the same text but
13       # instead with the option
14       # "compatible" (with vi) set...
15
16       # this block of comments I typed with option textwidth :
17       and (automatically), syntax=sh.  Notice how each line h.
18       separating space, all courtesy of vim's autoindent... n
19       text but instead with the option "compatible" (with vi)
20
```

Figure 14-13. Difference between Vim and vi autoindent

textwidth option isn't recognized, and now the text wraps only because option wrapmargin has a value.

smartindent

smartindent extends autoindent, slightly. It's useful, but if you are writing code in a C-like programming language with a fairly complex syntax, you are better served by using cindent instead.

smartindent automatically inserts indents when:

- A new line follows a line with a left brace ({).
- A new line begins with a keyword that's contained in the option cinwords.
- A new line is created preceding a line starting with a right brace (}), *if* the cursor is positioned on the line containing the brace and the user creates a new line using the O (open line above) command.
- A new line is a closing, or right, brace (}).

cindent

Regular Vim users who program in C-like languages will want to use either cindent or indentexpr for coding. Although indentexpr is more powerful, flexible, and customizable, cindent is more practical for most programming tasks. It has plenty of settings for most programmers' needs (and corporate standards). Try it for a while with its default settings, and then customize it if your standards differ.

If the `indentexpr` option has a defined value, it overrides `cindent`'s actions.

Three options define `cindent`'s behavior:

`cinkeys`
> Defines keyboard keys that signal Vim to reevaluate indentation

`cinoptions`
> Defines the indentation style

`cinwords`
> Defines keywords that signal when Vim should add an extra indent in subsequent lines

`cindent` uses the string defined by `cinkeys` as its ruleset to define how to indent. We'll examine the default value of `cinkeys` and then look at other settings you can define and how they work.

The cinkeys option

`cinkeys` is a comma-separated list of values:

> `0{,0},0),:,0#,!^X^F,o,O,e`

Here are the values, broken into their separate contexts, with brief descriptions for each behavior:

`0{`
> `0` (zero) sets a *beginning of line* context for the following character, `{`. That is, if you type the character `{` as the first character of a line, Vim will reevaluate the indentation for that line.
>
> Do not confuse the zero in this option with the behavior "use zero indentation here," a common practice in C indentation. The zero here means "if the character is typed at the beginning of the line," not "force the character to appear at the beginning of the line."
>
> The default indentation for `{` is zero: no added indentation beyond the current level. The following example shows typical results:
>
> ```
> main ()
> {
>     if ( argv[0] == (char *)NULL )
>     { ...
> ```

`0},0)`
> As in the previous description, these two settings define *beginning of line* context. Thus, if you type either `}` or `)` at the beginning of a line, Vim reevaluates indentation.

The default indentation for } matches the indentation defined for its matching open brace {.

The default indentation for) is one `shiftwidth`.

:

This is the C label or `case statement` context. If a : (colon) is typed at the end of a label or `case statement` statement, Vim reevaluates indentation.

The default indentation for : is column 1, the first column in a line. Do not confuse this with zero indentation, which leaves the new line at the same indentation level as the previous one. When the indentation is 1, the first character of a new line is shifted left *all the way* to the first column.

0#

Again, this is a *beginning of line* context. When # is the first character typed in a line, Vim reevaluates indentation.

Default indentation, as in the previous definition, shifts the entire line to the first column. This is consistent with the practice of beginning macros (`#define...`) in column 1.

!^F

The special character ! defines any following character as a *trigger* to reevaluate the indentation in the current line. In this case, the triggering character is `^F`, which stands for CTRL-F, so the default behavior is for Vim to reevaluate a line's indentation any time you type CTRL-F.

o

This context defines any new line you create, whether by pressing the ENTER key in *insert* mode or by using the o (open new line) command.

O

This context covers the creation of a new line *above* the current line using the O (open new line above) command.

e

This is the *else* context. If you begin a line with the word `else`, Vim reevaluates indentation. Vim does not recognize this context until the final "e" of *else* is typed.

cinkeys syntax rules.   Each `cinkeys` definition consists of an optional prefix (one of !, *, or 0) and the key for which indentation is reevaluated. The prefixes have the following meanings:

!

Indicates a key (default CTRL-F) that causes Vim to reevaluate indentation on the current line. You can add an additional key definition as a command (by using the += syntax) without overriding the preexisting command. In other words, you can provide multiple keys to trigger line indentation. Any key you add to the ! definition still performs its old function as well.

---

*

Tells Vim to reevaluate the current line indentation before inserting the key.

0

Sets a *beginning of line* context. The key you specify after the 0 triggers a reevaluation of indentation only when typed as the first character of a line.

> Be aware of the distinction in vi and Vim between "first character in a line" and "first column in a line." You already know that typing ^ moves to the first character of a line, not necessarily the first column (flush left); the same is true of inserting with I. In the same way, the 0 prefix applies to entering a character as the first character in a line, regardless of whether it is flush left.

cinkeys has special key names and provides ways to override any reserved characters, such as those used as prefix characters. Here are the special key options:

<>

Use this form to define keys literally. For special nonprinting keys, use the spelled-out versions. For example, you can define the literal character ":" with <:>. Another example for a nontyping key is to define the "up arrow" as <Up>.

^

Use the caret (^) to signify a control character. For example, ^F defines the key CTRL-F .

o, 0, e, :

We saw these special keys in the default value for cinkeys.

=word, =~word

Use these to define a word that should receive special behavior. Once the string *word* is matched, if it is the first text on a new line, Vim reevaluates indentation.

The form =~word is the same as =word except that it ignores case.

> The term *word* is an unfortunate misnomer. More properly, it represents *beginning of word*, because the trigger occurs as soon as the string matches, but it does not require that the matched end of string also be the end of word. Vim's built-in documentation gives the example of end matching both end and endif.

The cinwords option

cinwords defines keywords that, when typed, trigger extra indentation on the following line. The option's default value is:

```
if,else,while,do,for,switch
```

This covers the standard keywords in the C programming language.

These keywords are case-sensitive. In checking for them, Vim even ignores the setting of the `ignorecase` option. If you need variations for different cases of keywords, you must specify all combinations in the `cinwords` string.

The cinoptions option

`cinoptions` controls how Vim reindents lines of text in their C context. It includes settings to control a number of code formatting standards, such as:

- How far to indent a code block enclosed by braces
- Whether to insert a newline in front of a brace that follows a condition statement
- How to align blocks of code relative to their enclosing braces

`cinoptions` defines 28 settings with its default value:

```
s,e0,n0,f0,{0,}0,^0,:s,=s,l0,b0,gs,hs,ps,ts,is,+s,c3,C0,/0,(2s,us,U0,w0,W0,
    m0,j0,)20,*30
```

The very length of the option gives you a sense of how many ways Vim lets you customize indentation. Most customization with `cinoptions` defines slight differences in context blocks. Some customizations define how far to scan (how many lines forward and backward in the file to go) in order to establish the right context and properly evaluate indentation.

Settings that alter the amount of indentations for various contexts can increase or decrease levels of indentation. Also, you can redefine the number of columns to use for indentation. For example, setting `cinoptions=f5` causes an opening brace ({) to be indented five columns, so long as it is not inside any *other* braces.

Another way to define increments of indentation is by some multiplier (which doesn't have to be an integer) of `shiftwidth`. If, in the previous example, you append w to the definition (i.e., `cinoptions=f5w`), the opening brace shifts five `shiftwidth`s.

Insert a minus sign (-) before any numeric value to alter the indentation level to the left (a negative indentation).

This option and its string value is one to modify with great care. Remember that when you use = syntax, you redefine an option completely. Because `cinoptions` carries so many possible settings, use very fine-grained commands to make changes: += to add a setting, -= to remove an existing setting, and -= followed by += to change an existing setting.

The following is a brief list of the options you are most likely to change. It is a small subset of the settings in `cinoptions`, and many readers may find the other (or even *all*) settings useful to customize.

```
18
19 while (condition)
20 {
21     if (someothercondition)
22     {
23         printf("looks like I've got both conditions!\n");
24     }
25 }
26
```

Figure 14-14. cinoptions=s,f0,{0

```
27 while (condition)
28     {
29     if (someothercondition)
30         {
31         printf("looks like I've got both conditions!\n");
32         }
33     }
34 |
```

Figure 14-15. cinoptions=s,fs,{s

>n (default is s)

Any line where indentation is indicated should be indented *n* places. The default for this is s, meaning that the default indentation for a line is one shiftwidth.

f*n*, {*n*

The f defines how far to indent an opening unnested brace ({). The default value is zero, thus aligning braces with their logical counterpart. For example, a brace following a line with a while statement is placed under the "w" of the while.

The { behaves the same way as the f but applies to *nested* opening braces. Again, this one defaults to an indent level of zero.

Figures 14-14 and 14-15 show two examples of identical text entry in Vim, the first example with cinoptions=s,f0,{0, and the second with cinoptions=s,fs,{s. For both examples, option shiftwidth has the value 4 (four columns).

}*n*

Use this setting to define a closing brace's (}) offset from its matching brace. The default is zero (aligned with the matching brace).

^*n*

Add *n* to the current indentation inside a set of braces ({...}) if the opening brace is in column one.

:*n*, =*n*, b*n*

These three control indentation in case statements. With :, Vim indents case labels *n* characters from the position of its corresponding switch statement. The default is one shiftwidth.

The = setting defines the offset for lines of code from their corresponding case label. The default is to indent statements one `shiftwidth`.

The `b` setting defines where to place `break` statements. The default (zero) aligns `break` with the other statements within the corresponding `case` block. Any nonzero value aligns the `break` with its corresponding `case` label.

`)n, *n`

These two settings tell Vim how many lines to scan to find unclosed parentheses (default is 20 lines) and unclosed comments (default is 30 lines), respectively.

Ostensibly, these two settings limit how hard Vim has to work to look for matches. With today's powerful computers, you should consider ratcheting these values up to assure more complete scope management to match comments and parentheses. Try doubling each to 40 and 60 as a starting point.

indentexpr

`indentexpr`, if defined, overrides `cindent` so that you can define indentation rules and tailor them exactly to your language editing needs.

`indentexpr` defines an expression to be evaluated each time a new line is created in a file. This expression resolves to an integer that Vim uses as the indentation of the new line.

In addition, the option `indentkeys` can define useful keywords in the same way that `cinkeys` keywords define lines after which indentation is reevaluated.

The bad news is that it is a nontrivial project to write customized indentation rules from scratch for any language. The good news is it's likely that the work is already done. Look in the `$VIMRUNTIME/indent` directory to see whether your favorite language is represented. A quick peek today reveals more than 70 indent files.

The most common programming languages are represented, including *ada*, *awk*, *docbook* (the indent file is named `docbk`), *eiffel*, *fortran*, *html*, *java*, *lisp*, *pascal*, `perl`, *php*, *python*, *ruby*, *scheme*, *sh*, *sql*, and *zsh*. There is even an indent file defined for *xinetd*!

You can tell Vim to automatically detect your file type and load the indent file by putting the command `filetype indent on` in your `.vimrc` file. Now Vim will try to detect what file type you are editing and load a corresponding *indent* definition file for you. If the indent rules do not fill your needs—for example, if they indent in some unfamiliar or unwanted fashion—turn the definitions off with the command `:filetype indent off`.

We encourage power users to explore and learn from the indent definition files that come with Vim. And if you develop new definition files or improvements to existing ones, we encourage you to submit them to *vim.org* for possible addition to the Vim package.

A Final Word on Indentation

Before ending our discussion, it's worth noting a couple of points about working with automatic indenting:

When automatic indenting isn't
> Any time you act on a line in an edit session with automatic indenting and you change that line's indentation manually, Vim flags that line and will no longer try to automatically define its indentation.

Copy and paste
> When you paste text into your file where automatic indenting is turned on, Vim considers this regular input and applies all automatic indentation rules. In most cases, this is probably not what you intend. Any indentation in pasted text is tacked on to applied indentation rules. Typically the result is text that progressively skews to the right side of the screen with large indentation and no corresponding retreat to the left side.

To avoid this awkward situation and to paste text intact without side effects, set Vim's `paste` option before adding the imported text. `paste` comprehensively reconfigures all of Vim's automatic features to faithfully incorporate pasted text. To return to automatic mode, simply reset the `paste` option with the command `:set nopaste`.

Keyword and Dictionary Word Completion

Vim offers a comprehensive suite of *insertion-completion* capabilities. From programming language-specific keywords to filenames, dictionary words, and even entire lines, Vim knows how to offer possible completions to partially entered text. Not only that, but Vim abstracts the semantic of dictionary-based completion to include completions based on synonyms for the completed word from a thesaurus!

In this section we look at the different completion methods, their syntaxes, and descriptions of how they work with examples. The methods of completion include:

- Whole line
- Current file keywords
- `dictionary` option keywords
- `thesaurus` option keywords
- Current and *included* file keywords
- Tags (as in `ctags`)
- Filenames
- Macros
- Vim command line
- User-defined

- Omni
- Spelling suggestions
- `complete` option keywords

Except for `complete` keywords, all completion commands start with CTRL-X. The second key specifically defines the type of completion Vim attempts. For example, the command to autocomplete filenames is CTRL-X CTRL-F. (Not all the commands are so mnemonic, unfortunately.) Vim uses unmapped (default) keys, which allows you to shorten most of these commands to just the second keystroke by mapping the commands appropriately. (For instance, you can map CTRL-X CTRL-N to just CTRL-N.)

All completion methods have virtually identical behavior: they cycle through a list of candidate completions as you retype the second keystroke. Thus, if you choose filename autocompletion through CTRL-X CTRL-F and you don't get the right word on the first try, you can repeatedly press CTRL-F to see the other options. Additionally, if you press CTRL-N (for "next"), you move forward through the possibilities, whereas CTRL-P (for "previous") moves backward.

Let's look at some of these autocompletion methods with examples and consider how they might be useful.

Insertion Completion Commands

These methods range in function from simply looking for words in your current file to spanning the range of function, variable, macro, and other names throughout an entire suite of code. The final method combines features of the others for a nice compromise between power and sophistication.

> You may want to find your favorite completion method and map it to a single easy-to-use key. I map mine to the Tab key:
>
> ```
> :imap Tab <C-P>
> ```
>
> This sacrifices my ability to insert tabs easily, but it allows me to use the same key I use (available by default) in command-line environments such as DOS and shell (`xterm`, `konsole`, etc.) to complete partially typed information. (Remember, you can always insert a tab by quoting it with CTRL-V.) Mapping to the Tab key also corresponds to the normal completion key in Vim's command-line mode.

Completing whole lines

This is invoked through CTRL-X CTRL-L. The method looks backward in the current file for a line matching the characters you've typed. We'll try an example to give you a sense of how completion works.

```
 1 #           Reconstructed via infocmp from file: /etc/terminfo/r/rxv
 2 # (untranslatable capabilities removed to fit entry within 1023
 3 # This terminal widely used in our company...
 4 rxvt-unicode|rxvt-unicode terminal (X Window System):\
 5        :am:bw:eo:hs:km:mi:ms:xn:xo:\
 6        :co#80:it#8:li#24:lm#0:\
 7        :AL=\E[%dL:DC=\E[%dP:DL=\E[%dM:DO=\E[%dB:IC=\E[%d@:\
 8        :K1=\EOw:K2=\EOu:K3=\EOy:K4=\EOq:K5=\EOs:LE=\E[%dD:\
 9        :RI=\E[%dC:SF=\E[%dS:SR=\E[%dT:UP=\E[%dA:ae=\E(B:al=\E[L
```

Figure 14-16. Example of completion by line

```
 3 # This terminal widely used in our compa
 4 rxvt-unicode|rxvt-unicode terminal (X W
 5        :am:bw:eo:hs:km:mi:ms:xn:xo:\
 6        :co#80:it#8:li#24:lm#0:
 7
 8 # Thi
 9 rxvt-unicode2|rxvt-unicode2 terminal (X
 0        :AL=\E[%dL:DC=\E[%dP:DL=\E[%dM:
```

Figure 14-17. Partially typed line waiting for completion

```
 8 # This terminal widely used in our company...|
 9 # This section lists entries in a least-capable to most-cap
10 # This should only be used when the terminal emulator canno
11 # This entry is good for the 1.1.47 version of the Linux co
12 # This trick could work with other Intel consoles like the
13 # This terminal widely used in our company...
14       :cm=\E[%i%d:%dH:cr=^M:cs=\E[%i%d:%dr:ct=\E[3g:dc=\E
```

Figure 14-18. After typing CTRL-X CTRL-L

Consider a file that contains terminal, or console, definitions that characterize the features of terminals and how to manipulate them. Say your screen resembles Figure 14-16.

Note the highlighted line containing "This terminal widely used in our company...". You need this line in many places as you mark terminals as "widely used" for your company. Simply type enough of the line to make it unique, or close to unique, and then type CTRL-X CTRL-L. Thus, Figure 14-17 contains the partial input line:

    # Thi

CTRL-X CTRL-L causes Vim to show a set of possible completions for the line, based on lines previously entered in the file. The list of completions is shown in Figure 14-18.

It is hard to see in grayscale, but the screen offers a colored pop-up window containing multiple occurrences of lines matching the beginning of our partial line. Also displayed, but not visible in the screenshot, is information describing where the match is found.

```
   3 # This terminal widely used in our company...
   4 rxvt-unicode|rxvt-unicode terminal (X Window System):\
   5        :am:bw:eo:hs:km:mi:ms:xn:xo:\
   6        :co#80:it#8:li#24:lm#0:
   7
   8 # This terminal widely used in our company...
   9 rxvt-unicode2|rxvt-unicode2 terminal (X Window System)2:\
  10        :AL=\E[%dL:DC=\E[%dP:DL=\E[%dM:DO=\E[%dB:IC=\E[%d@
```

Figure 14-19. After typing CTRL-X CTRL-L and selecting our matching line

This method uses the `complete` option to define the scope for searching for matches. Scope is discussed in detail in the last method of this section.

The pop up[*] list highlights selections as you move forward (CTRL-N) or backward (CTRL-P) through the list. Press ENTER to select your match. If you do not want any of the choices in the list, type CTRL-E to halt the match method without substituting any text. Your cursor returns to its original position on the same partial input.

Figure 14-19 shows the results after we select an option from the list.

Completion by keyword in file

CTRL-X CTRL-N searches forward through the current file for keywords matching the keyword in front of the cursor. Once you enter those keystrokes, you can use CTRL-N and CTRL-P to search forward or backward, respectively. Press ENTER to select a match.

Note that "keyword" is loosely defined. While it may be keywords programmers are familiar with, it can really match any word in the file. Words are defined as a contiguous set of characters in the `iskeyword` option. The `iskeyword` defaults are pretty sane, but you can redefine the option if you want to include or leave out some punctuation. Characters in `iskeyword` can be specified either directly (such as `a-z`) or through ASCII code (such as using `97-122` to represent a–z).

For instance, the defaults allow an underscore as part of a word, but consider a period or hyphen to be a delimiter. This works fine for C-like languages, but may not be the best choice for other environments.

Completion by dictionary

CTRL-X CTRL-K searches forward through the files defined by the `dictionary` option for keywords matching the keyword in front of the cursor.

---

[*] The pop up is in `gvim`; Vim behaves slightly differently.

The default setup leaves the `dictionary` option undefined. There are common places to find dictionary files, and you can define your own. The most common dictionary files are:

- `/usr/dict/words` (Cygwin on XP)
- `/usr/share/dict/words` (FreeBSD)
- `$HOME/.mydict` (personal list of dictionary words)

Notice that for Windows XP, the dictionary word file is provided by Cygwin (*http://www.cygwin.com/*), a free software emulation suite of Unix utilities. Although installation of Cygwin is beyond the scope of this discussion, it is worth noting that you can selectively install small portions of it, and you may find it worthwhile to install the piece that contains the word dictionary.

Completion by thesaurus

CTRL-X CTRL-T searches forward through the files defined by the `thesaurus` option for keywords that match the keyword in front of the cursor.

This method offers an interesting twist. When Vim finds a match, if the line in the thesaurus file contains more than one word, Vim includes all the words in the list of completion candidates.

Ostensibly (and implied by the option's name), this method provides synonyms but allows *you* to define your own standard. Consider the example file containing these lines:

```
fun enjoyable desirable
funny hilarious lol rotfl lmao
retrieve getchar getcwd getdirentries getenv getgrent ...
```

The first two lines are typical English-language synonyms (matching "fun" and "funny," respectively), while the third line might be useful for C programmers who regularly insert function names that begin with `get`. The synonym we use for these functions is "retrieve."

In real life, we'd separate the English-language thesaurus from the C-language one, because Vim can search multiple thesauruses.

In input mode, type the word `fun`, then CTRL-X CTRL-T. Figure 14-20 shows the resulting pop up in `gvim`.

Notice the following:

- Vim matches *any* word it can find in a thesaurus entry, not just the first word of each line in the thesaurus file.
- Vim includes candidate words from all lines in the thesaurus that have a match with the keyword in front of the cursor. Thus, in this case, it finds the matches for both "fun" and "funny."

```
....                                ..................
1674              Unix</emphasis>.  While installatio
1675 fun
1676 fun        c:\home\ehannah\.mythesaurus otin
1677 enjoyable  c:\home\ehannah\.mythesaurus mpha
1678 desirable  c:\home\ehannah\.mythesaurus y.</
1679 funny      c:\home\ehannah\.mythesaurus
1680 hilarious  c:\home\ehannah\.mythesaurus
1681 lol        c:\home\ehannah\.mythesaurus
1682 rotfl      c:\home\ehannah\.mythesaurus
1683 lmao       c:\home\ehannah\.mythesaurus
1684           <title><emphasis>completion method<
1685           (<keycap>CTL-X CTL-T</keycap>) </ti
```

Figure 14-20. Thesaurus completion of "fun"

 Another interesting and perhaps unanticipated behavior of thesaurus is that the match can be on words on a line in the thesaurus file *other than* the first word. For instance, in the line from the previous example file:

```
funny hilarious lol rotfl lmao
```

If you type hilar and complete it, Vim will include in the list all words from hilarious on that line, i.e., "hilarious," "lol," "rotfl," and "lmao." Funny!

Did you notice the extra information in the list of candidates for completion? You can get information about where Vim found the match in the pop-up menu by adding the value preview to the completeopt option.

Now consider an example, using the same file as before, in which you type the partial word retrie. This matches "retrieve," a synonym we like as a mnemonic for "getting" stuff, and we include all "get" function names as synonyms. Now, CTRL-X CTRL-T gives us the pop-up menu (in gvim) of all of our functions as choices for completion. See Figure 14-21.

As with other completion methods, press ENTER to select the match.

Completion by keyword in current file and included files

CTRL-X CTRL-I searches forward through the current file and included files for keywords matching the keyword in front of the cursor. This method differs from the "search current file" method (CTRL-X CTRL-P) in that Vim inspects the current file for *include* file references and searches those files, too.

Vim uses the value in include to detect lines referencing *include* files. The default is a pattern telling Vim to find lines matching the standard C construct:

```
# include <somefile.h>
```

```
46    printf ("02 some line\n");
47    retrieve
48    retrieve           c:\home\ehannah\.mythesaurus
49    getchar            c:\home\ehannah\.mythesaurus
50    getcwd             c:\home\ehannah\.mythesaurus
51    getdirentries      c:\home\ehannah\.mythesaurus
52    getenv             c:\home\ehannah\.mythesaurus
53    getgrent           c:\home\ehannah\.mythesaurus
54    getgrgid           c:\home\ehannah\.mythesaurus
55    getgrnam           c:\home\ehannah\.mythesaurus
56    gethostbyaddr      c:\home\ehannah\.mythesaurus
57    gethostbyname      c:\home\ehannah\.mythesaurus
58    getmntent          c:\home\ehannah\.mythesaurus
59    getnetbyaddr       c:\home\ehannah\.mythesaurus
60    getnetbyname       c:\home\ehannah\.mythesaurus
61    getnetent          c:\home\ehannah\.mythesaurus
62    getopt             c:\home\ehannah\.mythesaurus
63    getopt_long        c:\home\ehannah\.mythesaurus
64    getpass            c:\home\ehannah\.mythesaurus
65    getprotobyname     c:\home\ehannah\.mythesaurus
66    getprotobynumber   c:\home\ehannah\.mythesaurus
67    getprotoent        c:\home\ehannah\.mythesaurus
```

Figure 14-21. Thesaurus completion of string "retrie"

In this case, Vim would find matches in the file `somefile.h` in the standard include file directories on the system. Vim also uses the `path` option as a list of directories to search for the included files.

Completion by tag

$\boxed{\text{CTRL-X}}$ $\boxed{\text{CTRL-]}}$ searches forward through the current file and included files for keywords matching *tags*. (See the earlier section "Using Tags" on page 123 for a discussion of tags.)

Completion by filename

$\boxed{\text{CTRL-X}}$ $\boxed{\text{CTRL-F}}$ searches for filenames matching the keyword in front of the cursor. Note that this causes Vim to complete the keyword with the *name of the file*, not with words found in files.

 As of Vim 7.1, Vim searches *only* in the current directory for files with possible filename matches. This is in contrast to many Vim features that use the `path` option to look for files. The built-in Vim documentation hints that this behavior is temporary, by pointing out that `path` isn't used "yet."

Completion by macro and definition names

CTRL-X CTRL-D searches forward through the current file and included files for macro names and definitions defined by the #define directive. This method inspects the current file for include file references and searches those files, too.

Completion method with Vim commands

This method, invoked through CTRL-X CTRL-V, is meant for use on the Vim command line and tries to guess the best completions for words. This context is provided to assist users developing Vim scripts.

Completion by user functions

This method, invoked through CTRL-X CTRL-U, lets you define the completion method with your own function. Vim uses the function pointed to by the option completefunc to make the completion. Refer to Chapter 12 for discussions about scripting and writing Vim functions.

Completion by omni function

This method, invoked through CTRL-X CTRL-O, uses user-defined functions much like the previous user function method. The significant difference is that this method expects the functions to be file type-specific, and hence, determined and loaded as a file is loaded. Omni completion files are already available for C, CSS, HTML, Java-Script, PHP, Python, Ruby, SQL, and XML. The built-in Vim documentation mentions that more scripts will be available soon for Vim 7.1, including an omni function file for C++. We encourage you to experiment with them.

Completion for spelling correction

This method is invoked through CTRL-X CTRL-S. The word in front of the cursor is used as the base word for which Vim offers candidates for completion. If the word appears to be badly spelled, Vim offers suggested "more correct" spellings.

Completion with the complete option

This is the most generic option, invoked through CTRL-N, and lets you combine all the other searches into one. For many users, this may be the most satisfactory because it requires little understanding of the nuances of the more specific methods.

Define where and how this completion acts by setting the comma-separated list of available sources in the complete option. Each available source is denoted by a single character. The choices include:

. *(period)*
    Search the current buffer

---

w

Search buffers in other windows (within the screen containing your Vim session)

b

Search other loaded buffers in the buffer list (which might not be visible in any Vim windows)

u

Search the unloaded buffers in the buffer list

U

Search the buffers *not* in the buffer list

k

Search the dictionary files (listed in the `dictionary` option)

kspell

Use the current spellchecking scheme (this is the only option that is not a single character)

s

Search the thesaurus files (listed in the `thesaurus` option)

i

Search the current and included files

d

Search the current and included files for defined macros

t,]

Search for tag completion

Some Final Comments on Vim Autocompletion

We've covered a lot of material related to autocompletion, but there's lots more. The autocompletion methods yield great returns for the time you invest in mastering their use. If you edit a *lot*, and if there's *any* notion or context of text to be completed, find the method best suited to that and learn it.

One final tip. Combinations with two keystrokes (more if you are a typical Unix user and count key combinations as "more than one") can be error-prone, especially given that they are combinations with the CTRL key. If you think you'd use autocompletion heavily, consider mapping your favorite autocompletion to just one keystroke or key combination. Large numbers of autocompletion commands abbreviated to half the length offer that much more efficiency.

The following example shows you why we find this customization so valuable. I map the Tab key to generic keyword matching, as mentioned earlier. While editing this book using DocBook XML tags, I have (using a conservative **grep** of the files) typed "emphasis" more than 1,200 times! Using keyword completion, I know the partial "emph" always matches to one choice, the "emphasis" tag I want. Thus, for each occurence of this word, I save at least three keystrokes (assuming perfect typing for the three initial letters), giving me a total savings of at least 3,600 keystrokes!

Here's another way to measure the efficiency of this method: I already know I type about four characters per second, thus gaining a savings in typing for *one keyword alone* of 3,600 divided by 4, or *15 minutes* time saved. For the same DocBook files, I complete another 20 to 30 keywords in the same fashion. The savings in time accrue quickly!

Tag Stacking

Tag stacking is described earlier in the section "Tag Stacks" on page 131. Besides moving back and forth among the tags you search for, you can choose among multiple matching tags. You can also do tag selection and window splitting with one command. The Vim ex mode commands for working with tags are provided in Table 14-1.

Table 14-1. Vim tag commands

Command	Function
ta[g][!] [*tagstring*]	Edit the file containing *tagstring* as defined in the tags file. The ! forces Vim to switch to the new file if the current buffer has been modified but not saved. The file may or may not be written out, depending on the setting of the autowrite option.
[*count*]ta[g][!]	Jump to the *count*'th newer entry in the tag stack.
[*count*]po[p][!]	Pop a cursor position off the stack, restoring the cursor to its previous position. If supplied, go to the *count*'th older entry.
tags	Display the contents of the tag stack.
ts[elect][!] [*tagstring*]	List the tags that match *tagstring*, using the information in the tags file(s). If no *tagstring* is given, the last tag name from the tag stack is used.
sts[elect][!] [*tagstring*]	Like :tselect, but splits the window for the selected tag.
[*count*]tn[ext][!]	Jump to the *count*'th next matching tag (default is 1).
[*count*]tp[revious][!]	Jump to the *count*'th previous matching tag (default is 1).
[*count*]tN[ext][!]	
[*count*]tr[ewind][!]	Jump to the first matching tag. With *count*, jump to the *count*'th matching tag.
tl[ast][!]	Jump to the last matching tag.

Normally, Vim shows you which matching tag out of how many it has jumped to. For example:

    tag 1 of >3

It uses a greater-than sign (>) to indicate that it has not yet tried all the matches. You can use :tnext or :tlast to try more matches. If this message is not displayed because of some other message, use :0tn to see it.

Here is the output of the `:tags` command, with the current location marked with a greater-than sign (`>`):

```
  # TO tag         FROM line in file
  1  1 main            1 harddisk2:text/vim/test
> 2  2 FuncA          58 -current-
  3  1 FuncC         357 harddisk2:text/vim/src/amiga.c
```

The `:tselect` command lets you pick from more than one matching tag. The "priority" (`pri` field) indicates the quality of the match (global versus static, exact case versus case-independent, etc.); this is described more fully in the `vim` documentation.

```
 nr pri kind tag             file ~
  1 F   f    mch_delay        os_amiga.c
                 mch_delay(msec, ignoreinput)
> 2 F   f    mch_delay        os_msdos.c
                 mch_delay(msec, ignoreinput)
  3 F   f    mch_delay        os_unix.c
                 mch_delay(msec, ignoreinput)
Enter nr of choice (<CR> to abort):
```

The `:tag` and `:tselect` commands can be given an argument that starts with /. In that case, the command uses it as a regular expression, and Vim will find all the tags that match the given regular expression. For example, `:tag /normal` will find the macro NORMAL, the function `normal_cmd`, and so on. Use `:tselect /normal` and enter the number of the tag you want.

The `vi` command mode commands are described in Table 14-2. Besides using the keyboard, as in the other editors, you can also use the mouse if mouse support is enabled in your version of Vim.

Table 14-2. Vim command mode tag commands

Command	Function
`^]` g <LeftMouse> CTRL-<LeftMouse>	Look up the location of the identifier under the cursor in the `tags` file, and move to that location. The current location is automatically pushed onto the tag stack.
`^T`	Return to the previous location in the tag stack, i.e., pop off one element. A preceding count specifies how many elements to pop off the stack.

The Vim options that affect tag searching are described in Table 14-3.

Table 14-3. Vim options for tag management

Option	Function
`taglength, tl`	Controls the number of significant characters in a tag that is to be looked up. The default value of zero indicates that all characters are significant.
`tags`	The value is a list of filenames in which to look for tags. As a special case, if a filename starts with ./, the dot is replaced with the directory part of the current file's pathname, making it possible to use `tags` files in a different directory. The default value is `"./tags,tags"`.

Option	Function
tagrelative	When set to true (the default) and using a tags file in another directory, filenames in that tags file are considered to be relative to the directory where the tags file is.

Vim can use Emacs-style etags files, but this is only for backward compatibility; the format is not documented in the Vim documentation, nor is the use of etags files encouraged.

Finally, Vim also looks up the entire word containing the cursor, not just the part of the word from the cursor location forward.

Syntax Highlighting

One of Vim's strongest enhancements to vi is its syntax highlighting. Vim's syntax formatting relies heavily on the use of color, but it also degrades gracefully on screens that do not support color. In this section we discuss three topics: getting started, customizing, and rolling your own. Syntax highlighting for Vim contains features that go beyond the scope of this book, so we focus on providing enough information to get you familiar with it and enable you to extend it to fit your needs.

 Because the impact of Vim's syntax highlighting is most dramatic in color, and this book isn't (in color), we strongly encourage you to try syntax highlighting to fully appreciate the power of color in defining context. I have never met a user who tried it and then did not continue to always use it.

Getting Started

Displaying a file's syntax highlighting is simple. Just issue the command:

```
:syntax enable
```

If all is well, and if you edit a file with a formal syntax, such as a programming language, you should see text in various colors, all determined by context and syntax. If nothing changed, try turning *syntax* on:

```
:syntax on
```

Enabling syntax should be enough by itself, but we have encountered situations where the additional command was required to turn on the syntax highlighting.

If you still see no syntax highlights, Vim may not know what your file type is and thus not understand which syntax is appropriate. There are a number of reasons this happens.

For example, if you create a new file and don't use a recognized suffix, or no suffix at all, Vim cannot determine the file type because the file is new and therefore empty. For instance, I write shell scripts without any `.sh` suffix. Each new shell script begins its editing life without syntax highlighting. Fortunately, once the file contains code, Vim knows how to figure out the file type and syntax highlighting works as expected.

It's also possible (though not likely) that Vim doesn't recognize your file type. This is very rare, and usually you just need to specify a file type explicitly, because someone has already written a syntax file for the language. Unfortunately, creating one from scratch is a complex undertaking, although we give you some tips later in this chapter.

You can force Vim to use the syntax highlighting of your choice by setting the syntax manually from the command line. When starting a new shell script, for instance, I always define the syntax with:

```
:set syntax=sh
```

The section "Dynamic File Type Configuration Through Scripting" on page 205 shows a clever and rather roundabout way to avoid this step.

When you enable syntax, Vim sets up syntax highlighting by going through a checklist. Without getting mired in too many technical details, we'll just say that Vim ultimately determines your file type, finds the appropriate syntax definition file, and loads it for you. The standard location for syntax files is the `$VIMRUNTIME/syntax` directory.

To get a sense of the comprehensive coverage of syntax definitions, the Vim syntax file directory contains *almost 500 syntax files*. Available syntaxes span the gamut from languages (C, Java, HTML) to content (`calendar`) to well-known configuration files (`fstab`, `xinetd`, `crontab`). If Vim doesn't recognize your file type, try looking in the `$VIMRUNTIME/syntax` directory for a syntax file that closely matches yours.

Customization

Once you start using syntax highlighting, you may find that some of the colors do not work for you. They may be difficult to see or just not suit your taste. Vim has a few ways to customize and tune colors.

Here are some things to try before taking more drastic measures (e.g., writing your own syntax, as described in the next section) to make syntax highlighting work for you.

Two of the most common and dramatic symptoms of syntax highlighting gone amok are:

- Bad contrast, with colors too similar and hard to see distinctly as different from each other
- Too many, or too varied, colors, which creates a harsh look to the text

Although these are subjective deficiencies, it's nice that Vim lets you make corrections. Two commands, `colorscheme` and `highlight`, and one option, `background`, can probably bring the colors to a satisfactory balance for most users.

There are a few other commands and options with which you can customize your syntax highlighting. After a brief introduction to syntax *groups*, we will talk about these commands and options in the following sections, with an emphasis on the three just mentioned.

Syntax groups

Vim classifies different types of text into groups. These groups each receive color and highlight definitions. Additionally, Vim allows groups of groups. You can address definitions at different levels. If you assign a definition to a group containing subgroups, unless otherwise defined, each subgroup inherits the parent group's definitions.

Some high-level groups for syntax highlighting include:

Comment
> Comments specific to the programming language, e.g.:
>
> ```
> // I am both a C++ and a JavaScript comment
> ```

Constant
> Any constant, e.g. `TRUE`

Identifier
> Variable and function names

Type
> Declarations, such as `int` and `struct` in C

Special
> Special characters, such as delimiters

Taking the "special" group from the previous list, we can look at an example of subgroups:

- SpecialChar
- Tag
- Delimiter
- SpecialComment
- Debug

With a basic understanding of syntax highlighting, groups, and subgroups, we now know enough to modify syntax highlighting to suit our tastes.

The colorscheme command

This command changes colors for different syntax highlights such as comments, keywords, or strings by redefining these syntax groups. Vim ships with the following color scheme choices:

- blue
- darkblue
- default
- delek
- desert
- elflord
- evening
- koehler
- morning
- murphy
- pablo
- peachpuff
- ron
- shine
- slate
- torte
- zellner

These files are in the directory `$VIMRUNTIME/colors`. You can activate any one of them with:

```
:colorscheme schemeName
```

 In non-GUI Vim, you can quickly cycle through the different schemes this way: type the partial command `:color`, press the Tab key to start command completion, press the Space bar, then repeatedly press the Tab key to cycle through the different choices.

In **gvim**, the choice is even easier. Click on the Edit menu, move the mouse over the Colorscheme submenu, and select the "tear off" (the line with scissors) menu. Now you can look at all the choices by clicking each button.

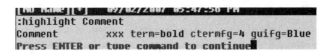

```
:highlight Comment
Comment           xxx term=bold ctermfg=4 guifg=Blue
Press ENTER or type command to continue
```

Figure 14-22. Highlight for comments

Setting the background option

When Vim sets colors, it first tries to determine what kind of background color your screen has. Vim has just two categories for background: dark or light. Based on Vim's determination, it sets colors differently for each, with the end result hopefully being a set of colors that works well with that background (one with good contrast and color compatibility). Although Vim does try very hard, a correct assessment is tricky, and an assignment to dark or light is subjective. Sometimes the contrasts render the session uncomfortable to view, and sometimes they are unreadable.

So, if the colors don't look good, try explicitly choosing a **background** setting. Make sure first to identify the setting:

```
:set background?
```

so that you know that you are changing the setting. Then, issue a command such as:

```
:set background=dark
```

Use the **background** option in tandem with the **colorscheme** command to fine-tune your screen colors. These two together can usually produce a satisfactory color palette that is comfortable to view.

The highlight command

Vim's **highlight** command lets you manipulate different groups and control how they are highlighted in your edit session. This command is powerful. You can inspect settings for various groups either as a list or by requesting specific group highlight information. For example:

```
:highlight comment
```

in my edit session returns Figure 14-22.

The output shows how comments in this file will appear. The **xxx** is dark gray on this page, but on the screen it's blue. The **term=bold** output means that on a terminal incapable of color, comments will be shown in bold. **ctermfg=4** means that on a color terminal, such as an **xterm** on a color monitor, the foreground color for comments will be the matching DOS color dark blue. Finally, **guifg=Blue** means the GUI interface will display comments with the foreground color blue.

```
No Name ||[+]     09/02/2007 07:06:56 PM
:hi Identifier
Identifier      xxx term=underline ctermfg=6 guifg=DarkCya
Press ENTER or type command to continue
```

Figure 14-23. Highlight for identifiers

The DOS color scheme is a more restricted set of colors than modern
GUI sets. For the DOS colors, there are eight: black, red, green, yel
low, blue, magenta, cyan, and white. Each of these can be set for text
foreground or background and optionally can be defined as "bright," a
brighter color on the screen. Vim uses analogous mappings for defining
text colors in non-GUI windows, e.g., xterms.

GUI windows offer virtually unlimited color definitions. Vim lets you
define some colors with common names such as Blue, but you can also
define these colors with red, green, and blue values. The format is
#rrggbb where the # is literal, and rr, gg, and bb are hex numbers rep-
resenting the level of each color. For example, red could be defined with
#ff0000.

Use the highlight command to change settings for groups whose colors you don't like.
For example, we can find that identifiers in this file are dark cyan for our GUI interface,
as shown in the output in Figure 14-23.

```
:highlight identifier
```

We can redefine the color for identifiers with the command:

```
:highlight identifiers guifg=red
```

Now all identifiers on the screen are (a rather ugly) red. This kind of customization is
fairly inflexible: it applies to all file types and does not adapt to different backgrounds
or color schemes.

To see how many highlight definitions exist and what their values are, again use high
light:

```
:highlight
```

Figure 14-24 shows a small sample of the results from the highlight command.

Note how some lines contain full definitions (listing term, ctermfg, and so on), whereas
others receive their attributes from parent groups (e.g., String links back to Constant).

Overriding syntax files

In the previous section, we learned how to define syntax group attributes for all instances of a group. Suppose you want to change a group for only one or a few syntax
definitions. Vim lets you do this with the after directory. This is a directory in which

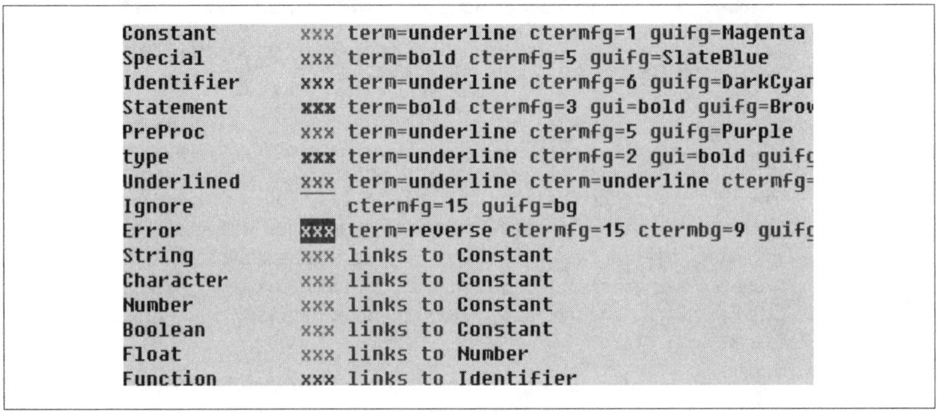

```
Constant        xxx term=underline ctermfg=1 guifg=Magenta
Special         xxx term=bold ctermfg=5 guifg=SlateBlue
Identifier      xxx term=underline ctermfg=6 guifg=DarkCyar
Statement       xxx term=bold ctermfg=3 gui=bold guifg=Brow
PreProc         xxx term=underline ctermfg=5 guifg=Purple
type            xxx term=underline ctermfg=2 gui=bold guifc
Underlined      xxx term=underline cterm=underline ctermfg=
Ignore              ctermfg=15 guifg=bg
Error           xxx term=reverse ctermfg=15 ctermbg=9 guifc
String          xxx links to Constant
Character       xxx links to Constant
Number          xxx links to Constant
Boolean         xxx links to Constant
Float           xxx links to Number
Function        xxx links to Identifier
```

Figure 14-24. Partial results from the highlight command

you can create any number of *after* syntax files that Vim will execute after the normal syntax file.

To do this, simply include highlight commands (or any processing commands—the notion of "after" processing is generic) in the specific file in a directory named after that is included in the runtimepath option. Now, when Vim sets up syntax highlighting rules for your file type, it will also execute your custom commands in the after file.

For example, let's apply a customization to XML files, which use the xml syntax. This means Vim loaded syntax definitions from a file in the syntax directory named xml.vim. As in the previous example, we want to define identifiers always to be red. So we create our own file named xml.vim in a directory named ~/.vim/after/syntax. In our xml.vim file we put the line:

```
highlight identifier ctermfg=red guifg=red
```

Before this customization works, we must ensure that ~/.vim/after/syntax is in the runtimepath path:

```
:set runtimepath+=~/.vim/after/syntax          In our .vimrc
```

To make the change permanent, of course, the line should go in our .vimrc file.

Now, whenever Vim loads syntax definitions for xml, it will override the definitions for *identifier* with our own customization.

Rolling Your Own

With the building blocks of the previous sections, we now have enough knowledge to write our own syntax files, simple as they might be. There are still many facets to learn before we can fully develop a syntax file.

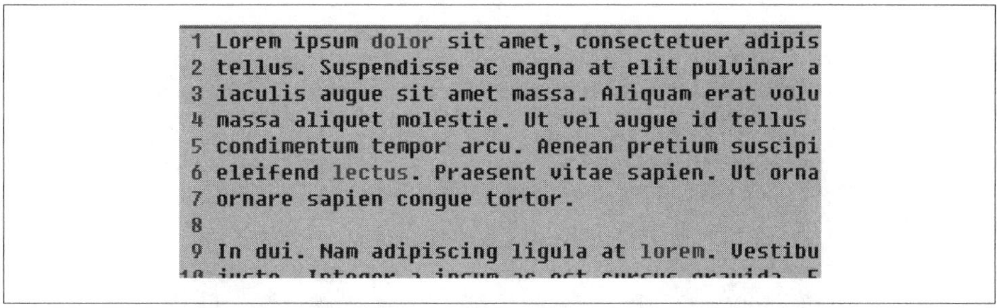

Figure 14-25. Latin file with keywords defined

We will incrementally build our own syntax file. Because syntax definitions can be extremely complex, let's consider something simple enough to be easily grasped, but complex enough to show its potential power.

Consider an excerpt from a generated Latin file, `loremipsum.latin`:

```
Lorem ipsum dolor sit amet, consectetuer adipiscing elit. Proin eget
tellus. Suspendisse ac magna at elit pulvinar aliquam. Pellentesque
iaculis augue sit amet massa. Aliquam erat volutpat. Donec et dui at
massa aliquet molestie. Ut vel augue id tellus hendrerit porta. Quisque
condimentum tempor arcu. Aenean pretium suscipit felis. Curabitur semper
eleifend lectus. Praesent vitae sapien. Ut ornare tempus mauris. Quisque
ornare sapien congue tortor.

In dui. Nam adipiscing ligula at lorem. Vestibulum gravida ipsum iaculis
justo. Integer a ipsum ac est cursus gravida. Etiam eu turpis. Nam laoreet
ligula mollis diam. In aliquam semper nisi. Nunc tristique tellus eu
erat. Ut purus. Nulla venenatis pede ac erat.

...
```

Create a new syntax by creating a new file of that syntax name, in this case `latin`. Its corresponding Vim file is `latin.vim`, which you can create in your personal Vim runtime directory, `$HOME/.vim`. Then, start your syntax definition simply by creating some keywords with the `syntax keyword` command. Choosing `lorem`, `dolor`, `nulla`, and `lectus` as our keywords, you can inaugurate the syntax file with the line:

```
syntax keyword identifier lorem dolor nulla lectus
```

There still isn't any syntax highlighting when you edit `loremipsum.latin`. More work needs to be done before highlighting is automatic. But for the time being, activate the syntax with the command:

```
:set syntax=latin
```

Because the `$HOME/.vim` directory is one of the directories in the `runtimepath` option, the text should now look something like Figure 14-25.

It is a little difficult to see, but the keywords you defined that are visible in this snapshot are dark gray instead of black, indicating a different color from the rest of the text. (The actual colors on the screen were black text with blue keywords.)

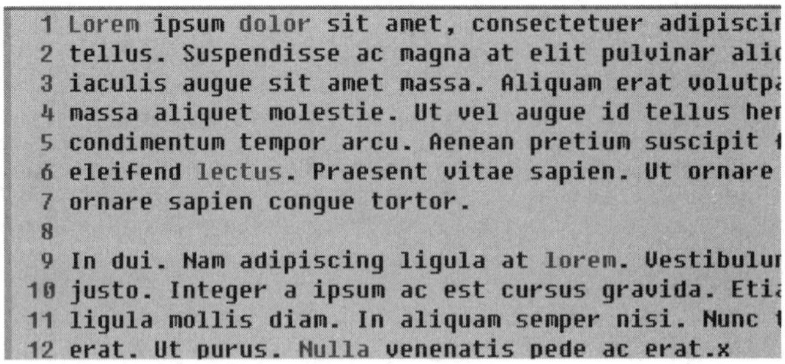

Figure 14-26. Latin file with keywords defined, ignoring case

You may have noticed that the first occurence of `Lorem` isn't highlighted. By default, syntax keywords are case-sensitive. Add the line at the top of our syntax file:

```
:syntax case ignore
```

and you should now see `Lorem` included as a highlighted keyword.

Before we try this again, let's make it all work automatically. After Vim tries to detect any file type, it optionally checks for other definitions, or even overriding definitions (which are not recommended), in a directory named `ftdetect` in your `runtimepath`. Therefore, create that directory under `$HOME/.vim` and create a file in it named `latin.vim` containing a single line:

```
au BufRead,BufNewFile *.latin set filetype=latin
```

This line tells Vim that any files with the suffix `.latin` are `latin` files, and therefore that Vim should execute the syntax file in `$HOME/.vim/syntax/latin.vim` when displaying them.

Now when you edit `loremipsum.latin`, you see Figure 14-26.

First, notice that the syntax was active right away, as Vim correctly detected your new syntax file type, `latin`. And keywords now match without any sensitivity to case.

For some more interesting extensions, define a `match` and assign it to group `Comment`. The `match` method uses a regular expression to define what is highlighted. For example, we will define all words beginning with s and ending with t to be `Comment` syntax (remember, this is just an example!). Our regular expression is: `\<s[^\t ]*t\>` (trust us). We also will define a region and highlight it as a `Number`. Regions are defined with a `start` and `end` regular expression.

Our region begins with `Suspendisse` and ends with `sapien\.`. To add even more of a twist, we decide that the keyword `lectus` is *contained* within our region. Our `latin.vim` syntax file now looks like:

```
syntax case ignore
syntax keyword identifier lorem dolor nulla lectus
syntax keyword identifier lectus  contained
```

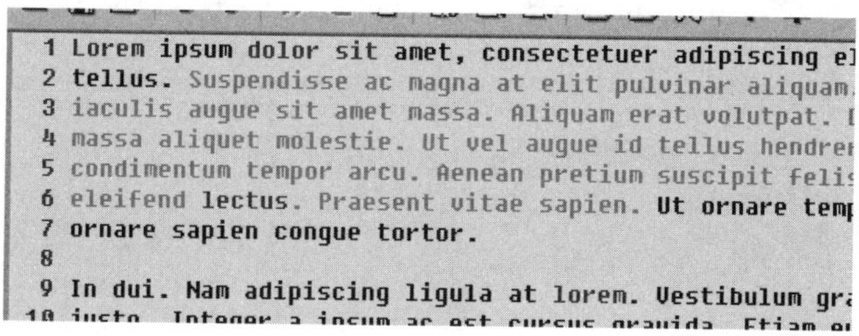

Figure 14-27. New latin syntax highlighting

```
syntax match comment /\<s[^\t ]*t\>/
syntax region number start=/Suspendisse/ end=/sapien\./ contains=identifier
```

Now, when we edit `loremipsum.latin`, we see Figure 14-27.

There are several things to notice, which you can see much more easily if you run the example and view the results in color:

- The new match highlights appear. On the first line, `sit` is highlighted in blue because it satisfies the regular expression for the `match`.

- The new region highlights appear. The entire section of the paragraph beginning with `Suspendisse` through `sapien.` is highlighted in purple (ick).

- The keywords are still highlighted as before.

- Within the highlighted region, the keyword `lectus` is still highlighted in green because we defined group `identifier` as `contained` and defined our region as `contains identifier`.

This example only begins to tap the rich powers of syntax highlighting. Although this particular example is somewhat useless, we hope that it demonstrates enough to convince you of its power and encourages you to experiment and create your own syntax definitions.

Compiling and Checking Errors with Vim

Vim isn't an Integrated Development Environment (IDE), but it tries to make life a little easier for programmers by incorporating compilation into the edit session and providing a quick and easy way to find and correct errors.

Additionally, Vim offers some convenience functions to track and navigate *locations* in your files. We discuss a simple example: the edit-compile-edit cycle using Vim's built-in features and some of its related commands and options, as well as the convenience functions. All of these depend on the same Vim `Quickfix List` window.

As a simple starting point, Vim lets you compile files using `make` each time you change one. Vim uses default behavior to manage the results of your build so that you can easily alternate between editing and compilation. Compilation errors appear in Vim's special Quickfix List window, where you can inspect, jump to, and correct errors.

For this topic we use a little C program that generates Fibonacci numbers. In its correct and compilable form, the code is:

```
# include <stdio.h>

int main(int argc, char *argv[])
  {
  /*
   * arg 1: starting value
   * arg 2: second value
   * arg 3: number of entries to print
   *
   */

  if (argc - 1 != 3)
    {
    printf ("Three command line args: (you used %d)\n", argc);
    printf ("usage: value 1, value 2, number of entries\n");
    return (1);
    }



  /* count = how many to print */
  int count = atoi(argv[3]);

  /* index = which to print */
  long int index;

  /* first and second passed in on command line */
  long int first, second;

  /* these get calculated */
  long int current, nMinusOne, nMinusTwo;

  first  = atoi(argv[1]);
  second = atoi(argv[2]);
  printf("%d fibonacci numbers with starting values: %d, %d\n", count, first,
      second);
  printf("====================================\n");

  /* print the first 2 from the starter values */
  printf("%d %04d\n", 1, first);
  printf("%d %04d  ratio (golden?) %.3f\n", 2, second, (double) second/first);

  nMinusTwo = first;
  nMinusOne = second;

  for (index=1; index<=count; index++)
    {
    current = nMinusTwo + nMinusOne;
    printf("%d %04d  ratio (golden?) %.3f\n",
```

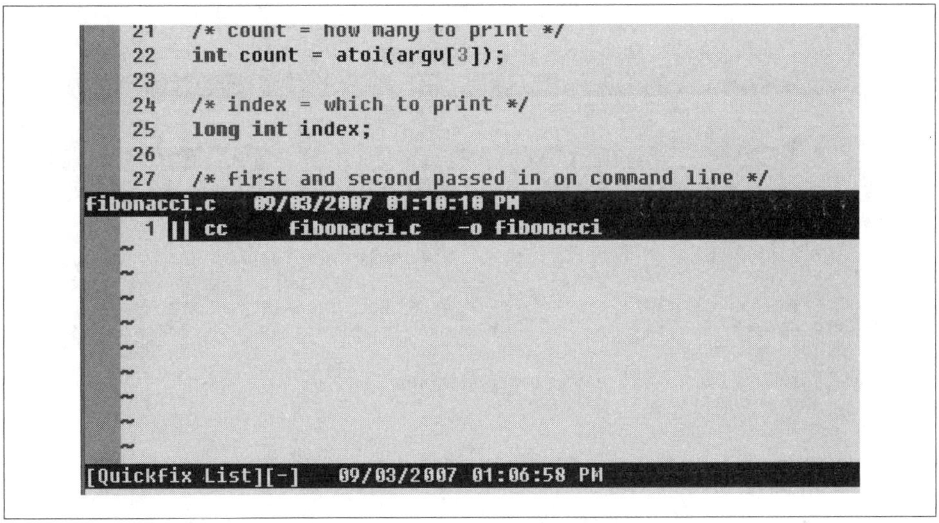

Figure 14-28. Quickfix List window after a clean compile

```
                index,
                current,
                (double) current/nMinusOne);
        nMinusTwo =  nMinusOne;
        nMinusOne = current;
        }
    }
```

From Vim, compile this program (assuming a filename of `fibonacci.c`) with the command:

```
:make fibonacci
```

By default, Vim passes the `make` command through to the external shell and captures the results in the special Quickfix List window. After compiling the previous code, the screen with the Quickfix List window looks something like Figure 14-28.

Next, we change enough lines in our program to introduce a healthy number of errors.

Change:

```
long int current, nMinusOne, nMinusTwo;
```

to the invalid declaration:

```
longish int current, nMinusOne, nMinusTwo;
```

Change:

```
nMinusTwo = first;
nMinusOne = second;
```

to misspelled variables `xfirst` and `xsecond`:

```
nMinusTwo = xfirst;
nMinusOne = xsecond;
```

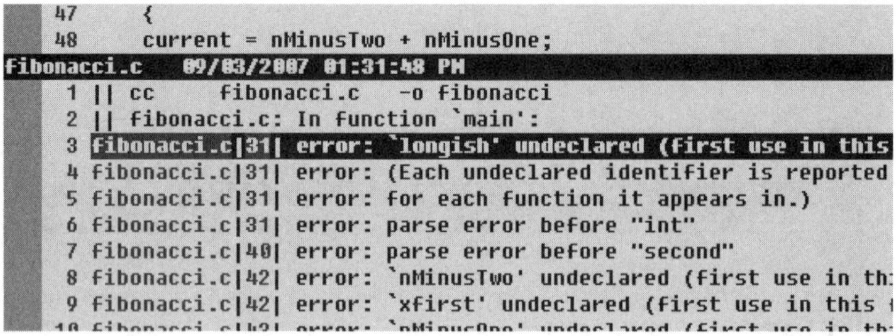

Figure 14-29. Quickfix List window after a compilation with errors

Change:

```
printf("%d %04d  ratio (golden?) %.3f\n", 2, second, (float) second/first);
```

to this, with missing commas:

```
printf("%d %04d  ratio (golden?) %.3f\n", 2 second (float) second/first);
```

Now recompile the program. Figure 14-29 shows what the Quickfix List window now contains.

Line 1 of the Quickfix List window shows the compile command executed. If there had been no errors, this would be the only line in the window. But because there are errors, line 3 begins the list of errors and their context.

Vim lists all errors in the Quickfix List window and lets you access the code, where errors are indicated in several ways. Vim starts with the convenience behavior by high-lighting the first error in the Quickfix List window. It then repositions the source file (scrolling if necessary) and places the cursor at the beginning of the source code line corresponding to the error.

As you fix errors, you can navigate to the next error in one of a couple ways: enter the command :cnext, or position the cursor over the error line in the Quickfix List window and press ENTER. Again, Vim scrolls the source file if necessary, and positions the cursor at the beginning of the offending source code line.

After you've made changes and are satisfied that you've corrected your errors, you're ready to begin the compile-edit cycle again using the same technique. If you have a standard developer's environment (which is almost always true for Unix/Linux machines), Vim's default behaviors will handle edit-compile-edit as described without any tweaking.

If Vim's defaults don't find a proper compile program, it has options you can use to define where utilities are located, to let you do your work. The details about programming environments and compilers are outside the scope of this discussion, but we present these Vim options as a starting point in case you need to play with your environment:

makeprg
> An option containing the name of the development environment's make or compile program.

:cnext, :cprevious
> Commands that move the cursor to *next* and *previous* error locations, as defined in the Quickfix List window, respectively.

:colder, :cnewer
> Vim remembers the last 10 lists of errors. These commands load the next *older* or next *newer* list of errors in the Quickfix List window. Each command takes an optional integer *n* to load the nth older or newer error list.

errorformat
> An option defining a format that Vim matches to find errors returned from a compile. Vim's built-in documentation gives much more detailed information on how this is defined, but the default almost always works. If you need to tune the option, view its details with:

> ```
> :help errorformat
> ```

More Uses for the Quickfix List Window

Vim also lets you build your own list of locations within files, specifying the locations through a grep-like syntax. The Quickfix List window returns the results you asked for in a format closely resembling the lines returned from the compilation process described earlier.

This feature is useful for such tasks as refactoring. As an example, we composed this manuscript in DocBook, a form similar to XML. At some point in the composition process we switched the notation for any occurence of "vim" from <emphasis> to <literal>. So, each occurence like:

```
<emphasis>vim</emphasis>
```

needed to be changed to:

```
<literal>vim</literal>
```

After executing this command:

```
:vimgrep /<emphasis>vim<\/emphasis>/ *.xml
```

the Quickfix List window contained the information shown in Figure 14-30.

Then it was a simple matter to navigate through all occurrences and quickly change to the new values.

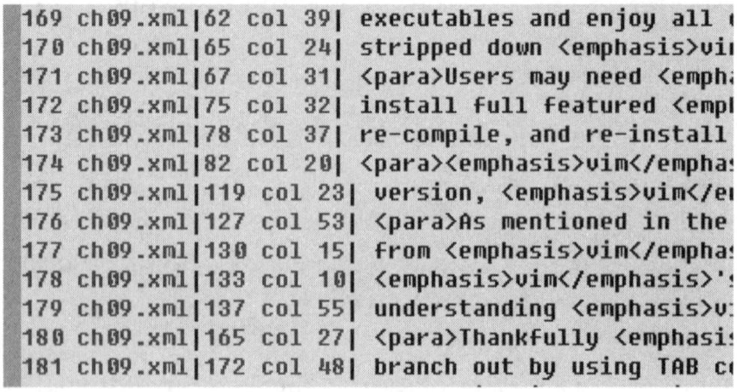

```
169 ch09.xml|62 col 39| executables and enjoy all
170 ch09.xml|65 col 24| stripped down <emphasis>vi
171 ch09.xml|67 col 31| <para>Users may need <empha
172 ch09.xml|75 col 32| install full featured <emp
173 ch09.xml|78 col 37| re-compile, and re-install
174 ch09.xml|82 col 20| <para><emphasis>vim</empha
175 ch09.xml|119 col 23| version, <emphasis>vim</e
176 ch09.xml|127 col 53| <para>As mentioned in the
177 ch09.xml|130 col 15| from <emphasis>vim</empha
178 ch09.xml|133 col 10| <emphasis>vim</emphasis>'
179 ch09.xml|137 col 55| understanding <emphasis>v
180 ch09.xml|165 col 27| <para>Thankfully <emphasi
181 ch09.xml|172 col 48| branch out by using TAB c
```

Figure 14-30. Quickfix List window after :vimgrep command

This example may seem to solve a problem more easily solved with this simple command:

```
:%s/<emphasis>vim<\/emphasis>/<literal>vim<\/literal>/g
```

But remember, vimgrep is more general and operates against multiple files. This is an example of what vimgrep does, not a definitive way to perform this task. In Vim, there are usually many ways to complete a task.

Some Final Thoughts on Vim for Writing Programs

We have looked at many powerful features in this chapter. Spend some time mastering these techniques and you'll gain great productivity. If you're a long-time **vi** user, you've already climbed one steep learning curve. The extra effort to learn Vim's additional features is worth a second learning curve.

If you're a programmer, we hope this chapter shows how much Vim offers for your programming tasks. We encourage you to try some of these features and even to extend Vim to your own needs. And maybe you will create extensions to give back to the Vim community. Now, go program!

Other Cool Stuff in Vim

Chapters 10 through 14 covered powerful Vim features and techniques we think you should know about to make effective use of the editor. This chapter takes a lighter look at Vim. It's a catch-all for some of the features that didn't fit into previous topics, ideas about editing and the Vim philosophy, and some fun things about Vim (not that the earlier chapters weren't fun!).

Editing Binary Files

Officially, Vim, like vi, is a *text* editor. But in pinch, Vim also lets you edit files containing data that is normally unreadable by humans.

Why would you ever want to edit a binary file? Aren't binary files binary for a reason? Aren't binary files typically generated by some application in a well-defined and specific format?

 While we enjoy Vim's binary editing feature, we do not present an in-depth discussion about potential serious issues to consider while editing binary files. For example, some binary files contain digital signatures or checksums to ensure file integrity. Editing these files risks damaging their integrity and could render them unusable. Therefore, do not consider this an endorsement of casual binary edits.

It's true that binary files are typically created by a computerized or analog process and are not intended to be edited manually. For example, digital cameras often store pictures in JPEG format, a compressed binary format for digital pictures. These are binary, but they have well-defined sections or blocks where standard information is stored (that is, they do if they're implemented according to specification). Digital pictures in JPEG format store picture meta-information (time of picture, resolution, camera settings, date, etc.) in reserved blocks separate from the compressed digital picture data. A practical application might use Vim's binary file editing feature to edit a directory of JPEG pictures to change all of the *year* fields in the "created" block to correct the picture's "date of creation" field.

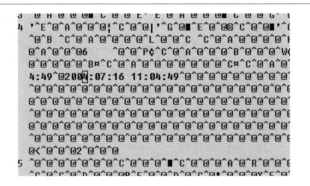

Figure 15-1. Editing a binary JPEG file

Figure 15-1 shows an editing session on a JPEG file. Notice how the cursor is positioned over the date field. You can directly edit information about this picture by changing these fields.

For power users familiar with a particular binary format, Vim can be extremely handy for making changes directly that might otherwise require tedious, repetitive access with other tools.

There are two main ways to edit binary files. You can set the `binary` option from the Vim command line:

```
set binary
```

or start Vim with the `-b` option.

To facilitate binary editing *and* protect Vim from damaging the file's integrity, Vim sets the following options accordingly:

- The `textwidth` and `wrapmargin` options are set to 0. This stops Vim from inserting spurious newline sequences into the file.

- The `modeline` and `expandtab` options are unset (`nomodeline` and `noexpandtab`). This stops Vim from expanding tabs to `shiftwidth` spaces, and prevents it from interpreting commands in a modeline, which potentially would set options that introduce unexpected and unwanted side effects.

 Be careful when moving from window to window, or buffer to buffer, when using binary mode. Vim uses entry and exit events to set and change options for switching buffers and windows, and you may confuse it into removing some of the protections just listed. We recommend a single-window, single-buffer session when editing binary files.

Digraphs: Non-ASCII Characters

Do you say that the *Messiah* is composed by George Frideric *Händel*, not George Frideric *Handel*? Do you think your *résumé* conveys a little more cachet than a *resume*? Use Vim's digraphs to enter special characters.

Even English-language text files occasionally need a special character, especially when making references to a globalized world. Text files in languages other than English need scads of special characters.

Vim lets you enter special characters in a number of ways, and two of them are relatively straightforward and intuitive. Both rely on defining a digraph through a prefix (CTRL-K) or the use of the BS (Backspace) key between two keyboard characters. (The other methods are more suited to entering characters by their raw numerical values, specified as decimal, hexadecimal, or octal numbers. While powerful, these methods do not lend themselves to easy mnemonics for digraphs.)

> The term *digraph* traditionally describes a two-letter combination that represents a single phonetic sound, such as the *ph* in "digraph" or "phonetic." Vim borrows the notion of "two-letter" combinations to describe its input mechanism for characters with special characteristics, typically accents or other markings such as the umlaut on *ä*. These special marks are properly called *diacritics*, or *diacritical marks*. In other words, Vim uses digraphs to create diacritics. Glad we could clear that up.

The first input method for diacritics is a three-character sequence consisting of CTRL-K, the base letter, and a punctuation character indicating the accent or mark to be added. For example, to create a c with a cedilla (ç), enter CTRL-K c,. To create an a with a grave accent (à), enter CTRL-K a!.

Greek letters can be created by a corresponding Latin letter followed by an asterisk (for instance, enter CTRL-K p* for a lowercase π). Russian letters can be created by a corresponding Latin letter followed by an equals sign or, in a few places, a percent sign. Use CTRL-K ?I (make sure to use a capital I) to enter an inverted question mark (¿) and CTRL-K ss to enter a German sharp S (ß).

To use Vim's second method, set the `digraph` option:

```
set digraph
```

Now create special characters by typing the first character of the two-character combination, then a backspace character (BS), and then the punctuation that creates a mark. Thus, enter ç through c BS , and à through a BS !.

Setting the `digraph` option doesn't preclude you from entering digraphs with the CTRL-K method. Consider using *only* the CTRL-K method if your typing is less than stellar.

SH	^A	1	SX	^B	2	EX	^C	3	ET	^D	4
UT	^K	11	FF	^L	12	CR	^M	13	SO	^N	14
NK	^U	21	SY	^U	22	EB	^W	23	CN	^X	24
US	^_	31	SP		32	Nb	#	35	DO	$	36
(!	{	123	!!	|	124	!)	}	125	'?	~	126
NL	■	133	SA	■	134	ES	■	135	HS	■	136
S3	■	143	DC	■	144	P1	'	145	P2	'	146
GC	■	153	SC	■	154	CI	■	155	ST	■	156
Pd	£	163	Cu	¤	164	Ye	¥	165	BB	¦	166
--	¬	173	Rg	®	174	'm	¯	175	DG	°	176
.M	·	183	',	¸	184	1S	¹	185	-o	º	186
A'	Á	193	A>	Â	194	A?	Ã	195	A:	Ä	196
E:	Ë	203	I!	Ì	204	I'	Í	205	I>	Î	206
O?	Õ	213	O:	Ö	214	*X	×	215	O/	Ø	216
ss	ß	223	a!	à	224	a'	á	225	a>	â	226
e'	é	233	e>	ê	234	e:	ë	235	i!	ì	236
o'	ó	243	o>	ô	244	o?	õ	245	o:	ö	246

Figure 15-2. Vim digraphs

Otherwise, you may find yourself inadvertently entering digraphs more often than you want as you backspace and type corrections.

Use the :digraph command to show all the default sequences; more verbose descriptions can be obtained with :help digraph-table. Figure 15-2 shows a partial list from the digraph command.

In the display, each digraph is represented by three columns. The display is a bit jumbled because Vim jams as many three-column combinations on each line as the screen permits. For each of the groups, column one shows the digraph's two-character combination, column two displays the digraph, and column three lists the decimal Unicode value for the digraph.

For your convenience, Table 15-1, lists the punctuation to use as the final character in the sequence to enter the most commonly needed accents and marks.

Table 15-1. How to enter accents and other marks

Mark	Character to enter as part of digraph
Acute accent (fiancé)	Apostrophe (')
Breve (publică)	Left parenthesis (
Caron (Dubček)	Less-than sign (<)
Cedilla (français)	Comma (,)
Circumflex or carot (português)	Greater-than sign (>)
Grave accent (voilà)	Exclamation point (!)
Macron (ātmā)	Hyphen (-)
Stroke (Søren)	Slash (/)
Tilde (señor)	Question mark (?)
Umlaut or diaeresis (Noël)	Colon (:)

Editing Files in Other Places

Thanks to seamless integration of network protocols, Vim lets you edit files on remote machines just as if they were local! If you simply specify a URL for a filename, Vim opens it in your window and writes your changes to it on the remote system (depending on your access rights). For instance, the following command edits a `.vimrc` file owned by user ehannah on the system mozart. The remote machine offers the SSH secure protocol on port 122 (this is a nonstandard port, providing additional security through obscurity):

```
$ vim scp://ehannah@mozart:122//home/ehannah/.vimrc
```

Because we're editing a file in ehannah's home directory on the remote machine, we can shorten the URL by using a simple filename. It's treated as a pathname relative to the user's home directory on the remote system:

```
$ vim scp://ehannah@mozart:122/.vimrc
```

Let's take apart the URL so you can learn how to build URLs for your particular environment:

scp:

> The first part, up to the colon, represents the transport protocol. In this example, the protocol is scp, a file copy protocol built on the Secure Shell (SSH) protocol. The following : is required.

//

> This introduces host information, which for most transport protocols takes the form [*user@*]*hostname*[*:port*].

ehannah@

> This is optional. For secure protocols such as scp, it specifies what user to log in as on the remote machine. When omitted, it defaults to your username on the local machine. When you are prompted for a password, you must enter the user's password on the remote machine.

mozart

> This is the remote machine's symbolic name, and it can also be specified as a numeric address, e.g., `192.168.1.106`.

:122

> This is optional and specifies the port on which the protocol is provided. The colon separates the port number from the preceding hostname. All standard protocols use well-known ports, so this element of the URL can be omitted if the standard port is used. In this example, 122 in *not* the standard port for the scp protocol, and because the administrator of the mozart system has chosen to provide the service on 122, this specification is required.

//home/ehannah/.vimrc

> This is the file on the remote machine we want to edit. We start with two slashes because we're specifying an absolute path. A relative path or simple filename requires only a single slash to separate it from the preceding hostname. A relative path is relative to the home directory of the user that you logged in as. So, in the example a relative path would be relative to ehannah's home directory, e.g., /home/ehannah.

Here is a partial list of the supported protocols:

- *ftp:* and *sftp:* (regular FTP and secure FTP)
- *scp:* (secure remote copy over SSH)
- *http:* (file transfer using standard browser protocol)
- *dav:* (a relatively new but popular proposed open standard for web transfer)
- *rcp:* (remote copy)

What we've described so far is enough to allow remote editing, but the process may not be as transparent as editing a file locally. That is, because of the intervening requirement to move data from remote hosts, you may be prompted for passwords to do your work. This can become tedious if you are used to periodically writing your file to disk while editing, as each of the "writes" is interrupted to prompt you to enter a password to complete the transaction.

All of the transport protocols in the preceding list allow you to configure the service to allow password-free access, but the details vary. Use the service's documentation for specific protocol details and configurations.

Navigating and Changing Directories

If you've used Vim a lot, you may have accidentally discovered that you can view a directory and move through it using keystrokes similar to those used with files.

Let's consider a directory containing many .c files, ex-050325 (this happens to be the directory containing the compilable source for the original vi editor). Edit ex-050325 with:

```
$ vim ex-050325
```

Figure 15-3 is a partial screenshot of something similar to what you might see.

Vim displays three types of information: introductory comments (preceded by equals signs), directories (displayed with trailing slashes), and files. Each directory or file is on its own line.

There are many ways to use this feature, but with little effort you can be immediately and intuitively productive with standard Vim motion commands (e.g., w to move to the

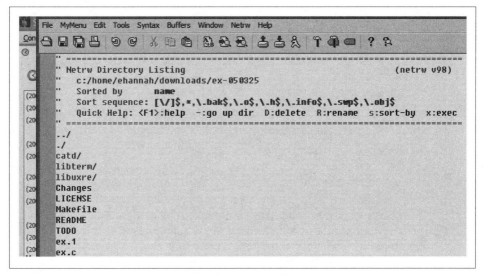

Figure 15-3. Vim "editing" the ex-050325 directory

next word, j or the down arrow to jump down one line) and by clicking the mouse over entries. Some particular features of directory mode include:

- When the cursor is positioned over a directory name, move to that directory by pressing the ENTER key.
- If the cursor is over a filename, pressing ENTER edits that file.

 If you want to keep the directory window around for further work in that directory, edit the file under the cursor by typing o, and Vim will split the window, editing the file in the newly created window. (This is also true for moving to another directory when the cursor is over a directory name; Vim splits the window and "edits" the directory to which you moved in the new window.)

- You can delete and rename files and directories. Rename a file or directory by typing capital R. Probably a little counterintuitively, Vim creates a command-line prompt with which you perform the rename. It should look something like Figure 15-4.

  To complete the rename, edit the second command-line argument.

  Deleting a file works similarly. Simply position the cursor over the filename you want to delete and type capital D. Vim prompts you with a verification dialog to delete the file. As with the rename function, Vim prompts for verification in the command-line area of the screen.

- One really nice advantage of editing directories is quick access to files through Vim's search function. For example, suppose you want to edit the file

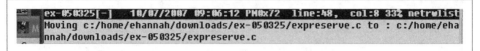

Figure 15-4. Prompt for rename in "edit directory"

`expreserve.c` in the `ex-050325` directory described earlier. To quickly navigate to and edit this file, you can search for part or all of the filename:

```
/expreserve.c
```

and with the cursor over that filename, press ENTER or o.

> When you read the online help for directory editing, you will see that Vim describes it as part of the entire suite of editing files with network protocols, which was described in the previous section. We have made directory editing its own topic in this chapter because it is useful, and it could get lost in the large volume of detail about network protocol editing.

Backups with Vim

Vim helps protect you from unintentionally losing data by letting you make a backup of the files you edit. For an edit session that has gone terribly wrong, this can be useful because you can recover your previous file.

Backups are controlled by the settings of two options: `backup` and `writebackup`. Where and how backups are created are controlled by four other options: `backupskip`, `backup copy`, `backupdir`, and `backupext`.

If both the `backup` and `writebackup` options are off (i.e., `nobackup` and `nowritebackup`), Vim makes no backup files for your edit sessions. If `backup` is on, Vim deletes any old backups and creates a backup for the current file. If `backup` is off and `writebackup` is on, Vim creates a backup file for the duration of the edit session and deletes the backup afterward.

The `backupdir` is a comma-separated list of directories in which Vim creates backup files. For example, if you want backups to always be created in your system's temporary directory, set `backupdir` to `"C:\TEMP"` for Windows or `"/tmp"` for Unix and Linux.

If you'd like to always create a backup of your file in the current directory, you can specify "." (a dot) as your backup directory. Or you could try to create a backup in a hidden subdirectory first if it exists, and then in the current directory if the hidden subdirectory doesn't exist. Do this by defining `backupdir`'s value to be something such as "./.mybackups,." (the single dot at the end denotes the file's current directory). This is a flexible option that supports many strategies for defining backup locations.

If you want to make backups for your edit sessions but not for all files, use the `backupskip` option to define a comma-separated list of patterns. Vim will not make a backup of any file matching one of the patterns. For example, you may never want to back up any files edited in the /tmp or /var/tmp directories. Prevent Vim from doing so by setting `backupskip` to "/tmp/*,/var/tmp/*".

By default, Vim creates your backup with the same filename as the original and the suffix ~ (a tilde). This is a fairly safe suffix, because filenames ending in that character are rare. Change the suffix to your preference with the `backupext` option. For example, if you want your backups to have the suffix .bu, set `backupext` to the string ".bu".

Finally, the `backupcopy` option defines *how* a backup copy is created. We recommend setting this option to `"auto"` to let Vim make a calculated choice of the best method for the backup.

HTML Your Text

Have you ever needed to present your code or text to a group? Have you ever tried to do a code review but were using someone else's Vim configuration and couldn't figure it out? Consider converting your text or code to HTML and viewing it from a browser.

Vim provides three methods to create an HTML version of your text. They all create a new buffer with the same name as the original file and the suffix .html Vim splits the current session window and displays the HTML version of the file in the new window:

gvim *"Convert to HTML"*
> This is the friendliest method, and is built into the gvim graphical editor (described in Chapter 13). Open the Syntax menu in gvim and select "Convert to HTML."

2html.vim *script*
> This is the underlying script invoked by the "Convert to HTML" menu option described in the previous item. Invoke it through the command:

```
:runtime!syntax/2html.vim
```

> It doesn't accept a range; it converts the whole buffer.

TOhtml *command*

This is more flexible than the `2html.vim` script, because you can specify an exact range of lines you want to convert. For instance, to convert lines 25 through 44 of a buffer, enter:

```
:25,44TOhtml
```

One advantage of using `gvim` for HTML conversion is that the GUI lets it accurately detect colors and create correct corresponding HTML directives. These methods still work in a non-GUI context, but the results are less assured to be accurate and may not be very useful.

It's up to you to manage the newly created file. Vim does not save it for you; it merely creates a buffer. We recommend providing a management policy to save and synchronize HTML versions of your text files. For example, you could create some autocommands to trigger the creation and saving of your HTML files.

The saved HTML file can be viewed in any web browser. Some people may not be familiar with ways to open files on the local system in their browsers. It's quite easy, though: virtually all browsers offer an Open File menu option in the File menu and display a file selection dialog to let you navigate to the folder containing the HTML file. If you plan on using this feature on a regular basis, we recommend building up a collection of bookmarks for all of your files.

What's the Difference?

Changes between different versions of a file are often subtle, and a tool that lets you view precise differences at a glance could save hours of work. Vim integrates the well known Unix `diff` command into a very sophisticated visualization interface invoked through its `vimdiff` command.

There are two equivalent ways to invoke this feature: as a standalone command and as an option to Vim:

```
$ vimdiff old_file new_file
$ vim -d old_file new_file
```

Typically, the first file to be compared is an old version of a file, and the second is a newer version, but that is by convention only. Indeed, it's possible to make a case for reversing the order.

Figure 15-5 shows an example of `vimdiff` output. Because of limited real estate, we've squeezed the width and turned off Vim's `wrap` option to allow illustration of the differences.

```
 4 # Know what <block> terminal is on it+    4 # Know what terminal is on it. The c
 5 # terminal are the lowest common deno+   5 # terminal are the lowest common denor
 6 # The last one, "other", is like unkn+   6 # The last one, "other", is like unknc
 7 # that insists that a "real" unknown +   7 # that insists that a "real" unknown t
 8 <block>                                  8 #
 9                                          9
10 dumb:\                                  10 dumb:\
11 +-- 15 lines: :am:\-------------------+ 11 +-- 15 lines: :am:\---------------
26          :co#132:li#66:\              26          :co#132:li#66:\
27          :bl=^G:cr=^M:do=^J:ff=^L:le=^+ 27          :bl=^G:cr=^M:do=^J:ff=^L:le=^
28                                         28
29 #### ANSI terminals and terminal emul+ 29 #### ANSI terminals and terminal emula
30 #                                        30 #
31 # See near the end of this file for d+ 31 # See near the end of this file for de
32 # Don't mess with these entries! Lot+  32 # Don't <block>mess with these entries! L
33 #                                        33 #
34 # This section lists entries in a lea+ 34 # This section lists entries in a leas
35 # if you're in doubt about what `ANSI+ 35 # if you're in doubt about what `ANSI
36 # order and back off from the first t+ 36 # order and back off from the first th
37                                         37
38 # (ansi: changed ":pt:" to ":it#8:" -+ 38 # (ansi: changed ":pt:" to ":it#8:" --
39 ansi-mini|any ansi terminal with pess+ 39 ansi-mini|any ansi terminal with pessi
40          :am:bs:\                      40          :am:bs:\
41          :co#80:it#8:li#24:\           ----------------------------------------
42          :ce=\E[K:cl=\E[;H\E[2J:cm=\E[+ ----------------------------------------
43          :ho=\E[H:le=\E[D:nd=\E[C:up=\+ 41          :ho=\E[H:le=\E[D:nd=\E[C:up=\E
44                                         42
45 # Color controls corresponding to the+ 43 # Color controls corresponding to the
```

Figure 15-5. vimdiff results

Though the figure does not convey the full impact of the visual content (particularly because colors are reduced to gray), it shows some key characteristic behaviors:

- On line 4, you can see a dark block on the left line that isn't on the right line. This is a highlighted word indicating a difference between the two lines. Similarly, on line 32, the righthand line contains a highlighted word that is not on the left.

- On line 11 of both sides, Vim has created a 15-line *fold*. These 15 lines in both files are identical, so Vim folds them to maximize useful "diff" information on the screen.

- Lines 41–42 on the left are highlighted, whereas in the corresponding positions on the right, strings of hyphens (-) indicate that the lines are missing. The line numbering differs from this point on, because the right side has two lines fewer, but corresponding lines in the two files still line up horizontally.

The `vimdiff` feature comes with all Unix-like Vim installations because the `diff` command is a Unix standard. Non-Unix Vim installations should come with Vim's own version of `diff`. Vim allows drop-in replacements of `diff` commands as long as they create standard `diff` output.

The `diffexpr` variable defines the replacement expression for the default `vimdiff` behavior and is typically implemented as a script that operates on the following variables:

`v:fname_in`
    The first input file to be compared

```
v:fname_new
```
> The second file to be compared

```
v:fname_out
```
> A file that captures the `diff` output

Undoing Undos

Beyond the convenience of undoing an arbitrary number of edits, Vim offers an interesting twist called *branching* undos.

To use this feature, first decide how much control you want over undoing edits. Use the `undolevels` option to define the number of undoable changes you can make in an edit session. The default is 1,000, which is probably more than enough for most users. If you want `vi` compatibility, set `undolevels` to zero:

```
:set undolevels=0
```

In `vi`, the undo command `u` is basically a toggle between the file's current state and its most recent change. The first *undo* reverts to the state before the last change. The next *undo* redoes the undone change. Vim behaves quite differently, and therefore the commands are implemented differently.

Instead of toggling the most recent change, repeated invocations of Vim's undo rolls back the state of the file through the most recent changes, in order, for as many changes as defined by the `undolevels` option. Because the undo command `u` only moves backward, we need a command to roll forward and "redo" changes. Vim does this with the redo command, `:redo`, or the CTRL-R key. The CTRL-R key accepts a numeric prefix to redo several changes at once.

When rolling forward and backward through changes with the redo (CTRL-R) and undo (u) commands, Vim maintains a map of the file's state and knows when the last possible undo has been performed. When all possible undos are done, Vim resets the file's *modified* status, which allows quitting without the ! suffix. Although this is a modest benefit for general user interaction, it is more useful for behind-the-scenes scripting where the modified state of the file is important.

For most users, simply undoing and redoing changes is sufficient. But consider a more complex scenario. What if you make seven changes to a file, and undo three? So far, so good, nothing unusual to consider. But now, suppose that after undoing three out of seven changes, you then make a change different from the next forward change in Vim's collection of changes? Vim defines that point in the change history as a *branch* from which different paths of changes occur. With that path you can now move back and forth chronologically, with the added twist that at a branch point you can move forward along any of the different paths of recorded changes.

For more complete descriptions of how to navigate changes as a tree, use Vim's help command:

```
:help usr_32.txt
```

Now, Where Was I?

Most text editors start editing files at line 1, column 1. That is, each time the editor is started, the file is loaded and editing begins from line 1. If you edit a file many times, progressing through it, you would find it more convenient to begin an edit session where the last one ended. Vim lets you do just that.

There are two different methods to save edit session information for future uses: the `viminfo` option and the `mksession` command.

The viminfo Option

Vim uses the `viminfo` option to define what, how, and where to save edit session information. The option is a string with comma-delimited parameters that tell Vim how much information to save and where to save it. Some of `viminfo`'s suboptions are defined by the following:

<n

>   Tells Vim to save lines for each register, up to a maximum of *n* lines.

>   If you do not specify any value for this option, *all* lines are saved. While at first this may seem to be the normal desire, consider whether you commonly edit very large files and make large changes to those files. For example, if you commonly edit a 10,000-line file and delete all lines (possibly to pare it down from rapid growth caused by some external application) and then save it, all 10,000 lines get saved in the `viminfo` file for that entry. If you do this often for many files, the `viminfo` file will grow very large. You may then notice long delays when starting Vim, even for files not related to the large file, because Vim must process the `viminfo` file each time it starts up.
>
>   We recommend specifying some sane but useful limit. This author uses 50.

/n

>   The number of search pattern history items to be saved. If not specified, Vim uses the value in the `history` option.

:n

>   The maximum number of commands from the command-line history to save. If not specified, Vim uses the value in the `history` option.

'n

> The maximum number of files for which Vim maintains information. If you define the `viminfo` option, this parameter is required.

Here is what Vim saves in the `viminfo` file:

- Command-line history
- Search string history
- Input-line history
- Registers
- File marks (e.g., a mark created by `mx` is saved and can be moved to when re-editing the file by typing `'x`)
- Last search and substitute patterns
- Buffer list
- Global variables

This option is really handy for sustaining continuity across edit sessions. For example, if you edit a large file in which you are changing a pattern, the search pattern is remembered as well as where the cursor is positioned in the file. To continue searching in a new session, you need only type `n` to move to the next occurrence of the search pattern.

The mksession Command

Vim saves all edit information specific to a session with its `mksession` command. The `sessionoptions` option contains a comma-separated string specifying which components of a session to save. This way of saving edit session information is much more comprehensive but much more specific than `viminfo`. Saving session information this way is specific to all of the files, buffers, windows, etc. in the current edit session, and `mksession` saves the information so that the entire session can be reconstructed. All of the files being edited and all of the settings for all options, even window sizes, are saved so that reloading the information brings back an exact recreation of the session. Contrast this with `viminfo`, which only restores edit information on a per-file basis.

To save a session this way, enter:

    :mksession [*filename*]

where *filename* specifies a file in which to save the session information. Vim creates a script file that, when executed later with the **source** command, reconstructs the session. (The default filename, if none was specified, is `Session.vim`.). So, if you save a session with the command:

    :mksession mysession.vim

you could later reestablish the session with the command:

```
:source mysession.vim
```

Here is what you can save from a session, and the parameter in the `sessionoptions` option to save it:

`blank`
> Empty windows

`buffers`
> Hidden and unloaded buffers

`curdir`
> The current directory

`folds`
> Manually created folds, opened/closed folds, and local fold options

 It wouldn't make any sense to save anything but manually created folds. Automatically created folds will be automatically recreated!

`globals`
> Global variables, which start with an uppercase letter and contain at least one lowercase letter

`help`
> The help window

`localoptions`
> Options defined locally to a window

`options`
> Options set by `:set`

`resize`
> Size of the Vim window

`sesdir`
> The directory in which the session file is located

`slash`
> Backslashes in filenames replaced with forward slashes

`tabpages`
> All tab pages

 If you do not specify this in the `sessionoptions` string, only the current tab session is saved as a standalone entity. This gives you the flexibility of defining sessions at either the tab level or globally across all tabs.

unix
> Unix end-of-line format

winpos
> Position of Vim window on the screen

winsize
> Size of buffer windows on the screen

So, for example, if you want to save a session to retain all information for all buffers, all folds, global variables, all options, window size, and window position, you would define the `sessionoptions` option with:

```
:set sessionoptions=buffers,folds,globals,options,resize,winpos
```

What's My Line (Size)?

Vim allows lines of virtually unlimited lengths. You can have them either wrap onto multiple screen lines, so you can see them all without horizontal scrolling, or you can display the beginning of each line on one screen line and scroll to the right to see hidden parts.

If you prefer one line of text per screen line, turn off the `wrap` option:

```
set nowrap
```

With `nowrap`, Vim displays as many characters as the screen width permits. Think of the screen as a view port or window through which the wide line is viewed. For example, a 100-character line contains 20 characters too many for a screen that is 80 columns wide. Depending on what character is displayed in the screen's first column, Vim determines which characters in the 100-character line are not displayed. For example, if the screen's first column is the line's 5th character, characters 1–4 are to the left of the visible screen and therefore invisible, that is, not displayed. Characters 5–84 are visible in the screen, and the remaining characters from 85–100 are to the right of the screen and are also invisible.

Vim manages how the line is displayed as you move left and right through the long line. Vim shifts the line left and right a minimum of `sidescroll` characters. You can set its value as follows:

```
set sidescroll=n
```

where n is the number of columns to scroll. We recommend setting `sidescroll` to 1, because modern PCs easily provide the processing power necessary to smoothly shift the screen one column at a time. If your screen slows down and response times lag, you may need to bump the value to something higher to minimize the screen redraws.

The `sidescroll` value defines a *minimum* shift. As you probably expect, Vim shifts far enough to complete any motion commands. For example, typing `w` moves the cursor to the next word in the line. However, Vim's treatment of the movement is a bit tricky.

If the next word is partially visible (on the right), Vim moves to the first character of that word but does not shift the line. The next `w` command will shift the line to the left far enough to position the cursor over the first character of the next word, but only far enough to expose this first character.

You can control this behavior with the `sidescrolloff` option. `sidescrolloff` defines the minimum number of columns to maintain to the right and left of the cursor. So, for example, if you defined `sidescrolloff` to be 10, Vim maintains at least 10 characters of context as the cursor nears either side of the screen. Now when you move left and right on a line, your cursor will never get closer than (in this case) 10 columns from either side of the screen, as Vim shifts enough text into view to maintain that context. This is probably a better way to configure Vim in `nowrap` mode.

Vim provides convenient visual cues with the `listchar` option. `listchar` defines how to display characters when Vim's `list` option is set. Vim also provides two settings in this option that control whether to use characters to indicate if there are more characters to the left or right of the visible screen for long lines. For example:

```
set listchars=extends:>
set listchars+=precedes:<
```

tells Vim to display a `<` in column 1 if a long line contains more characters to the left of the visible screen, and a `>` in the last column to indicate there are more characters to the right of the visible screen. Figure 15-6 shows an example.

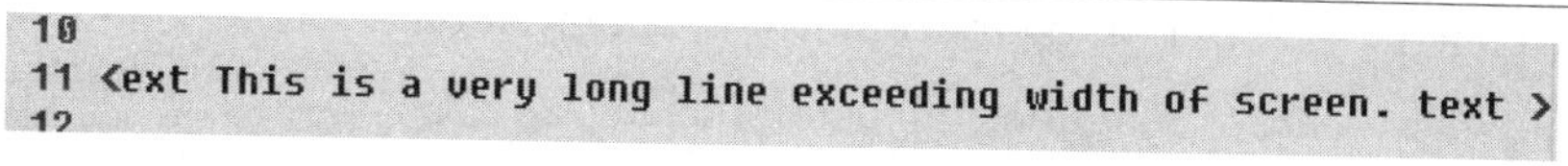

```
10
11 <ext This is a very long line exceeding width of screen. text >
12
```

Figure 15-6. A long line in nowrap mode

In contrast, if you prefer to see a whole line without scrolling, tell Vim to wrap the lines with the `wrap` option:

```
set wrap
```

Now the line appears as in Figure 15-7.

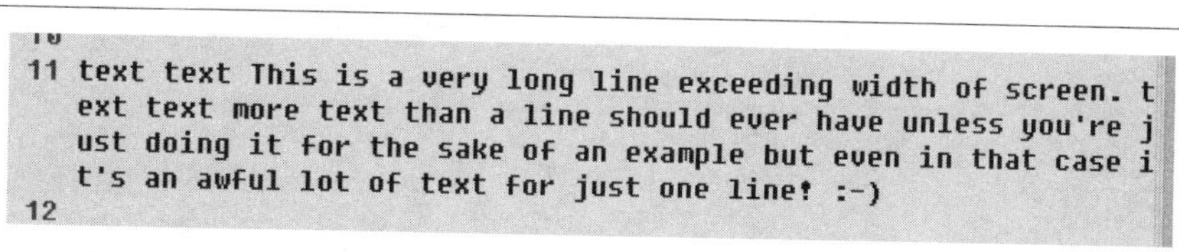

```
10
11 text text This is a very long line exceeding width of screen. t
   ext text more text than a line should ever have unless you're j
   ust doing it for the sake of an example but even in that case i
   t's an awful lot of text for just one line! :-)
   12
```

Figure 15-7. A long line in wrap mode

Very long lines that can't be entirely displayed on the screen are displayed with the single character `@` in the first position, until the cursor and file are positioned in such a way that the line can be displayed completely. The line in Figure 15-7 appears as shown in Figure 15-8 when it is near the bottom of the screen.

Figure 15-8. Long line indicator

Abbreviations of Vim Commands and Options

There are so many commands and options in Vim that we recommend learning them by name first. Almost all commands and options (at least any that have more than a few characters) have some associated short form. These can save time, but *be sure* you know what you're abbreviating! This author has had some embarrassing and unexpected results using short forms thought to be one thing that turned out to be something quite different.

As you become more experienced and develop your favorite subset of Vim commands and options, using some of the abbreviated forms for commands and options saves time. Vim typically tries for Unix-like abbreviations for options and allows for the shortest unique initial substring for commands' abbreviations.

Some abbreviations for common commands include:

n	next
prev	previous
q	quit
se	set
w	write

Some abbreviations for common options include:

ai	autoindent
bg	background
ff	fileformat
ft	filetype
ic	ignorecase
li	list
nu	number
sc	showcommand (*not* showcase)
sm	showmatch

```
sw    shiftwidth

wm    wrapmargin
```

Short forms for commands and options save time when you know your commands and options well. But for scripting and setting up sessions with commands in your .vimrc or .gvimrc files, you're more likely to save time in the long run by sticking with full command and option names. Your configuration file and scripts are easier to read and debug when you use full names.

 Note that this is not the approach taken with the suite of Vim script files (syntax, autoindent, colorscheme, etc.) in the Vim distribution, though we take no issue with their approach. We just recommend, for ease of managing your own scripts, that you stay with full names.

A Few Quickies (Not Necessarily Vim-Specific)

We now offer several techniques—some of which are offered by basic vi as well as Vim—that are worth remembering and having handy:

A quick swap
> A common typing error is to enter two characters in the wrong order. Position the cursor over the first wayward character and type xp (delete character, put character).

Another quick swap
> Got two lines you'd rather swap? Position the cursor on the top line, and type ddp (delete line, put line after current line).

Quick help
> Don't forget about Vim's built-in help. A quick tap on the F1 function key splits your screen and displays the introduction to the online help.

What was that great command I used?
> In its simplest form, Vim lets you access recently executed commands by using the arrow keys in the command line. Moving up and down with the arrow keys, Vim displays recent commands, any one of which you may edit. Whether or not you edit a command from Vim's history, you can execute the command by pressing the ENTER key.

> You can get even more sophisticated by invoking Vim's built-in command history editing. Do this by entering CTRL-F on the command line. A small "command" window opens up (with the default height of 7) in which you can navigate with normal Vim motion commands. You can search as if in a normal Vim buffer, and make changes.

In the command edit window, you can easily find a recent command, modify it if necessary, and execute it by pressing ENTER. You can write the buffer to a filename of your choice, to record the command history for future reference.

A bit of humor

Try entering the command:

```
:help sure
```

and read Vim's reply.

More Resources

Here are two links for HTML renditions of Vim's built-in help for the two most recent major Vim releases:

Vim 6.2
   http://www.vim.org/htmldoc/help.html

Vim 7
   http://vimdoc.sourceforge.net/htmldoc/usr_toc.html

Additionally, *http://vimdoc.sourceforge.net/vimfaq.html* is a Vim Frequently Asked Questions list. It doesn't link questions to answers, but it is all on one page. We recommend scrolling down to the section with the answers and scanning from there.

The official Vim page used to host tips on Vim, but because of problems with spammers, the administrators moved the tips to a wiki where spam is more easily managed. That wiki is here: *http://vim.wikia.com/wiki/Category:Integration*.

Other vi Clones

Part III covers other popular clones of **vi** that have grown up in parallel with Vim. This part contains the following chapters:

- Chapter 16, *nvi: New vi*
- Chapter 17, *Elvis*
- Chapter 18, *vile: vi Like Emacs*

nvi: New vi

nvi is short for "new vi." It was developed initially at the University of California at Berkeley (UCB), home of the famous Berkeley Software Distribution (BSD) versions of Unix. It was used for writing this chapter.

Author and History

The original vi was developed at UCB in the late 1970s by Bill Joy, then a computer science graduate student, and later a founder and vice president of Sun Microsystems.

Prior to nvi, Bill Joy first built ex, by starting with and heavily enhancing the sixth edition ed editor. The first enhancement was open mode, done with Chuck Haley. Between 1976 and 1979, ex evolved into vi. Mark Horton then came to Berkeley, added macros "and other features,"[*] and did much of the labor on vi to make it work on a large number of terminals and Unix systems. By 4.1 BSD (1981), the vi editor already had essentially all of the features we have described in Part I of this book.

Despite all of the changes, vi's core was (and is) the original Unix ed editor. As such, it was code that could not be freely distributed. By the early 1990s, when they were working on 4.4 BSD, the BSD developers wanted a version of vi that could be freely distributed in source code form.

Keith Bostic of UCB started with elvis 1.8,[†] which was a freely distributable vi clone, and began turning it into a "bug for bug compatible" clone of vi. nvi also complies with the POSIX Command Language and Utilities Standard (IEEE P1003.1) where it makes sense to do so.

Although no longer affiliated with UCB, Keith Bostic continues to distribute nvi. The current version at the time of this writing is nvi 1.79.

---

[*] From the nvi reference manual. Unfortunately, it does not say which features.

[†] Although little or no original elvis code is left.

nvi is important because it is the "official" Berkeley version of vi. It is part of 4.4BSD-Lite II, and it is the vi version used on the various popular BSD variants, such as NetBSD and FreeBSD.

Important Command-Line Arguments

In a pure BSD environment, nvi is installed under the names ex, vi, and view. Typically they are all links to the same executable, and nvi looks at how it is invoked to determine its behavior. (Unix vi works this way, too.) It allows the Q command from vi mode to switch it into ex mode. The view variant is like vi, except that the readonly option is set initially.

nvi has a number of command-line options. The most useful are described here:

-c *command*

> Execute *command* upon startup. This is the POSIX version of the historical +command syntax, but nvi is not limited to positioning commands. (The old syntax is also accepted.)

-F

> Don't copy the entire file when starting to edit. This may be faster, but it allows the possibility of someone else changing the file while you're working on it.

-r

> Recover specified files, or if no files are listed on the command line, list all the files that can be recovered.

-R

> Start in read-only mode, setting the readonly option.

-s

> Enter batch (script) mode. This is only for ex and is intended for running editing scripts. Prompts and nonerror messages are disabled. This is the POSIX version of the historic "-" argument; nvi supports both.

-S

> Run with the secure option set, disallowing access to external programs.‡

-t *tag*

> Start editing at the specified *tag*.

-w *size*

> Set the initial window size to *size* lines.

---

‡ As with anything labeled "secure," blind trust is usually inappropriate. Keith Bostic says, though, that you *can* trust nvi's secure option.

Online Help and Other Documentation

nvi comes with quite comprehensive printable documentation. In particular, it comes with troff source, formatted ASCII, and formatted PostScript for the following documents:

The vi reference manual
> The reference manual for nvi. This manual describes all of the nvi command-line options, commands, options, and ex commands.

The vi manpage
> The manpage for nvi.

The vi tutorial
> This document is a tutorial introduction to editing with vi.

The ex reference manual
> The reference manual for ex. This manual is the original one for ex; it is a bit out-of-date with respect to the facilities in nvi.

Also included are ASCII files that document some of the nvi internals and provide a list of features that should be implemented, along with files that can be used as an online tutorial to vi.

The online help built into nvi is minimal, consisting of two commands, :exusage and :viusage. These commands provide one-line summaries of each ex and vi command. This is usually sufficient to remind you about how something works, but not very good for learning about new or obscure features in nvi.

You can give a command as an argument to the :exusage and :viusage commands, in which case nvi will display the help just for that command. nvi prints one line explaining what the command does, and a one-line summary of the command's usage.

Initialization

If the -s or "-" options have been specified, then nvi will bypass all initializations. Otherwise, nvi performs the following steps:

1. Read and execute the file /etc/vi.exrc. It must be owned either by root or by you.

2. Execute the value of the NEXINIT environment variable if it exists; otherwise, use EXINIT if it exists. Only one will be used, not both. Bypass executing $HOME/.nexrc or $HOME/.exrc.

3. If $HOME/.nexrc exists, read and execute it. Otherwise, if $HOME/.exrc exists, read and execute it. Only one will be used.

4. If the exrc option has been set, then look for and execute either ./.nexrc if it exists, or ./.exrc. Only one will be used.

nvi will not execute any file that is writable by anyone other than the file's owner.

The nvi documentation suggests putting common initialization actions into your .exrc file (i.e., options and commands for Unix vi), and having your .nexrc file execute :source .exrc before or after the nvi-specific initializations.

Multiwindow Editing

To create a new window in nvi, you use a capitalized version of one of the ex editing commands: Edit, Fg, Next, Previous, Tag, or Visual. (As usual, these commands can be abbreviated.) If your cursor is in the top half of the screen, the new window is created on the bottom half, and vice versa. You then switch to another window with CTRL-W:

```
<preface id="VI6-CH-0">
<title>Preface </title>

<para>
Text editing is one of the most common uses of any computer system, and
<command>vi</command> is one of the most useful standard text editors
on your system.
With <command>vi</command> you can create new files, or edit any existing
Unix text file.
</para>
ch00.sgm: unmodified: line 1
# Makefile for vi book
#
# Arnold Robbins

CHAPTERS = ch00_6.sgm ch00_5.sgm ch00.sgm ch01.sgm ch02.sgm ch03.sgm \
    ch04.sgm ch05.sgm ch06.sgm ch07.sgm ch08.sgm
APPENDICES = appa.sgm appb.sgm appc.sgm appd.sgm

POSTSCRIPT = ch00_6.ps ch00_5.ps ch00.ps ch01.ps ch02.ps ch03.ps \
    ch04.ps ch05.ps ch06.ps ch07.ps ch08.ps \
Makefile: unmodified: line 1
```

This example shows nvi editing two files, ch00.sgm and Makefile. The split screen is the result of typing nvi ch00.sgm followed by :Edit Makefile. The last line of each window acts as the status line, and it's where colon commands are executed for that window. The status lines are highlighted in reverse video.

The windowing ex mode commands and what they do are described in Table 16-1.

Table 16-1. nvi window management commands

Command	Function
bg	Hide the current window. It can be recalled with the fg and Fg commands.
di[splay] b[uffers]	Display all buffers, including named, unnamed, and numeric buffers.
di[splay] s[creens]	Display the filenames of all backgrounded windows.
Edit *filename*	Edit *filename* in a new window.

Command	Function
Edit /tmp	Create a new window editing an empty buffer. /tmp is interpreted specially to create a new temporary file.
fg *filename*	Uncover *filename* into the current window. The previous file moves to the background.
Fg *filename*	Uncover *filename* in a new window. The current window is split, instead of redistributing the screen space among all open windows.
Next	Edit the next file in the argument list in a new window.
Previous	Edit the previous file in the argument list in a new window. (The corresponding previous command, which moves back to the previous file, exists in nvi; it is not in Unix vi.)
resize ±*nrows*	Increase or decrease the size of the current window by *nrows* rows.
Tag *tagstring*	Edit the file containing *tagstring* in a new window.

The CTRL-W command cycles between windows, top to bottom. The :q and ZZ commands exit the current window.

You may have multiple windows open on the same file. Changes made in one window are reflected in the other, although changes made in nvi's insert mode are not seen in the other window until after you finalize the change by typing ESC. You will not be prompted to save your changes until you issue a command that would cause nvi to leave the last window open upon a file.

GUI Interfaces

nvi does not provide a graphical user interface (GUI) version.

Extended Regular Expressions

We introduced extended regular expressions earlier in the section "Extended Regular Expressions" on page 128. Here, we just summarize the metacharacters that nvi provides. nvi also supports the POSIX bracket expressions, [[:alnum:]], and so on.

You use :set extended to enable extended regular expression matching:

|

  Indicates alternation. The left and right sides need not be just single characters.

(...)

  Used for grouping, to allow the application of additional regular expression operators.

  When extended is set, text grouped with parentheses acts like text grouped in \(...\) in regular vi; the actual text matched can be retrieved in the replacement part of a substitute command with \1, \2, etc. In this case, \(represents a literal left parenthesis.

+

> Matches one or more of the preceding regular expressions. This is either a single character or a group of characters enclosed in parentheses.

?

> Matches zero or one occurrence of the preceding regular expression.

{...}

> Defines an *interval expression*. Interval expressions describe counted numbers of repetitions. In the following descriptions, *n* and *m* represent integer constants:
>
> **{n}**
>
> > Matches exactly *n* repetitions of the previous regular expression.
>
> **{n,}**
>
> > Matches *n* or more repetitions of the previous regular expression.
>
> **{n,m}**
>
> > Matches *n* to *m* repetitions.
>
> When extended is not set, nvi provides the same functionality with \{ and \}.

As might be expected, when extended is set, you should precede metacharacters with a backslash in order to match them literally.

Improvements for Editing

This section describes the features of nvi that make simple text editing easier and more powerful.

Command-Line History and Completion

nvi saves your ex command lines and makes it possible for you to edit them for resubmission.

This facility is controlled with the cedit option, whose value is a string.

When you type the first character of this string on the colon command line, nvi opens a new window on the command history that you can then edit. On any given line when you hit ENTER, nvi executes that line. ESC is a good choice for this option. (Use ^V ^[to enter it.)

Because the ENTER key actually executes the command, be careful to use either the j or ↓ keys to move down from one line to the next.

In addition to being able to edit your command line, you can also do filename expansion. This feature is controlled with the filec option.

When you type the first character of this string on the colon command line, nvi treats the blank delimited word in front of the cursor as if it had an * appended to it and does shell-style filename expansion. ESC is also a good choice for this option. (Use ^V ^[to enter it.) When this character is the same as for the `cedit` option, the command-line editing is performed only when it is entered as the first character on the colon command line.

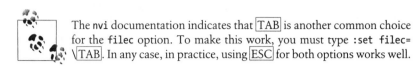 The `nvi` documentation indicates that TAB is another common choice for the `filec` option. To make this work, you must type `:set filec= \`TAB. In any case, in practice, using ESC for both options works well.

It is easiest to set these options in your `.nexrc` file:

```
set cedit=^[
set filec=^[
```

Tag Stacks

Tag stacking is described earlier in the section "Tag Stacks" on page 131. `nvi`'s tag stack is the simplest of the four clones. Tables 16-2 and 16-3 show the commands it uses.

Table 16-2. nvi tag commands

Command	Function
di[splay] t[ags]	Display the tag stack.
ta[g][!] *tagstring*	Edit the file containing *tagstring* as defined in the **tags** file. The ! forces `nvi` to switch to the new file if the current buffer has been modified but not saved.
Ta[g][!] *tagstring*	Just like `:tag`, except that the file is edited in a new window.
tagp[op][!] *tagloc*	Pop to the given tag, or to the most recently used tag if no *tagloc* is supplied. The location may be either a filename of the tag of interest or a number indicating a position in the stack.
tagt[op][!]	Pop to the oldest tag in the stack, clearing the stack in the process.

Table 16-3. nvi command mode tag commands

Command	Function
^]	Look up the location of the identifier under the cursor in the **tags** file, and move to that location. The current location is automatically pushed onto the tag stack.
^T	Return to the previous location in the tag stack, i.e., pop off one element.

You can set the **tags** option to a list of filenames where `nvi` should look for a tag. This provides a simplistic search path mechanism. The default value is `"tags /var/db/ libc.tags /sys/kern/tags"`, which on a 4.4 BSD system looks in the current directory, and then in the files for the C library and the operating system source code.

The **taglength** option controls how many characters in a tag string are significant. The default value of zero means to use all the characters.

nvi behaves like vi: it uses the "word" under the cursor starting at the current cursor position. If your cursor is on the *i* in *main*, nvi searches for the identifier *in*, not *main*.

nvi relies on the traditional tags file format. Unfortunately, this format is very limited. In particular, it has no concept of programming language *scope*, which allows the same identifier to be used in different contexts to mean different things. The problem is exacerbated by C++, which explicitly allows function name *overloading*, i.e., the use of the same name for different functions.

nvi gets around the tags file limitations by using a different mechanism entirely: the cscope program. cscope, once proprietary, is now an open source program available from the Bell Labs World-Wide Exptools project (see *http://www.bell-labs.com/project/wwexptools/*). It reads C source files and builds a database describing the program. nvi provides commands that query the database and allow you to process the results. Because cscope is not universally available, we do not cover its use here. Details of the nvi commands are provided in the nvi documentation.

The extended tags file format produced by Exuberant ctags does not produce any errors with nvi 1.79; however, nvi does not take advantage of this format, either.

Infinite Undo

In vi, the dot (.) command generally acts as the "do again" command; it repeats the last editing action you performed, be it a deletion, insertion, or replacement.

nvi generalizes the dot command into a full "redo" command, applying it even if the last command was u for "undo."

Thus, to begin a series of "undo" commands, first type a u. Then, for each . (dot) that you type, nvi will continue to undo changes, moving the file progressively closer to its original state.

Eventually, you will reach the initial state of your file. At that point, typing . will just ring the bell (or flash the screen). You can now begin redoing by typing u to "undo the undos" and then using . to reapply successive changes.

nvi does not allow you to provide a count to either the u or . command.

Arbitrary Length Lines and Binary Data

nvi can edit files with arbitrary length lines and with an arbitrary number of lines.

nvi automatically handles binary data. No special command-line options or ex options are required. You use ^X followed by one or two hexadecimal digits to enter any 8-bit character into your file.

Incremental Searching

Enable incremental searching in nvi using :set searchincr.

The cursor moves through the file as you type, always being placed on the first character of the text that matches.

Left-Right Scrolling

Enable left-right scrolling in nvi using :set leftright. The value of sidescroll controls the number of characters by which nvi shifts the screen when scrolling left to right.

Programming Assistance

nvi does not provide specific programming assistance facilities.

Interesting Features

nvi is the most minimal of the clones, without a large number of additional features that have not yet been covered. However, it does have several important features worthy of mention:

Internationalization support
Most of the informational and warning messages in nvi can be replaced with translations into a different language, using a facility known as a "message catalog." nvi implements this facility itself, using a straightforward mechanism documented in the file catalog/README in the nvi distribution. Message catalogs are provided for Dutch, English, French, German, Russian, Spanish, and Swedish.

Arbitrary buffer names
Historically, vi buffer names are limited to the 26 characters of the alphabet. nvi allows you to use any character as a buffer name.

Special interpretation of /tmp
For any ex command that needs a filename argument, if you use the special name /tmp, nvi will replace it with the name of a unique temporary file.

Sources and Supported Operating Systems

nvi can be obtained from *http://www.bostic.com/vi*. This is a web page from which you can download the current version,[§] and can also ask to be added to a mailing list that sends notifications about new versions of nvi and new features.

[§] A GUI version of nvi is under development; see the web page for contact information if you're interested.

The source code for nvi is freely distributable. The licensing terms are described in the LICENSE file in the distribution, and they permit distribution in source and binary form.

nvi builds and runs under Unix. It can also be built to run under LynxOS 2.4.0, and possibly later versions. It may build and run on other POSIX-compliant systems as well, but the documentation does not contain a specific list of known operating systems.

Compiling nvi is straightforward. Retrieve the distribution via ftp. Uncompress and untar it, run the configure program, and then run make:

```
$ gzip -d < nvi.tar.gz | tar -xvpf -
...
$ cd nvi-1.79; ./configure
...
$ make
...
```

nvi should configure and build with no problems. Use make install to install it.

Should you need to report a bug or problem in nvi, the person to contact is Keith Bostic, at *bostic@bostic.com*.

Elvis

`elvis` was written and is maintained by Steve Kirkendall. An earlier version became the basis for `nvi`. This chapter was originally written using `elvis`.

Author and History

With our thanks for his help, we'll let Steve Kirkendall give the history in his own words:

> I started writing `elvis` 1.0 after an early clone called `stevie` crashed on me, causing me to lose a few hours' work and totally destroying my confidence in that program. Also, `stevie` stored the edit buffer in RAM, which simply wasn't practical in Minix. So I started writing my own clone, which stored its edit buffer in a file. And even if my editor crashed, the edited text could still be retrieved from that file.

> `elvis` 2.x is almost completely separate from 1.x. I wrote this, my second `vi` clone, because my first one inherited too many limitations from the real `vi`, and from Minix. The biggest change is the support for multiple edit buffers and multiple windows, neither of which could be retrofitted into 1.x very easily. I also wanted to shed the line-length limitation, and have online help written in HTML.

As to the name "elvis," Steve says that at least part of the reason he chose the name was to see how many people would ask him why he chose the name![*] It is also common for `vi` clones to have the letters "vi" somewhere in their names.

Important Command-Line Arguments

`elvis` is not typically installed as `vi`, though it can be. If invoked as `ex`, it operates as a line editor and allows the `Q` command from `vi` mode to switch into `ex` mode.

`elvis` has a number of command-line options. The most useful are described here:

`-a`
  Load each file named on the command line into a separate window.

---

[*] ☺ In around eight years, I was only number four! —A.R.

-c *command*

Execute *command* upon startup. This is the POSIX version of the historical +command syntax. (The old syntax is also accepted.)

-f *filename*

Use *filename* for the session file instead of the default name. Session files are discussed later in this chapter.

-G *gui*

Use the given interface. The default is the `termcap` interface. Other choices include `x11`, `windows`, `curses`, `open`, and `quit`. Not all the interfaces may be compiled into your version of `elvis`.

-i

Start editing in input mode instead of in command mode. This may be easier for novice users.

-o *logfile*

Redirect the startup messages out to a file, instead of `stdout/stderr`. This is of critical importance to MS Windows users because Windows discards anything written to standard output and standard error, which made WinElvis configuration problems almost impossible to diagnose. With `-o` *filename* you can send the diagnostic info to a file and view it later.

-r

Perform recovery after a crash.

-R

Start editing each file in read-only mode.

-s

Read an `ex` script from standard input and execute (per the POSIX standard). This bypasses all initialization scripts.

-S

Set the option `security=safer` for the whole session, not just execution of `.exrc` files. This adds a certain amount of security, but it should not necessarily be trusted blindly.

-SS

Set the option `security=restricted`, which is even more paranoid than `security=safer`.

-t *tag*

Start editing at the specified *tag*.

-V

Output more verbose status information. Useful for diagnosing problems with initialization files.

-?

Print a summary of the possible options.

Online Help and Other Documentation

`elvis` is very interesting in this department. The online help is comprehensive and written entirely in HTML. This makes is easy to view in your favorite web browser. `elvis` also has an HTML display mode (discussed later), which makes it easy and pleasant to view the online help from within `elvis` itself.

When viewing HTML files, you use the tag commands (^] and ^T) to go to different topics and then return, making it easy to browse the help files. We applaud this innovation in online help.

Of course, `elvis` also comes with Unix manpages.

Initialization

This section describes `elvis`'s session files and itemizes the steps it takes during initialization.

The Session File

`elvis` is intended to eventually meet Common Open System Environment (COSE) standards. These require that programs be able to save their state and return to that saved state at a later time.

To be able to do this, `elvis` maintains all its state in a session file. Normally `elvis` creates the session file when it starts and removes it when it exits, but if `elvis` crashes, a leftover session file can be used to implement recovery of the edited files.

Initialization Steps

`elvis` performs the following initialization steps. Interestingly, much of the customization for `elvis` is moved out of editor options and into initialization files:

1. Initialize all hardcoded options.
2. Select an interface from those compiled into `elvis`. `elvis` will choose the "best" of the ones that are compiled in and that can work. For example, the X11 interface is considered to be better than the `termcap` interface, but it may not be usable if the X Window System is not currently running.

   The selected interface can process the command line for initialization options that are specific to it.
3. Create the session file if it doesn't exist; otherwise, read it (in preparation for recovery).

4. Initialize the `elvispath` option from the `ELVISPATH` environment variable. Otherwise, give it a default value. `"~/.elvislib:/usr/local/lib/elvis"` is a typical value, but the actual value will depend on how `elvis` was configured and built.

5. Search `elvispath` for an `ex` script named `elvis.ini` and run it. The default `elvis.ini` file performs the following actions:

   • Chooses a digraph table based on the current operating system. (Digraphs are a way to define the system's extended ASCII character set and how characters from the extended set should be entered.)

   • Sets options based on the program's name (for example, `ex` versus `vi` mode).

   • Handles system-dependent tweaks, such as setting the colors for X11 and adding menus to the interface.

   • Picks an initialization filename, either `.exrc` for Unix or `elvis.rc` for non-Unix systems. Call this file `f`.

   • If the `EXINIT` environment variable exists, executes its value. Otherwise, it executes `:source ~/f`, where `f` is the filename chosen previously.

   • If the `exrc` option has been set, runs the `safely source` command on `f` in the current directory.

   • For X11, sets the normal, bold, and italic fonts, if they have not been set already.

6. Load the pre- and post-read and pre- and post-write command files, if they exist. Also load the `elvis.msg` file. All of these files are described later in this chapter.

7. Load and display the first file named on the command line.

8. If the `-a` option was given, load and display the rest of the files, each in its own window.

Multiwindow Editing

To create a new window in `elvis`, you use the `ex` command `:split`. You then use one of the regular `ex` commands, such as `:e` *filename* or `:n` to edit a new file. This is the simplest method; other, shorter methods are described later in this chapter. You can switch back and forth between windows with CTRL-W CTRL-W :

```
<preface id="VI6-CH-0">
<title>Preface </title>

<para>
Text editing is one of the most common uses of any computer system, and
<command>vi</command> is one of the most useful standard text editors
on your system.
With <command>vi</command> you can create new files, or edit any
existing Unix text file.

# Makefile for vi book
#
# Arnold Robbins

CHAPTERS = ch00_6.sgm ch00_5.sgm ch00.sgm ch01.sgm ch02.sgm ch03.sgm \
        ch04.sgm ch05.sgm ch06.sgm ch07.sgm ch08.sgm
APPENDICES = appa.sgm appb.sgm appc.sgm appd.sgm

POSTSCRIPT = ch00_6.ps ch00_5.ps ch00.ps ch01.ps ch02.ps ch03.ps \
        ch04.ps ch05.ps ch06.ps ch07.ps ch08.ps \
        appa.ps appb.ps appc.ps appd.ps
```

The split screen is the result of typing elvis ch00.sgm followed by :split Makefile.

Like nvi, elvis gives each window its own status line. elvis is unique in that it uses a
highlighted line of underscores, instead of reverse video, for the status line. ex colon
commands are carried out on each window's status line.

Table 17-1 describes the windowing ex mode commands and what they do.

Table 17-1. elvis window management commands

Command	Function
sp[lit] [*file*]	Create a new window, and load it with *file* if supplied. Otherwise, the new window shows the current file.
new sne[w]	Create a new empty buffer, and then create a new window to show that buffer.
sn[ext] [*file...*]	Create a new window, showing the next file in the argument list. The current file is not affected.
sN[ext]	Create a new window, showing the *previous* file in the argument list. The current file is not affected.
sre[wind][!]	Create a new window, showing the first file in the argument list. Reset the "current" file to be the first one with respect to the :next command. The current file is not affected.
sl[ast]	Create a new window, showing the last file in the argument list. The current file is not affected.
sta[g][!] *tag*	Create a new window showing the file where the requested *tag* is found.
sa[ll]	Create a new window for any files named in the argument list that don't already have a window.
wi[ndow] [*target*]	With no *target*, list all windows. The possible values for *target* are described in Table 17-2.

Command	Function
close	Close the current window. The buffer that the window was displaying remains intact. If it was modified, the other elvis commands that quit will prevent you from quitting until you explicitly save or discard the buffer.
wquit	Write the buffer back to the file and close the window. The file is saved, regardless of whether it has been modified.
qall	Issues a :q command for each window. Buffers without windows are not affected.

Table 17-2 describes the windowing ex arguments and their meanings.

Table 17-2. Arguments to the elvis window command

Argument	Meaning
+	Switch to the next window, like ^W k.
++	Switch to the next window, wrapping like ^W ^W.
-	Switch to the previous window, like ^W j.
--	Switch to the previous window, wrapping.
num	Switch to the window whose windowid=*num*.
buffer-name	Switch to the window editing the named buffer.

elvis provides a number of vi mode commands for moving between windows. They are summarized in Table 17-3.

Table 17-3. elvis window commands from vi command mode

Command	Function
^W c	Hide the buffer and close the window. This is identical to the :close command.
^W d	Toggle the display mode between syntax mode and the other display modes (html, man, tex) if that's appropriate. This makes editing web pages a little more convenient. This is a per-window option. Display modes are discussed in the later section "Display Modes" on page 337.
^W j	Move down to the next window.
^W k	Move up to the previous window.
^W n	Create a new window, and create a new buffer to be displayed in the window. It is similar to the :snew command.
^W q	Save the buffer and close the window, identical to ZZ.
^W s	Split the current window, equivalent to :split.
^W S	Toggle the wrap option. This option controls whether long lines wrap or whether the whole screen scrolls to the right. This is a per-window option. This option is discussed in the later section "Left-Right Scrolling" on page 331.
^W]	Create a new window, then look up the tag underneath the cursor. It is similar to the :stag command.
[*count*] ^W ^W	Move to next window, or to the *count*th window.

Command	Function
^W +	Increase the size of the current window (`termcap` interface only).
^W -	Reduce the size of the current window (`termcap` interface only).
^W \	Make the current window as large as possible (`termcap` interface only).

GUI Interfaces

The screenshots and explanation for this section were supplied by Steve Kirkendall. We thank him.

elvis's X11 interface provides a scrollbar and mouse support, and it allows you to select which fonts to use. There is no way to change fonts after elvis has created the first window. The fonts must all be monospace fonts, typically some variation of a Courier or other fixed-width font.

elvis's X11 interface supports multiple fonts and colors, a blinking cursor that changes shape to indicate your editing mode (insert versus command), a scrollbar, anti-aliased text, an image file to use for the background (with optional tint), a user-specified icon image, and mouse actions. The mouse can be used for selecting text, cutting and pasting between applications, and performing tag searches. In addition, there is a configurable toolbar, dialog windows, a status bar, and the `-client` flag.

> The MS Windows GUI interface also supports a background image file, using the same command and using XPM format files, so that the same background image file may be used in both environments.

The Basic Window

The basic elvis window is shown in Figure 17-1.

elvis provides a separate text search pop-up dialog box, which is shown in Figure 17-2.

The look and feel are intended to resemble Motif, but elvis doesn't actually use the Motif libraries.

Command-line options let you choose the four different fonts that elvis uses: normal, italic, bold, and "control," which is the font for the toolbar text and button labels. You may also specify foreground and background colors, the initial window geometry, and whether elvis should start out iconified.

The `-client` option causes elvis to look for an already running elvis process and send it a message requesting it to start editing the files named on the command line. Doing it this way allows you to share yanked text and other information between the files elvis is currently editing and the new files.

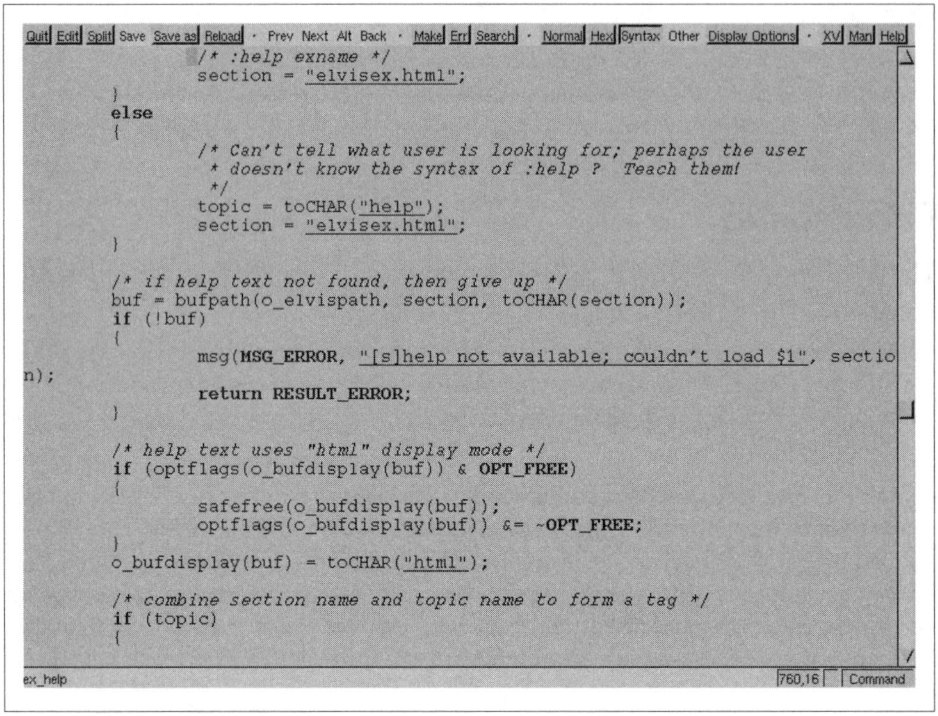

Figure 17-1. The elvis GUI window

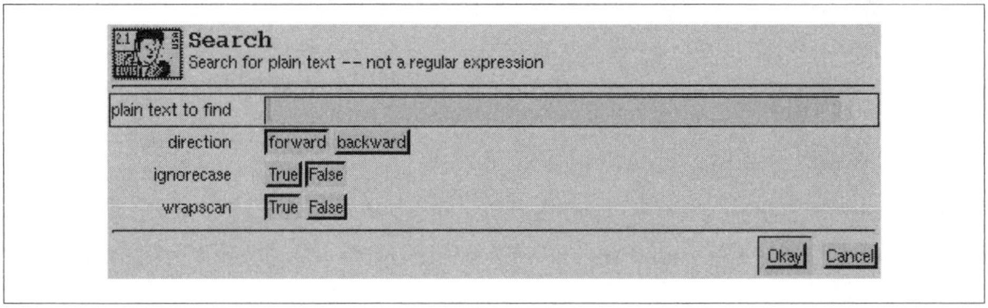

Figure 17-2. The elvis search dialog

Besides the toolbar, there is also a status bar that displays status messages and any available information about toolbar buttons.

Mouse Behavior

The mouse behavior tries to strike a balance between `xterm` and what makes sense for an editor. To do this correctly, `elvis` distinguishes between clicking and dragging.

Dragging the mouse always selects text. Dragging with button 1 pressed selects characters, dragging with button 2 selects a rectangular area, and dragging with button 3 selects whole lines. (Buttons 1, 2, and 3 correspond to the left, middle, and right buttons for a right-handed user. The order will be the opposite for a left-handed user.) These operations correspond to elvis's v, ^V, and V commands, respectively. (These commands are described later in this chapter.) When you release the button at the end of the drag, the selected text is immediately copied into an X11 cut buffer, so you can paste it into another application, such as xterm. The text remains selected, so you can apply an operator command to it.

Clicking button 1 cancels any pending selection and moves the cursor to the clicked-on character. Clicking button 3 moves the cursor without canceling the pending selection; you use this to extend a pending selection.

Clicking button 2 "pastes" text from the X11 cut buffer (such as xterm). If you're entering an ex command line, the text will be pasted into the command line as though you had typed it. If you're in visual command mode or input mode, the text will be pasted into your edit buffer. When pasting, it doesn't matter where you click in the window; elvis always inserts the text at the position of the text cursor.

Double-clicking button 1 simulates a ^] keystroke, causing elvis to perform tag lookup on the clicked-on word. If elvis happens to be displaying an HTML document, then tag lookup pursues hypertext links, so you can double-click on any underlined text to view the topic that describes that text. Double-clicking button 3 simulates a ^T keystroke, taking you back to where you did the last tag lookup.

The Toolbar

The X11 interface supports a user-configurable toolbar. By default, the toolbar is enabled unless your ~/.exrc file has a set notoolbar command.

The default toolbar already has some buttons defined. You use the :gui command to reconfigure the toolbar.

There are a number of commands. In particular, you can reconfigure the toolbar to suit your tastes, deleting one or all of the existing buttons, adding new ones, and controlling the spacing between buttons or groups of buttons. Here is a simple example:

```
:gui Make:make
:gui Make " Rebuild the program
:gui Quit:q
:gui Quit?!modified
```

These commands add two new buttons. The first line adds a button named Make, which will execute the :make command when pressed. (The :make command is described later in this chapter.) The second line adds descriptive text for the Make button that shows up in the status line when the button is pressed. In this case, the " does not start a comment; rather it is an operator for the :gui command.

The second button, named Quit, is created by the third line. It exits the program. The fourth line changes its behavior. If the condition (!modified) is true, the button will behave normally. But if it's false, the button will ignore any mouse clicks, and it will also be displayed as being "flat" instead of having the normal 3-D appearance. Thus, if the current file is modified, you won't be able to use the Quit button to exit.

You can create pop-up dialogs that appear when a toolbar button is pressed. The dialog can set the value(s) of predefined variables (options) that can then be tested from the ex command associated with the button. There are 26 predefined variables, named a-z, that are set aside for user "programs" of this sort to use. This example associates a dialog with a new button named Split:

```
:gui Split"Create a new window, showing a given file
:gui Split;"File to load:" (file) f = filename
:gui Split:split (f)
```

The first command associates descriptive text with the Split button. The second command creates the pop-up dialog: its prompt is File to load: and it will set the file name option. The (file) indicates that any string may be entered, but that the TAB key may be used for filename completion. The f = filename copies the value of filename into f. Finally, the third command actually executes the :split command on the value of f, which will be the new filename supplied by the user.

The facility is quite flexible; see the online help for the full details.

Options

A large number of options control the X11 interface. You typically set these in your .exrc file. There are options and abbreviations for setting the various fonts, and for enabling and configuring the toolbar, status bar, scrollbars, and the cursor. Other options control the cursor's behavior when you switch windows with ^W ^W and whether the cursor goes back to the original xterm when elvis exits.

The online documentation describes all of the X11-related ex options. Here, we describe some of the more interesting ones:

autoiconify
> Normally, when the ^W ^W command switches focus to an iconified window, that window is de-iconified. When autoiconify is true, elvis will iconify the old window, so that the number of open elvis windows remains constant.

blinktime
> The value is a number between 1 and 10 that indicates for how many 10ths of a second the cursor should be visible and then invisible. A value of 0 disables blinking.

firstx, firsty, stagger
> firstx and firsty control the position of the first window that elvis creates. If not set, the -geometry option or the window manager controls placement. If stagger is

set to a nonzero value, any new windows are created that many pixels down and to the right of the current window. Setting it to zero lets the window manager do the placement.

stopshell

Stores a command that runs an interactive shell, for the ex commands :shell and :stop, and for the ^Z visual command. The default value is xterm &, which starts an interactive terminal emulator in another window.

xscrollbar

Values left and right place the scrollbar on the indicated side of the window, and none disables the scrollbar. The default is right.

elvis can be configured via X resources.[†] The resource values can be overridden by command-line flags, or by explicit :set or :color commands in the initialization scripts. elvis's resources are listed in Table 17-4.

Table 17-4. elvis X resources

Resource class (name is lowercase of class)	Type	Default value
Elvis.Toolbar	Boolean	true
Elvis.Statusbar	Boolean	true
Elvis.Font	Font	fixed
Elvis.Geometry	Geometry	80x34
Elvis.Foreground	Color	black
Elvis.Background	Color	gray90
Elvis.MultiClickTimeout	Timeout	3
Elvis.Control.Font	Font	variable
Elvis.Cursor.Foreground	Color	red
Elvis.Cursor.Selected	Color	red
Elvis.Cursor.BlinkTime	Timeout	3
Elvis.Tool.Foreground	Color	black
Elvis.Tool.Background	Color	gray75
Elvis.Scrollbar.Foreground	Color	gray75
Elvis.Scrollbar.Background	Color	gray60
Elvis.Scrollbar.Width	Number	11
Elvis.Scrollbar.Repeat	Timeout	4
Elvis.Scrollbar.Position	Edge	right

[†] X resources are a way to configure X11 applications based on a set of name/value pairs stored in memory by the X server. They are not used very much by the current crop of desktop environments, such as KDE and GNOME. Nonetheless, you can still set them using the xrdb command.

The "Timeout" type gives a time value, in 10ths of a second. The "Edge" type gives a scrollbar position, one of left, right, or none.

For example, if your X resource database contains the line elvis.font: 10x20, the default text font would be 10x20. This value would be used if the normalfont option was unset.

Extended Regular Expressions

We introduced extended regular expressions earlier in the section "Extended Regular Expressions" on page 128. The additional metacharacters available in elvis are:

\|
: Indicates alternation.

\(...\)
: Used for grouping, to allow the application of additional regular expression operators.

\+
: Matches one or more of the preceding regular expressions.

\?
: Matches zero or one of the preceding regular expressions.

\@
: Matches the word under the cursor.

\=
: Indicates where to put the cursor when the text is matched. For instance, hel\=lo would put the cursor on the second *l* in the next occurrence of *hello*.

\{...\}
: Describes an interval expression, such as x\{1,3\} to match *x*, *xx*, or *xxx*.

POSIX bracket expressions (character classes, etc.) are available.

Improved Editing Facilities

This section describes the features of elvis that make simple text editing easier and more powerful.

Command-Line History and Completion

Everything you type on the ex command line is saved in a buffer named Elvis ex history. This is accessible like any other elvis buffer, but it is not directly useful when just viewed in a window.

To access the history, you use the arrow keys to display previous commands and to edit them. Use ↑ and ↓ to page through the list, and ← and → to move around on a command line. You can insert characters by typing, and you can erase them by backspacing over them. Much as when editing in a regular vi buffer, the backspace does remove the characters, but the line is not updated as you type, so be careful!

When entering text into the Elvis ex history buffer (i.e., on the colon command line), the TAB key can be used for filename expansion. The preceding word is assumed to be a partial filename, and elvis searches for all matching files. If there are multiple matches, it fills in as many characters of the name as possible, and then beeps; or, if no additional characters are implied by the matching filenames, elvis lists all matching names and redisplays the command line. If there is a single match, elvis completes the name and appends a tab character. If there are no matches, elvis simply inserts a tab character.

To get a real tab character, precede it with a ^V. You can also disable filename completion entirely by setting the Elvis ex history buffer's inputtab option to tab, via the following command:

```
:(Elvis ex history)set inputtab=tab
```

Tag Stacks

Tag stacking is described earlier in the section "Tag Stacks" on page 131. In elvis, tag stacking is very straightforward, as shown in Tables 17-5 and 17-6.

Table 17-5. elvis tag commands

Command	Function
ta[g][!] [*tagstring*]	Edit the file containing *tagstring* as defined in the tags file. The ! forces elvis to switch to the new file if the current buffer has been modified but not saved.
stac[k]	Display the current tag stack.
po[p][!]	Pop a cursor position off the stack, restoring the cursor to its previous position.

Table 17-6. elvis command mode tag commands

Command	Function
^]	Look up the location of the identifier under the cursor in the tags file, and move to that location. The current location is automatically pushed onto the tag stack.
^T	Return to the previous location in the tag stack, i.e., pop off one element.

Unlike traditional vi, when you type ^], elvis looks up the entire word containing the cursor, not just the part of the word from the cursor location forward.

In HTML mode (discussed in the later section "Display Modes" on page 337), the commands all work the same, except that :tag expects to be given a URL instead of a tag name. URLs don't depend on having a tags file, so the tags file is ignored when in HTML mode. elvis supports file:, http:, and ftp: URLs. It can also write via FTP. Simply give a URL wherever elvis expects a filename. To access your own account on an FTP site (instead of the anonymous account), the directory name portion of the URL must begin with /~. elvis will read your ~/.netrc file to find the right name and password. The html display mode makes good use of these features! (The network functions work in Windows and OS/2, too.)

Several :set options affect how elvis works with tags, as described in Table 17-7.

Table 17-7. elvis options for tag management

Option	Function
taglength, tl	Control the number of significant characters in a tag that is to be looked up. The default value of zero indicates that all characters are significant.
tags, tagpath	The value is a list of directories and/or filenames in which to look for tags files. elvis looks for a file named tags in any entry that is a directory. Entries in the list are colon-separated (or semicolon-separated on DOS/Windows), in order to allow spaces in directory names. The default value is just tags, which looks for a file named tags in the current directory. This can be overridden by setting the TAGPATH environment variable.
tagstack	When set to true, elvis stacks each location on the tag stack. Use :set notagstack to disable tag stacking.

elvis supports the extended tags file format described in Chapter 8. elvis comes with its own version of ctags (named elvtags, to avoid conflict with the standard version). It generates the enhanced format described earlier. Here is an example of the special !_TAG_ lines it produces:

```
!_TAG_FILE_FORMAT      2          /supported features/
!_TAG_FILE_SORTED      1          /0=unsorted, 1=sorted/
!_TAG_PROGRAM_AUTHOR   Steve Kirkendall      /kirkenda@cs.pdx.edu/
!_TAG_PROGRAM_NAME     Elvis Ctags    //
!_TAG_PROGRAM_URL      ftp://ftp.cs.pdx.edu/pub/elvis/README.html  //
!_TAG_PROGRAM_VERSION  2.1    //
```

In elvis, each window has its own tag stack.

In general, elvis does some innovative things with tags. When reading overloaded tags, it tries to guess which one you're looking for and presents the most likely one first. If you reject it (by hitting ^] again, or typing :tag again), it then presents you with the next most likely match, and so on. It also notes the attributes of the tags that you reject or accept and uses those to improve its guessing heuristic for later searches.

The :tag command's syntax has been extended to allow you to search for tags by features other than just the tag name. There are too many details to go into here; see the chapter in the online help that describes the use of tags.

There is also a :browse command, which finds all matching tags at once and builds an HTML table from them. From this table, you can follow hypertext links to any matching tags you want.

Finally, there is the tagprg option, which, if set, discards the built-in tag searching algorithm and instead runs an external program to perform the search.

Infinite Undo

With elvis, before being able to undo and redo multiple levels of changes, you must first set the undolevels option to the number of levels of "undo" that elvis should allow. A negative value disallows *any* undoing (which is not terribly useful). The elvis documentation warns that each level of undo uses around 6K bytes of the session file (the file that describes your editing session), and thus can eat up disk space rather quickly. It recommends not setting undolevels any higher than 100 and "probably much lower."

Once you've set undolevels to a nonzero value, you enter text as normal. Then, each successive u command undoes one change. To redo (undo the undo), you use the (rather mnemonic) ^R (Ctrl-R) command.

In elvis, the default value of undolevels is zero, which causes elvis to mimic Unix vi. The option applies per buffer being edited; see the earlier section "Initialization Steps" on page 319 for a description of how to set it for every file that you edit.

Once undolevels has been set, adding a count to either the u or ^R commands undoes or redoes the given number of changes.

Arbitrary Length Lines and Binary Data

elvis can edit files with arbitrary length lines and with an arbitrary number of lines.

Under Unix, elvis does not treat a binary file differently from any other file. On other systems, it uses the elvis.brf file to set the binary option. This avoids newline translation issues. You can enter 8-bit text by typing ^X followed by two hexadecimal digits. Using the hex display mode is an excellent way to edit binary files. The elvis.brf file and the hex display mode are described in the later section "Interesting Features" on page 335.

Left-Right Scrolling

You enable left-right scrolling in elvis using :set nowrap. The value of sidescroll controls the number of characters by which elvis shifts the screen when scrolling left to right. The ^W S command toggles the value of this option.

Visual Mode

elvis allows you to select regions one character at a time, one line at a time, or rectangularly, using the commands shown in Table 17-8.

Table 17-8. elvis block mode command characters

Command	Function
v	Start region selection, character-at-a-time mode.
V	Start region selection, line-at-a-time mode.
^V	Start region selection, rectangular mode.

elvis highlights the text (using reverse video) as you are selecting it. To make your selection, simply use the normal motion keys. The screen here shows a rectangular region:

```
The 6th edition of <citetitle>Learning the vi Editor</citetitle>
brings the book into the late 1990&rsquo;s.
In particular, besides the &ldquo;original&rdquo; version of
<command>vi</command> that comes as a standard part of every Unix
system, there are now a number of freely available &ldquo;clones&rdquo;
or work-alike editors.
```

elvis permits only a few operations on selected areas of text. Some operations work only on whole lines, even if you've selected a region that does not contain whole lines (see Table 17-9).

Table 17-9. elvis block mode operations

Command	Operation
c, d, y	Change, delete, or yank text. Only d works exactly on rectangles.
<, >, !	Shift text left or right, and filter text. These operate on the whole lines containing the marked region.

After using the d command to delete the region, the screen now looks like this:

```
The 6th edition of <citetitle>Learning the vi Editor</citetitle>
brings the 90&rsquo;s.
In particulo;original&rdquo; version of
<command>vi as a standard part of every
system, there are n available &ldquo;clones&rdquo;
or work-alike editors.
```

Programming Assistance

elvis's programming assistance capabilities are described in this section.

Edit-Compile Speedup

elvis provides commands that make it easier to stay within the editor while working on a program. You can recompile a single file, rebuild your entire program, and work through compiler errors one at a time. The elvis commands are summarized in Table 17-10.

Table 17-10. elvis program development commands

Command	Option	Function
cc[!] [*args*]	ccprg	Run the C compiler. Useful for recompiling an individual file.
mak[e][!] [*args*]	makeprg	Recompile everything that needs recompiling (usually via make).
er[rlist][!] [*file*]		Move to the next error's location.

The cc command recompiles an individual source file. You run it from the colon command line. For example, if you are editing the file hello.c and you type :cc, elvis will compile hello.c for you.

If you supply additional arguments to the :cc command, those arguments will be passed on to the C compiler. In this case, you need to supply *all* the arguments, including the filename.

The :cc command works by executing the text of the ccprg option. The default value is "cc ($1?$1:$2)". elvis sets $2 to the name of the current source file, and $1 to the arguments you give to the :cc command. The value of ccprg thus uses your arguments if they are present; otherwise, it just passes the current file's name to the system cc command. (You can, of course, change ccprg to suit your taste.)

Similarly, the :make command is intended to recompile everything that needs recompiling. It does this by executing the contents of the makeprg option, which by default is "make $1". Thus, you could type :make hello to make just the hello program, or just :make to make everything.

elvis captures the output of the compile or make and looks for things that look like filenames and line numbers. When it finds likely candidates, it treats them as such and moves to the location of the first error. The :errlist command moves to each successive error location in turn. elvis displays the error message text in the status line as you move to each location.

If you supply a *filename* argument to :errlist, elvis will load a fresh batch of error messages from that file, and move to the location of the first error.

The vi mode command * (asterisk) is equivalent to :errlist. This is more convenient to use when you have a lot of errors to step through.

Finally, one really nice feature is that elvis compensates for changes in the file. As you add or delete lines, elvis keeps track, so that when you go to the next error, you end up on the correct line—which is not necessarily the one with the same absolute line number as in the compiler's error message.

Syntax Highlighting

To cause elvis to do syntax highlighting, use the `:display syntax` command. This is a per-window command. (The other elvis display modes are described in "Display Modes" on page 337.)

You specify the appearance of text directly, using the `:color` command. You first give the type of text to highlight. For example, in the syntax display mode, some of the possibilities are:

comment
> How to display comments

function
> How to display identifiers that are function names

keyword
> How to display identifiers that are keywords

prep
> How to display C and C++ preprocessor directives

string
> How to display string constants (such as "Don't panic!" in awk)

variable
> How to display for variables, fields, and so on

other
> How to display things that don't fall into the other categories but that should not be displayed in the normal font (e.g., type names defined with the C typedef keyword)

Next, you indicate the font face, one of normal, bold, italic, underlined, emphasized, boxed, graphic, proportional, or fixed. (These can be abbreviated to a single letter.) You can then follow the face with a color. For example:

```
:color function bold yellow
```

The description of each language's comments, functions, keywords, etc., is stored in the elvis.syn file. This file comes with a number of specifications in it already. As an example, here is the syntax specification for awk:

```
# Awk.  This is actually for Thompson Automation's AWK compiler, which is
# somewhat beefier than the standard AWK interpreter.
language tawk awk
extension .awk
keyword BEGIN BEGINFILE END ENDFILE INIT break continue do else for function
keyword global if in local next return while
comment #
```

```
function (
string "
regexp /
useregexp (,~
other allcaps
```

The format is mostly self-explanatory and is fully documented in the elvis online documentation.

The reason elvis associates fonts and colors with different parts of a file's syntax is its ability to print files as they're shown on the screen (see the discussion of the :lpr command in the later section "Display Modes" on page 337).

On a nonbitmapped display, such as the Linux console, all of the fonts map into the one used by the console driver. This makes it rather difficult to distinguish normal from italic, for example. However, on some displays (such as the Linux console), elvis compensates by changing the color of the different fonts. If you have a GNU/Linux system with elvis, use it to edit a convenient C source file and you will see different parts of the code in different colors. The effect is rather pleasant; we regret that we can't reproduce it here in print.

In elvis, the syntax colors are per-window attributes. You can change the color for the italic font in one window, and it will not affect the color for the italic font in another window. This is true even if both windows are showing the same file.

Syntax coloring makes program editing much more interesting and lively. But you have to be careful in your choice of colors!

Interesting Features

elvis has a number of interesting features:

Internationalization support

Like nvi, elvis also has a home-grown method for allowing translations of messages into different languages. The elvis.msg file is searched for along the elvis path and loaded into a buffer named Elvis messages.

Messages have the form "*terse message:long message.*" Before printing a message, elvis looks up the terse form, and if there is a corresponding long form, that message is used. Otherwise, the terse message is used.

Display modes

This is perhaps the most interesting of elvis's features. For certain kinds of files, elvis formats the file content on the screen, giving a surprisingly good approximation of a WYSIWYG effect. elvis can also use the same formatting for printing the buffer to several kinds of printers. Display modes get their own subsection later in this chapter.

Pre- and post-operation command files

elvis loads four files (if they exist) that allow you to customize its behavior before and after reading and writing a file. This feature also gets its own subsection, later.

Open mode

elvis is the only one of the clones that actually implements vi's open mode. (Think of open mode as like vi, but with only a one-line window. The "advantage" of open mode is that it can be used on terminals that don't have cursor motion capabilities.)

Security

The :safely command sets the security option for execution of non-home-directory .exrc files, or any other untrusted files. When security=safer is set, "certain commands are disabled, wildcard expansion in filenames is disabled, and certain options are locked (including the security option itself)." The elvis documentation provides the details; however, don't blindly trust elvis to provide complete security for you.

Built-in calculator

elvis extends the ex command language with a built-in calculator (sometimes referred to as an expression evaluator in the documentation). It understands C expression syntax, and is most used in the :if, :calc, and :eval commands. See the online help for details, as well as examples in the elvis distribution's sample initialization files.

Macro debugger

elvis has a debugger for vi macros (the :map command). This can be useful when writing complicated input or command maps.

Macros for ex mode

The :alias command provides for defining ex macros. It is intended to resemble the alias command in csh. For example, there is a :safer alias for the :safely command, which provides backward compatibility with earlier versions of elvis.

Smarter % command

The visual % command has been extended to recognize #if, #else, and #endif directives if you're using the syntax display mode.

Built-in spellchecker

In syntax display mode, the spellchecker is smart enough to check the tags file for program symbols and a natural-language dictionary for comments. See :help set spell.

Text folding

Text folding allows you to hide and reveal certain parts of a file, which is useful for working with structured text. See :help :fold.

Highlighting selected lines

Steve tells us: "elvis can add a highlight to selected lines. See :help :region. For example, the commands :load since and then :rcssince will highlight lines that have been changed since the last time the file was checked into RCS."

Display Modes

elvis has several display modes. Depending on the kind of file, elvis produces a formatted version of the file, producing a WYSIWYG effect. The display modes are outlined in Table 17-11.

Table 17-11. elvis display modes

Mode	Display appearance
normal	No formatting; displays your text as it exists in the file.
syntax	Like normal, but with syntax coloring turned on.
hex	An interactive hex dump, reminiscent of mainframe hex dumps. Good for editing binary files.
html	A simple web page formatter. The tag commands can be used to follow links and return to the original starting point.
man	Simple manpage formatter. Like the output of nroff -man.
tex	A simple subset of the TeX formatter.

The :normal command will switch the display from one of the formatted views to normal mode. Use :display *mode* to switch back. As a shortcut, the ^W d command will toggle the display modes for the window.

Of the available modes, html and man are the most WYSIWYG in nature. The online documentation clearly defines the subset of both markup languages that elvis understands.

elvis uses the html mode for displaying its online help, which is written in HTML and has *many* cross-referencing links within it.

The example here shows elvis editing one of the HTML help files. The screen is split. Both windows show the same buffer; the bottom window is using the html display mode, whereas the top is using the normal display mode:

```
<html><head>
<title>Elvis 2.0 Sessions</title>
</head><body>

<h1>10. SESSIONS, INITIALIZATION, AND RECOVERY</h1>

This section of the manual describes the life-cycle of an
edit session. We begin with the definition of an
<a href="#SESSION">edit session</a> and
what that means to elvis.
This is followed by sections discussing
<a href="#INIT">initialization</a>
and <a href="#RECOVER">recovery after a crash.</a>
_____


10.0 SESSIONS, INITIALIZATION, AND RECOVERY
```

> This section of the manual describes the life-cycle of an
> edit session. We begin with the definition of an **edit
> session** and what that means to elvis. This is
> followed by sections discussing **initialization** and
> **recovery after a crash.**
>
> **10.1 Sessions**

The man mode is also interesting, since normally you have to format and print a manpage to be sure you've done a decent job of laying it out. The following quote from the online help seems appropriate:

> Troff source was never designed to be interactively edited, and although I did the best I could, attempting to edit in man mode is still a disorienting experience. I suggest you get in the habit of using normal mode when making changes, and man mode to preview the effect of those changes. The ^W d command makes switching between modes a pretty easy thing to do.

As an interesting adjunct, both the html and man modes also work with the :color command described later in "Syntax Highlighting" on page 334. This is particularly nice with man mode. For example, by default on a Linux console, only bold text (.B) is distinguishable from normal text. But with syntax coloring on, both bold and italic (.I) text become distinct. The mode commands are summarized in Table 17-12.

Table 17-12. elvis display mode commands

Command	Function
di[splay] [*mode* [*lang*]]	Change the display mode to *mode*. Use *lang* for syntax mode.
no[rmal]	Same as :display normal, but much easier to type.

Associated with each window is the bufdisplay option, which should be set to one of the supported display modes. The standard elvis.arf file (see the next subsection) will look at the extension of the buffer's filename and attempt to set the display to a more interesting mode than normal.

Finally, elvis can also apply its WYSIWYG formatting to printing the contents of a buffer. The :lpr command formats a line range (or the whole buffer, by default) for printing. You can print to a file or down a pipe to a command. By default, elvis prints to a pipe that executes the system print spooling command.

The :lpr command is controlled by several options, described in Table 17-13.

Table 17-13. elvis options for print management

Option	Function
lptype, lp	The printer type.
lpconvert, lpcvt	If set, convert Latin-8 extended ASCII to PC-8 extended ASCII.
lpcrlf, lpc	The printer needs CR/LF to end each line.
lpout, lpo	The file or command to print to.

Option	Function
lpcolumns, lpcols	The printer's width.
lpwrap, lpw	Simulate line wrapping.
lplines, lprows	The length of the printer's page.
lpformfeed, lpff	Send a form feed after the last page.
lpoptions, lpopt	Control of various printer features. This matters only for PostScript printers.
lpcolor, lpcl	Enables color printing for PostScript and MS Windows printers.
lpcontrast, lpct	Controls shading and contrast; for use with the lpcolor option.

Most of the options are self-explanatory. elvis supports several printer types, as described in Table 17-14.

Table 17-14. Values for the lptype option

Name	Printer Type
ps	PostScript, one logical page per sheet of paper.
ps2	PostScript, two logical pages per sheet of paper.
epson	Most dot-matrix printers; no graphic characters supported.
pana	Panasonic dot-matrix printers.
ibm	Dot-matrix printers with IBM graphic characters.
hp	Hewlett-Packard printers, and most non-PostScript laser printers.
cr	Line printers; overtyping is done with carriage return.
bs	Overtyping is done via backspace characters. This setting is the closest to traditional Unix nroff.
dumb	Plain ASCII, no font control.

If you have a PostScript printer, by all means use an lptype of ps or ps2. Use the latter to save paper, which is particularly handy when printing drafts.

Pre- and Post-Operation Control Files

elvis gives you the ability to control its actions at four points when reading and writing files: before and after reading a file, and before and after writing a file. It does this by executing the contents of four **ex** scripts at those respective points. These scripts are searched for using the directories listed in the **elvispath** option:

elvis.brf

This file is executed Before Reading a File (.brf). The default version looks at the file's extension and attempts to guess whether the file is binary. If it is, the **binary** option is turned on, to prevent elvis from converting newlines (which may be actual CR/LF pairs in the file) into line feeds internally.

`elvis.arf`

> This file is executed After Reading a File (`.arf`). The default version examines the file's extension in order to turn on syntax highlighting.

`elvis.bwf`

> This file is executed Before Writing a File (`.bwf`), in particular, before completely replacing an original file with the contents of the buffer. The default version implements copying the original file to a file with a `.bak` extension. You must set the `backup` option for this to work.

`elvis.awf`

> This file is executed After Writing a File (`.awf`). There is no default file for this, although it might be a good place to add hooks into a source code control system.

The use of command files to control these actions is quite powerful. It allows you to easily tailor `elvis`'s behavior to suit your needs; in other editors these kinds of features are much more hardwired into the code.

In addition, `elvis` supports Vim-style autocommands with `:autocmd`. See the online help for details.

elvis Futures

Steve Kirkendall informs us that there are a few things he has implemented but not yet released, as described in the following list:

- An interface to the GDB (GNU debugger) for use in software development
- A persistence feature similar to Vim's `viminfo` file
- The ability to embed one syntax within another, such as JavaScript embedded in HTML

Sources and Supported Operating Systems

The official WWW location for `elvis` is *ftp://ftp.cs.pdx.edu/pub/elvis/README.html*. From there, you can download the `elvis` distribution or get it directly, using `ftp` from *ftp://ftp.cs.pdx.edu/pub/elvis/elvis-2.2_0.tar.gz*.

The source code for `elvis` is freely distributable. `elvis` is distributed under the terms of `perl`'s Artistic License. The licensing terms are described in the `doc/license.html` file in the distribution.

`elvis` works under Unix, OS/2, MS-DOS, and modern versions of MS Windows. The Unix and Windows ports provide a graphical user interface. The MS-DOS version includes mouse support.

Compiling `elvis` is straightforward. Retrieve the distribution via `ftp` or via a web browser. Uncompress and untar it,[‡] run the `configure` program, and then run `make`:

```
$ gzip -d < elvis-2.2_0.tar.gz | tar -xvpf -
...
$ cd elvis-2.2_0; ./configure
...
$ make
...
```

`elvis` should configure and build with no problems. Use `make install` to install it.

 The default configuration causes `elvis` to install itself in standard system directories, such as `/usr/bin`, `/usr/share`, and so on. If you wish to have things installed in `/usr/local`, use the `--prefix` option to the `configure` script.

Should you need to report a bug or problem in `elvis`, the person to contact is Steve Kirkendall at *kirkenda@cs.pdx.edu*.

[‡] The `untar.c` program available from the `elvis` `ftp` site is a very portable, simple program for unpacking `gziped` `tar` files on non-Unix systems.

vile: vi Like Emacs

vile stands for "vi Like Emacs." It started out as a copy of version 3.9 of MicroEMACS that was modified to have the "finger-feel" of vi. Thomas Dickey and Paul Fox are the maintainers. Over the years (since 1990), there have been other contributors, including Kevin Buettner and Clark Morgan.

The current version is 9.6, released late in 2007. The screenshots in this chapter were made with 9.5s (a pre-release beta). Until the late 1990s, version numbers advanced roughly one per year; starting with 1999, the scheme is about 0.1 per year—and someday will reach 10.

This chapter was written using vile.

Authors and History

Paul Fox describes the early vile history this way:

> vile's design goal has always been a little different than that of the other clones. vile has never *really* attempted to be a "clone" at all, though most people find it close enough. I started it because in 1990 I wanted to be able to edit multiple files in multiple windows, I had been using vi for 10 years already, and the sources to MicroEMACS came floating past my newsreader at a job where I had too much time on my hands. I started by changing the existing keymaps in the obvious way, and ran full-tilt into the "Hey! Where's 'insert' mode?" problem. So I hacked a little more, and hacked a little more, and eventually released in '91 or '92. (Starting soon thereafter, major version numbers tracked the year of release: 7.3 was the third release in '97.)

> But my goal has always been to preserve finger-feel (as opposed to the display visuals), and, selfishly, to preserve finger-feel most for the commands I use. ☺ vile has quite an amazing ex mode, that works very well—it just *looks* really odd, and a couple of commands that are beyond the scope of the current parser are missing. For the same reasons, vile also won't fully parse existing .exrc files, since I don't really think that's so important —it does simple ones, but more sophisticated ones need some tweaking. But when you toss in vile's built-in command/macro language, you quickly forget you ever cared about .exrc.

Thomas Dickey started working on vile in December of 1992, initially just contributing patches, and later doing more significant features and extensions, such as line numbering, name completion, and animating the buffer list window. He explains: "Integrating features together is more important to my design goals than implementing a large number of features."

In February of 1994, Kevin Buettner started working on vile. Initially, he supplied bug fixes for the X11 version, xvile, and then improvements, such as scrollbars. This evolved into support for the Motif, OpenLook, and Athena widget sets. Because the Athena widgets were, surprisingly, not "universally available in a bug-free form," he wrote a version that used the raw Xt toolkit. This version ended up providing superior functionality to the Athena version. Kevin also contributed the initial support in vile for GNU Autoconf.

The Win32 GUI port, called winvile, started in 1997, and continued on with extensions, including an OLE server and a Visual Studio add-in.

In the current version of vile, the perl interface and major modes (discussed later) are stable. They are used as a basis for other features, such as a server (using the perl interface) and syntax highlighting based on the major modes. For the near term, future work will focus on improving the locale support.

Important Command-Line Arguments

Although vile does not expect to be invoked as either vi or ex, it can be invoked as view, in which case it will treat each file as read-only. Unlike the other clones, it does *not* have a line-editor mode.

Here are the important vile command-line arguments:

-c *command*, + *command*

    vile will execute the given ex-style command. Any number of -c options may be given.

-h

    Invokes vile on the help file.

-R

    Invokes vile in "read-only" mode; no writes are permitted while in this mode. (This will also be true if vile is invoked as view, or if readonly mode is set in the startup file.)

-t *tag*

    Start editing at the specified *tag*. The -T option is equivalent and can be used when X11 option parsing eats the -t.

-v

    Invokes vile in "view" mode; no changes are permitted to any buffer while in this mode.

`-?`

> `vile` prints a short usage summary and then exits.

`@cmdfile`

> `vile` will run the specified file as its startup file, and will bypass any normal startup file (i.e., `.vilerc`) or environment variable (i.e., `VILEINIT`).

A few often-used options are obsolete since `vile` implements the POSIX `-c` (or `+`) option:

`-g N`

> `vile` will begin editing on the first file at the specified line number. This can also be given as `+N`.

`-s pattern`

> In the first file, `vile` will execute an initial search for the given pattern. This can also be given as `+/pattern`.

Online Help and Other Documentation

`vile` currently comes with a single (rather large) ASCII text file, `vile.hlp`. The `:help` command (which can be abbreviated to `:h`) opens a new window on that file. You can then search for information on a particular topic, using standard `vi` search techniques. Because it is a flat ASCII file, it is also easy to print out and read through.

In addition to the help file, `vile` has a number of built-in commands for displaying information about the facilities and state of the editor. Some of the most useful commands are:

`:show-commands`

> Creates a new window that shows a complete list of all `vile` commands, with a brief description of each one. The information is placed in its own buffer that can be treated just like any other `vile` buffer. In particular, it is easy to write it out to a file for later printing.

`:apropos`

> Shows all commands whose names contain a given substring. This is easier than just randomly searching through the help file to find information on a particular topic.

`:describe-key`

> Prompts you for a key or key sequence, and then shows the description of that command. For instance, the `x` key implements the `delete-next-character` function.

`:describe-function`

> Prompts you for a function name, and then shows the description of that function. For instance, the `delete-next-character` function deletes a given number of characters to the right of the current cursor position.

The :apropos, :describe-function, and :describe-key commands all give the descriptive information, plus all other synonyms (since a function may have more than one name, for convenience), all other keys that are bound to it (since many key sequences may be bound to the same function), and whether the command is a "motion" or an "operator." A good example of this is the output of :describe-function next-line:

```
"next-line"              ^J      ^N      j      #-B
    or    "down-arrow"
    or    "down-line"
    or    "forward-line"
    (motion:  move down CNT lines )
```

This shows all four of its names and its key bindings. (The sequence #-B is vile's terminal-independent representation of the up arrow—use :show-key-names for a complete list.)

The VILE_STARTUP_PATH environment variable can be set to a colon-separated search path for the help file.* The VILE_HELP_FILE environment variable can be used to override the name of the help file (typically vile.hlp).

The combination of online searchable help, built-in command and key descriptions, and command completion makes the help facility straightforward to use.

Initialization

xvile performs extra initialization for its menus, before the other steps:

1. (xvile only.) Use the value of the XVILE_MENU environment variable for the name of the menu description file, if provided. Otherwise, it uses .vilemenu. This file sets the default menus for the X11 interface.†

After that, the different versions vile, xvile, and winvile perform the same two-stage initialization. The first stage uses a mixture of environment variables and files:

2. Execute the file named on the command line with @cmdfile options, if any. Bypass any other initialization steps that would otherwise be done.

3. If the VILEINIT environment variable exists, execute its value. Otherwise, look for an initialization file.

4. If the VILE_STARTUP_FILE environment variable exists, use that as the name of the startup file. If not, on Unix use .vilerc, and on other systems use vile.rc.

5. Look for the startup file in the current directory, and then in the user's home directory. Use whichever one is found first.

The second stage uses the initialization commands:

---

* The Win32 port uses a semicolon as a list-separator; the OpenVMS port uses commas.

† winvile's menus are not configurable; they provide features that are supported only in Win32.

---

6. Load the first file specified on the command line into a memory buffer.

7. Execute the commands given with -c options, applying them by default to the first file.

Like the other clones, vile lets you place common initialization actions into your .exrc file (i.e., options and commands for Unix vi and/or the other clones), and use your .vilerc file to execute :source .exrc before or after the vile-specific initializations.

Multiwindow Editing

vile is somewhat different from the other clones. It started life as a version of Micro-EMACS, and then was modified into an editor with the "finger-feel" of vi.

One of the things that versions of Emacs have always done is handle multiple windows and multiple files; as such, vile was the first vi-like program to provide multiple windows and editing buffers.

As in elvis and Vim, the :split command‡ creates a new window, and then you can use the ex command :e *filename* to edit a new file in the new window. After that, things become different; in particular, the vi command mode keys to switch among windows are very different.

Figure 18-1 depicts a split screen that results from typing vile ch12.xml§ followed by :split and :e !zcat chapter.xml.gz.

Like Vim, all windows share the bottom line for execution of ex commands. Each window has its own status line, with the current window indicated by filling its status line with equals signs. The status line also acquires an I in the second column when in insert mode, and [modified] is appended after the filename when the file has been changed but not yet written out.

vile is also like Emacs in that commands are bound to key sequences. Table 18-1 presents the commands and their key sequences. In some cases, two sets of key sequences do the same operation, for example, the delete-other-windows command.

Table 18-1. vile window management commands

Command	Key sequence(s)	Function
delete-other-windows	^O, ^X 1	Eliminate all windows except the current one.
delete-window	^K, ^X 0	Destroy the current window, unless it is the last one.

‡ That this works is an artifact of vile allowing you to abbreviate commands. The actual command name is split-current-window.

§ The alert reader may have noticed that this is not Chapter 12. The chapters were renumbered during the development of the seventh edition.

```
 ┌────────────────────────────── /users/tom/vi-book/ch12.xml - vile ──────────────────────────────┐
 <chapter label="12" id="vi6-ch-12">
 <!--
   vile:docbookmode
   -->
 <title>vile&mdash;vi Like Emacs</title>

 <para><emphasis>vile</emphasis> stands for "vi Like Emacs."
 It started out as a copy of Version 3.9 of MicroEMACS
 that was modified to have the "finger feel" of <emphasis>vi</emphasis>.
 Thomas Dickey and Paul Fox are the maintainers.█
 === ch12.xml [docbookmode] ==============================================(10,48) 0% ==
 <?xml version="1.0"?>
 <!DOCTYPE book PUBLIC "-//OASIS//DTD DocBook XML V4.4//EN"
 "http://www.oasis-open.org/docbook/xml/4.4/docbookx.dtd" [
 <!ENTITY latex "!!LATEX!!">
 <!ENTITY tex "!!TEX!!">

 <!ENTITY ch12 SYSTEM "ch12.xml">
 ]>
 <book fpi="9780596529833">
 <title>Learning the vi and vim Editors</title>
 <bookinfo>
 [!zcat chapter.xml.] [xmlmode read-only] is !zcat chapter.xml.gz (2,1) 3%
```

Figure 18-1. Editing this chapter in vile

Command	Key sequence(s)	Function
edit-file, E, e	^X e	Bring given (or under-cursor, for ^X e) file or existing buffer into window.
find-file	^X e	Like edit-file.
grow-window	V	Increase the size of the current window by *count* lines.
move-next-window-down	^A ^E	Move next window down (or buffer up) by *count* lines.
move-next-window-up	^A ^Y	Move next window up (or buffer down) by *count* lines.
move-window-left	^X ^L	Scroll window to left by *count* columns, or a half screen if *count* is unspecified.
move-window-right	^X ^R	Scroll window to right by *count* columns, or a half screen if *count* is unspecified.
next-window	^X o	Move to the next window.
position-window	z *where*	Reframe with cursor specified by *where*, as follows: center (., M, m), top ($\boxed{\text{ENTER}}$, H, t), or bottom (-, L, b).
previous-window	^X O	Move to the previous window.
resize-window		Change the current window to *count* lines. *count* is supplied as a prefix argument.
restore-window		Return to window saved with save-window.
save-window		Mark a window for later return with restore-window.
scroll-next-window-down	^A ^D	Move next window down by *count* half screens. *count* is supplied as a prefix argument.

Command	Key sequence(s)	Function
scroll-next-window-up	^A ^U	Move next window up by *count* half screens. *count* is supplied as a prefix argument.
shrink-window	v	Decrease the size of the current window by *count* lines. *count* is supplied as a prefix argument.
split-current-window	^X 2	Split the window in half; a *count* of 1 or 2 chooses which becomes current. *count* is supplied as a prefix argument.
view-file		Bring given file or existing buffer into window, and mark it "view-only."
set-window		Bring existing buffer into window.
historical-buffer	_	Display a list of the first nine buffers. A digit moves to the given buffer; _ moves to the most recently edited file. Tab (and back-tab) rotate the list, making it simple to navigate in a list of long buffer names.
toggle-buffer-list	*	Pop up/down a window showing *all* the vile buffers.

GUI Interfaces

The screen shots and the explanation in this section were supplied by Kevin Buettner, Thomas Dickey, and Paul Fox. We thank them.

There are several X11 interfaces for vile, each utilizing a different toolkit based on the Xt library. There is a plain "No Toolkit" version that does not use a toolkit, but it has custom scrollbars and a bulletin board widget for geometry management. There are versions that use the Motif, Athena, or OpenLook toolkits.[||] The Motif and Athena versions are the best supported, and have menu support.

There is a "single" Win32 GUI—with variations to support OLE and Unicode. On the surface, they look the same.

Fortunately, the basic interface is the same for all versions. There is a single top-level window that can be split into two or more panes. The panes, in turn, may be used to display multiple views of a buffer, multiple buffers, or a mixture of both. In vile parlance these panes are called "windows," but to avoid confusion, we will continue to call them "panes" in the following discussion.

Building xvile

Although there are binary packages for xvile, you may wish to compile it on a platform with no package support.

[||] Sun Microsystems dropped support for OpenLook before releasing Solaris 9 in 2002.

When building `xvile`, you have to choose which toolkit version to use. This is done when you configure `vile` with the `configure` command.# The relevant options are:

`--with-screen=`*value*
> Specify terminal driver. The default is `tcap`, for the `termcap`/`terminfo` driver. Other values include `curses`, `ncurses`, `ncursesw`, `X11`, `OpenLook`, `Motif`, `Athena`, `Xaw`, `Xaw3d`, `neXtaw`, and `ansi`.

`--with-x`
> Use the X Window System. This is the "No Toolkit" version.

`--with-Xaw-scrollbars`
> Use `Xaw` scrollbars rather than the `vile` custom scrollbars.

`--with-drag-extension`
> Use the drag/scrolling extension with `Xaw`.

xvile Basic Appearance and Functionality

The following figures show `xvile`'s Motif interface. It is similar to the Athena interface.

Figure 18-2 shows three panes:

1. The manpage for `vile`, which shows the use of underlining and boldface.
2. A buffer `misc.c`, from `tin`, which shows syntax highlighting (this time with colors—grayscaled for printing—for preprocessor statements, comments, and keywords).
3. A three-line pane, which is active (noted by a darker status line), named [`Completions`], for filename completions. The pane is coordinated with the minibuffer (the colon command line): the first line reads `Completions prefixed by /usr/build/in/tin-1.9.2+/src/m:`, and the minibuffer reads `Find file: m`. The rest of the pane contains the actual filenames that match. The first line of [`Completions`] and the contents change as the user completes the filename (and presses TAB to tell `vile` to show the reduced set of choices).

Figure 18-3 also shows three panes:

1. The [`Help`] pane, which of course shows the most important feature of an editor (how to exit without modifying your files). ☺
2. The [`Buffer List`], which indicates that `charset.c` is the # (previous) buffer. The % (current) buffer is not shown on the list, since only the "visible" buffers are displayed in this copy of [`Buffer List`]. Supplying an argument to the * command would have shown the invisible buffers as well. Buffers 0 and 2 are `charset.c` and `misc.c`. They have been loaded, so their sizes (12425 and 89340) are displayed in the [`Buffer List`]. Buffer 1 (`<vile.1>`) holds a formatted manpage generated by a

---

The `configure` script should work for any Unix (or similar) platform. For building on OpenVMS, use the `vmsbuild.com` script. Build instructions are in comments at the top of the script.

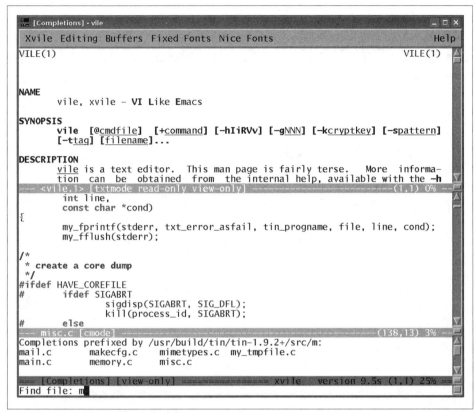

Figure 18-2. The xvile GUI window

macro and does not correspond to a file.[*] Buffer 3 (`color.c`) has not been loaded, so a u is displayed in the first column, and the size is shown as zero.

3. The [Completions] buffer is active. This time it displays tag completions for the partial match *co*, and the *Completions prefixed* message is not shown because the buffer is scrolled down, which is another side effect of pressing TAB : vile cycles through a scrolling action so that all of the choices will be shown, even when the window is small.[†]

Generated buffers such as [Help] and [Buffer List] are "scratch" buffers. When popped down, they are closed, and their content is discarded. There are other buffers, e.g., those containing scripts, which are "invisible." Both are normally not shown in [Buffer List].

---

[*] The angle-brackets in the name `<vile.1>` are a convention to avoid naming conflicts, since two buffers are not allowed to have the same name.

[†] The [Completions] buffer is automatically sized, showing no more lines than necessary. If it is too large for the available space, vile borrows up to ¾ of the space from an adjacent pane.

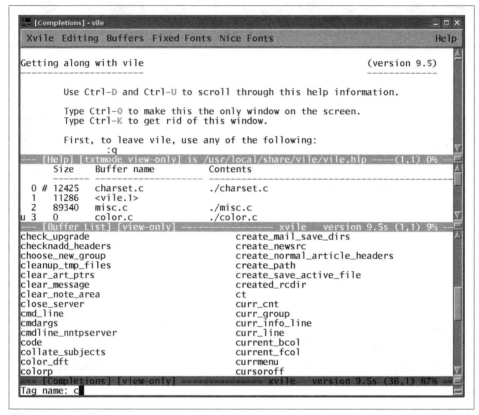

Figure 18-3. Buffers and completions in vile

Scrollbars

At the right of each pane is a scrollbar that may be used in the customary fashion to move about in the buffer. Note, however, that the customary fashion varies from toolkit to toolkit. In the Athena and "No Toolkit" versions, the middle mouse button may be used to drag the "thumb" or visible indicator around. The left and right mouse buttons move down or up (respectively) in the buffer. The amount moved depends on the location of the mouse cursor on the scrollbar. Placing it near the top will scroll by as little as one line. When placed near the bottom, the text will scroll by as much as a full pane.

The Motif scrollbar is probably more familiar. The leftmost mouse button is used for all operations. Clicking on the little arrows will move up or down by one line. The scrollbar indicator may be dragged in order to move about, and scrolling up or down by an entire pane can be accomplished by clicking above or below the indicator.

In each version, there is a small handle above or below (i.e., between) scrollbars that may be used to adjust the size of two adjacent panes. In the "No Toolkit" version of

---

xvile, the pane resize handle blends in with the status line of two adjacent panes. In the other versions, the resize handle is more distinguishable. But in each case, the mouse cursor will change to a heavy vertical double arrow when placed above the resize handle. The windows may be resized by clicking on and dragging the handle.

A pane can be split into two by holding the Ctrl key down and clicking the left mouse button on a scrollbar. Then you will have two views of a particular buffer. Other vile commands may be used to replace one of the views with another buffer if desired. A pane may be deleted by holding the Ctrl key down and clicking the middle mouse button. Sometimes after creating a lot of panes, you find yourself wanting to use all of the window real estate for just one pane. To do this, Ctrl-click the right mouse button; all other panes will be removed, leaving the entire xvile window containing only the pane on which you clicked. These actions are summarized in Table 18-2.

Table 18-2. vile pane management commands

Command	Function
Ctrl-left button	On a scrollbar, split the pane.
Ctrl-middle button	Delete a pane.
Ctrl-right button	Make the clicked pane the only pane.

Setting the cursor position and mouse motions

Within the text area of a pane, the cursor may be set by clicking the left mouse button. This not only sets the cursor position, but also sets the pane in which editing is being done. To set just the pane but preserve the old position, click on the status line below the text you wish to edit.

A mouse click is viewed as a motion, just like 4j is considered a motion. To delete five lines, you could enter d4j, which will delete the current line and the four below it. You can do the same thing with a mouse click. Position your cursor at the place you want to start deleting from and then press d. After this, click in the buffer at the point to which you wish to delete. Mouse clicks are real motions and may be used with other operators as well.

Selections

Selections may be made by holding the left mouse button down and dragging with the mouse. This is called the PRIMARY selection. Release of the mouse button causes the selection to be yanked and made available (if desired) for pasting. You can force the selected region to be rectangular by holding the Ctrl key down while dragging with the left button depressed. If the dragging motion goes out of the current window, text will be scrolled in the appropriate direction, if possible, to accommodate selections larger than the window. The speed at which the scrolling occurs will increase with the passage of time, making it practical to select large regions of text quickly.

Individual words or lines may be selected by double- or triple-clicking on them.

A selection may be extended by clicking the right mouse button. As with the left button, the selection can be adjusted or scrolled by holding the right button down and dragging with it. Selections may be extended in any window open to the same buffer as the one in which the selection was started. That is, if you have two views of a buffer (in two different panes), one containing the start of the buffer and the other the end, it is possible to select the entire buffer by clicking the left button at the beginning of the pane that shows the beginning of the buffer and then clicking the right button in the pane that shows the end of the buffer. Also, selections may be extended in a rectangular fashion by holding the Ctrl key down in conjunction with the right mouse button.

The middle button is used for pasting the selection. By default, it pastes at the last text cursor position. If the Shift key is held down while clicking the middle button, the paste occurs at the position of the mouse cursor.

A selection may be cleared (if owned by xvile) by double-clicking on one of the status lines.

Clipboard

Data may be exchanged between many X applications via the PRIMARY selection. This selection is set and manipulated as described previously.

Other applications use the CLIPBOARD selection to exchange data between applications. On many Sun keyboards, selected text is moved to the clipboard by pressing the COPY key and pasted by pressing the PASTE key. If you find that you cannot paste text selected in xvile into other applications (or vice versa), it may well be that these applications use the CLIPBOARD selection instead of the PRIMARY selection. (The other mechanism used among really old applications involves the use of a ring of cut buffers.)

xvile provides two commands for manipulating the clipboard: copy-to-clipboard and paste-from-clipboard. When copy-to-clipboard is executed, the contents of the current selection are copied to the special clipboard kill register (denoted by ; in the register list). When an application requests the clipboard selection, xvile gives it the contents of this kill register. The paste-from-clipboard command requests clipboard data from the current owner of the CLIPBOARD selection.

Users of Sun systems may want to put the following key bindings in their .vilerc file in order to make use of the COPY and PASTE keys found on their keyboards:

```
bind-key copy-to-clipboard #-^
bind-key paste-from-clipboard #-*
```

Key bindings are described in detail later in this chapter.

Resources

xvile has many resources that can be used to control appearance and behavior. Font choice is particularly important if you want italic or oblique fonts to be displayed properly. vile's documentation has a complete list of resources, as well a sample set of .Xdefault entries.

Adding menus

The Motif and Athena versions have menu support. Menu items, which are user-definable, are read from the .vilemenu file, in the current or home directory.

xvile allows three types of menu items:

- Built-in, i.e., specific to the menuing system, such as rereading the .vilerc file or spawning a new copy of xvile
- Direct invocation of built-in commands (e.g., displaying the [Buffer List])
- Invocation of arbitrary command strings (e.g., running interactive macros, such as a search command)

We make a distinction between the last two because the authors prefer making vile able to check the validity of commands before they are executed.

Building winvile

Binaries are available for each release of winvile, but you may wish to compile one of the interim patch versions. The sources provide makefiles for the Microsoft (makefile.wnt) and Borland (makefile.tbc) compilers. The former has more features, providing options for building with OLE, perl, and built-in syntax highlighting. The Win32 GUI can be built with either compiler environment.

winvile Basic Appearance and Functionality

Figures 18-4 and 18-5 show winvile's Win32 GUI interface. On the surface, it is much like the "No Toolkit" X11 interface, having scrollbars. Underneath the surface—which is easily accessed—it is more elaborate than the Motif interface.

Figure 18-4 shows a view of winvile editing Unicode data:

- The font dialog is initially set to the fixed-pitch system font. Like xvile, the font can be set when winvile is started, or via a script. It can also be set via an OLE server. Finally, as shown here, it can use the Win32 common controls.
- The data is Unicode UTF-16, with no byte order mark. It is underlined, since the highlighting palette used underlining and cyan for coloring quoted strings.
- The default system font cannot display the characters in the file. winvile sees that the font is small, and displays the Unicode data in hexadecimal form.

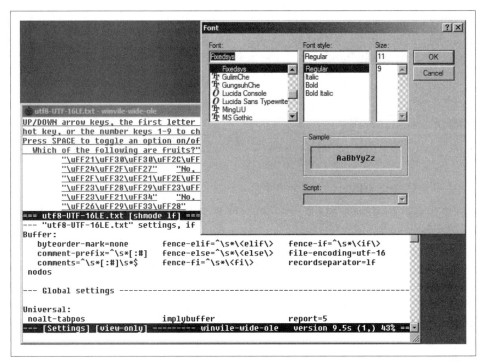

Figure 18-4. winvile with non-Unicode font

Figure 18-5 shows the result of selecting a more capable font. If you select the system font again, `winvile` will show the hexadecimal values again. If you prefer to see the wide characters as hexadecimal all the time, `vile` has an option setting for this purpose.

Figure 18-6 shows some of the `winvile` menu functions, which include:

- `winvile` extends the system menu, which is accessed by right-clicking on the title bar of the window.

  It also has the same selections on a right-click pop-up menu, eliminating the need to go up to the title bar. That is enabled by the "Menu" entry at the bottom.

- The menus provide the open, save, print, and font operations typical of GUI applications. You can also set `winvile`'s current working directory with the *CD* entry.

  The corresponding dialogs are also accessible from the Win32 console version, though without a menu.

- `winvile` also allows you to browse the Windows *Favorites* folder.

- The recent files (and recent folders) entries select from a user-configurable number of "recent" files (or folders). `winvile` saves the names in the user's registry data, making them available for each instance of `winvile` that might be running.

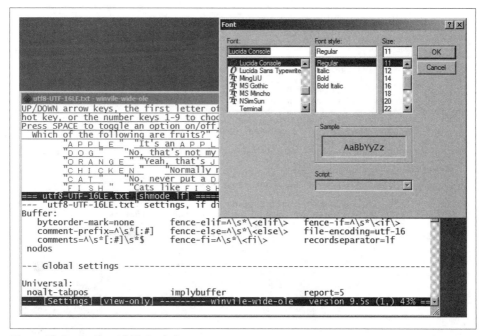

Figure 18-5. winvile with Unicode font

Extended Regular Expressions

We introduced extended regular expressions earlier in the section "Extended Regular Expressions" on page 128. `vile` provides essentially the same facilities as `nvi`'s `extended` option. This includes the POSIX bracket expressions for character classes, `[[:alnum::]]`, with some extensions (additional classes and abbreviations), and interval expressions, such as `{,10}`. The syntax is somewhat different from `nvi`, relying on additional backslash-escaped characters:

`\|`

  Indicates alternation: `house\|home`.

`\+`

  Matches one or more of the preceding regular expression.

`\?`

  Matches zero or one of the preceding regular expression.

`\(...\)`

  Provides grouping for `*`, `\+`, and `\?`, as well as making matched subtexts available in the replacement part of a substitute command (`\1`, `\2`, etc.).

`\s, \S`

  Match whitespace and nonwhitespace characters, respectively.

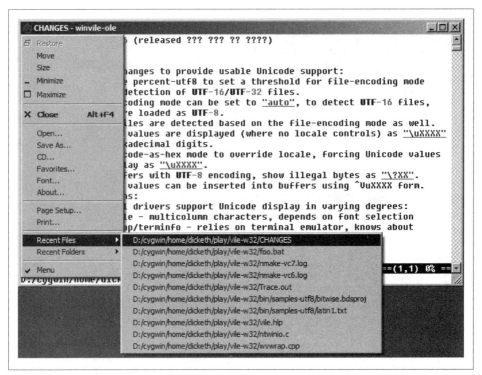

Figure 18-6. The winvile recent files menu

`\w, \W`

Match "word-constituent" characters (alphanumerics and the underscore, "_") and non-word-constituent characters, respectively. For example, `\w\+` would match C/C++ identifiers and keywords.[‡]

`\d, \D`

Match digits and nondigits, respectively.

`\p, \P`

Match printable and nonprintable characters, respectively. Whitespace is considered to be printable.

`vile` allows the escape sequences `\b`, `\f`, `\r`, `\t`, and `\n` to appear in the replacement part of a substitute command. They stand for backspace, form feed, carriage return, tab, and newline, respectively. Also, from the `vile` documentation:

> Note that `vile` mimics `perl`'s handling of `\u\L\1\E` instead of `vi`'s. Given `:s/\(abc\)/\u \L\1\E/`, `vi` will replace with *abc* whereas `vile` and `perl` will replace with *Abc*. This is somewhat more useful for capitalizing words.

[‡] For the pedantic among you, it also matches identifiers that start with a leading digit; usually this isn't much of a problem.

Improved Editing Facilities

This section describes the features of vile that make simple text editing easier and more powerful.

Command-Line History and Completion

vile records your ex commands in a buffer named [History]. This feature is controlled with the history option, which is true by default. Turning it off disables the history feature and removes the [History] buffer. The command show-history splits the screen and displays the [History] buffer in a new window.

The colon command line is really a minibuffer. You can use it to recall lines from the [History] buffer and edit them.

You use the ↑ and ↓ keys to scroll backward and forward in the history, and ← and → to move around within the line. Your current delete character (usually BACK-SPACE) can be used to delete characters. Any other characters you type will be inserted at the current cursor position.

You can toggle the minibuffer into vi mode by typing the mini-edit character (by default, ^G). When you do this, vile will highlight the minibuffer using the mechanism specified by the mini-hilite option. The default is reverse, for reverse video. In vi mode, you can use vi-style commands for positioning. You can also use other vile commands that are appropriate to editing within a single line, such as i, I, a, and A. vile decides which commands to accept based on its command tables, which allows your key bindings to work in the minibuffer, too.

An interesting feature is that vile will use the history to show you previous data that corresponds to the command you're entering. For instance, after typing :set followed by a space, vile will prompt you with Global value:. At that point, you can use ↑ to see previous global variables that you have set, should you wish to change one of them.

The ex command line provides completion of various sorts. As you type the name of a command, you can hit the TAB key at any point. vile fills out the rest of the command name as much as possible. If you type a TAB a second time, vile creates a new window that shows you all the possible completions.

Completion applies to built-in and user-defined vile commands, tags, filenames, modes (described later in this chapter), variables, enumerated values (such as color names), and to the terminal characters (the character settings such as backspace, suspend, and so on, derived from your stty settings).

As a side note, this leads to an interesting phenomenon. In vi-style editors, commands may have long names, but they tend to be unique in the first few characters, since abbreviations are accepted. In Emacs-style editors, command names often are not unique in the first several characters, but command completion still allows you to get away with less typing.

Tag Stacks

Tag stacking is described earlier in the section "Tag Stacks" on page 131. In vile, tag stacking is available and straightforward. It is somewhat different than the other clones, most notably in the vi mode commands that are used for tag searching and popping the tag stack. Table 18-3 shows the vile tag commands.

Table 18-3. vile tag commands

Command	Function
next-tag	Continues searching through the tags file for more matches.
pop[!]	Pops a cursor position off the stack, restoring the cursor to its previous position.
show-tagstack	Creates a new window that displays the tag stack. The display changes as tags are pushed onto or popped off of the stack.
ta[g][!] [*tagstring*]	Edit the file containing *tagstring* as defined in the tags file. The ! forces vile to switch to the new file if the current buffer has been modified but not saved.

The vi mode commands are described in Table 18-4.

Table 18-4. vile command mode tag commands

Command	Function
^]	Look up the location of the identifier under the cursor in the tags file, and move to that location. The current location is automatically pushed onto the tag stack.
^T, ^X ^]	Return to the previous location in the tag stack, i.e., pop off one element.
^A ^]	Same as the :next-tag command.

As in the other editors, options control how vile manages the tag-related commands, as shown in Table 18-5.

Table 18-5. vile options for tag management

Option	Function
pin-tagstack	Makes tag searches and pop ups not change the current window, thereby "pinning" it. This option is false by default.
tagignorecase	Makes tag searches ignore case. This option is false by default.
taglength	Controls the number of significant characters in a tag that is to be looked up. The default value of zero indicates that all characters are significant.
tagrelative	When using a tags file in another directory, filenames in that tags file are considered to be relative to the directory where the tags file is.

Option	Function
tags	Can be set to a whitespace-separated list of **tags** files to use for looking up tags. **vile** loads all **tags** files into separate buffers that are hidden by default, but that can be edited if you wish. You can place environment variables and shell wildcards into **tags**.
tagword	Uses the whole word under the cursor for the tag lookup, not just the subword starting at the current cursor position. This option is disabled by default, which keeps **vile** compatible with **vi**.

Infinite Undo

vile is similar in principle but different in practice from the other editors. Like **elvis** and Vim, you can set an undo limit, but like **nvi**, the **.** command will do the next undo or redo as appropriate. Separate **vi** mode commands implement successive undo and redo.

vile uses the **undolimit** option to control how many changes it will store. The default is 10, meaning that you can undo up to the 10 most recent changes. Setting it to zero allows true "infinite undo," but this may consume a lot of memory.

To start an undo, first use either the u or ^X u commands. Then, each successive **.** command will do another undo. Like **vi**, two u commands just toggle the state of the change; however, each ^X u command does another undo.

The ^X r command does a redo. Typing **.** after the first ^X r will do successive redos. You can provide a count to the ^X u and ^X r commands, in which case **vile** performs the requested number of undos or redos.

Arbitrary Length Lines and Binary Data

vile can edit files with arbitrary length lines, and with an arbitrary number of lines.

vile automatically handles binary data. No special command lines or options are required. To enter 8-bit text, type ^V followed by an x and two hexadecimal digits, or a 0 and three octal digits, or three decimal digits.

You can also enter 16-bit Unicode values by typing ^V followed by a u and up to four hexadecimal digits. If the current buffer's **file-encoding** option is one of the Unicode flavors (utf-8, utf-16, or utf-32), **vile** stores it directly as UTF-8, displaying it according to the capabilities of the terminal or display.

This leads us into the topic of localization.

Locale support

For many years, **vile** had only rudimentary locale support. In part this was because locale support on the various platforms was rudimentary (except for vendor Unix systems). It had its own character type tables (i.e., control, numeric, printable, punctuation, as well as application-specific filename, wildcard, shell), allowing you to specify which of those non-ASCII characters were printable.

Times change, and `vile` continues to evolve according to its users' needs. Here is a brief summary of those changes, ordered logically rather than in the order they were developed:

- Rather than having a fixed notion of the character types, `vile` imports the host's character type tables and then provides commands to modify the data via scripts.[§]
- `vile` regular expressions support POSIX character classes, as well as classes corresponding to `vile`'s own character types.
- `vile` supports extraction of tokens from the screen, e.g., for `tags`, for scripting, etc. Once, these tokens were a mixture of character-type tests with special parsing logic. Now, they are purely regular expressions, with no need for the parsing logic.
- Editing a file containing 8-bit data—e.g., data encoded in ISO-8859-7 (Greek)— when the host's locale encoding uses UTF-8 can be challenging. When `vile` starts up, it checks whether the host locale ends with UTF-8 (or similar), e.g., `el_GR.UTF-8`. If so, it then supports editing in the corresponding 8-bit locale, e.g., `el_GR`.
- Similarly, when editing files in a host environment supporting UTF-8, there are files encoded in UTF-8. In the newest release, you can tell `vile` to write a file in various Unicode encodings, and to read the same encodings. The 8-bit editing model is carried forward, translating to the 8-bit encoding for buffers that are marked as 8-bit, and directly editing (i.e., with no translation) the Unicode buffers.

These are all extensions; at each stage the older features are still retained.

There are other aspects of localization that are not addressed in `vile`, such as message formatting and text collating order.

File formats

When `vile` reads a file, it makes several guesses about its content, in order to present you with useful data:

- It checks whether the file permissions allow you to write to the file.
- It checks for line endings, which may be different flavors of CR, LF, or CR/LF.
- It checks for Unicode byte order marks.
- It checks for Unicode multibyte encodings.

Based on these checks, `vile` may set properties (called "modes") of the newly read buffer that apply to that buffer. In addition, it may translate the data as it is read:

[§] This feature is useful even on the vendor Unix systems, which do not always deliver correct tables.

- It removes the line endings from each line, remembering the associated `recordseparator` mode.
- If the file is missing a final line ending, `vile` sets the `nonewline` option.
- It translates UTF-16 and UTF-32 data into UTF-8, remembering the associated `file-encoding` option.

When you tell `vile` to write a buffer to a file, it uses these local option settings to reconstruct the file.

Incremental Searching

As mentioned earlier in the section "Incremental Searching" on page 136, you perform incremental searching in `vile` using the ^X S and ^X R commands. It is not necessary to set an option to enable incremental searching.

The cursor moves through the file as you type, always being placed on the first character of the text that matches. ^X S incrementally searches forward through the file, whereas ^X R incrementally searches backward.

You may wish to add the following commands (described later in "The vile Editing Model" on page 368) to your `.vilerc` file to make the more familiar / and ? search commands work incrementally:

```
bind-key incremental-search /
bind-key reverse-incremental-search ?
```

Also of interest is the "visual match" facility, which highlights *all* occurrences of the matched expression. For a `.vilerc` file:

```
set visual-matches reverse
```

directs `vile` to use reverse video for visual matching. Since the highlighting can sometimes be visually distracting, the = command turns off any current highlighting until you enter a new search pattern.

Left-Right Scrolling

As mentioned earlier in the section "Left-Right Scrolling" on page 137, you enable left-right scrolling in `vile` using `:set nolinewrap`. Unlike the other editors, left-right scrolling is the default. Long lines are marked at the left and right edges with < and >. The value of `sideways` controls the number of characters by which `vile` shifts the screen when scrolling left to right. With `sideways` set to zero, each scroll moves the screen by one third. Otherwise, the screen scrolls by the desired number of characters.

Visual Mode

vile is different from elvis and Vim in the way you highlight the text you want to operate on. It uses the "quoted motion" command, q.

You enter q at the beginning of the region, any other vi motions to get to the opposite end of the region, and then another q to end the quoted motion. vile highlights the marked text.

Arguments to the q command determine what kind of highlighting it will do. 1q (same as q) does an exact highlighting, 2q does line-at-a-time highlighting, and 3q does rectangular highlighting.

Typically, you use a quoted motion in conjunction with an operator, such as d or y. Thus, d3qjjwq deletes the rectangle indicated by the motions. When used without an operator, the region is left highlighted. It can be referred to later using ^S. Thus, d ^S will delete the highlighted region.

In addition, rectangular regions can be indicated through the use of marks.[||] As you know, a mark can be used to refer to either a specific character (when referred to with `) or a specific line (when referred to with '). In addition, referring to the mark (say, a mark set with mb) with `b instead of 'b can change the nature of the operation being done—d'b will delete a set of lines, and d`b will delete two partial lines and the lines in between. Using the ` form of mark reference gives a more "exact" region than the ' form of mark reference.

vile adds a third form of mark reference. The \ command can be used as another way of referring to a mark. By itself, it behaves just like ` and moves the cursor to the character at which the mark was set. When combined with an operator, however, the behavior is quite different. The mark reference becomes "rectangular," such that the action d\b will delete the rectangle of characters whose corners are marked by the cursor and the character that holds mark b:

Keystrokes	Results
| ma | ```
The 6th edition of <citetitle>Learning the vi Editor</citetitle>
brings the book into the late 1990&rsquo;s.
In particular, besides the &ldquo;original&rdquo; version of
<command>vi</command> that comes as a standard part of every Unix system,
there are now a number of freely available &ldquo;clones&rdquo;
or work-alike editors.
``` |
| | Set mark a at the *b* in *book*. |
| 3jfr | ```
The 6th edition of <citetitle>Learning the vi Editor</citetitle>
brings the book into the late 1990&rsquo;s.
In particular, besides the &ldquo;original&rdquo; version of
<command >vi</command> that comes as a standard part of every Unix system,
there are now a number of freely available &ldquo;clones&rdquo;
or work-alike editors.
``` |
| | Move the cursor to the *r* in *number* to mark the opposite corner. |

[||] Thanks to Paul Fox for this explanation.

Keystrokes	Results
^A ~\a	The 6th edition of \<citetitle>Learning the vi Editor\</citetitle> brings the BOOK INTO The late 1990’s. In particulAR, BESIDES the “original” version of \<command>vi\</COMMAND> that comes as a standard part of every Unix system, there are nOW A NUMBER of freely available “clones” or work-alike editors.
	Toggle the case of the rectangle bounded with mark **a**.

The commands that define arbitrary regions and operate upon them are summarized in Table 18-6.

Table 18-6. vile block mode operations

Command	Operation
q	Start and end a quoted motion.
^A r	Open up a rectangle.
>	Shift text to the right. Same as ^A r when the region is rectangular.
<	Shift text to the left. Same as **d** when the region is rectangular.
y	Yank the whole region. vile remembers that it was rectangular.
c	Change the region. For a nonrectangular region, delete all the text between the end points and enter insert mode. For a rectangular region, prompt for the text to fill the lines.
^A u	Change the case of the region to all uppercase.
^A l	Change the case of the region to all lowercase.
^A ~	Toggle the case of all alphabetic characters in the region.
^A SPACE	Fill the region with spaces.
p, P	Put the text back. vile does a rectangular put if the original text was rectangular.
^A p, ^A P	Force previously yanked text to be put back as if it were rectangular. The width of the longest yanked line is used for the rectangle's width.

Programming Assistance

vile's programming assistance capabilities are discussed in this section.

Edit-Compile Speedup

vile uses two straightforward **vi** mode commands to manage program development, shown in Table 18-7.

Table 18-7. vile program development vi mode commands

Command	Function
^X !*command* ENTER	Run *command*, saving the output in a buffer named [Output].
^X ^X	Find the next error. vile parses the output and moves to the location of each successive error.

vile understands the *Entering directory XXX* and *Leaving directory XXX* messages that GNU `make` generates, allowing it to find the correct file, even if it's in a different directory.

The error messages are parsed using regular expressions in the buffer [`Error Expressions`]. `vile` automatically creates this buffer, and then it uses the buffer when you use `^X ^X`. You can add expressions to it as needed, and it has an extended syntax that allows you to specify where filenames, line numbers, columns, and so on appear in the error messages. Full details are provided in the online help, but you probably won't need to make any changes, as it works pretty well "out of the box."

`vile`'s error finder also compensates for changes in the file, keeping track of additions and deletions as you progress to each error.

The error finder applies to the most recent buffer created by reading from a shell command. For example, `^X!command` produces a buffer named [`Output`], and `:e !command` produces a buffer named [`!command`]. The error finder will be set appropriately.

You can point the error finder at an arbitrary buffer (not just the output of shell commands) using the `:error-buffer` command. This lets you use the error finder on the output of previous compiler or `egrep` runs.

Syntax Highlighting

`vile` supports syntax highlighting in all configurations. It uses custom *syntax filter* programs to perform syntax coloring. These may be built into `vile` or run as external programs. `vile` sends the contents of the buffer to be colored by the syntax filter, reads a marked-up version of it, and applies the markup to color the buffer.

> Built-in filters are faster than external programs, and eliminate interference from your shell when displaying in a terminal. For some platforms, the syntax filters can be dynamically loaded. This allows the editor executable to be smaller, though not as fast as with the built-in filters.

There are currently 71 programs, as well as a separate program for Unix manpages. Some of the programs are used for more than one type of file. For instance, C, C++, and Java have similar syntax, but use different keywords.

`vile` provides macros that run the syntax filters on demand, or automatically as you modify the buffer. These are summarized in Table 18-8.

Table 18-8. vile syntax highlighting commands

Command	Key binding	Function
`:HighlightFilter`		Invoke syntax-highlighting filter on the current buffer. `vile` chooses a filter based on an extended property of the

Command	Key binding	Function
		buffer, called a *major mode* (discussed later in the section "Major Modes" on page 370).
		If the filters are built-in, `vile`'s initialization sets the *auto-color* mode to invoke this macro five seconds after you stop modifying a buffer.
`:HighlightFilterMsg`	`^X-q`	Attach highlighting to the current buffer using `HighlightFilter`. Display a message on completion.[a]
`:HighlightClear`	`^X-Q`	Clear all highlighting from the current buffer. This does not alter the buffer's major mode.
`:set-highlighting majormode`		Change the buffer's major mode to *majormode* and run the syntax highlighter.
`:show-filtermsgs`		Show syntax-filter error messages for the current buffer. If the *syntax filter* finds any errors, it reports them, and `vile` displays them in the `[Filter Messages]` buffer and sets the error buffer to allow you to step through the places where an error is found.

[a] When syntax highlighting was first implemented in `vile` in the mid-1990s, it was important to show that it was completed. Times change—machines are faster.

Each time a *syntax filter* runs, it reads one or more external files containing the keywords to be highlighted, along with their corresponding color and video attributes (bold, underline, italic). It searches for these files (suffixed `.keywords`) using the name of the buffer's *majormode*. The search rules are documented in the online help. You can use the `:which-keywords` macro to show the locations where `vile` will look for the files, and where it finds them. See Example 18-1.

Example 18-1. Sample output of ":which-keywords cmode"

```
Show which keyword-files are tested for:
        cmode                           ❶
(* marks found-files)

$cwd                                    ❷
  ./.c.keywords
$HOME
  ~/.c.keywords
  ~/.vile/c.keywords
$startup-path                           ❸
* /usr/local/share/vile/c.keywords
```

❶ The *major mode*, which always ends with "mode"

❷ Your current working directory

❸ `vile`'s search path for scripts

Whether the configuration is X11, terminal (`termcap`, `terminfo`, `curses`), or Windows, `vile`'s syntax filters use a common set of colors, defined in classes: `Action`, `Comment`, `Error`, `Ident`, `Ident2`, `Keyword`, `Keyword2`, `Literal`, `Number`, `Preproc`, and `Type`. Most of the keyword definitions refer to a class. Doing this allows you to modify all of the colors by changing just one file, normally your $HOME/.vile.keywords file. The online help gives details on customizing the syntax colors.

On the one hand, because syntax highlighting is accomplished with an external program, it should be possible to write any number of highlighters for different languages. On the other hand, because the facilities are rather low-level, doing so is not for nonprogrammers. The online help describes how the highlight filters should work.

The directory *ftp://invisible-island.net/vile/utilities* contains user-contributed filters for coloring makefiles, input, perl, HTML, and troff. It even contains a macro that will color the lines in RCS files according to their age!

Interesting Features

vile has a number of interesting features that are the topic of this section:

The vile *editing model*
> vile's editing model is somewhat different from vi's. Based on concepts from Emacs, it provides key rebinding and a more dynamic command line.

Major modes
> vile supports editing "modes." These are groups of option settings that make it convenient for editing different kinds of files.

The procedure language
> vile's procedure language allows you to define functions and macros that make the editor more programmable and flexible.

Miscellaneous small features
> A number of smaller features make day-to-day editing easier.

The vile Editing Model

In vi and the other clones, editing functionality is "hardwired" into the editor. The association between command characters and what they do is built into the code. For example, the x key deletes characters, and the i key enters insert mode. Without resorting to severe trickery, you cannot switch the functionality of the two keys (if it can even be done at all).

vile's editing model, derived from Emacs through MicroEMACS, is different. The editor has defined, named functions, each of which performs a single editing task, such as delete-next-character or delete-previous-character. Many of the functions are then bound to keystrokes, such as binding delete-next-character to x.[#]

[#] vile 9.6 has 421 defined functions (including some that are available only in the X11 or Win32 configurations), with predefined key bindings for about 260.

vile has different flavors of key bindings for its insert, command, and selection modes. Here we are describing the bindings for the normal editing mode. Changing bindings is very easy to do. Use the `:bind-key` command, and as arguments, give the name of the function and then the key sequence to bind the function to. As mentioned earlier, you might put the following commands into your `.vilerc` file:

```
bind-key incremental-search /
bind-key reverse-incremental-search ?
```

These commands change the / and ? search commands to do incremental searching.

In addition to predefined functions, vile contains a simple programming language that allows you to write procedures. You can then bind the command for executing a procedure to a keystroke sequence. GNU Emacs uses a variant of Lisp for its language, which is extremely powerful. vile has a somewhat simpler, less general-purpose language.

Also, as in Emacs, the vile command line is very interactive. Many commands display a default value for their operand, which you can either edit if inappropriate or select by hitting ENTER. As you type vi mode editing commands, such as those that change or delete characters, you will see feedback about the operation in the status line.

The "amazing" ex mode that Paul referred to earlier is best reflected in the behavior of the `:s` (substitute) command. It prompts for each part of the command: the search pattern, the replacement text, and any flags.

As an example, let's assume you wish to change all instances of *perl* to *awk* everywhere in your file. In the other editors, you'd simply type `:1,$s/perl/awk/g` ENTER, and that's what would appear on the command line. The following examples describe what you see on the vile colon command line *as you type*:

Keystrokes	Results
`:1,$s`	The first part of the substitute command.
`/`	`substitute pattern: █` vile prompts you for the pattern to search for. Any previous pattern is placed there for you to reuse.
`perl/`	`replacement string: █` At the next / delimiter, vile prompts you for the replacement text. Any previous text is placed there for you to reuse.
`awk/`	`(g)lobally, ([1-9])th occurrence on line, (c)onfirm, and/or (p)rint result: █` At the final delimiter, vile prompts for the optional flags. Enter any desired flags, then press ENTER.

vile follows through with this style of behavior on all appropriate ex commands. For example, the read command (`:r`) prompts you with the name of the last file you read. To read that file again, just hit ENTER.

Finally, `vile`'s ex command parser is weaker than in the other editors. For example, you cannot use search patterns to specify line ranges (`:/now/,/forever/s/perl/awk/g`), and the move command (`m`) is not implemented. In practice, what's not implemented does not seem to hinder you very much.

Major Modes

A *major mode*[*] is a collection of option settings that apply when editing a certain class of file. These options apply on a per-buffer basis, such as the tab-stop settings.

`vile` provides three types of options:

- *Universal*, applied to the program
- *Buffer*, applied to the content of a memory buffer
- *Window*, applied to windows ("panes," in our terminology)

The *buffer*—and *window*—option settings can be global or local values. Any buffer (or window, depending on the option) can have its own private (local) option value. If it does not have a private value, it uses the global value. Major modes add a level between the *buffer* global and local values by providing option values that a buffer uses if it does not have a private value.

`vile` has two built-in major modes: `cmode`, for editing C and C++ programs, and `vile` mode, for its scripts that are loaded into memory buffers. With `cmode`, you can use `%` to match C preprocessor conditionals (`#if`, `#else`, and `#endif`). `vile` will do automatic source code indentation based on the placement of braces (`{` and `}`), and it will do smart formatting of C comments. The `tabstop` and `shiftwidth` options are set on a per-major-mode basis as well.

Using major modes, you can apply the same features to programs written in other languages. This example, courtesy of Thomas Dickey, defines a new major mode, `shmode`, for editing Bourne shell scripts. (This is useful for any Bourne-style shell, such as `ksh`, `bash`, or `zsh`.)

```
define-mode sh
set shsuf "\.sh$"
set shpre "^#!\\s*\/.*sh\\>$"
define-submode sh comment-prefix "^\\s*/[:#]"
define-submode sh comments        "^\\s*/\\?[:#]\\s+/\\?\\s*$"
define-submode sh fence-if        "^\\s*\\<if\\>"
define-submode sh fence-elif      "^\\s*\\<elif\\>"
define-submode sh fence-else      "^\\s*\\<else\\>"
define-submode sh fence-fi        "^\\s*\\<fi\\>"
```

[*] `vile`'s documentation spells it as a single word.

The shsuf (shell suffix) variable describes the filename suffix that indicates a file is a shell script. The shpre (shell preamble) variable describes a first line of the file that indicates that the file contains shell code. The define-submode commands then add options that apply only to buffers where the corresponding major mode is set. The examples here set up the smart comment formatting and the smart % command matching for shell programs.

The example shown is more verbose than needed. vile's scripting language recognizes a more concise description using ~with:

```
define-mode sh
~with define-submode sh
        suf              "\.sh$"
        pre              "^#!\\s*\/.*sh\\>$"
        comment-prefix   "^\\s*/[:#]"
        comments         "^\\s*/\\?[:#]\\s+/\\?\\s*$"
        fence-if         "^\\s*\\<if\\>"
        fence-elif       "^\\s*\\<elif\\>"
        fence-else       "^\\s*\\<else\\>"
        fence-fi         "^\\s*\\<fi\\>"
~endwith
```

With its initialization scripts, vile provides 90 predefined major modes. Use the :show-majormodes command to see the definitions of the available major modes.

The suffix and prefix are criteria used by vile to decide which major mode to apply, when it reads a file into a buffer.[†] Table 18-9 lists all of the criteria.

Table 18-9. Major mode criteria

Criteria	Description
after	Force the defined major mode to be checked after the given major mode. Normally, major modes are checked in the order in which they are defined.
before	Force the defined major mode to be checked before the given major mode. Normally, major modes are checked in the order in which they are defined.
mode-filename (mf)	A regular expression describing filenames for which the corresponding major mode will be set. The expression is applied only to the portion of the complete pathname after removing the directory name.
mode-pathname (mp)	A regular expression describing pathnames for which the corresponding major mode will be set.
preamble (pre)	A regular expression describing the first line of filenames for which the corresponding major mode will be set.
qualifiers	Tells how to combine the preamble and suffixes criteria. Use all to tell vile to use both, and any to use either.
suffixes (suf)	A regular expression describing filename suffixes for which the corresponding major mode will be set. The expression is applied only to the portion of the filename starting with the first period.

[†] These criteria are a fourth category of option, counting universal, buffer, and window. They are not listed with the others in Table B-5 because you set them in an entirely different way.

You can always tell `vile` to use a specific major mode; for example:

```
:setl cmode
```

will set it to "c" mode.‡ But that does not update the syntax highlighting. Use the macro:

```
:set-h cmode
```

(`set-highlighting`; see Table 18-8), which does both parts.

The Procedure Language

`vile`'s procedure language is almost unchanged from that of MicroEMACS. Comments begin with a semicolon or a double quote character. Environment variable names (editor options) start with a `$`, and user variable names start with `%`. A number of built-in functions exist for doing comparisons and testing conditions; their names all begin with `&`. Flow control commands and certain others begin with `~`. An `@` with a string prompts the user for input, and the user's answer is returned. This rather whimsical example from the `macros.doc` file should give you a taste of the language's flavor:

```
~if &sequal %curplace "timespace vortex"
        insert-string "First, rematerialize\n"
~endif
~if &sequal %planet "earth"      ;If we have landed on earth...
        ~if &sequal %time "late 20th century"  ;and we are then
                write-message "Contact U.N.I.T."
        ~else
                insert-string "Investigate the situation....\n"
                insert-string "(SAY 'stay here Sara')\n"
        ~endif
~elseif &sequal %planet "luna"  ;If we have landed on our neighbor...
        write-message "Keep the door closed"
~else
        setv %conditions @"Atmosphere conditions outside? "
        ~if &sequal %conditions "safe"
                insert-string &cat "Go outside......" "\n"
                insert-string "lock the door\n"
        ~else
                insert-string "Dematerialize..try somewhen else"
                newline
        ~endif
~endif
```

You can store these procedures into a numbered macro or give them names that can be bound to keystrokes. The procedure just shown is most useful when using the Tardis `vile` port. ☺

This more realistic example from Paul Fox runs `grep`, searching for the word under the cursor in all C source files. It then puts the results in a buffer named after the word,

---

‡ The `setl` command sets the local properties of the buffer. The command `:set cmode` sets the default major mode if `vile` is unable to recognize the file.

and sets things up so that the built-in error finder (^X ^X) will use this output as its list of lines to visit. Finally, the macro is bound to ^A g. The ~force command allows the following command to fail without generating an error message:

```
14 store-macro
        set-variable %grepfor $identifier
        edit-file &cat "!egrep -n " &cat %grepfor " *.[ch]"
        ~force rename-buffer %grepfor
        error-buffer $cbufname
~endm
bind-key execute-macro-14 ^A-g
```

User-defined procedures can have parameters, much like the Bourne shell—but the parameters can be limited to specific data types. This makes procedures work as expected with vile's editing model (and command-history mechanism). The procedures are not completely interchangeable with the built-in commands, since there is not yet a mechanism for making the undo feature treat a whole macro as a single operation.

Finally, the read-hook and write-hook variables can be set to names of procedures to run after reading and before writing a file, respectively. This allows you to do things similar to the pre- and post-operation files in elvis and the autocommand facility in Vim.

The language is quite capable, including flow control and comparison features, as well as variables that provide access to a large amount of vile's internal state. The macros.doc file in the vile distribution describes the language in detail.

Miscellaneous Small Features

Several other, smaller features are worth mentioning:

Piping into vile

If you make vile the last command in a pipeline, it will create a buffer named [Standard Input] and edit that buffer for you. This is perhaps the "pager to end all pagers."

Editing Windows files

When set to true, the dos option causes vile to strip carriage returns at the end of a line in files when reading, and to write them back out again. This makes it easy to edit Windows files on a Unix or GNU/Linux system.

Text reformatting

The ^A f command reformats text, performing word wrapping on selected text. It understands C and shell comments (lines with a leading * or #) and quoted email (a leading >). It is similar to the Unix fmt command, but faster.

Formatting the information line

The modeline-format variable is a string that controls the way vile formats the status line. This is the line at the bottom of each window that describes the buffer's status, such as its name, current major mode, modification status, insert versus command mode, and so on.§

The string consists of *printf*(3)-style percent sequences. For example, %b represents the buffer name, %m the major mode, and %l the line number if ruler has been set. Characters in the string that are not part of a format specifier are output verbatim.

vile has many other features. The vi finger-feel makes it easy to switch to vile from another editor. The programmability provides flexibility, and its interactive nature and use of defaults is perhaps friendlier than traditional vi for the novice.

Sources and Supported Operating Systems

The official WWW location for vile is *http://invisible-island.net/vile/vile.html*. The ftp location is *ftp://invisible-island.net/vile/vile.tar.gz*. The file vile.tar.gz is always a symbolic link to the current version.

vile is written in ANSI C. It builds and runs on Unix, OpenVMS, MS-DOS, Win32 console and Win32 GUI, BeOS, QNX, and OS/2.

Compiling vile is straightforward. Retrieve the distribution via ftp or from the web page. Uncompress and untar it, run the configure program, and then run make:

```
$ gzip -d < vile.tar.gz | tar -xvpf -
...
$ cd vile-*; ./configure
...
$ make
...
```

vile should configure and build with no problems. Use make install to install it.

 If you want syntax coloring to work smoothly, you may wish to run configure with the option --with-builtin-filters. You should use flex (version 2.54a or newer) rather than lex, since Unix versions of that tool do not perform well. The configure script will also not accept a version of flex that is too old.

Should you need to report a bug or problem in vile, send email to the address *vile@nongnu.org*. This is the preferred way to report bugs. If necessary, you can contact Thomas Dickey directly at *dickey@invisible-island.net*.

---

§ vile's documentation refers to this as the *modeline*. However, since vile also implements the vi modeline feature, we are calling it a status line, to reduce confusion.

Appendixes

Part IV provides reference material that should be of interest to a vi user. This part contains the appendixes:

- Appendix A, *The vi, ex, and Vim Editors*
- Appendix B, *Setting Options*
- Appendix C, *Problem Checklists*
- Appendix D, *vi and the Internet*

The vi, ex, and Vim Editors

This appendix summarizes the standard features of **vi** in quick-reference format. Commands entered at the colon (known as **ex** commands because they date back to the original creation of that editor) are included, as well as the most popular Vim features.

This appendix presents the following topics:

- Command-line syntax
- Review of **vi** operations
- Alphabetical list of keys in command mode
- **vi** commands
- **vi** configuration
- **ex** basics
- Alphabetical summary of **ex** commands

Command-Line Syntax

The three most common ways of starting a **vi** session are:

```
vi [options] file
vi [options] +num file
vi [options] +/pattern file
```

You can open *file* for editing, optionally at line *num* or at the first line matching *pattern*. If no *file* is specified, **vi** opens with an empty buffer.

Command-Line Options

Because **vi** and **ex** are the same program, they share the same options. However, some options only make sense for one version of the program. Options specific to Vim are so marked:

+[*num*]

Start editing at line number *num*, or the last line of the file if *num* is omitted.

+/pattern

> Start editing at the first line matching *pattern*. (For **ex**, this fails if nowrapscan is set in your .exrc startup file, since **ex** starts editing at the last line of a file.)

+?pattern

> Start editing at the last line matching *pattern*.

-b

> Edit the file in binary mode. {Vim}

-c *command*

> Run the given **ex** command upon startup. Only one -c option is permitted for **vi**; Vim accepts up to 10. An older form of this option, *+command*, is still supported.

--cmd *command*

> Like -c, but execute the command before any resource files are read. {Vim}

-C

> Solaris **vi**: same as -x, but assume the file is encrypted already.
>
> Vim: start the editor in **vi**-compatible mode.

-d

> Run in diff mode. Works like vimdiff. {Vim}

-D

> Debugging mode for use with scripts. {Vim}

-e

> Run as **ex** (line-editing rather than full-screen mode).

-h

> Print help message, then exit. {Vim}

-i *file*

> Use the specified *file* instead of the default (~/.viminfo) to save or restore Vim's state. {Vim}

-l

> Enter Lisp mode for running Lisp programs (not supported in all versions).

-L

> List files that were saved due to an aborted editor session or system crash (not supported in all versions). For Vim, this option is the same as -r.

-m

> Start the editor with the write option turned off so that the user cannot write to files. {Vim}

-M

> Do not allow text in files to be modified. {Vim}

-n

> Do not use a swap file; record changes in memory only. {Vim}

`--noplugin`
> Do not load any plug-ins. {Vim}

`-N`
> Run Vim in a non-**vi**-compatible mode. {Vim}

`-o[`*num*`]`
> Start Vim with *num* open windows. The default is to open one window for each file. {Vim}

`-O[`*num*`]`
> Start Vim with *num* open windows arranged horizontally (split vertically) on the screen. {Vim}

`-r [`*file*`]`
> Recovery mode; recover and resume editing on *file* after an aborted editor session or system crash. Without *file*, list files available for recovery.

`-R`
> Edit files in read-only mode.

`-s`

> Silent; do not display prompts. Useful when running a script. This behavior also can be set through the older - option. For Vim, applies only when used together with -e.

`-s` *scriptfile*
> Read and execute commands given in the specified *scriptfile* as if they were typed in from the keyboard. {Vim}

`-S` *commandfile*
> Read and execute commands given in *commandfile* after loading any files for editing specified on the command line. Shorthand for `vim -c 'source `*commandfile*`'`. {Vim}

`-t` *tag*
> Edit the file containing *tag*, and position the cursor at its definition.

`-T` *type*
> Set the option terminal type. This value overrides the $TERM environment variable. {Vim}

`-u` *file*
> Read configuration information from the specified resource file instead of the default `.vimrc` resource file. If the *file* argument is NONE, Vim will read no resource files, load no plug-ins, and run in compatible mode. If the argument is NORC, it will read no resource files, but it will load plug-ins. {Vim}

`-v`
> Run in full-screen mode (default for **vi**).

`--version`
> Print version information, then exit. {Vim}

-V[*num*]

> Verbose mode; print messages about what options are being set and what files are being read or written. You can set a level of verbosity to increase or decrease the number of messages received. The default value is 10 for high verbosity. {Vim}

-w *rows*

> Set the window size so *rows* lines at a time are displayed; useful when editing over a slow dial-up line (or long distance Internet connection). Older versions of vi do not permit a space between the option and its argument. Vim does not support this option.

-W *scriptfile*

> Write all typed commands from the current session to the specified *scriptfile*. The file created can be used with the -s command. {Vim}

-x

> Prompt for a key that will be used to try to encrypt or decrypt a file using crypt (not supported in all versions).*

-y

> Modeless vi; run Vim in insert mode only, without a command mode. This is the same as invoking Vim as evim. {Vim}

-Z

> Start Vim in restricted mode. Do not allow shell commands or suspension of the editor. {Vim}

Although most people know ex commands only by their use within vi, the editor also exists as a separate program and can be invoked from the shell (for instance, to edit files as part of a script). Within ex, you can enter the vi or visual command to start vi. Similarly, within vi, you can enter Q to quit the vi editor and enter ex.

You can exit ex in several ways:

:x	Exit (save changes and quit).
:q!	Quit without saving changes.
:vi	Enter the vi editor.

Review of vi Operations

This section provides a review of the following:

- vi modes
- Syntax of vi commands
- Status-line commands

---

* The crypt command's encryption is weak. Don't use it for serious secrets.

Command Mode

Once the file is opened, you are in command mode. From command mode, you can:

- Invoke insert mode
- Issue editing commands
- Move the cursor to a different position in the file
- Invoke ex commands
- Invoke a Unix shell
- Save the current version of the file
- Exit vi

Insert Mode

In insert mode, you can enter new text in the file. You normally enter insert mode with the i command. Press the ESC key to exit insert mode and return to command mode. The full list of commands that enter insert mode is provided later in the section "Insert Commands" on page 386.

Syntax of vi Commands

In vi, editing commands have the following general form:

    [n] operator [m] motion

The basic editing *operators* are:

c   Begin a change.

d   Begin a deletion.

y   Begin a yank (or copy).

If the current line is the object of the operation, the *motion* is the same as the operator: cc, dd, yy. Otherwise, the editing operators act on objects specified by cursor-movement commands or pattern-matching commands. (For example, cf. changes up to the next period.) *n* and *m* are the number of times the operation is performed, or the number of objects the operation is performed on. If both *n* and *m* are specified, the effect is $n \times m$.

An object of operation can be any of the following text blocks:

word
    Includes characters up to a whitespace character (space or tab) or punctuation mark. A capitalized object is a variant form that recognizes only whitespace.

sentence
    Up to ., !, or ?, followed by two spaces.

paragraph
> Up to the next blank line or paragraph macro defined by the **para=** option.

section
> Up to the next **nroff/troff** section heading defined by the **sect=** option.

motion
> Up to the character or other text object as specified by a motion specifier, including pattern searches.

Examples

2cw	Change the next two words.
d}	Delete up to the next paragraph.
d^	Delete back to the beginning of the line.
5yy	Copy the next five lines.
y]]	Copy up to the next section.
cG	Change to the end of the edit buffer.

More commands and examples may be found in the section "Changing and deleting text" on page 387 later in this appendix.

Visual mode (Vim only)

Vim provides an additional facility, "visual mode." This allows you to highlight blocks of text, which then become the object of edit commands such as deletion or saving (yanking). Graphical versions of Vim allow you to use the mouse to highlight text in a similar fashion. See the earlier section "Visual Mode Motion" on page 168 for more information.

v	Select text in visual mode one character at a time.
V	Select text in visual mode one line at a time.
CTRL-V	Select text in visual mode in blocks.

Status-Line Commands

Most commands are not echoed on the screen as you input them. However, the status line at the bottom of the screen is used to edit these commands:

/	Search forward for a pattern.
?	Search backward for a pattern.
:	Invoke an **ex** command.
!	Invoke a Unix command that takes as its input an object in the buffer and replaces it with output from the command. You type a motion command after the ! to describe what should be passed to the Unix command. The command itself is entered on the status line.

Commands that are entered on the status line must be entered by pressing the ENTER key. In addition, error messages and output from the CTRL-G command are displayed on the status line.

vi Commands

vi supplies a large set of single-key commands when in command mode. Vim supplies additional multikey commands.

Movement Commands

Some versions of vi do not recognize extended keyboard keys (e.g., arrow keys, page up, page down, home, insert, and delete); some do. All versions, however, recognize the keys in this section. Many users of vi prefer to use these keys, as it helps them keep their fingers on the home row of the keyboard. A number preceding a command repeats the movement. Movement commands are also used after an operator. The operator works on the text that is moved.

Character

h, j, k, l	Left, down, up, right (←, ↓, ↑, →)
Spacebar	Right
BACKSPACE	Left
CTRL-H	Left

Text

w, b	Forward, backward by "word" (letters, numbers, and underscores make up words).
W, B	Forward, backward by "WORD" (only whitespace separates items).
e	End of word.
E	End of WORD.
ge	End of previous word. {Vim}
gE	End of previous WORD. {Vim}
), (	Beginning of next, current sentence.
}, {	Beginning of next, current paragraph.
]], [[	Beginning of next, current section.
][, []	End of next, current section. {Vim}

Lines

Long lines in a file may show up on the screen as multiple lines. (They *wrap* around from one screen line to the next.) Although most commands work on the lines as defined in the file, a few commands work on lines as they appear on the screen. The Vim option `wrap` allows you to control how long lines are displayed.

0, $	First, last position of current line.
^, _	First nonblank character of current line.
+, -	First nonblank character of next, previous line.
ENTER	First nonblank character of next line.
num |	Column *num* of current line.
g0, g$	First, last position of screen line. {Vim}
g^	First nonblank character of screen line. {Vim}
gm	Middle of screen line. {Vim}
gk, gj	Move up, down one screen line. {Vim}
H	Top line of screen (Home position).
M	Middle line of screen.
L	Last line of screen.
num H	*num* lines after top line.
num L	*num* lines before last line.

Screens

CTRL-F, CTRL-B	Scroll forward, backward one screen.
CTRL-D, CTRL-U	Scroll down, up one-half screen.
CTRL-E, CTRL-Y	Show one more line at bottom, top of screen.
z ENTER	Reposition line with cursor to top of screen.
z.	Reposition line with cursor to middle of screen.
z-	Reposition line with cursor to bottom of screen.
CTRL-L	Redraw screen (without scrolling).
CTRL-R	vi: redraw screen (without scrolling).
	Vim: redo last undone change.

Searches

/ *pattern*	Search forward for *pattern*. End with ENTER.
/ *pattern* /+ *num*	Go to line *num* after *pattern*. Forward search for *pattern*.
/ *pattern* /- *num*	Go to line *num* before *pattern*. Forward search for *pattern*.
? *pattern*	Search backward for *pattern*. End with ENTER.
? *pattern* ?+ *num*	Go to line *num* after *pattern*. Backward search for *pattern*.
? *pattern* ?- *num*	Go to line *num* before *pattern*. Backward search for *pattern*.
:noh	Suspend search highlighting until next search. {Vim}
n	Repeat previous search.

N	Repeat search in opposite direction.
/	Repeat previous search forward.
?	Repeat previous search backward.
*	Search forward for word under cursor. Matches only exact words. {Vim}
#	Search backward for word under cursor. Matches only exact words. {Vim}
g*	Search backward for word under cursor. Matches the characters of this word when embedded in a longer word. {Vim}
g#	Search backward for word under cursor. Matches the characters of this word when embedded in a longer word. {Vim}
%	Find match of current parenthesis, brace, or bracket.
f x	Move cursor forward to x on current line.
F x	Move cursor backward to x on current line.
t x	Move cursor forward to character before x in current line.
T x	Move cursor backward to character after x in current line.
,	Reverse search direction of last f, F, t, or T.
;	Repeat last f, F, t, or T.

Line numbering

CTRL-G	Display current line number.
gg	Move to first line in file. {Vim}
num G	Move to line number num.
G	Move to last line in file.
: num	Move to line number num.

Marks

m x	Place mark x at current position.
` x	(Backquote.) Move cursor to mark x.
' x	(Apostrophe.) Move to start of line containing x.
``	(Backquotes.) Return to position before most recent jump.
''	(Apostrophes.) Like preceding, but return to start of line.
'"	(Apostrophe quote.) Move to position when last editing the file. {Vim}
`[, `]	(Backquote bracket.) Move to beginning/end of previous text operation. {Vim}
'[, ']	(Apostrophe bracket.) Like preceding, but return to start of line where operation occurred. {Vim}
`.	(Backquote period.) Move to last change in file. {Vim}
'.	(Apostrophe period.) Like preceding, but return to start of line. {Vim}
'0	(Apostrophe zero.) Position where you last exited Vim. {Vim}
:marks	List active marks. {Vim}

Insert Commands

a	Append after cursor.
A	Append to end of line.
c	Begin change operation.
C	Change to end of line.
gI	Insert at beginning of line. {Vim}
i	Insert before cursor.
I	Insert at beginning of line.
o	Open a line below cursor.
O	Open a line above cursor.
R	Begin overwriting text.
s	Substitute a character.
S	Substitute entire line.
ESC	Terminate insert mode.

The following commands work in insert mode:

BACKSPACE	Delete previous character.
DELETE	Delete current character.
TAB	Insert a tab.
CTRL-A	Repeat last insertion. {Vim}
CTRL-D	Shift line left to previous shiftwidth. {Vim}
CTRL-E	Insert character found just below cursor. {Vim}
CTRL-H	Delete previous character (same as backspace).
CTRL-I	Insert a tab.
CTRL-K	Begin insertion of multikeystroke character.
CTRL-N	Insert next completion of the pattern to the left of the cursor. {Vim}
CTRL-P	Insert previous completion of the pattern to the left of the cursor. {Vim}
CTRL-T	Shift line right to next shiftwidth. {Vim}
CTRL-U	Delete current line.
CTRL-V	Insert next character verbatim.
CTRL-W	Delete previous word.
CTRL-Y	Insert character found just above cursor. {Vim}
CTRL-[	(ESC) Terminate insert mode.

Some of the control characters listed in the previous table are set by stty. Your terminal settings may differ.

Edit Commands

Recall that c, d, and y are the basic editing operators.

Changing and deleting text

The following list is not exhaustive, but it illustrates the most common operations:

cw	Change word.
cc	Change line.
c$	Change text from current position to end-of-line.
C	Same as c$.
dd	Delete current line.
num dd	Delete *num* lines.
d$	Delete text from current position to end-of-line.
D	Same as d$.
dw	Delete a word.
d}	Delete up to next paragraph.
d^	Delete back to beginning of line.
d/ *pat*	Delete up to first occurrence of pattern.
dn	Delete up to next occurrence of pattern.
df *x*	Delete up to and including *x* on current line.
dt *x*	Delete up to (but not including) *x* on current line.
dL	Delete up to last line on screen.
dG	Delete to end of file.
gqap	Reformat current paragraph to `textwidth`. {Vim}
g~w	Switch case of word. {Vim}
guw	Change word to lowercase. {Vim}
gUw	Change word to uppercase. {Vim}
p	Insert last deleted or yanked text after cursor.
gp	Same as p, but leave cursor at end of inserted text. {Vim}
gP	Same as P, but leave cursor at end of inserted text. {Vim}
]p	Same as p, but match current indention. {Vim}
[p	Same as P, but match current indention. {Vim}
P	Insert last deleted or yanked text before cursor.
r *x*	Replace character with *x*.
R *text*	Replace with new *text* (overwrite), beginning at cursor. ESC ends replace mode.
s	Substitute character.
4s	Substitute four characters.
S	Substitute entire line.
u	Undo last change.

CTRL-R	Redo last change. {Vim}
U	Restore current line.
x	Delete current cursor position.
X	Delete back one character.
5X	Delete previous five characters.
.	Repeat last change.
~	Reverse case and move cursor right.
CTRL-A	Increment number under cursor. {Vim}
CTRL-X	Decrement number under cursor. {Vim}

Copying and moving

Register names are the letters **a–z**. Uppercase names append text to the corresponding register.

Y	Copy current line.
yy	Copy current line.
" *x* yy	Copy current line to register *x*.
ye	Copy text to end of word.
yw	Like ye, but include the whitespace after the word.
y$	Copy rest of line.
" *x* dd	Delete current line into register *x*.
" *x* d	Delete into register *x*.
" *x* p	Put contents of register *x*.
y]]	Copy up to next section heading.
J	Join current line to next line.
gJ	Same as J, but without inserting a space. {Vim}
:j	Same as J.
:j!	Same as gJ.

Saving and Exiting

Writing a file means overwriting the file with the current text.

ZZ	Quit **vi**, writing the file only if changes were made.
:x	Same as ZZ.
:wq	Write file and quit.
:w	Write file.
:w *file*	Save copy to *file*.
: *n* , *m* w *file*	Write lines *n* to *m* to new *file*.
: *n* , *m* w >> *file*	Append lines *n* to *m* to existing *file*.

`:w!`	Write file (overriding protection).
`:w!` *file*	Overwrite *file* with current text.
`:w %. new`	Write current buffer named *file* as *file*.new.
`:q`	Quit `vi` (fails if changes were made).
`:q!`	Quit `vi` (discarding edits).
`Q`	Quit `vi` and invoke `ex`.
`:vi`	Return to `vi` after `Q` command.
`%`	Replaced with current filename in editing commands.
`#`	Replaced with alternate filename in editing commands.

Accessing Multiple Files

`:e` *file*	Edit another *file*; current file becomes alternate.
`:e!`	Return to version of current file at time of last write.
`:e + file`	Begin editing at end of *file*.
`:e +num file`	Open *file* at line *num*.
`:e #`	Open to previous position in alternate file.
`:ta` *tag*	Edit file at location *tag*.
`:n`	Edit next file in the list of files.
`:n!`	Force next file.
`:n` *files*	Specify new list of *files*.
`:rewind`	Edit first file in the list.
CTRL-G	Show current file and line number.
`:args`	Display list of files to be edited.
`:prev`	Edit previous file in the list of files.

Window Commands (Vim)

The following table lists common commands for controlling windows in Vim. See also the `split`, `vsplit`, and `resize` commands in the later section "Alphabetical Summary of ex Commands" on page 395. For brevity, control characters are marked in the following list by ^.

`:new`	Open a new window.
`:new` *file*	Open *file* in a new window.
`:sp` [*file*]	Split the current window. With *file*, edit that file in the new window.
`:sv` [*file*]	Same as `:sp`, but make new window read-only.
`:sn` [*file*]	Edit next file in file list in new window.
`:vsp` [*file*]	Like `:sp`, but split vertically instead of horizontally.
`:clo`	Close current window.

`:hid`	Hide current window, unless it is the only visible window.
`:on`	Make current window the only visible one.
`:res` *num*	Resize window to *num* lines.
`:wa`	Write all changed buffers to their files.
`:qa`	Close all buffers and exit.
`^W s`	Same as `:sp`.
`^W n`	Same as `:new`.
`^W ^`	Open new window with alternate (previously edited) file.
`^W c`	Same as `:clo`.
`^W o`	Same as `:only`.
`^W j, ^W k`	Move cursor to next/previous window.
`^W p`	Move cursor to previous window.
`^W h, ^W l`	Move cursor to window on left/right of screen.
`^W t, ^W b`	Move cursor to window on top/bottom of screen.
`^W K, ^W B`	Move current window to top/bottom of screen.
`^W H, ^W L`	Move current window to far left/right of screen.
`^W r, ^W R`	Rotate windows down/up.
`^W +, ^W -`	Increase/decrease current window size.
`^W =`	Make all windows same height.

Interacting with the System

`:r` *file*	Read in contents of *file* after cursor.
`:r !`*command*	Read in output from *command* after current line.
`:` *num* `r !`*command*	Like previous, but place after line *num* (0 for top of file).
`:!`*command*	Run *command*, then return.
`!`*motion command*	Send the text covered by *motion* to Unix *command*; replace with output.
`:` *n* `,` *m* `!`*command*	Send lines *n–m* to *command*; replace with output.
num`!!`*command*	Send *num* lines to Unix *command*; replace with output.
`:!!`	Repeat last system command.
`:sh`	Create subshell; return to editor with *EOF*.
CTRL-Z	Suspend editor, resume with **fg**.
`:so` *file*	Read and execute **ex** commands from *file*.

Macros

`:ab` *in out*	Use *in* as abbreviation for *out* in insert mode.
`:unab` *in*	Remove abbreviation for *in*.
`:ab`	List abbreviations.

:map *string* *sequence*	Map characters *string* as *sequence* of commands. Use #1, #2, etc., for the function keys.
:unmap *string*	Remove map for characters *string*.
:map	List character strings that are mapped.
:map! *string* *sequence*	Map characters *string* to input mode *sequence*.
:unmap! *string*	Remove input mode map (you may need to quote the characters with CTRL-V).
:map!	List character strings that are mapped for input mode.
q *x*	Record typed characters into register specified by letter *x*. If letter is uppercase, append to register. {Vim}
q	Stop recording. {Vim}
@ *x*	Execute the register specified by letter *x*. Use @@ to repeat the last @ command.

In **vi**, the following characters are unused in command mode and can be mapped as user-defined commands:

Letters
  g, K, q, V, and v

Control keys
  ^A, ^K, ^O, ^W, ^X, ^_, and ^\

Symbols
  _, *, \, =, and #

 The = is used by **vi** if Lisp mode is set. Different versions of **vi** may use some of these characters, so test them before using.

Vim does not use ^K, ^_, _, or \.

Miscellaneous Commands

<	Shift text described by following motion command left by one shiftwidth. {Vim}
>	Shift text described by following motion command right by one shiftwidth. {Vim}
<<	Shift line left one shiftwidth (default is eight spaces).
>>	Shift line right one shiftwidth (default is eight spaces).
>}	Shift right to end of paragraph.
<%	Shift left until matching parenthesis, brace, or bracket. (Cursor must be on the matching symbol.)
==	Indent line in C-style, or using program specified in `equalprg` option. {Vim}
g	Start many multiple character commands in Vim.
K	Look up word under cursor in manpages (or program defined in `keywordprg`). {Vim}

^O	Return to previous jump. {Vim}
^Q	Same as ^V. {Vim} (On some terminals, resume data flow.)
^T	Return to the previous location in the tag stack. (Solaris vi, Vim, nvi, elvis, and vile.)
^]	Perform a tag lookup on the text under the cursor.
^\	Enter ex line-editing mode.
^^	(Caret key with Ctrl key pressed.) Return to previously edited file.

vi Configuration

This section describes the following:

- The :set command
- Options available with :set
- Example .exrc file

The :set Command

The :set command allows you to specify options that change characteristics of your editing environment. Options may be put in the ~/.exrc file or set during a vi session.

The colon does not need to be typed if the command is put in .exrc:

:set x	Enable Boolean option x; show value of other options.
:set no x	Disable option x.
:set x = value	Give value to option x.
:set	Show changed options.
:set all	Show all options.
:set x ?	Show value of option x.

Appendix B provides tables of :set options for Solaris vi, Vim, nvi, elvis, and vile. Please see that appendix for more information.

Example .exrc File

In an ex script file, comments start with the double quote character. The following lines of code are an example of a customized .exrc file:

```
set nowrapscan              " Searches don't wrap at end of file
set wrapmargin=7            " Wrap text at 7 columns from right margin
set sections=SeAhBhChDh nomesg    " Set troff macros, disallow message
map q :w^M:n^M              " Alias to move to next file
map v dwElp                 " Move a word
ab ORA O'Reilly Media, Inc. " Input shortcut
```

The q alias isn't needed for Vim, which has the :wn command. The v alias would hide the Vim command v, which enters character-at-a-time visual mode operation.

ex Basics

The ex line editor serves as the foundation for the screen editor vi. Commands in ex work on the current line or on a range of lines in a file. Most often, you use ex from within vi. In vi, ex commands are preceded by a colon and entered by pressing ENTER.

You can also invoke ex on its own—from the command line—just as you would invoke vi. (You could execute an ex script this way.) Or you can use the vi command Q to quit the vi editor and enter ex.

Syntax of ex Commands

To enter an ex command from vi, type:

```
:[address] command [options]
```

An initial : indicates an ex command. As you type the command, it is echoed on the status line. Execute the command by pressing the ENTER key. *Address* is the line number or range of lines that are the object of *command*. *Options* and *addresses* are described later. ex commands are described in the later section "Alphabetical Summary of ex Commands" on page 395.

You can exit ex in several ways:

:x	Exit (save changes and quit).
:q!	Quit without saving changes.
:vi	Switch to the vi editor on the current file.

Addresses

If no address is given, the current line is the object of the command. If the address specifies a range of lines, the format is:

```
x,y
```

where *x* and *y* are the first and last addressed lines (*x* must precede *y* in the buffer). *x* and *y* each may be a line number or a symbol. Using ; instead of , sets the current line to *x* before interpreting *y*. The notation 1,$ addresses all lines in the file, as does %.

Address Symbols

1,$	All lines in the file.
x , y	Lines x through y.
x ; y	Lines x through y, with current line reset to x.
0	Top of file.
.	Current line.
num	Absolute line number num.
$	Last line.
%	All lines; same as 1,$.
x - n	n lines before x.
x + n	n lines after x.
-[num]	One or num lines previous.
+[num]	One or num lines ahead.
' x	(Apostrophe.) Line marked with x.
' '	(Apostrophe apostrophe.) Previous mark.
/pattern/	Forward to line matching pattern.
?pattern?	Backward to line matching pattern.

See Chapter 6 for more information on using patterns.

Options

!

Indicates a variant form of the command, overriding the normal behavior. The !
must come immediately after the command.

count

The number of times the command is to be repeated. Unlike in vi commands,
count cannot precede the command, because a number preceding an ex command
is treated as a line address. For example, d3 deletes three lines, beginning with the
current line; 3d deletes line 3.

file

The name of a file that is affected by the command. % stands for the current file;
stands for the previous file.

Alphabetical Summary of ex Commands

ex commands can be entered by specifying any unique abbreviation. In the following list of reference entries, the full name appears as the heading of the reference entry, and the shortest possible abbreviation is shown in the syntax line below it. Examples are assumed to be typed from **vi**, so they include the : prompt.

---

abbreviate

ab [*string text*]

Define *string* when typed to be translated into *text*. If *string* and *text* are not specified, list all current abbreviations.

Examples

Note: ^M appears when you type ^V followed by ENTER.

```
:ab ora O'Reilly Media, Inc.
:ab id Name:^MRank:^MPhone:
```

---

append

[*address*] a[!]
text
.

Append new *text* at specified *address*, or at present address if none is specified. Add a ! to toggle the autoindent setting that is used during input. That is, if autoindent was enabled, ! disables it. Enter new text after entering the command. Terminate input of new text by entering a line consisting of just a period.

Example

```
:a                          Begin appending to current line
Append this line
and this line too.
.                           Terminate input of text to append
```

---

args

ar
args *file* ...

Print the members of the argument list (files named on the command line), with the current argument printed in brackets ([ ]).

The second syntax is for Vim, which allows you to reset the list of files to be edited.

---

bdelete

[*num*] bd[!] [*num*]

Unload buffer *num* and remove it from the buffer list. Add a ! to force removal of an unsaved buffer. The buffer may also be specified by filename. If no buffer is specified, remove the current buffer. {Vim}

buffer

[*num*] b[!] [*num*]

Begin editing buffer *num* in the buffer list. Add a ! to force a switch from an unsaved buffer. The buffer may also be specified by filename. If no buffer is specified, continue editing the current buffer. {Vim}

buffers

buffers[!]

Print the members of the buffer list. Some buffers (e.g., deleted buffers) will not be listed. Add ! to show unlisted buffers. ls is another abbreviation for this command. {Vim}

cd

cd *dir*
chdir *dir*

Change the current directory within the editor to *dir*.

center

[*address*] ce [*width*]

Center the line within the specified *width*. If *width* is not specified, use textwidth. {Vim}

change

[*address*] c[!]
text
.

Replace the specified lines with *text*. Add a ! to switch the autoindent setting during input of *text*. Terminate input by entering a line consisting of just a period.

close

clo[!]

Close current window unless it is the last window. If buffer in window is not open in another window, unload it from memory. This command will not close a buffer with unsaved changes, but you may add ! to hide it instead. {Vim}

copy

[*address*] co *destination*

Copy the lines included in *address* to the specified *destination* address. The command t (short for "to") is a synonym for copy.

Example

    :1,10 co 50   *Copy first 10 lines to just after line 50*

delete

[*address*] d [*register*] [*count*]

Delete the lines included in *address*. If *register* is specified, save or append the text to the named register. Register names are the lowercase letters a–z. Uppercase names append text to the corresponding register. If *count* is specified, delete that many lines.

Examples

    :/Part I/,/Part II/-1d   *Delete to line above "Part II"*
    :/main/+d   *Delete line below "main"*
    :.,$d x   *Delete from this line to last line into register x*

edit

e[!] [+*num*] [*filename*]

Begin editing on *filename*. If no *filename* is given, start over with a copy of the current file. Add a ! to edit the new file even if the current file has not been saved since the last change. With the +*num* argument, begin editing on line *num*. Alternatively, *num* may be a pattern, of the form /*pattern*.

Examples

    :e file   *Edit file in current editing buffer*
    :e +/^Index #   *Edit alternate file at pattern match*
    :e!   *Start over again on current file*

file

f [*filename*]

Change the filename for the current buffer to *filename*. The next time the buffer is written, it will be written to file *filename*. When the name is changed, the buffer's "not edited" flag is set, to indicate that you are not editing an existing file. If the new filename is the same as a file that already exists on the disk, you will need to use :w! to overwrite the existing file. When specifying a filename, the % character can be used to indicate the current filename. A # can be used to indicate the alternate filename. If no *filename* is specified, print the current name and status of the buffer.

Example

    :f %.new

fold

address fo

Fold the lines specified by *address*. A fold collapses several lines on the screen into one line, which can later be unfolded. It doesn't affect the text of the file. {Vim}

foldclose

[*address*] foldc[!]

Close folds in the specified *address*, or at the present address if none is specified. Add a ! to close more than one level of folds. {Vim}

foldopen

[*address*] foldo[!]

Open folds in the specified *address*, or at the present address if none is specified. Add a ! to open more than one level of folds. {Vim}

global

[*address*] g[!]/*pattern*/[*commands*]

Execute *commands* on all lines that contain *pattern* or, if *address* is specified, on all lines within that range. If *commands* are not specified, print all such lines. Add a ! to execute *commands* on all lines *not* containing *pattern*. See also v, later in this list.

Examples

:g/Unix/p	*Print all lines containing "Unix"*
:g/Name:/s/tom/Tom/	*Change "tom" to "Tom" on all lines containing "Name:"*

hide

hid

Close current window unless it is the last window, but do not remove the buffer from memory. This command is safe to use on an unsaved buffer. {Vim}

insert

[*address*] i[!]
text
.

Insert *text* at line before the specified *address*, or at present address if none is specified. Add a ! to switch the autoindent setting during input of *text*. Terminate input of new text by entering a line consisting of just a period.

join

[*address*] j[!] [*count*]

Place the text in the specified range on one line, with whitespace adjusted to provide two space characters after a period (.), no space characters before a), and one space character otherwise. Add a ! to prevent whitespace adjustment.

Example

:1,5j!	*Join first five lines, preserving whitespace*

jumps

ju

Print jump list used with CTRL-I and CTRL-O commands. The jump list is a record of most movement commands that skip over multiple lines. It records the position of the cursor before each jump. {Vim}

k

[*address*] k *char*

Same as mark; see mark later in this list.

left

[*address*] le [*count*]

Left-align lines specified by *address*, or current line if no address is specified. Indent lines by *count* spaces. {Vim}

list

[*address*] l [*count*]

Print the specified lines so that tabs display as ^I and the ends of lines display as $. l is like a temporary version of :set list.

map

map[!] [*string commands*]

Define a keyboard macro named *string* as the specified sequence of *commands*. *string* is usually a single character or the sequence #*num*, the latter representing a function key on the keyboard. Use a ! to create a macro for input mode. With no arguments, list the currently defined macros.

Examples

:map K dwwP	*Transpose two words*
:map q :w^M:n^M	*Write current file; go to next*
:map! + ^[bi(^[ea)	*Enclose previous word in parentheses*

 Vim has K and q commands, which the example aliases would hide.

mark

[*address*] ma *char*

Mark the specified line with *char*, a single lowercase letter. Same as k. Return later to the line with 'x (apostrophe plus x, where x is the same as *char*). Vim also uses uppercase and numeric characters for marks. Lowercase letters work the same as in vi. Uppercase letters are associated with filenames and can be used between multiple files. Numbered marks, however, are maintained in a special `viminfo` file and cannot be set using this command.

marks

marks [*chars*]

Print list of marks specified by *chars*, or all current marks if no *chars* specified. {Vim}

Example

:marks abc   *Print marks a, b, and c*

mkexrc

mk[!] *file*

Create an `.exrc` file containing **set** commands for changed **ex** options and key mappings. This saves the current option settings, allowing you to restore them later. {Vim}

move

[*address*] m *destination*

Move the lines specified by *address* to the *destination* address.

Example

:.,/Note/m /END/   *Move text block to after line containing "END"*

new

[*count*] new

Create a new window *count* lines high with an empty buffer. {Vim}

next

n[!] [[+*num*] *filelist*]

Edit the next file from the command-line argument list. Use **args** to list these files. If *filelist* is provided, replace the current argument list with *filelist* and begin editing on the first file. With the +*num* argument, begin editing on line *num*. Alternatively, *num* may be a pattern, of the form /*pattern*.

Example

:n chap*   *Start editing all "chapter" files*

---

nohlsearch

noh

Temporarily stop highlighting all matches to a search when using the hlsearch option. Highlighting is resumed with the next search. {Vim}

---

number

[*address*] nu [*count*]

Print each line specified by *address*, preceded by its buffer line number. Use # as an alternate abbreviation for number. *count* specifies the number of lines to show, starting with *address*.

---

only

on [!]

Make the current window be the only one on the screen. Windows open on modified buffers are not removed from the screen (hidden), unless you also use the ! character. {Vim}

---

open

[*address*] o [/*pattern*/]

Enter open mode (vi) at the lines specified by *address*, or at the lines matching *pattern*. Exit open mode with Q. Open mode lets you use the regular vi commands, but only one line at a time. It can be useful on slow dial-up lines (or on very distant Internet ssh connections).

---

preserve

pre

Save the current editor buffer as though the system were about to crash.

---

previous

prev[!]

Edit the previous file from the command-line argument list. {Vim}

---

print

[*address*] p [*count*]

Print the lines specified by *address*. *count* specifies the number of lines to print, starting with *address*. P is another abbreviation.

Example

    :100;+5p   *Show line 100 and the next 5 lines*

put

[*address*] pu [*char*]

Place previously deleted or yanked lines from the named register specified by *char*, to the line specified by *address*. If *char* is not specified, the last deleted or yanked text is restored.

qall

qa[!]

Close all windows and terminate the current editing session. Use ! to discard changes made since the last save. {Vim}

quit

q[!]

Terminate the current editing session. Use ! to discard changes made since the last save. If the editing session includes additional files in the argument list that were never accessed, quit by typing q! or by typing q twice. Vim closes the editing window only if there are still other windows open on the screen.

read

[*address*] r *filename*

Copy the text of *filename* after the line specified by *address*. If *filename* is not specified, the current filename is used.

Example

    :0r $HOME/data   *Read file in at top of current file*

read

[*address*] r !*command*

Read the output of shell *command* into the text after the line specified by *address*.

Example

    :$r !spell %   *Place results of spellchecking at end of file*

recover

rec [*file*]

Recover *file* from the system save area.

redo

red

Restore last undone change. Same as CTRL-R. {Vim}

resize

res [[±]*num*]

Resize current window to be *num* lines high. If + or - is specified, increase or decrease the current window height by *num* lines. {Vim}

rewind

rew[!]

Rewind the argument list and begin editing the first file in the list. Add a ! to rewind even if the current file has not been saved since the last change.

right

[*address*] ri [*width*]

Right-align lines specified by *address*, or current line if no address is specified, to column *width*. Use textwidth option if no *width* is specified. {Vim}

sbnext

`[count] sbn [count]`

Split the current window and begin editing the *count* next buffer from the buffer list. If no count is specified, edit the next buffer in the buffer list. {Vim}

sbuffer

`[num] sb [num]`

Split the current window and begin editing buffer *num* from the buffer list in the new window. The buffer to be edited may also be specified by filename. If no buffer is specified, open the current buffer in the new window. {Vim}

set

`se parameter1 parameter2 ...`

Set a value to an option with each *parameter*, or if no *parameter* is supplied, print all options that have been changed from their defaults. For Boolean options, each *parameter* can be phrased as *option* or no*option*; other options can be assigned with the syntax *option=value*. Specify all to list current settings. The form set *option*? displays the value of *option*. See the tables that list set options in Appendix B.

Examples

```
:set nows wm=10
:set all
```

shell

`sh`

Create a new shell. Resume editing when the shell terminates.

snext

`[count] sn [[+num] filelist]`

Split the current window and begin editing the next file from the command-line argument list. If *count* is provided, edit the *count* next file. If *filelist* is provided, replace the current argument list with *filelist* and begin editing the first file. With the +*n* argument, begin editing on line *num*. Alternately, *num* may be a pattern of the form /*pattern*. {Vim}

source

so *file*

Read (source) and execute **ex** commands from *file*.

Example

    :so $HOME/.exrc

split

[*count*] sp [*+num*] [*filename*]

Split the current window and load *filename* in the new window, or the same buffer in both windows if no file is specified. **Make the** new window *count* lines high, or if *count* is not specified, split the window into equal parts. With the +*n* argument, begin editing on line *num*. *num* may also be a pattern of the form */pattern*. {Vim}

sprevious

[*count*] spr [*+num*]

Split the current window and begin editing the previous file from the command-line argument list in the new window. If *count* is specified, edit the *count* previous file. With the +*num* argument, begin editing on line *num*. *num* may also be a pattern of the form */pattern*. {Vim}

stop

st

Suspend the editing session. Same as CTRL-Z. Use the shell **fg** command to resume the session.

substitute

[*address*] s [*/pattern/replacement/*] [*options*] [*count*]

Replace the first instance of *pattern* on each of the specified lines with *replacement*. If *pattern* and *replacement* are omitted, **repeat** last substitution. *count* specifies the number of lines on which to substitute, starting with *address*. (Spelling out the command name does not work in Solaris **vi**.)

Options

c   Prompt for confirmation before **each change.**

g   Substitute all instances of *pattern* on each line (global).

p   Print the last line on which a substitution was made.

Examples

`:1,10s/yes/no/g`	*Substitute on first 10 lines*
`:%s/[Hh]ello/Hi/gc`	*Confirm global substitutions*
`:s/Fortran/\U&/ 3`	*Uppercase "Fortran" on next three lines*
`:g/^[0-9][0-9]*/s//Line &:/`	*For every line beginning with one or more digits, add "Line" and a*

colon

suspend

`su`

Suspend the editing session. Same as CTRL-Z. Use the shell `fg` command to resume the session.

sview

`[count] sv [+num] [filename]`

Same as the `split` command, but set the `readonly` option for the new buffer. {Vim}

t

`[address] t destination`

Copy the lines included in *address* to the specified *destination* address. t is equivalent to `copy`.

Example

`:%t$`	*Copy the file and add it to the end*

tag

`[address] ta tag`

In the `tags` file, locate the file and line matching *tag* and start editing there.

Example

Run `ctags`, then switch to the file containing *myfunction*:

```
:!ctags *.c
:tag myfunction
```

tags

tags

Print list of tags in the tag stack. {Vim}

unabbreviate

una *word*

Remove *word* from the list of abbreviations.

undo

u

Reverse the changes made by the last editing command. In vi the undo command will undo itself, redoing what you undid. Vim supports multiple levels of undo. Use redo to redo an undone change in Vim.

unhide

[*count*] unh

Split screen to show one window for each active buffer in the buffer list. If specified, limit the number of windows to *count*. {Vim}

unmap

unm[!] *string*

Remove *string* from the list of keyboard macros. Use ! to remove a macro for input mode.

v

[*address*] v/*pattern*/[*command*]

Execute *command* on all lines *not* containing *pattern*. If *command* is not specified, print all such lines. v is equivalent to g!. See global, earlier in this list.

Example

    :v/#include/d   *Delete all lines except "#include" lines*

version

ve

Print the editor's current version number and date of last change.

view

vie[[+*num*] *filename*]

Same as **edit**, but set file to **readonly**. When executed in **ex** mode, return to normal or visual mode. {Vim}

visual

[*address*] vi [*type*] [*count*]

Enter visual mode (**vi**) at the line specified by *address*. Return to **ex** mode with **Q**. *type* can be one of -, ^, or . (see the **z** command, later in this section). *count* specifies an initial window size.

visual

vi [+*num*] *file*

Begin editing *file* in visual mode (**vi**), optionally at line *num*. Alternately, *num* may be a pattern, of the form /*pattern*. {Vim}

vsplit

[*count*] vs [+*num*] [*filename*]

Same as the **split** command, but split the screen vertically. The *count* argument can be used to specify a width for the new window. {Vim}

wall

wa[!]

Write all changed buffers with filenames. Add ! to force writing of any buffers marked readonly. {Vim}

wnext

[*count*] wn[!] [[+*num*] *filename*]

Write current buffer and open next file in argument list, or the *count* next file if specified. If *filename* is specified, edit it next. With the *+num* argument, begin editing on line *num*. *num* may also be a pattern of the form */pattern*. {Vim}

wq

wq[!]

Write and quit the file in one action. The file is always written. The ! flag forces the editor to write over any current contents of *file*.

wqall

wqa[!]

Write all changed buffers and quit the editor. Add ! to force writing of any buffers marked readonly. xall is another alias for this command. {Vim}

write

[*address*] w[!] [[>>] *file*]

Write lines specified by *address* to *file*, or write full contents of buffer if *address* is not specified. If *file* is also omitted, save the contents of the buffer to the current filename. If >> *file* is used, append lines to the end of the specified *file*. Add a ! to force the editor to write over any current contents of *file*.

Examples

    :1,10w name_list   *Copy first 10 lines to file* name_list
    :50w >> name_list   *Now append line 50*

write

[*address*] w !*command*

Write lines specified by *address* to *command*.

Example

    :1,66w !pr -h myfile | lp   *Print first page of file*

X

X

Prompt for an encryption key. This can be preferable to `:set key`, as typing the key is not echoed to the console. To remove an encryption key, just reset the **key** option to an empty value. {Vim}

xit

x

Write the file if it was changed since the last write, and then quit.

yank

[*address*] y [*char*] [*count*]

Place lines specified by *address* in named register *char*. Register names are the lowercase letters a–z. Uppercase names append text to the corresponding register. If no *char* is given, place lines in the general register. *count* specifies the number of lines to yank, starting with *address*.

Example

    :101,200 ya a   *Copy lines 100–200 to register "a"*

z

[*address*] z [*type*] [*count*]

Print a window of text with the line specified by *address* at the top. *count* specifies the number of lines to be displayed.

Type

+

Place specified line at the top of the window (default).

-

Place specified line at the bottom of the window.

.

Place specified line in the center of the window.

^

Print the previous window.

=

Place specified line in the center of the window and leave the current line at this line.

&

[*address*] & [*options*] [*count*]

Repeat the previous substitute (**s**) command. *count* specifies the number of lines on which to substitute, starting with *address*. *options* are the same as for the substitute command.

Examples

:s/Overdue/Paid/	*Substitute once on current line*
:g/Status/&	*Redo substitution on all "Status" lines*

@

[*address*] @ [*char*]

Execute contents of register specified by *char*. If *address* is given, move cursor to the specified address first. If *char* is @, repeat the last @ command.

=

[*address*] =

Print the line number of the line indicated by *address*. The default is the line number of the last line.

!

[*address*] !*command*

Execute Unix *command* in a shell. If *address* is specified, use the lines contained in *address* as standard input to *command*, and replace those lines with the output and error output. (This is called *filtering* the text through the *command*.)

Examples

:!ls	*List files in the current directory*
:11,20!sort -f	*Sort lines 11–20 of current file*

< >

[*address*] < [*count*]
  or
[*address*] > [*count*]

Shift lines specified by *address* either left (<) or right (>). Only leading spaces and tabs are added or removed when shifting lines. *count* specifies the number of lines to shift, starting with *address*. The `shiftwidth` option controls the number of columns that are shifted. Repeating the ‹ or › increases the shift amount. For example, :>>> shifts three times as much as :>.

~

[*address*] ~ [*count*]

Replace the last-used regular expression (even if from a search, and not from an s command) with the replacement pattern from the most recent s (substitute) command. This is rather obscure; see Chapter 6 for details.

address

address

Print the lines specified in *address*.

ENTER

Print the next line in the file. (For ex only, not from the : prompt in vi.)

Setting Options

This appendix describes the important **set** command options for Solaris **vi**, **nvi** 1.79, **elvis** 2.2, Vim 7.1, and **vile** 9.6.

Solaris vi Options

Table B-1 contains brief descriptions of the important **set** command options. In the first column, options are listed in alphabetical order; if the option can be abbreviated, that abbreviation is shown in parentheses. The second column shows the default setting that **vi** uses unless you issue an explicit **set** command (either manually or in the **.exrc** file). The last column describes what the option does, when enabled.

Table B-1. Solaris vi set options

Option	Default	Description
autoindent (ai)	noai	In insert mode, indents each line to the same level as the line above or below. Use with the **shiftwidth** option.
autoprint (ap)	ap	Display changes after each editor command. (For global replacement, display last replacement.)
autowrite (aw)	noaw	Automatically write (save) the file if changed before opening another file with :n or before giving a Unix command with :!.
beautify (bf)	nobf	Ignore all control characters during input (except tab, newline, or form feed).
directory (dir)	/tmp	Names directory in which **ex/vi** stores buffer files. (Directory must be writable.)
edcompatible	noedcompatible	Remember the flags used with the most recent substitute command (global, confirming), and use them for the next substitute command. Despite the name, no version of **ed** actually does this.
errorbells (eb)	errorbells	Sound bell when an error occurs.
exrc (ex)	noexrc	Allow the execution of **.exrc** files that reside outside the user's home directory.

Option	Default	Description
flash (fp)	nofp	Flash the screen instead of ringing the bell.
hardtabs (ht)	8	Define boundaries for terminal hardware tabs.
ignorecase (ic)	noic	Disregard case during a search.
lisp	nolisp	Insert indents in appropriate Lisp format. ( ), { }, [[, and]] are modified to have meaning for Lisp.
list	nolist	Print tabs as ^I; mark ends of lines with $. (Use list to tell whether end character is a tab or a space.)
magic	magic	Wildcard characters . (dot), * (asterisk), and [] (brackets) have special meaning in patterns.
mesg	mesg	Permit system messages to display on terminal while editing in vi.
novice	nonovice	Require the use of long ex command names, such as copy or read.
number (nu)	nonu	Display line numbers on left of screen during editing session.
open	open	Allow entry to *open* or *visual* mode from ex. Although not in Solaris vi, this option has traditionally been in vi, and may be in your Unix's version of vi.
optimize (opt)	noopt	Abolish carriage returns at the end of lines when printing multiple lines; this speeds output on dumb terminals when printing lines with leading whitespace (spaces or tabs).
paragraphs (para)	IPLPPPQP LIpplpipbp	Define paragraph delimiters for movement by { or }. The pairs of characters in the value are the names of troff macros that begin paragraphs.
prompt	prompt	Display the ex prompt (:) when vi's Q command is given.
readonly (ro)	noro	Any writes (saves) of a file fail unless you use ! after the write (works with w, ZZ, or autowrite).
redraw (re)		vi redraws the screen whenever edits are made (in other words, insert mode pushes over existing characters, and deleted lines immediately close up). Default depends on line speed and terminal type. noredraw is useful at slow speeds on a dumb terminal: deleted lines show up as @, and inserted text appears to overwrite existing text until you press ESC.
remap	remap	Allow nested map sequences.
report	5	Display a message on the status line whenever you make an edit that affects at least a certain number of lines. For example, 6dd reports the message "6 lines deleted."
scroll	[½ *window*]	Number of lines to scroll with ^D and ^U commands.
sections (sect)	SHNHH HU	Define section delimiters for [[and]] movement. The pairs of characters in the value are the names of troff macros that begin sections.
shell (sh)	/bin/sh	Pathname of shell used for shell escape (:!) and shell command (:sh). Default value is derived from shell environment, which varies on different systems.

Option	Default	Description
shiftwidth (sw)	8	Define number of spaces in backward (^D) tabs when using the autoindent option, and for the << and >> commands.
showmatch (sm)	nosm	In vi, when) or } is entered, cursor moves briefly to matching (or {. (If no match, ring the error message bell.) Very useful for programming.
showmode	noshowmode	In insert mode, display a message on the prompt line indicating the type of insert you are making, for example, "OPEN MODE" or "APPEND MODE."
slowopen (slow)		Hold off display during insert. Default depends on line speed and terminal type.
tabstop (ts)	8	Define number of spaces that a tab indents during editing session. (Printer still uses system tab of 8.)
taglength (tl)	0	Define number of characters that are significant for tags. Default (zero) means that all characters are significant.
tags	tags /usr/lib/tags	Define pathname of files containing tags. (See the Unix ctags command.) By default, vi searches the file tags in the current directory and /usr/lib/tags.
tagstack	tagstack	Enable stacking of tag locations on a stack.
term		Set terminal type.
terse	noterse	Display shorter error messages.
timeout (to)	timeout	Keyboard maps time out after 1 second.[a]
ttytype		Set terminal type. This is just another name for term.
warn	warn	Display the warning message, "No write since last change."
window (w)		Show a certain number of lines of the file on the screen. Default depends on line speed and terminal type.
wrapmargin (wm)	0	Define right margin. If greater than zero, automatically inserts carriage returns to break lines.
wrapscan (ws)	ws	Searches wrap around either end of file.
writeany (wa)	nowa	Allow saving to any file.

[a] When you have mappings of several keys (for example, :map zzz 3dw), you probably want to use notimeout. Otherwise, you need to type zzz within one second. When you have an insert mode mapping for a cursor key (for example, :map! ^[OB ^[ja), you should use timeout. Otherwise, vi won't react to ESC until you type another key.

nvi 1.79 Options

nvi 1.79 has a total of 78 options that affect its behavior. Table B-2 summarizes the most important ones. Most options described in Table B-1 are not repeated here.

Table B-2. nvi 1.79 set options

Option	Default	Description
backup		A string describing a backup filename to use. The current contents of a file are saved in this file before writing the

Option	Default	Description
		new data out. A first character of N causes nvi to include a version number at the end of the file; version numbers are always incremented. "N%.bak" is a reasonable example.
cdpath	Environment variable CDPATH, or current directory	A search path for the :cd command.
cedit		When the first character of this string is entered on the colon command line, nvi opens a new window on the command history that you can then edit. Hitting EN-TER on any given line executes that line. ESC is a good choice for this option. (Use ^V ^[to enter it.)
comment	nocomment	If the first nonempty line begins with /*, //, or #, nvi skips the comment text before displaying the file. This avoids displaying long, boring legal notices.
directory (dir)	Environment variable TMPDIR, or /tmp	The directory where nvi puts its temporary files.
extended	noextended	Searches use egrep-style extended regular expressions.
filec		When the first character of this string is entered on the colon command line, nvi treats the blank delimited word in front of the cursor as if it had an * appended to it and does shell-style filename expansion. ESC is also a good choice for this option. (Use ^V ^[to enter it.) When this character is the same as for the cedit option, command-line editing is performed only when the character is entered as the first character on the colon command line.
iclower	noiclower	Make all regular expression searches case-insensitive, as long as the search pattern contains no uppercase letters.
leftright	noleftright	Long lines scroll the screen left to right, instead of wrapping.
lock	lock	nvi attempts to get an exclusive lock on the file. Editing a file that cannot be locked creates a read-only session.
octal	nooctal	Display unknown characters in octal, instead of in hexadecimal.
path		A colon-separated list of directories in which nvi will look for the file to be edited.
recdir	/var/tmp/vi.recover	The directory where recovery files are stored.
ruler	noruler	Displays the row and column of the cursor.
searchincr	nosearchincr	Searches are done incrementally.
secure	nosecure	Turn off access to external programs via text filtering (:r!, :w!), disable the vi mode ! and ^Z commands, and the ex mode !, shell, stop, and suspend commands. Once set, it cannot be changed.
shellmeta	~{[*?$`'"\	When any of these characters appear in a filename argument to an ex command, the argument is expanded by the program named by the shell option.

Option	Default	Description
showmode (smd)	noshowmode	Display a string in the status line showing the current mode. Display an * if the file has been modified.
sidescroll	16	The number of columns by which the screen is shifted left or right when leftright is true.
taglength (tl)	0	Defines number of characters that are significant for tags. Default (zero) means that all characters are significant.
tags (tag)	tags /var/db/libc.tags /sys/kern/tags	The list of possible tag files.
tildeop	notildeop	The ~ command takes an associated motion, not just a preceding count.
wraplen (wl)	0	Identical to the wrapmargin option, except that it specifies the number of characters from the left margin at which the line will be split. The value of wrapmargin overrides wraplen.

elvis 2.2 Options

elvis 2.2 has a total of 225 options that affect its behavior. Table B-3 summarizes the most important ones. Most options described in Table B-1 are not repeated here.

Table B-3. elvis 2.2 set options

Option	Default	Description
autoiconify (aic)	noautoiconify	Iconify the old window when de-iconifying a new one. X11 only.
backup (bk)	nobackup	Make a backup file (xxx.bak) before writing the current file out to disk.
binary (bin)		The buffer's data is not text. This option is set automatically.
boldfont (xfb)		The name of the bold font. X11 only.
bufdisplay (bd)	normal	The default display mode for the buffer (hex, html, man, normal, syntax, or tex).
ccprg (cp)	cc ($1?$1:$2)	The shell command for :cc.
directory (dir)		Where to store temporary files. The default is system-dependent.
display (mode)	normal	The name of current display mode, set by the :display command.
elvispath (epath)		A list of directories in which to search for configuration files. The default is system-dependent.
focusnew (fn)	focusnew	Force keyboard focus into the new window. X11 only.
font (fnt)		The name of the normal font, for the Windows and X11 interfaces.
gdefault (gd)	nogdefault	Cause the substitute command to change all instances.
home (home)	$HOME	The home directory for ~ in filenames.
italicfont (xfi)		The name of the italic font. X11 only.

Option	Default	Description
locked (lock)	nolocked	Make the buffer read-only and cause most commands that would modify the buffer to fail. Usually set automatically for read-only HTML files.
lpcolor (lpcl)	nolpcl	Use color when printing; for :lpr.
lpcolumns (lpcols)	80	The width of a printer page; for :lpr.
lpcrlf (lpc)	nolpcrlf	The printer needs CR/LF for newline in the file; for :lpr.
lpformfeed (lpff)	nolpformfeed	Send a form feed after the last page; for :lpr.
lpheader (lph)	nolph	Print a header at the top of the page; for :lpr.
lplines (lprows)	60	The length of a printer page; for :lpr.
lpout (lpo)		The printer file or filter, for :lpr. A typical value might be !lpr. The default is system-dependent.
lptype (lpt)	dumb	The printer type, for :lpr. The value should be one of: ps, ps2, epson, pana, ibm, hp, cr, bs, dumb, html, or ansi.
lpwrap (lpw)	lpwrap	Simulate line wrap; for :lpr.
makeprg (mp)	make $1	The shell command for :make.
prefersyntax (psyn)	never	Control use of syntax mode. Useful for HTML and manpages to show the input instead of the formatted contents. With a value of never, never use syntax mode. With writable, do so for writable files. With local, do so for files in the current directory. With always, always use syntax mode.
ruler (ru)	noruler	Display the cursor's line and column.
security (sec)	normal	One of normal (standard vi behavior), safer (attempt to prevent writing malicious scripts), or restricted (try to make elvis safe for use as a restricted editor). In general, use the :safely command to set this; don't do it directly.
showmarkups (smu)	noshowmarkups	For the man and html modes, show the markup at the cursor position, but not elsewhere.
sidescroll (ss)	0	The sideways scrolling amount. Zero mimics vi, making lines wrap.
smartargs (sa)	nosmartargs	Place the arguments for a function on the screen based on a tags file lookup after typing the function name and the func tion character (usually a left parenthesis).
spell (sp)	nospell	Highlight misspelled words. This also works with programs, based on lookups in a tags file.
taglength (tl)	0	Defines the number of characters that are significant for tags. Default (zero) means that all characters are significant.
tags (tagpath)	tags	The list of possible tag files.
tagstack (tsk)	tagstack	Remember the origin of tag searches on a stack.
undolevels (ul)	0	The number of undoable commands. Zero mimics vi. You probably want to set this to a bigger number.
warpback (wb)	nowarpback	Upon exit, move the pointer back to the xterm that started elvis. X11 only.
warpto (wt)	don't	How ^W ^W forces pointer movement: don't for no movement, scrollbar moves the pointer to the scrollbar, origin moves the

Option	Default	Description
		pointer to the upper left corner, and `corners` moves it to the corners furthest from and nearest to the current cursor position. This forces the X display to pan, to make sure the window is entirely onscreen.

Vim 7.1 Options

Vim 7.1 has a total of 295 (!) options that affect its behavior. Table B-4 summarizes the most important ones. Most options described in Table B-1 are not repeated here.

The summaries in this table are by necessity very brief. Much more information about each option may be found in the Vim online help.

Table B-4. Vim 7.1 set options

Option	Default	Description
autoread (ar)	noautoread	Detect whether a file inside Vim has been modified externally, not by Vim, and automatically refresh the Vim buffer with the changed version of the file.
background (bg)	dark or light	Vim tries to use background and foreground colors that are appropriate to the particular terminal. The default depends on the current terminal or windowing system.
backspace (bs)	0	Control whether you can backspace over a newline and/or over the start of insert. Values are: 0 for vi compatibility; 1 to backspace over newlines; and 2 to backspace over the start of insert. Using a value of 3 allows both.
backup (bk)	nobackup	Make a backup before overwriting a file, then leave it around after the file has been successfully written. To have a backup file just while the file is being written, use the `writebackup` option.
backupdir (bdir)	., ~/tmp/, ~/	A list of directories for the backup file, separated with commas. The backup file is created in the first directory in the list where this is possible. If empty, you cannot create a backup file. The name . (dot) means the same directory as where the edited file is.
backupext (bex)	~	The string that is appended to a filename to make the name of the backup file.
binary (bin)	nobinary	Change a number of other options to make it easier to edit binary files. The previous values of these options are remembered and restored when `bin` is switched back off. Each buffer has its own set of saved option values. This option should be set before editing a binary file. You can also use the `-b` command-line option.
cindent (cin)	nocindent	Enable automatic smart C program indenting.

Option	Default	Description
cinkeys (cink)	0{,0},:,0#,!^F, o,O,e	A list of keys that, when typed in insert mode, cause reindenting of the current line. Only happens if cindent is on.
cinoptions (cino)		Affects the way cindent reindents lines in a C program. See the online help for details.
cinwords (cinw)	if, else, while, do, for, switch	These keywords start an extra indent in the next line when smartindent or cindent is set. For cindent this is done only at an appropriate place (inside {...}).
comments (com)		A comma-separated list of strings that can start a comment line. See the online help for details.
compatible (cp)	cp; nocp when a .vimrc file is found	Makes Vim behave more like vi in too many ways to describe here. It is on by default, to avoid surprises. Having a .vimrc turns off the vi compatibility; usually this is a desirable side effect.
completeopt (cot)	menu,preview	A comma-separated list of options for insert mode completion.
cpoptions (cpo)	aABceFs	A sequence of single character flags, each one indicating a different way in which Vim will or will not exactly mimic vi. When empty, the Vim defaults are used. See the online help for details.
cursorcolumn (cuc)	nocursorcolumn	Highlight the screen column of the cursor with CursorColumn highlighting. This is useful for lining up text vertically. Can slow down screen display.
cursorline (cul)	nocursorline	Highlight the screen line of the cursor with Cursor Row highlighting. Makes it easy to find the current line in the edit session. Use in conjunction with cursorcolumn for a crosshairs effect. Can slow down screen display.
define (def)	^#\s*define	A search pattern that describes macro definitions. The default value is for C programs. For C++, use ^\(#\s*define\ |[a-z]*\s*const\s*[a-z]*\). When using the :set command, you need to double the backslashes.
directory (dir)	., ~/tmp, /tmp	A list of directory names for the swap file, separated with commas. The swap file will be created in the first directory where this is possible. If empty, no swap file will be used and recovery is impossible! The name . (dot) means to put the swap file in the same directory as the edited file. Using . first in the list is recommended so that editing the same file twice will result in a warning.
equalprg (ep)		External program to use for = command. When this option is empty, the internal formatting functions are used.
errorfile (ef)	errors.err	Name of the error file for the quickfix mode. When the -q command-line argument is used, errorfile is set to the following argument.

Option	Default	Description
errorformat (efm)	(Too long to print)	Scanf-like description of the format for the lines in the error file.
expandtab (et)	noexpandtab	When inserting a tab, expand it to the appropriate number of spaces.
fileformat (ff)	unix	Describes the convention to terminate lines when reading/writing the current buffer. Possible values are dos (CR/LF), unix (LF), and mac (CR). Vim usually sets this automatically.
fileformats (ffs)	dos,unix	List the line-terminating conventions that Vim tries to apply to a file when reading. Multiple names enable automatic end-of-line detection when reading a file.
formatoptions (fo)	Vim default: tcq; vi default: vt	A sequence of letters that describes how automatic formatting is to be done. See the online help for details.
gdefault (gd)	nogdefault	Cause the substitute command to change all instances.
guifont (gfn)		A comma-separated list of fonts to try when starting the GUI version of Vim.
hidden (hid)	nohidden	Hide the current buffer when it is unloaded from a window, instead of abandoning it.
history (hi)	Vim default: 20; vi default: 0	Control how many ex commands, search strings, and expressions are remembered in the command history.
hlsearch (hls)	nohlsearch	Highlight all matches of the most recent search pattern.
icon	noicon	Vim attempts to change the name of the icon associated with the window where it is running. Overridden by the iconstring option.
iconstring		String value used for the icon name of the window.
include (inc)	^#\s*include	Define a search pattern for finding include commands. The default value is for C programs.
incsearch (is)	noincsearch	Enable incremental searching.
isfname (isf)	@,48-57,/,.,-,_, +,,,$,:,~	A list of characters that can be included in file and path names. Non-Unix systems have different default values. The @ character stands for any alphabetic character. It is also used in the other is XXX options, described next.
isident (isi)	@,48-57,_,192-255	A list of characters that can be included in identifiers. Non-Unix systems may have different default values.
iskeyword (isk)	@,48-57,_,192-255	A list of characters that can be included in keywords. Non-Unix systems may have different default values. Keywords are used in searching and recognizing with many commands, such as w, [i, and many more.

Option	Default	Description
isprint (isp)	@,161-255	A list of characters that can be displayed directly to the screen. Non-Unix systems may have different default values.
makeef (mef)	/tmp/vim##.err	The error file name for the :make command. Non-Unix systems have different default values. The ## is replaced by a number to make the name unique.
makeprg (mp)	make	The program to use for the :make command. % and # in the value are expanded.
modifiable (ma)	modifiable	When turned off, do not allow any changes in the buffer.
mouse		Enable the mouse in non-GUI versions of Vim. This works for MS-DOS, Win32, QNX pterm, and xterm. See the online help for details.
mousehide (mh)	nomousehide	Hide the mouse pointer during typing. Restores the pointer when the mouse is moved.
paste	nopaste	Change a large number of options so that pasting into a Vim window with a mouse does not mangle the pasted text. Turning it off restores those options to their previous values. See the online help for details.
ruler (ru)	noruler	Show the line and column number of the cursor position.
secure	nosecure	Disable certain kinds of commands in the startup file. Automatically enabled if you don't own the .vimrc and .exrc files.
shellpipe (sp)		The shell string to use for capturing the output from :make into a file. The default value depends upon the shell.
shellredir (srr)		The shell string for capturing the output of a filter into a temporary file. The default value depends upon the shell.
showmode (smd)	Vim default: smd; vi default: nosmd	Put a message in the status line for insert, replace, and visual modes.
sidescroll (ss)	0	How many columns to scroll horizontally. The value zero puts the cursor in the middle of the screen.
smartcase (scs)	nosmartcase	Override the ignorecase option if the search pattern contains uppercase characters.
spell	nospell	Turn on spellchecking.
suffixes	*.bak,~,.o,.h,.info,.swp	When multiple files match a pattern during file-name completion, the value of this variable sets a priority among them, in order to pick the one Vim will use.
taglength (tl)	0	Define number of characters that are significant for tags. Default (zero) means that all characters are significant.

Option	Default	Description
tagrelative (tr)	Vim default: tr; vi default: notr	Filenames in a tags file from another directory are taken to be relative to the directory where the tags file is.
tags (tag)	./tags,tags	Filenames for the :tag command, separated by spaces or commas. The leading ./ is replaced with the full path to the current file.
tildeop (top)	notildeop	Make the ~ command behave like an operator.
undolevels (ul)	1000	The maximum number of changes that can be undone. A value of 0 means vi compatibility: one level of undo and u undoes itself. Non-Unix systems may have different default values.
viminfo (vi)		Read the viminfo file upon startup, and write it upon exiting. The value is complex; it controls the different kinds of information that Vim will store in the file. See the online help for details.
writebackup (wb)	writebackup	Make a backup before overwriting a file. The backup is removed after the file is successfully written, unless the backup option is also on.

vile 9.6 Options

vile 9.6 has 167 options (called "modes" in vile), which are denoted *universal*, *buffer*, or *window* modes according to their use. There are also 101 *environment variables*, which are more useful in scripts than for direct user manipulation.[*] Not all are available on every platform; some apply only to X11 or Win32.

Table B-5 shows the compiled-in default values for the most important of vile's options. The initialization scripts, such as vileinit.rc, override several of those values. Most options described in Table B-1 are not repeated here.

Table B-5. vile 9.6 set options

Option	Default	Description
alt-tabpos (atp)	noatp	Controls whether the cursor sits at the left or right end of the whitespace representing a tab character.
animated	animated	Automatically updates the contents of scratch buffers when their contents change.
autobuffer (ab)	autobuffer	Uses "most-recently-used" style buffering; the buffers are sorted in order of use. Otherwise, buffers remain in the order in which they were edited.
autocolor (ac)	0	Automatic syntax coloring. If set to zero, automatic syntax coloring is disabled. Otherwise, it should be set to a small positive

---

[*] These include variables that are set or used as a side effect of other commands. Owing to their focus on scripting, their descriptions are also not suitable for this table since they tend to be lengthy—read the online help for details.

Option	Default	Description
		integer that represents the number of milliseconds to wait for a "quiet interval" before invoking the `autocolor-hook` hook.
autosave (as)	noautosave	Automatic file saving. Writes the file after every `autosavecnt` characters of inserted text.
autosavecnt (ascnt)	256	Specifies after how many inserted characters automatic saves take place.
backspacelimit (bl)	backspacelimit	If disabled, then in insert mode you can backspace past the point at which the insert began.
backup-style	off	Controls how backup files are created when writing a file. Possible values are `off`, `.bak` for DOS-style backups, and `tilde` for Emacs-style `hello.c~` backups under Unix.
bcolor	default	Sets the background color on systems that support it.
byteorder-mark (bom)	auto	Controls the check for a prefix used to distinguish different types of UTF encoding. The default value `auto` tells `vile` to inspect the file; specific values tell it to use that value.
check-modtime	nocheck-modtime	Issues a "file newer than buffer" warning if the file has changed since it was last read or written, and prompts for confirmation.
cindent	nocindent	Enable C-style indentation, which helps maintain current indentation level automatically during insert, like `autoindent`.
cindent-chars	:#{}( )[]	The list of characters interpreted by the `cindent` mode. These include # to indent to column 1, and : to indent further, as after a label. Listing a pair of characters that are also in `fence-pairs` causes text enclosed by the pair to be further indented.
cmode	off	A built-in major mode for C code.
color-scheme (cs)	default	Specify by name an aggregate of `fcolor`, `bcolor`, `video-attrs`, and `$palette` defined via the `define-color-scheme` command.
comment-prefix	^\s*\(\(\s*[#*>] \)|\(///*\)\)\+	Describes the leading part of a line that should be left alone when reformatting comments. The default value is good for `Makefile`, shell and C comments, and email.
comments	^\s*/\?\ (\s*[#*>/]\)\)\+/ \?\s*$	A regular expression defining commented paragraph delimiters. Its purpose is to preserve paragraphs inside comments when reformatting.
cursor-tokens	regex	Controls whether `vile` uses regular expressions or character classes for parsing tokens from the screen for various commands. This uses an enumeration: `both`, `cclass`, and `regex`.
dirc	nodirc	`vile` checks each name when scanning directories for filename completion. This allows you to distinguish between directory names and filenames in the prompt.
dos	nodos	Strips out the CR from CR/LF pairs when reading files, and puts them back when writing. New buffers for nonexistent files inherit the line style of the operating system, whatever the value of `dos`.
fcolor	default	Sets the foreground color on systems that support it.
fence-begin	/*	Regular expressions for the start and end of simple non-nestable fences, such as C comments.
fence-end	*/	

Option	Default	Description
fence-if	^\s*#\s*if	Regular expressions marking the start, "else if", "else", and end of line-oriented, nested fences, such as C-preprocessor control lines.
fence-elif	^\s*#\s*elif\>	
fence-else	^\s*#\s*else\>	
fence-fi	^\s*#\s*endif\>	
fence-pairs	{}()[]	Each pair of characters denotes a set of "fences" that should be matched with %.
file-encoding	auto	Specifies the character encoding of the buffer contents, e.g., one of 8bit, ascii, auto, utf-8, utf-16, or utf-32.
filtername (fn)		Specifies a syntax-highlighting filter, for a given major mode.
for-buffers (fb)	mixed	Specifies whether globbing or regular expressions are used to select buffer names in the for-buffers and kill-buffer commands.
glob	!echo %s	Controls how wildcard characters (e.g., * and ?) are treated in prompts for filenames. A value of off disables expansion, and on uses the internal globber, which can handle normal shell wildcards and ~ notation. The default value for Unix guarantees compatibility with your shell.
highlight (hl)	highlight	Enables or disables syntax highlighting in the corresponding buffers.
history (hi)	history	Logs commands from the colon command line (minibuffer) in the [History] buffer.
horizscroll (hs)	horizscroll	Moving off the end of a long line shifts the whole screen sideways. If not set, only the current line shifts.
ignoresuffix (is)	\(\.orig|~\)$	Strips the given pattern from a filename before matching it for major mode suffixes.
linewrap (lw)	nolinewrap	Wraps long logical lines onto multiple screen lines.
maplonger	nomaplonger	The map facility matches against the longest possible mapped sequence, not the shortest.
meta-insert-bind ings (mib)	mib	Controls behavior of 8-bit characters during insert. Normally, key bindings are operational only when in command mode; when in insert mode, all characters are self-inserting. If this mode is on, and a metacharacter (i.e., a character with the eighth bit set) is typed that is bound to a function, then that function binding will be honored and executed from within insert mode. Any unbound metacharacters will remain self-inserting.
mini-hilite (mh)	reverse	Defines the highlight attribute to use when the user toggles the editing mode in the minibuffer.
modeline	nomodeline	Controls whether a vi-like mode line feature is enabled.
modelines	5	Controls the number of lines from each end of the buffer to scan for vi-like mode lines.
overlap-matches	overlap-matches	Modifies the highlighting shown by visual-matches to control whether overlapping matches are shown.
percent-crlf	50	Percentage of total lines that must end with CR/LF for vile to automatically convert buffer's recordseparator to crlf.

Option	Default	Description
percent-utf8	90	Percentage of total characters that contain embedded nulls, making them look like UTF-16 or UTF-32 encodings. If the file-encoding option is set to auto and the match is higher than this threshold, vile will load the buffer data as UTF-8.
popup-choices (pc)	delayed	Controls the use of a pop-up window for help in doing completion. The value is either off for no window, immediate for an immediate pop up, or delayed to wait for a second Tab key.
popup-msgs (pm)	nopopup-msgs	When enabled, vile pops up the [Messages] buffer, showing the text that was written to the message line.
recordseparator (rs)	lf[a]	Specify format of files that vile reads and writes. Formats are lf (for Unix), crlf (for DOS), cr (for Macintosh), and default (lf or crlf, depending on the platform).
resolve-links	noresolve-links	If set, vile fully resolves filenames in case some path components are symbolic links. This helps avoid multiple unintentional edits of the same physical file via different pathnames.
ruler	noruler	Shows the current line and column in the status line, as well as what percentage of the current buffer's lines are in front of the cursor.
showchar (sc)	noshowchar	Shows the value of the current character in the status line.
showformat (sf)	foreign	Controls when/whether recordseparator information is shown in the status line. Values are: always, differs (to show when the local mode differs from the global), local (to show whenever a local mode is set), foreign (to show when the recordseparator differs from the native default), and never.
showmode (smd)	showmode	Displays an indicator on the status line for insert and replace modes.
sideways	0	Controls by how many characters the screen scrolls to the left or right. The value of 0 moves the screen by one-third.
tabinsert (ti)	tabinsert	Allows the physical insertion of tab characters into the buffer. If turned off (notabinsert), vile will never insert a tab into a buffer; instead it will always insert the appropriate number of spaces.
tagignorecase (tc)	notagignorecase	Makes tag searches ignore case.
taglength (tl)	0	Defines the number of characters that are significant for tags. Default (zero) means that all characters are significant. This does not affect tags picked up from the cursor; they are always matched exactly. (This is different from the other editors).
tagrelative (tr)	notagrelative	When using a tags file in another directory, filenames in that tags file are considered to be relative to the directory where the tags file is.
tags	tags	A space-separated list of files in which to look up tag references.
tagword (tw)	notagword	Use the whole word under the cursor for the tag lookup, not just the subword starting at the current cursor position.
undolimit (ul)	10	Limits how many changes may be undone. The value zero means "no limit."

Option	Default	Description
unicode-as-hex (uh)	nounicode-as-hex	If displaying a buffer whose file encoding says it is one of the Unicode flavors (e.g., utf-8, utf-16, or utf-32), shows the values that are non-ASCII in \u*XXXX* format even if the display is capable of showing these as regular characters.
unprintable-as-octal (uo)	nounprintable-as-octal	Displays nonprinting characters with the eighth bit set in octal. Otherwise, uses hexadecimal. Nonprinting characters whose eighth bit is not set are always displayed in control character notation.
visual-matches	none	Controls highlighting of all matching occurrences of a search pattern. The possible values are none for no highlighting, or underline, bold, and reverse for those kinds of highlighting. Colors may also be used on systems that support it.
xterm-fkeys	noxterm-fkeys	Supports xterm's modified function keys by generating system bindings for the Shift-, Ctrl-, and Alt- modifiers of each function key listed in the terminal description.
xterm-mouse	noxterm-mouse	Allows use of the mouse from inside an xterm. See the online help for details.
xterm-title	noxterm-title	Enables title bar updates if you are running within an xterm. Each time you switch to a different buffer, vile can update the title. This uses the same tests of the TERM variable as the xterm-mouse mode.

a This depends on the platform for which vile is compiled.

Problem Checklists

This appendix consolidates the problem checklists that are provided throughout Part I. Here they are presented in one place for ease of reference.

Problems Opening Files

- *When you invoke* vi, *the message* [open mode] *appears.*

  Your terminal type is probably incorrectly identified. Quit the editing session immediately by typing :q. Check the environment variable $TERM. It should be set to the name of your terminal. Alternatively, ask your system administrator to provide an adequate terminal type setting.

- *You see one of the following messages:*

  ```
  Visual needs addressable cursor or upline capability
  Bad termcap entry
  Termcap entry too long
  terminal:  Unknown terminal type
  Block device required
  Not a typewriter
  ```

  Either your terminal type is undefined, or there's probably something wrong with your terminfo or termcap entry. Enter :q to quit. Check your $TERM environment variable, or ask your system administrator to select a terminal type for your environment.

- *A* [new file] *message appears when you think a file already exists.*

  Check that you have used the correct case in the filename (filenames are often case-sensitive). If you have, you are probably in the wrong directory. Enter :q to quit. Then check to see that you are in the correct directory for that file (enter pwd at the Unix prompt). If you are in the right directory, check the list of files in the directory (with ls) to see whether the file exists under a slightly different name.

- *You invoke* vi, *but you get a colon prompt (indicating that you're in* ex *line-editing mode).*

  You probably typed an interrupt before vi could draw the screen. Enter vi by typing vi at the ex prompt (:).

- *One of the following messages appears:*

  ```
  [Read only]
  File is read only
  Permission denied
  ```

  "Read only" means that you can only look at the file; you cannot save any changes you make. You may have invoked vi in *view mode* (with view or vi -R), or you do not have write permission for the file. See the next section, "Problems Saving Files" on page 432.

- *One of the following messages appears:*

  ```
  Bad file number
  Block special file
  Character special file
  Directory
  Executable
  Non-ascii file
  file non-ASCII
  ```

  The file you've called up to edit is not a regular text file. Type :q! to quit, then check the file you wish to edit, perhaps with the file command.

- *When you type* :q *because of one of the previously mentioned difficulties, this message appears:*

  ```
  No write since last change (:quit! overrides).
  ```

  You have modified the file without realizing it. Type :q! to leave vi. Your changes from this session will not be saved in the file.

Problems Saving Files

- *You try to write your file, but you get one of the following messages:*

  ```
  File exists
  File file exists - use w!
  [Existing file]
  File is read only
  ```

  Type :w! *file* to overwrite the existing file, or type :w *newfile* to save the edited version in a new file.

- *You want to write a file, but you don't have write permission for it. You get the message "Permission denied."*

  Use :w *newfile* to write out the buffer into a new file. If you have write permission for the directory, you can use mv to replace the original version with your copy of it. If you don't have write permission for the directory, type `:w `*`pathname/file`* to write out the buffer to a directory in which you do have write permission (such as your home directory, or `/tmp`).

- *You try to write your file, but you get a message telling you that the file system is full.*

  Type `:!rm `*`junkfile`* to delete a (large) unneeded file and free some space. (Starting an `ex` command line with an exclamation point gives you access to Unix.)

  Or type `:!df` to see whether there's any space on another file system. If there is, choose a directory on that file system and write your file to it with `:w `*`pathname`*. (`df` is the Unix command to check a disk's free space.)

- *The system puts you into open mode and tells you that the file system is full.*

  The disk with `vi`'s temporary files is filled up. Type `:!ls /tmp` to see whether there are any files you can remove to gain some disk space.* If there are, create a temporary Unix shell from which you can remove files or issue other Unix commands. You can create a shell by typing `:sh`; type CTRL-D or `exit` to terminate the shell and return to `vi`. (On most Unix systems, when using a job-control shell, you can simply type CTRL-Z to suspend `vi` and return to the Unix prompt; type `fg` to return to `vi`.) Once you've freed up some space, write your file with `:w!`.

- *You try to write your file, but you get a message telling you that your disk quota has been reached.*

  Try to force the system to save your buffer with the `ex` command `:pre` (short for `:preserve`). If that doesn't work, look for some files to remove. Use `:sh` (or CTRL-Z if you are using a job-control system) to move out of `vi` and remove files. Use CTRL-D (or `fg`) to return to `vi` when you're done. Then write your file with `:w!`.

Problems Getting to Visual Mode

- *While editing in* vi, *you accidentally end up in the* ex *editor.*

  A `Q` in the command mode of `vi` invokes `ex`. Any time you are in `ex`, the command `vi` returns you to the `vi` editor.

Problems with vi Commands

- *When you type commands, text jumps around on the screen and nothing works the way it's supposed to.*

  Make sure you're not typing the `J` command when you mean `j`.

---

* Your `vi` may keep its temporary files in `/usr/tmp`, `/var/tmp`, or your current directory; you may need to poke around a bit to figure out where exactly you've run out of room.

You may have hit the CAPS LOCK key without noticing it. vi is case-sensitive; that is, uppercase commands (I, A, J, etc.) are different from lowercase commands (i, a, j), so all your commands are being interpreted not as lowercase but as uppercase commands. Press the CAPS LOCK key again to return to lowercase, press ESC to ensure that you are in command mode, then type either U to restore the last line changed or u to undo the last command. You'll probably also have to do some additional editing to fully restore the garbled part of your file.

Problems with Deletions

- *You've deleted the wrong text and you want to get it back.*

  There are several ways to recover deleted text. If you've just deleted something and you realize you want it back, simply type u to undo the last command (for example, a dd). This works only if you haven't given any further commands, since u undoes only the most recent command. On the other hand, a U will restore the line to its pristine state, the way it was before *any* changes were applied to it.

  You can still recover a recent deletion, however, by using the p command, since vi saves the last nine deletions in nine numbered deletion buffers. If you know, for example, that the third deletion back is the one you want to restore, type:

      "3p

  to "put" the contents of buffer number 3 on the line below the cursor. This works only for a deleted *line*. Words, or a portion of a line, are not saved in a buffer. If you want to restore a deleted word or line fragment, and u won't work, use the p command by itself. This restores whatever you've last deleted.

vi and the Internet

*Sure, vi is user friendly. It's just particular about who it
makes friends with.*

Being the "standard" Unix screen editor since at least 1980 has enshrined vi firmly in
Unix culture.

vi helped build Unix, and Unix in turn built the foundation for today's Internet. Thus,
it was inevitable that there be at least one Internet web site devoted to vi. This appendix
describes some of the vi resources that are available for the vi connoisseur.

Where to Start

There is surely no activity with more built-in obsolescence than publishing World Wide
Web sites in a printed book. We have tried to publish URLs that we hope will have a
reasonable lifetime.

In the meantime, the "Tips" section of the elvis documentation lists interesting vi-
related web sites (that's where we started), and the Usenet comp.editors newsgroup is
also a good place to look.

vi Web Sites

There are two primary vi-related web sites, the *vi Lover's Home Page*, by Thomer M.
Gil, and the *Vi Pages*, by Sven Guckes. Each contains a large number of links to interesting vi-related items.

The vi Lover's Home Page

The *vi Lover's Home Page* can be found at *http://www.thomer.com/vi/vi.html*. This site
contains the following items:

- A table of all known vi clones, with links to the source code or binary distributions

- Links to other **vi** sites, including the *Vi Pages*, by Sven Guckes
- A large number of links to **vi** documentation, manuals, help, and tutorials, at a number of different levels
- **vi** macros for writing HTML documents and solving the Towers of Hanoi, and FTP sites for other macro sets
- Miscellaneous **vi** links: poems, a story about the "real history" of **vi**, **vi** versus Emacs discussions, and **vi** coffee mugs (see the section "vi for Java Lovers" on page 437)

There are other things there, too; this makes a great starting point.

The Vi Pages

The *Vi Pages* can be found at *http://www.vi-editor.org.*[*] This site contains the following items:

- A detailed comparison of options and features among different **vi** clones
- Screenshots of different versions of **vi**
- A table listing many **vi** clones, as well as a list with contact information (name, address, URL) for the clones
- Pointers to several FAQ files
- Some cute quotes about **vi**, such as the one that opened this chapter
- Other links, including a link to the **vi** coffee mugs

The *vi Lover's Home Page* refers to this web site as "the only Vi site on this planet better than the one you're looking at." This site is also well worth checking out.

vi Powered!

One of the cuter items we found is the *vi Powered* logo (Figure D-1). This is a small GIF file you can add to your personal web page to show that you used **vi** to create it.

Figure D-1. vi Powered!

The original home page for the *vi Powered* logo was *http://www.abast.es/~avelle/vi.html*. That page was written in Spanish and is no longer available. The English home page is at *http://www.darryl.com/vi.shtml*. Instructions for adding the logo are at *http://www.darryl.com/addlogo.html*. Doing so consists of several simple steps:

---

[*] This site is mirrored at *http://www.saki.com.au/mirror/vi/index.php3*.

1. Download the logo. Enter *http://www.darryl.com/vipower.gif* into your (graphical) web browser, and then save it to a file, or use a command-line web retrieval utility, such as `wget`.

2. Add the following code to your web page in an appropriate place:

```
<A HREF="http://www.darryl.com/vi.html">
<IMG SRC="vipower.gif">
</A>
```

This puts the logo into your page and makes it into a hypertext link that, when selected, will go to the *vi Powered* home page. You may wish to add an `ALT="This Web Page is vi Powered"` attribute to the `<IMG>` tag, for users of nongraphical browsers.

3. Add the following code to the `<HEAD>` section of your web page:

```
<META name="editor" content="/usr/bin/vi">
```

Just as the Real Programmer will eschew a WYSIWYG word processor in favor of `troff`, so too will Real Webmasters eschew fancy HTML authoring tools in favor of `vi`. You can use the *vi Powered* logo to display this fact with pride. ☺

You can find the Vim logo, in several variations, at *http://www.vim.org/logos.php*. A number of *Vim Powered* logos for web sites are at *http://www.vim.org/buttons.php*.

vi for Java Lovers

Despite the title, this subsection is about the java you drink, not the Java you program in.[†]

Our hypothetical Real Programmer, while using `vi` to write her C++ code, her `troff` documentation, and her web page, undoubtedly will want a cup of coffee now and then. She can now drink her coffee from a mug with a `vi` command reference printed on it!

When we first found `vi` reference mugs, they were available in sets of four from a dedicated web site. That site seems to have disappeared. However, `vi` reference mugs, T-shirts, sweatshirts, and mouse pads are now available from a different site: *http://www.cafepress.com/geekcheat/366808*.

Online vi Tutorial

The two home pages we've mentioned have a large number of links to documentation on `vi`. Of special note, though, is a nine-part online tutorial from *Unix World* magazine, by Walter Zintz. The starting-off point is here: *http://www.networkcomputing.com/unixworld/tutorial/009/009.html*. (The link for this has moved around; it may not be

---

[†] Still, it's somehow fitting that Java came from Sun Microsystems, where Bill Joy—`vi`'s original author—is a founder and former vice president.

Figure D-2. The story of vigor—part I

up-to-date on the vi home pages, but this URL worked when we tried it early in 2008.) The tutorial covers the following topics:

- Editor fundamentals
- Line-mode addresses
- The g (global) command
- The substitute command
- The editing environment (the set command, tags, and EXINIT and .exrc)
- Addresses and columns
- The replacement commands, r and R
- Automatic indentation
- Macros

Also available with the tutorial is an online quiz that you can use to see how well you've absorbed the material in the tutorial. Or you can just try the quiz directly, to see how well we've done with this book!

A Different vi Clone

Depicted in Figures D-2 through D-9 is the story of **vigor**, a *different* vi clone.

The source code for **vigor** is available at *http://vigor.sourceforge.net*.

Amaze Your Friends!

In the long term, perhaps the most useful items are in the collection of vi-related information in the FTP archives at *alf.uib.no*. The original archives were at *ftp://afl.uib.no/ pub/vi*. This site has gone away, but you can find the archives mirrored at *ftp://ftp.uu.net/*

Figure D-3. The story of vigor—part II

Figure D-4. The story of vigor—part III

pub/text-processing/vi.‡ The file **INDEX** in that directory describes what's in the archives and lists additional mirrors that may be geographically closer to you.

Unfortunately, these files were last updated in May of 1995. Fortunately, vi's basic functionality has not changed, and the information and macros in the archive are still useful. The archive has four subdirectories:

docs
:   Documentation on vi, and also some comp.editors postings.

macros
:   vi macros.

comp.editors
:   Various materials posted to comp.editors.

---

‡ You may have better luck accessing this site with a command-line FTP client than with a web browser.

Figure D-5. The story of vigor—part IV

Figure D-6. The story of vigor—part V

programs

> Source code for vi clones for various platforms (and other programs). Take things from here with caution, as much of it is out of date.

The docs and macros are the most interesting. The docs directory has a large number of articles and references, including beginners' guides, explanations of bugs, quick references, and many short "how to" kinds of articles (e.g., how to capitalize just the first letter of a sentence in vi). There's even a song about vi!

The macros directory has over 50 files in it that do different things. We mention just three of them here. (Files whose names end in .Z are compressed with the Unix compress program. They can be uncompressed with either uncompress or gunzip.)

Figure D-7. The story of vigor—part VI

Figure D-8. The story of vigor—part VII

evi.tar.Z

An Emacs "emulator." The idea behind it is to turn `vi` into a modeless editor (one that is always in input mode, with commands done with control keys). It is actually done with a shell script that replaces the `EXINIT` environment variable.

hanoi.Z

This is perhaps the most famous of the unusual uses of `vi`: a set of macros that solve the Towers of Hanoi programming problem. This program simply displays the moves; it does not actually draw the disks. For fun, we have reprinted it in the sidebar later in this chapter.

turing.tar.Z

This program uses `vi` to implement an actual Turing machine! It's rather amazing to watch it execute the programs.

There are many, many more interesting macros, including `perl` and RCS modes.

Figure D-9. The story of vigor—part VIII

The Towers of Hanoi, vi Version

```
" From: gregm@otc.otca.oz.au (Greg McFarlane)
" Newsgroups: comp.sources.d,alt.sources,comp.editors
" Subject: VI SOLVES HANOI
" Date: 19 Feb 91 01:32:14 GMT
"
" Submitted-by: gregm@otc.otca.oz.au
" Archive-name: hanoi.vi.macros/part01
"
" Everyone seems to be writing stupid Tower of Hanoi programs.
" Well, here is the stupidest of them all: the hanoi solving
" vi macros.
"
" Save this article, unshar it, and run uudecode on
" hanoi.vi.macros.uu. This will give you the macro file
" hanoi.vi.macros.
" Then run vi (with no file: just type "vi") and type:
"     :so hanoi.vi.macros
"     g
" and watch it go.
"
" The default height of the tower is 7 but can be easily changed
" by editing the macro file.
"
" The disks aren't actually shown in this version, only numbers
" representing each disk, but I believe it is possible to write
" some macros to show the disks moving about as well. Any takers?
"
" (For maze solving macros, see alt.sources or comp.editors)
"
" Greg
"
" ------------ REAL FILE STARTS HERE ---------------
set remap
set noterse
set wrapscan
" to set the height of the tower, change the digit in the following
```

```
        " two lines to the height you want (select from 1 to 9)
        map t 7
        map! t 7
        map L 1G/t^MX/^O^M$P1GJ$An$BGCOe$XOEOF$X/T^M@f^M@h^M$A1GJ@fOl$Xn$PU
        map g IL
        map I KMYNOQNOSkRTV
        map J /^O[^t]*$^M
        map X x
        map P p
        map U L
        map A
        map B "hyl
        map C "fp
        map e "fy2l
        map E "hp
        map F "hy2l
        map K 1Go^[
        map M dG
        map N yy
        map O p
        map q tllD
        map Y oO123456789Z^[Oq
        map Q oiT^[
        map R $rn
        map S $r$
        map T koO^MO^M^M^[
        map V Go/^[
```

Tastes Great, Less Filling

```
vi is [[13~^[[15~^[[15~^[[19~^[[18~^ a
muk[^[[29~^[[34~^[[26~^[[32~^ch better editor than this emacs. I know
I^[[14~'ll get flamed for this but the truth has to be
said. ^[[D^[[D^[[D^[[D ^[[D^[^[[D^[[D^[[B^
exit ^X^C quit :x :wq dang it :w:w:w :x ^C^C^Z^D
```

— Jesper Lauridsen from `alt.religion.emacs`

We can't discuss **vi** as part of Unix culture without acknowledging what is perhaps the longest running debate in the Unix community:[§] **vi** versus Emacs.

Discussions about which is better have cropped up on `comp.editors` (and other news-groups) for years and years. (This is illustrated nicely in Figure D-10.) You will find summaries of some of these discussions in the many web sites described earlier. You will find pointers to more recent versions on the web pages.

Some of the better arguments in favor of **vi** are:

- **vi** is available on every Unix system. If you are installing systems, or moving from system to system, you might have to use **vi** anyway.

[§] OK, it's really a religious war, but we're trying to be nice. (The other religious war, BSD versus System V, was settled by POSIX. System V won, although BSD received significant concessions. ☺)

Figure D-10. It's not a religious war. Really!

- You can usually keep your fingers on the home row of the keyboard. This is a big plus for touch typists.
- Commands are one (or sometimes two) regular characters; they are much easier to type than all of the control and metacharacters that Emacs requires.
- vi is generally smaller and less resource-intensive than Emacs. Startup times are appreciably faster, sometimes up to a factor of 10.
- Now that the vi clones have added features such as incremental searching, multiple windows, and buffers, GUI interfaces, syntax highlighting and smart indenting, and programmability via extension languages, the functional gap between the two editors has narrowed significantly, if not disappeared entirely.

To be complete, two more items should be mentioned. First, there are actually two versions of Emacs that are popular: the original GNU Emacs and XEmacs, which is derived from an earlier version of GNU Emacs. Both have advantages and disadvantages, and their own sets of devotees.‖

Second, although GNU Emacs has always had vi-emulation packages, they are usually not very good. However, the "viper mode" is now reputed to be an excellent vi emulation. It can serve as a bridge for learning Emacs for those who are interested in doing so.

To conclude, always remember that you are the final judge of a program's utility. You should use the tools that make you the most productive, and for many tasks, vi and its clones are excellent tools.

‖ Who undoubtedly share a joint distaste for vi! ☺

vi Quotes

Finally, here are some more **vi** quotes, courtesy of Bram Moolenaar, Vim's author:

> THEOREM: **vi** is perfect.
>
> PROOF: VI in roman numerals is 6. The natural numbers less than 6 which divide 6 are 1, 2, and 3. 1 + 2 + 3 = 6. So 6 is a perfect number. Therefore, **vi** is perfect.
>
> — Arthur Tateishi

A reaction from Nathan T. Oelger:

> So, where does the above leave Vim? VIM in roman numerals might be: $(1000 - (5 + 1))$ = 994, which happens to be equal to 2*496+2. 496 is divisible by 1, 2, 4, 8, 16, 31, 62, 124, and 248 and 1+2+4+8+16+31+62+124+248 = 496. So, 496 is a perfect number. Therefore, Vim is twice as perfect as **vi**, *plus* a couple extra bits of goodies. ☺
>
> That is, Vim is *better* than perfect.

This quote seems to sum it up for the true **vi** lover:

> To me **vi** is zen. To use **vi** is to practice zen. Every command is a koan. Profound to the user, unintelligible to the uninitiated. You discover truth every time you use it.
>
> — Satish Reddy

Index

Symbols

! (exclamation point)
  buffers, interaction with, 187
  cinkeys syntax rules, 254
  ex commands starting with, 11
  mapping keys for insert mode, 109
  overriding save warnings, 64
  for Unix commands, 99, 101
(pound sign)
  for alternate filename, 67
  buffers, describing, 187
  meta-information, extracting, 149
  show line numbers command, 59
$ (dollar sign)
  cursor movement command, 17, 38
  for last file line (ex), 60
  marking end of change region, 20
  metacharacter, 75
$MYGVIMRC variable, 220
% (percent sign)
  buffers, describing, 187
  for current filename, 67
  every line symbol (ex), 72
  matching brackets, 122
  meta-information, extracting, 149
  representing every line (ex), 60
& (ampersand)
  metacharacter, 78
  to repeat last command, 80
' (apostrophe)
  " (move to mark) command, 44, 53
  marking lines (vile), 364
  move to mark command, 53
(underscore), using in file names, 7

* (asterisk)
  cinkeys syntax rules, 255
* (asterisk) metacharacter, 74
+ (plus sign), 377
  \+ metacharacter, 169, 328, 357
  buffers, describing, 187
  metacharacter, 128, 312
  move cursor command, 15, 38
  for next file lines (ex), 60
  running commands when starting vi, 48
+-- marker, as a fold placeholder, 244
+/ option, 378
+? option, 378
, (comma)
  for line ranges (ex), 56, 58
  repeat search command, 42
- (hyphen)
  buffers, describing, 187
  manual folding and, 246
  move cursor command, 15, 38
  for previous file lines (ex), 60
-? option (elvis), 318
-? option (vile), 345
-b option, 378
-e option, 378
-h option, 378
. (dot)
  current line symbol (ex), 60
  echo command and, 199
  filenames and, 7
  meta-information, extracting, 149
  metacharacter, 74
  repeat command, 28, 72
  undo/redo (nvi), 314
.viminfo file, 148

We'd like to hear your suggestions for improving our indexes. Send email to *index@oreilly.com*.

directory buffer, 188
"Disk quota has been reached" message, 11
:display (di) command
    elvis editor, 338
    nvi editor, 310, 313
display modes, elvis, 334, 337–339
:display syntax command (elvis), 334, 337–
    339
dL command, 387
dn command, 387
documentation
    elvis editor, 319
    nvi editor, 309
    vi-related archives (FTP), 438
    vi-related web sites, 435
    vile editor, 345
dollar sign ($)
    cursor movement command, 17, 38
    for last file line (ex), 60
    marking end of change region, 20
    metacharacter, 75
dot (.)
    current line symbol (ex), 60
    echo command and, 199
    filenames and, 7
    meta-information, extracting, 149
    metacharacter, 74
    repeat command, 28, 72
    undo/redo (nvi), 314
double quote (XXX_DQUOTE) command, 51,
    52
dt command, 387
dumb values (lptype option), 339
dw command, 387
d^ command, 387
d} command, 387

E

:e (edit file) command (ex), 67, 397
    :e! command, 67
e (move cursor) command, 38
E (move cursor) command, 39
:e command, 389
\E metacharacter, 79
\e metacharacter, 79, 170
:e! ENTER command, 10
eadirection option, 185
"easy gvim" (MS Windows), 219
echo command, 197

echoing of commands, 5
Eclipse, 239
ed line editor, 3
ed text editor, 3
edcompatible option, 80
:edit command, 187
:Edit command (nvi), 310
edit commands, 387
edit-compile speedup, 139
    elvis editor, 333
    vile editor, 365
editing, 13–33
    clone improvements over vi, 134–138, 312–
        315, 328–332, 359–365
    customizing editing environment, 95
    ex commands on command line, 135
        elvis editor, 328
        nvi editor, 312
        vile editor, 359
    ex editor for, 58
    lists of files, 108
    multiple files, 65
    read-only mode, 49
    recovering the buffer, 50
    replacing text (see replacing text)
    source code, advice for, 120
        indentation control, 120
        matching brackets, 122
        using tags, 123, 129–134
    transparent for Vim, 149
    using multiple windows, 126–127
        elvis editor, 320–323
        nvi editor, 310–311
        vile editor, 347
    vile editing model, 368
else blocks, 196
elseif blocks, 196
elvis (vi clone), 307, 317–341
    documentation and online help, 319
    extended regular expressions, 328
    feature summary, 140
    future of, 340
    GUI interfaces for, 323–328
    important command-line arguments, 317–
        318
    improvements over vi, 328–332
    infinite undo facility, 136
    initialization of, 319
    interesting features, 335–340

:q! command, 64
Q command, 57
:q (quoted motion) command (vile), 364
:q! command, 10, 380
    quitting, 9
qa command, 403
:qall command (elvis), 322
question mark (?)
    \? metacharacter, 328, 357
    metacharacter, 128, 312
    search command, 5, 40
quickfix buffer, 187
Quickfix List window, 279
quipty option, 238
Quit button (elvis), 326
:quit command, 192
quitting vi, 63
XXX_DQUOTE (yank from buffer) command,
    51, 52
quote (XXX_DQUOTE) command, 51, 52
quoted motion (q) command (vile), 364
quotes about vi, 445

R

:r (read) command (ex), 65, 403
r (replace character) command, 22, 31
R (replace character) command, 22, 30, 386
\r metacharacter, 170
-R option, 49, 50, 379
    vile editor, 344
-r option, 50
    elvis editor, 318
    nvi editor, 308
range of lines, 58, 62
rcp (remote copy), 290
:read command (ex), 65
    reading Unix command output, 100
read-hook option (vile), 373
"Read Only" files, 432
"[Read only]" message, 8
read-only mode, 49
read-only registers (Vim), 149
rec command, 404
recovering deletions, 25, 51
recovering the buffer, 50
red command, 404
redrawing screen, 37
reformatting text (vile), 373
regular expressions, 74, 128–129

elvis editor, 328
metacharacters
    in replacement strings, 78
    in search patterns, 74
    substitution tricks, 80
nvi editor, 311–312
pattern-matching examples, 81
vile editor, 357–358
Vim editor, 169–171
relative line addressing (ex), 60
relative pathnames, 7
renaming buffer (ex), 64
repeating commands, 28–29
    :g command for (example), 92
    global substitutions, 80
    pattern searches, 40, 42
    searching numbered buffers, 51
replacing text, 18, 19
    by characters, 22
    globally, 71
        confirming substitutions, 72
        context sensitivity, 73
        replacement-string metacharacters, 78
        substitution tricks, 80
    by lines, 21–22
    searching and, 42
    by words, 20–21
repositioning screen, 36
res command, 404
:resize command, 184
    nvi, 311
resize parameter (sessionoptions option), 299
:resize-window command (vile), 348
:restore-window command (vile), 348
:reverse-incremental-search command (vile),
    363
rew command, 404
:rew, :rewind commands (ex), 67
right margin, setting, 16
right/left scrolling, 137
    elvis editor, 331
    nvi editor, 315
    vile editor, 363
rm command (Unix), 11
ruler option, 138

S

s (substitute) command, 22, 30–31, 386
S (substitute) command, 22, 30–31, 386

V

About the Authors

Arnold Robbins is a professional programmer and technical author who's been working with various Unix systems since 1980, and with GNU/Linux systems since 1996. As a member of the POSIX 1003.2 balloting group, he helped shape the POSIX standard for *awk*. He is currently the maintainer of *gawk* and its documentation. A software engineer at Intel, Arnold is the author and/or coauthor of several bestselling titles from O'Reilly, including *Unix in a Nutshell*, *Effective awk Programming*, *sed & awk*, *Learning the Korn Shell*, and *Classic Shell Scripting*.

Elbert Hannah is a professional software engineer and software architect recently finishing a 21-year career in the telcom industry. He wrote a full screen editor in assembler in 1983 as his first professional assignment, and has had special interest in editors since. He loves connecting Unix to anything and once wrote a stream editor program to automate JCL edits for mainframe monthly configurations by streaming mainframe JCL to a stream editor on an RJE-connected Unix box.

Linda Lamb is a former employee of O'Reilly Media, Inc., where she worked in various capacities, including technical writer, editor of technical books, and marketing manager. She also worked on O'Reilly's series of consumer health books, Patient Centered Guides.

Colophon

The animal on the cover of *Learning the vi and Vim Editors*, Seventh Edition, is a tarsier, a nocturnal mammal related to the lemur. Its generic name, Tarsius, is derived from the animal's very long ankle bone, the tarsus. The tarsier is a native of the East Indies jungles from Sumatra to the Philippines and Sulawesi, where it lives in the trees, leaping from branch to branch with extreme agility and speed.

A small animal, the tarsier's body is only 6 inches long, followed by a 10-inch tufted tail. It is covered in soft, brown or gray silky fur, and has a round face and huge eyes. Its arms and legs are long and slender, as are its digits, which are tipped with rounded, fleshy pads to improve its grip on trees. Tarsiers are active only at night, hiding during the day in tangles of vines or in the tops of tall trees. They subsist mainly on insects and, though very curious animals, tend to be loners.

The cover image is a 19th-century engraving from the Dover Pictorial Archive. The cover font is Adobe's ITC Garamond. The text font is Linotype Birka, the heading font is Adobe Myriad Condensed, and the code font is LucasFont's TheSansMonoCondensed.

Related Titles from O'Reilly

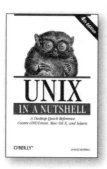

Our books are available at most retail and online bookstores.

To order direct: 1-800-998-9938 • *order@oreilly.com* • *www.oreilly.com*

Online editions of most O'Reilly titles are available by subscription at *safari.oreilly.com*

The O'Reilly Advantage

Stay Current and Save Money